Reappraisals

Reappraisals

REFLECTIONS ON THE FORGOTTEN

TWENTIETH CENTURY

TONY JUDT

WITHDRAWN

THE PENGUIN PRESS

NEW YORK

2008

THE PENGUIN PRESS
Published by the Penguin Group

Penguin Group (USA) Inc., 375 Hudson Street, New York, New York 10014, U.S.A. • Penguin Group (Canada), 90 Eglinton Avenue East, Suite 700, Toronto, Ontario, Canada M4P 2Y3 (a division of Pearson Penguin Canada Inc.) • Penguin Books Ltd, 80 Strand, London WC2R 0RL, England • Penguin Ireland, 25 St. Stephen's Green, Dublin 2, Ireland (a division of Penguin Books Ltd) • Penguin Books Australia Ltd, 250 Camberwell Road, Camberwell, Victoria 3124, Australia (a division of Pearson Australia Group Pty Ltd) • Penguin Books India Pvt Ltd, 11 Community Centre, Panchsheel Park, New Delhi - 110 017, India • Penguin Group (NZ), 67 Apollo Drive, Rosedale, North Shore 0632, New Zealand (a division of Pearson New Zealand Ltd) • Penguin Books (South Africa) (Pty) Ltd, 24 Sturdee Avenue, Rosebank, Johannesburg 2196, South Africa

Penguin Books Ltd, Registered Offices:
80 Strand, London WC2R 0RL, England

First published in 2008 by The Penguin Press,
a member of Penguin Group (USA) Inc.

The original publishers of these essays are acknowledged on page 433.

"The Social Question Redivivus" is reprinted by permission of *Foreign Affairs* (volume 76, no. 5, September/October 1997). Copyright 1997 by the Council on Foreign Relations, Inc.

Excerpt from "MCMXIV" from *Collected Poems* by Philip Larkin. Copyright © 1988, 2003 by the Estate of Philip Larkin. Reprinted by permission of Farrar, Straus and Giroux, LLC., and Faber and Faber Ltd.

Excerpt from "The Survivor" from *Collected Poems* by Primo Levi, translated by Ruth Feldman and Brian Swann. English translation copyright © 1988 by Ruth Feldman and Brian Swann. Reprinted by permission of Faber and Faber, Inc., an affiliate of Farrar, Straus, and Giroux, LLC.

LIBRARY OF CONGRESS CATALOGING IN PUBLICATION DATA AVAILABLE
ISBN: 978–59420–136–3

Printed in the United States of America
1 3 5 7 9 10 8 6 4 2

DESIGNED BY AMANDA DEWEY

For AK and GL

CONTENTS

Part Three

LOST IN TRANSITION: PLACES AND MEMORIES   *179*

Part Four

THE AMERICAN (HALF-) CENTURY   *297*

ACKNOWLEDGMENTS

With few exceptions these essays were written at the invitation of a journal or newspaper editor. So much the better: left to himself, an author—or at any rate, this author—would in all likelihood stick to familiar material. So I am grateful to those who over the years have urged me to address fresh subjects in unfamiliar formats and milieux: Michael Handelsaltz of *HaAretz*, Adam Shatz (formerly at *The Nation*, now *The London Review of Books*), Mary-Kay Wilmers (*The London Review of Books*), Leon Wieseltier (*The New Republic*), and Fareed Zakaria (formerly at *Foreign Affairs*, now with *Newsweek International*). I owe special thanks, once more, to Robert Silvers of *The New York Review of Books*, who emboldened me to write about United States foreign policy and who was the first to encourage me to address the problem of Israel.

It is a pleasure once again to express my gratitude to Sarah Chalfant and Andrew Wylie at The Wylie Agency for their advice and encouragement, and to Scott Moyers at the Penguin Press for his continuing support and interest. This book is dedicated to the memory of Annie Kriegel and George Lichtheim, two outstanding historians, polemicists, and interpreters of their century: she in Paris, he in London. Without their motivating example—and their support at a crucial juncture—it is unlikely that I would have embarked upon an academic career. The publication of these essays affords a welcome opportunity to acknowledge that debt.

—*New York, September 2007*

Reappraisals

INTRODUCTION

The World We Have Lost

T he essays in this book were written over a span of twelve years, between 1994 and 2006. They cover quite a broad swath of subject matter—from French Marxists to American foreign policy, from the economics of globalization to the memory of evil—and they range in geography from Belgium to Israel. But they have two dominant concerns. The first is the role of ideas and the responsibility of intellectuals: The earliest essay reproduced here discusses Albert Camus, the most recent is devoted to Leszek Kołakowski. My second concern is with the place of recent history in an age of forgetting: the difficulty we seem to experience in making sense of the turbulent century that has just ended and in learning from it.

These themes are of course closely interconnected. And they are intimately bound up with the moment of their writing. In decades to come we shall, I think, look back upon the half generation separating the fall of Communism in 1989–91 from the catastrophic American occupation of Iraq as the years the locust ate: a decade and a half of wasted opportunity and political incompetence on both sides of the Atlantic. With too much confidence and too little reflection we put the twentieth century behind us and strode boldly into its successor swaddled in self-serving half-truths: the triumph of the West, the end of History, the unipolar

American moment, the ineluctable march of globalization and the free market.

In our Manichaean enthusiasms we in the West made haste to dispense whenever possible with the economic, intellectual, and institutional baggage of the twentieth century and encouraged others to do likewise. The belief that *that* was then and *this* is now, that all we had to learn from the past was not to repeat it, embraced much more than just the defunct institutions of Cold War–era Communism and its Marxist ideological membrane. Not only did we fail to learn very much from the past—this would hardly have been remarkable. But we have become stridently insistent—in our economic calculations, our political practices, our international strategies, even our educational priorities—that *the past has nothing of interest to teach us.* Ours, we insist, is a new world; its risks and opportunities are without precedent.

Writing in the nineties, and again in the wake of September 11, 2001, I was struck more than once by this perverse contemporary insistence on *not* understanding the context of our present dilemmas, at home and abroad; on *not* listening with greater care to some of the wiser heads of earlier decades; on seeking actively to *forget* rather than to remember, to deny continuity and proclaim novelty on every possible occasion. This always seemed a trifle solipsistic. And as the international events of the early twenty-first century have begun to suggest, it might also be rather imprudent. The recent past may yet be with us for a few years longer. This book is an attempt to bring it into sharper focus.

THE TWENTIETH CENTURY is hardly behind us, but already its quarrels and its dogmas, its ideals and its fears are slipping into the obscurity of mis-memory. Incessantly invoked as "lessons," they are in reality ignored and untaught. This is not altogether surprising. The recent past is the hardest to know and understand. Moreover, the world has undergone a remarkable transformation since 1989, and such transformations always bring a sense of distance and displacement for those who remember how things were before. In the decades following the French Revolution the *douceur de vivre* of the vanished *ancien régime* was much regretted by older commentators. One hundred years later, evocations and memoirs of pre–World War I Europe typically depicted (and still depict) a lost civilization, a world whose illusions had quite literally been blown apart: "Never such innocence again."[1]

But there is a difference. Contemporaries might have regretted the world before the French Revolution, or the lost cultural and political landscape of Europe before August 1914. But they had not *forgotten* them. Far from it: For much of the nineteenth century Europeans were obsessed with the causes and meaning of the French revolutionary transformations. The political and philosophical debates of the Enlightenment were not consumed in the fires of revolution. On the contrary, the French Revolution and its consequences were widely attributed to that same Enlightenment, which thus emerged—for friend and foe alike—as the acknowledged source of the political dogmas and social programs of the century that followed.

In a similar vein, while everyone after 1918 agreed that things would never be the same again, the particular shape that a postwar world should take was everywhere conceived and contested in the long shadow of nineteenth-century experience and thought. Neoclassical economics, liberalism, Marxism (and its Communist stepchild) "revolution," the bourgeoisie and the proletariat, imperialism and "industrialism"—in short, the building blocks of the twentieth-century political world— were all nineteenth-century artifacts. Even those who, along with Virginia Woolf, believed that "in or about December 1910, human character changed"—that the cultural upheaval of Europe's fin de siècle had radically shifted the terms of intellectual exchange—nonetheless devoted a surprising amount of energy to shadowboxing with their predecessors.[2] The past hung heavy across the present.

Today, in contrast, we wear the last century rather lightly. To be sure, we have memorialized it everywhere: museums, shrines, inscriptions, "heritage sites," even historical theme parks are all public reminders of "the Past." But there is a strikingly selective quality to the twentieth century that we have chosen to commemorate. The overwhelming majority of places of official twentieth-century memory are either avowedly nostalgio-triumphalist—praising famous men and celebrating famous victories—or else, and increasingly, opportunities for the acknowledgment and recollection of selective suffering. In the latter case they are typically the occasion for the teaching of a certain sort of political lesson: about things that were done and should never be forgotten, about mistakes that were made and should not be made again.

The twentieth century is thus on the path to becoming a moral memory palace: a pedagogically serviceable Chamber of Historical Horrors whose way stations are labeled "Munich" or "Pearl Harbor," "Auschwitz" or "Gulag," "Armenia" or "Bosnia" or "Rwanda," with "9-11" as a sort of supererogatory coda, a bloody postscript for those who would forget the lessons of the century or who never properly learned them. The problem with this lapidary representation of the last century as a uniquely horrible time from which we have now, thankfully, emerged is not the description—the twentieth century *was* in many ways a truly awful era, an age of brutality and mass suffering perhaps unequaled in the historical record. The problem is the message: that all of *that* is now behind us, that its meaning is clear, and that we may now advance— unencumbered by past errors—into a different and better era.

But such official commemoration, however benign its motives, does not enhance our appreciation and awareness of the past. It serves as a substitute, a surrogate. Instead of teaching children recent history, we walk them through museums and memorials. Worse still, we encourage citizens and students to see the past—and its lessons—through the particular vector of their own suffering (or that of their ancestors). Today, the "common" interpretation of the recent past is thus composed of the manifold fragments of separate pasts, each of them (Jewish, Polish, Serb, Armenian, German, Asian-American, Palestinian, Irish, homosexual . . .) marked by its own distinctive and assertive victimhood.

The resulting mosaic does not bind us to a shared past, it separates us from it. Whatever the shortcomings of the older national narratives once taught in school, however selective their focus and ruthlessly instrumental their message, they had at least the advantage of providing a nation with past references for present experience. Traditional history, as taught to generations of schoolchildren and college students, gave the present a meaning by reference to the past: Today's names, places, inscriptions, ideas, and allusions could be slotted into a memorized narrative of yesterday. In our time, however, this process has gone into reverse. The past now has no agreed narrative shape of its own. It acquires meaning only by reference to our many and often contrasting present concerns.

This disconcertingly alien character of the past—such that it has to be domesticated with some contemporary significance or lesson before we can approach it—is doubtless in part the result of the sheer speed of contemporary change. "Globalization," shorthand for everything from the Internet to the unprecedented scale of transnational economic exchange, has churned up people's lives in ways that their parents or grandparents would be hard put to imagine. Much of what had for decades, even centuries, seemed familiar and permanent is now passing rapidly into oblivion.

The expansion of communication, together with the fragmentation of information, offers a striking contrast with communities of even the quite recent past. Until the last decades of the twentieth century, most people in the world had limited access to information; but within any one state or nation or community they were all likely to know many of the same things, thanks to national education, state-controlled radio and television, and a common print culture. Today, the opposite applies. Most people in the world outside of sub-Saharan Africa have access to a near infinity of data. But in the absence of any common culture beyond a small elite, and not always even there, the particular information and ideas that people select or encounter are determined by a multiplicity of tastes, affinities, and interests. As the years pass, each one of us has less in common with the fast-multiplying worlds of our contemporaries, not to speak of the world of our forebears.

All of this is surely true—and it has disturbing implications for the future of democratic governance. Nevertheless, disruptive change, even global transformation, is not in itself unprecedented. The economic "globalization" of the late nineteenth century was no less disruptive, except that its implications were initially felt and understood by far fewer people. What is significant about the *present* age of transformations is the unique insouciance with which we have abandoned not just the practices of the past—this is normal enough and not so very alarming—but their very memory. A world just recently lost is already half forgotten.

What, then, is it that have we misplaced in our haste to put the twentieth century behind us? Curious as it may seem, we (or at least we

Americans) have forgotten the meaning of war. In part this is, perhaps, because the impact of war in the twentieth century, though global in reach, was not everywhere the same. For most of continental Europe and much of Asia, the twentieth century, at least until the 1970s, was a time of virtually unbroken war: continental war, colonial war, civil war. War in the last century signified occupation, displacement, deprivation, destruction, and mass murder. Countries that lost wars often lost population, territory, security, and independence. But even those countries that emerged formally victorious had similar experiences and usually remembered war much as the losers did. Italy after World War I, China after World War II, and France after both wars might be cases in point. And then there are the surprisingly frequent instances of countries that won a war but "lost the peace": gratuitously wasting the opportunities afforded them by their victory. Israel in the decades following its victory in June 1967 remains the most telling example.

Moreover, war in the twentieth century frequently meant civil war: often under the cover of occupation or "liberation." Civil war played a significant role in the widespread "ethnic cleansing" and forced population transfers of the twentieth century, from India and Turkey to Spain and Yugoslavia. Like foreign occupation, civil war is one of the great "shared" memories of the past hundred years. In many countries "putting the past behind us"—i.e., agreeing to overcome or forget (or deny) a recent memory of internecine conflict and intercommunal violence—has been a primary goal of postwar governments: sometimes achieved, sometimes overachieved.

The United States avoided all that. Americans experienced the twentieth century in a far more positive light. The U.S. was never occupied. It did not lose vast numbers of citizens, or huge swaths of national territory, as a result of occupation or dismemberment. Although humiliated in neocolonial wars (in Vietnam and now in Iraq), it has never suffered the consequences of defeat. Despite the ambivalence of its most recent undertakings, most Americans still feel that the wars their country has fought were "good wars." The USA was enriched rather than impoverished by its role in the two world wars and by their outcome, in which respect it has nothing in common with Britain, the only other major country to emerge unambiguously victorious from those struggles but at the cost of near-bankruptcy and the loss of empire. And compared with the other major twentieth-century combatants, the U.S. lost relatively few soldiers in battle and suffered hardly any civilian casualties.

As a consequence, the United States today is the only advanced country that still glorifies and exalts the military, a sentiment familiar in Europe before 1945 but quite unknown today. America's politicians and statesmen surround themselves with the symbols and trappings of armed prowess; its commentators mock and scorn countries that hesitate to engage themselves in armed conflict. It is this differential recollection of war and its impact, rather than any structural difference between the U.S. and otherwise comparable countries, which accounts for their contrasting responses to international affairs today.

It also, perhaps, accounts for the distinctive quality of much American writing—scholarly and popular—on the cold war and its outcome. In European accounts of the fall of Communism and the Iron Curtain, the dominant sentiment is one of relief at the final closing of a long, unhappy chapter. Here in the U.S., however, the same story is typically recorded in a triumphalist key.[3] For many American commentators and policymakers the message of the last century is that war *works*. The implications of this reading of history have already been felt in the decision to attack Iraq in 2003. For Washington, war remains an option—in this case the first option. For the rest of the developed world it has become a last resort.

After war, the second characteristic of the twentieth century was the rise and subsequent fall of the state. This applies in two distinct but related senses. The first describes the emergence of autonomous nation-states during the early decades of the century, and the recent diminution of their powers at the hands of multinational corporations, transnational institutions, and the accelerated movement of people, money, and goods outside their control. Concerning this process there is little dispute, though it seems likely that those who regard the outcome—a "flat world"—as both desirable and inevitable may be in for a surprise, as populations in search of economic and physical security turn back to the political symbols, legal resources, and physical barriers that only a territorial state can provide.

But the state in my second sense has a more directly political significance.

In part as a result of war—the organization and resources required to fight it, the authority and collective effort involved in making good its consequences—the twentieth-century state acquired unprecedented capacities and resources. In their benevolent form these became what we now call the "welfare state" and what the French, more precisely, term "l'état providence": the providential state, underwriting needs and minimizing risks. Malevolently, these same centralized resources formed the basis of authoritarian and totalitarian states in Germany, Russia, and beyond—sometimes providential, always repressive.

For much of the second half of the twentieth century, it was widely accepted that the modern state could—and therefore should—perform the providential role; ideally, without intruding excessively upon the liberties of its subjects, but where intrusion was unavoidable, then in exchange for social benefits that could not otherwise be made universally available. In the course of the last third of the century, however, it became increasingly commonplace to treat the state not as the natural benefactor of first resort but as a source of economic inefficiency and social intrusion best excluded from citizens' affairs wherever possible. When combined with the fall of Communism, and the accompanying discrediting of the socialist project in all its forms, this discounting of the state has become the default condition of public discourse in much of the developed world.

As a consequence, when now we speak of economic "reform" or the need to render social services more "efficient," we mean that the state's part in the affair should be reduced. The privatization of public services or publicly owned businesses is now regarded as self-evidently a good thing. The state, it is conventionally assumed on all sides, is an impediment to the smooth running of human affairs: In Britain both Tory and Labour governments, under Margaret Thatcher and Tony Blair, have talked down the public sector as dowdy, unexciting, and inefficient. In Western societies taxation—the extraction of resources from subjects and citizens for the pursuit of state business and the provision of public services—had risen steadily for some two hundred years, from the late eighteenth century through the 1970s, accelerating in the course of the years 1910–1960 thanks to the imposition of progressive income tax, inheritance tax, and the taxation of land and capital. Since that time, however, taxes have typically fallen, or else become indirect and regressive (taxing purchases rather than wealth), and the state's reach has been proportionately reduced.

Whether this is good or bad—and for whom—is a matter for discussion. What is indisputable is that this public policy reversal has come upon the developed world quite suddenly (and not only the developed world, for it is now enforced by the International Monetary Fund and other agencies upon less developed countries as well). It was not always self-evident that the state is bad for you; until very recently there were many people in Europe, Asia, and Latin America, and not a few in the U.S., who believed the contrary. Were this not the case, neither the New Deal, nor Lyndon Johnson's Great Society program, nor many of the institutions and practices that now characterize Western Europe would have come about.

The fact that Fascists and Communists *also* explicitly sought a dominant role for the state does not in itself disqualify the public sector from a prominent place in free societies; nor did the fall of Communism resolve in favor of the unregulated market the question as to the optimum balance of freedom and efficiency. This is something any visitor to the social-democratic countries of northern Europe can confirm. The state, as the history of the last century copiously illustrates, does some things rather well and other things quite badly. There are some things the private sector, or the market, can do better and many things they cannot do at all. We need to learn once again to "think the state," free of the prejudices we have acquired against it in the triumphalist wake of the West's cold war victory. We need to learn how to acknowledge the shortcomings of the state *and* to present the case for the state without apology. As I conclude in Chapter XIV, we all know, at the end of the twentieth century, that you can have too much state. But . . . you can also have too little.

The twentieth-century welfare state is conventionally dismissed today as European and "socialist"—usually in formulations like this: "I believe history will record that it was Chinese capitalism that put an end to European socialism."[4] European it may be (if we allow that Canada, New Zealand, and—in respect of social security and national health for the aged—the USA are all for this purpose "European"); but "socialist"? The epithet reveals once again a curious unfamiliarity with the recent past. Outside of Scandinavia—in Austria, Germany, France, Italy, Holland, and elsewhere—it was not socialists but *Christian Democrats* who played the greatest part in installing and administering the core institutions of the activist welfare state. Even in Britain, where the post–World War II Labour government of Clement Attlee indeed inaugurated the welfare state as we knew it, it was the wartime government of Winston Churchill that commissioned and approved the Report by William Beveridge (himself a Liberal) that established the principles of public welfare provision: principles—and practices—that were reaffirmed and underwritten by every Conservative government that followed until 1979.

The welfare state, in short, was born of a cross-party twentieth-century consensus. It was implemented, in most cases, by liberals or conservatives who had entered public life well before 1914 and for whom the public provision of universal medical services, old age pensions, unemployment and sickness insurance, free education, subsidized public transport, and the other prerequisites of a stable civil order represented not the first stage of twentieth-century socialism but the culmination of late-nineteenth-century reformist liberalism. A similar perspective informed the thinking of many New Dealers in the United States.

Moreover, and here the memory of war played once again an important role, the twentieth-century "socialist" welfare states were constructed not as an advance guard of egalitarian revolution but to provide a barrier against the return of the past: against economic depression and its polarizing, violent political outcome in the desperate politics of Fascism and Communism alike. The welfare states were thus *prophylactic* states. They were designed quite consciously to meet the widespread yearning for security and stability that John Maynard Keynes and others foresaw long before the end of World War II, and they succeeded beyond anyone's expectations. Thanks to half a century of prosperity and safety, we in the West have forgotten the political and social traumas of mass insecurity. And thus we have forgotten why we have inherited those welfare states and what brought them about.

The paradox, of course, is that the very success of the mixed-economy welfare states, in providing the social stability and ideological demobilization which made possible the prosperity of the past half century, has led a younger political generation to take that same stability and ideological quiescence for granted and demand the elimination of the "impediment" of the taxing, regulating, and generally interfering state. Whether the economic case for this is as secure as it now appears—whether regulation and social provision were truly an impediment to "growth" and "efficiency" and not perhaps their facilitating condition—is debatable. But what is striking is how far we have lost the capacity even to conceive of public policy beyond a narrowly construed economism. We have forgotten how to think politically.

This, too, is one of the paradoxical legacies of the twentieth century. The exhaustion of political energies in the orgy of violence and repression from 1914 through 1945 and beyond has deprived us of much of the political inheritance of the past two hundred years. "Left" and "Right"— terminology inherited from the French Revolution—are not quite without meaning today, but they no longer describe (as they still did within recent memory) the political allegiances of most citizens in democratic societies. We are skeptical, if not actively suspicious, of all-embracing political goals: The grand narratives of Nation and History and Progress that characterized the political families of the twentieth century seem discredited beyond recall. And so we describe our collective purposes in exclusively economic terms—prosperity, growth, GDP, efficiency, output, interest rates, and stock market performances—as though these were not just means to some collectively sought social or political ends but were necessary and sufficient ends in themselves.

In an unpolitical age, there is much to be said for politicians thinking and talking economically: This is, after all, how most people today conceive of their own life chances and interests, and any project of public policy that ignored this truth would not get very far. But that is only how things are *now*. They have not always looked this way, and we have no good reason for supposing that they will look this way in the future. It is not only nature that abhors a vacuum: Democracies in which there are no significant political choices to be made, where economic policy is all that really matters—and where economic policy is now largely determined by nonpolitical actors (central banks, international agencies, or transnational corporations)—must either cease to be functioning democracies or accommodate once again the politics of frustration, of populist

resentment. Post-Communist Central and Eastern Europe offers one illustration of how this can happen; the political trajectory of comparably
fragile democracies elsewhere, from South Asia to Latin America, provides another. Outside of North America and Western Europe, it would
seem, the twentieth century is with us still.

OF ALL THE TRANSFORMATIONS of the past three decades, the disappearance of "intellectuals" is perhaps the most symptomatic. The twentieth century was the century of the intellectual: The very term first came
into use (pejoratively) at the turn of the century and from the outset it
described men and women in the world of learning, literature, and the
arts who applied themselves to debating and influencing public opinion
and policy. The intellectual was by definition committed—"engaged":
usually to an ideal, a dogma, a project. The first "intellectuals" were the
writers who defended Captain Alfred Dreyfus against the accusation of
treason, invoking on his behalf the primacy of universal abstractions:
"truth," "justice," and "rights." Their counterparts, the "anti-Dreyfusards"
(also intellectuals, though they abhorred the term), invoked abstractions
of their own, though less universal in nature: "honor," "nation," "*patrie*,"
"France."

So long as public policy debate was framed in such all-embracing
generalities, whether ethical or political, intellectuals shaped—and in
some countries dominated—public discourse. In states where public opposition and criticism was (is) repressed, individual intellectuals assumed
de facto the role of spokesmen for the public interest and for the people,
against authority and the state. But even in open societies the twentieth-
century intellectual acquired a certain public status, benefiting not only
from the right of free expression but also from the near-universal literacy
of the advanced societies, which assured him or her an audience.

It is easy in retrospect to dismiss the engaged intellectuals of the last
century. The propensity for self-aggrandizement, preening contentedly
in the admiring mirror of an audience of like-minded fellow thinkers,
was easy to indulge. Because intellectuals were in so many cases politically
"engaged" at a time when political engagement took one to extremes, and
because their engagement typically took the form of the written word,

many have left a record of pronouncements and affiliations that have not worn well. Some served as spokesmen for power or for a constituency, trimming their beliefs and pronouncements to circumstance and interest: what Edward Said once called "the fawning elasticity with regard to one's own side" has indeed "disfigured the history of intellectuals."

Moreover, as Raymond Aron once remarked apropos his French contemporaries, intellectuals seemed all too often to make a point of *not* knowing what they were talking about, especially in technical fields such as economics or military affairs. And for all their talk of "responsibility," a disconcerting number of prominent intellectuals on Right and Left alike proved strikingly irresponsible in their insouciant propensity for encouraging violence to others at a safe distance from themselves. "Mistaken ideas always end in bloodshed," Camus wrote, "but in every case it is someone else's blood. That is why some of our thinkers feel free to say just about anything."

All true. And yet: The intellectual—free-thinking or politically committed, detached or engaged—was also a defining glory of the twentieth century. A mere listing of the most interesting political writers, social commentators, or public moralists of the age, from Émile Zola to Václav Havel, from Karl Kraus to Margarete Buber-Neumann, from Alva Myrdal to Sidney Hook, would fill this introduction and more. We have all but forgotten not only *who* these people were but just how large was their audience and how widespread their influence. And to the extent that we do have a shared recollection of intellectuals, it is all too often reduced to the stereotype of a rather narrow band of left-leaning Western "progressives" who dominated their own stage from the 1950s through the 1980s: Jean-Paul Sartre, Michel Foucault, Günter Grass, Susan Sontag.

The real intellectual action, however, was elsewhere. In the Soviet Union and Eastern Europe, opposition to Communist repression was for many years confined to a handful of courageous individuals "writing for the desk drawer." In interwar Europe both Fascism and "anti-Fascism" could draw on a talented pool of literary advocates and spokespersons: We may not be altogether comfortable acknowledging the number and quality of nationalist and Fascist intellectuals in those years, but at least until 1941 the influence of writers like Ernst Jünger in Germany, Pierre Drieu La Rochelle and Louis-Ferdinand Céline in France, Mircea Eliade in Romania, or Henri de Man in Belgium was probably greater than that of their left-leaning contemporaries whom we more readily celebrate today: André Malraux, John Dewey, or even George Orwell.

But above all, the twentieth century saw the emergence of a new intellectual type: the rootless "voyager in the century." Typically such persons had passed from political or ideological commitment in the wake of the Russian Revolution into a world-weary skepticism: compatible with a sort of disabused, pessimistic liberalism but at a tangent to national or ideological allegiances. Many of these representative twentieth-century intellectuals were Jewish (though few remained practicing Jews and fewer still became active Zionists), overwhelmingly from the Jewish communities of Eastern and Central Europe: "chance survivors of a deluge" in Hannah Arendt's words. Many, too, came from cities and provinces that for all their cultural cosmopolitanism, were geographically peripheral: Königsberg, Cernovitz, Vilna, Sarajevo, Alexandria, Calcutta, or Algiers. Most were exiled in one way or another and would have shared, on their own terms, Edward Said's bewilderment at the appeal of patriotism: "I still have not been able to understand what it means to love a country."

Taken all in all, these men and women constituted a twentieth-century "Republic of Letters": a virtual community of conversation and argument whose influence reflected and illuminated the tragic choices of the age. Some of them are represented in the essays in this book. Of these, Arendt and Albert Camus may be the only names still familiar to a broad audience. Primo Levi is of course widely read today, but not, perhaps, in ways he might have wished. Manès Sperber is sadly forgotten, though his distinctively Jewish trajectory is perhaps the most emblematic of them all. Arthur Koestler, whose life, allegiances, and writings established him for many decades as the intellectual archetype of the age, is no longer a household name. There was a time when every college student had read—or wanted to read—*Darkness at Noon*. Today, Koestler's best-selling novel of the Moscow show trials is an acquired, minority taste.

If young readers find Koestler's themes alien and his concerns exotic, this is because we have lost touch not only with the great intellectuals of the past century but also with the ideas and ideals that moved them.

Outside North Korea, no one under the age of forty today has an adult memory of life in a Communist society.[5] It is now so long since a self-confident "Marxism" was the conventional ideological reference point of the intellectual Left that it is quite difficult to convey to a younger generation what it stood for and why it aroused such passionate sentiments for and against. There is much to be said for consigning defunct dogmas to the dustbin of history, particularly when they have been responsible for so much suffering. But we pay a price: The allegiances of the past—and thus the past itself—become utterly incomprehensible.

If we are to understand the world whence we have just emerged, we need to remind ourselves of the power of ideas. And we need to recall the remarkable grip exercised by the Marxist idea in particular upon the imagination of the twentieth century. Many of the most interesting minds of the age were drawn to it, if only for a while: on its own account or because the collapse of liberalism and the challenge of Fascism offered no apparent alternative. Many others, some of whom were never in the least tempted by the mirage of Revolution, nevertheless devoted much of their lives to engaging and combating Marxism. They took its challenge very seriously indeed and often understood it better than its acolytes.

The Jewish intellectuals of interwar and postwar Central Europe were especially drawn to Marxism: in part by the Promethean ambition of the project, but also thanks to the complete collapse of their world, the impossibility of returning to the past or continuing in the old ways, the seeming inevitability of building an utterly different, new world. "Żydokommuna" ("Judeo-Communism") may be an anti-Semitic term of abuse in Polish nationalist circles, but for a few crucial years it also described a reality. The remarkable Jewish contribution to the history of modern Eastern Europe cannot be disentangled from the unique attraction to Central European Jewish intellectuals of the Marxist project. In retrospect, of course, the intellectual and personal enthusiasms and engagements of the age seem tragically out of proportion to the gray, grim outcome. But that is not how things seemed at the time.

Because all this passion now appears spent, and the counter-passions it aroused accordingly redundant, commentators today are inclined to dismiss the ideological "culture wars" of the twentieth century, the doctrinal challenges and counter-challenges, as a closed book. Communism confronted capitalism (or liberalism): It lost, both in the terrain of ideas and on the ground, and is thus behind us. But in dismissing the failed promises and false prophets of the past, we are also a little too quick to underestimate—or simply to forget—their appeal. Why, after all, were so many talented minds (not to speak of many millions of voters and activists) attracted to these promises and those prophets? Because of the horrors and fears of the age? Perhaps. But were the circumstances of the twentieth century really so unusual, so unique and unrepeatable that we can be sure that whatever propelled men and women toward the grand narratives of revolution and renewal will not come again? Are the sunlit uplands of "peace, democracy, and the free market" truly here to stay?[6]

WE ARE PREDISPOSED today to look back upon the twentieth century as an age of political extremes, of tragic mistakes and wrongheaded choices; an age of delusion from which we have now, thankfully, emerged. But are we not just as deluded? In our newfound worship of the private sector and the market have we not simply inverted the faith of an earlier generation in "public ownership" and "the state," or in "planning"? Nothing is more ideological, after all, than the proposition that all affairs and policies, private and public, must turn upon the globalizing economy, its unavoidable laws, and its insatiable demands. Indeed, this worship of economic necessity and its iron laws was also a core premise of Marxism. In transiting from the twentieth century to the twenty-first, have we not just abandoned one nineteenth-century belief system and substituted another in its place?

We are no less confused, it seems, in the moral lessons we claim to have drawn from the past century. Modern secular society has long been uncomfortable with the idea of "evil." Liberals are embarrassed by its uncompromising ethical absolutism and religious overtones. The great political religions of the twentieth century preferred more rationalistic, instrumental accounts of good and bad, right and wrong. But in the wake of World War II, the Nazi destruction of the Jews, and a growing international awareness of the scale of Communist crimes, "evil" crept slowly back into moral and even political discourse. Hannah Arendt was perhaps the first to recognize this, when she wrote in 1945 that "the problem of evil will be the fundamental question of postwar intellectual life in Europe"; but it is Leszek Kołakowski, a very different sort of philosopher working in an avowedly religious tradition, who has put the matter best: "The Devil is part of our experience. Our generation has seen enough of it for the message to be taken extremely seriously. Evil, I contend, is not contingent, it is not the absence, or deformation, or the subversion of virtue (or whatever else we may think of as its opposite), but a stubborn and unredeemable fact."

But now that the concept of "evil" has reentered discursive usage, we don't know what to do with it. In Western usage today the word is deployed primarily to denote the "unique" evil of Hitler and the Nazis. But here we become confused. Sometimes the genocide of the Jews—the "Holocaust"—is presented as a singular crime, the twentieth-century incarnation of an evil never matched before or since, an example and a warning: "Never again." But at other times we are all too ready to invoke that same evil for comparative purposes, finding genocidal intentions, "axes of evil" and "Hitlers" everywhere from Iraq to North Korea, and warning of an impending repeat of the unique and unrepeatable every time someone smears anti-Semitic graffiti on a synagogue wall or expresses nostalgia for Stalin. In all this we have lost sight of what it was about twentieth-century radical ideologies that proved so seductive and thus truly *diabolical.* Sixty years ago Arendt feared that we would not know how to speak of evil and would thus never grasp its significance. Today we speak of it all the time—with the same result.

Much the same confusion attends our contemporary obsession with "terror," "terrorism," and "terrorists." To state what should be obvious, there is nothing new about terrorism and it is hard to know what to make of a historian who can claim that terrorism is a "post–Cold War phenomenon" (see Chapter XXI). Even if we exclude assassinations or attempted assassinations of presidents and monarchs and confine ourselves to those who kill unarmed civilians in pursuit of a political objective, terrorists have been with us for well over a hundred years. There have been Russian terrorists, Indian terrorists, Arab terrorists, Basque terrorists, Malay terrorists, and dozens of others besides. There have been and still are Christian terrorists, Jewish terrorists, and Muslim terrorists. There were

Yugoslav ("partisan") terrorists settling scores in World War II; Zionist terrorists blowing up Arab marketplaces in Palestine before 1948; American-financed Irish terrorists in Margaret Thatcher's London; U.S.-armed *mujahaddin* terrorists in 1980s Afghanistan, and so on.

No one who has lived in Spain, Italy, Germany, Turkey, Japan, the UK, or France, not to speak of more habitually violent lands, could have failed to notice the omnipresence of terrorists—using guns, knives, bombs, chemicals, cars, trains, planes, and much else—over the course of the twentieth century right up to and beyond the year 2000. The only—*only*—thing that has changed is the September 2001 unleashing of homicidal terrorism within the United States. Even that is not wholly unprecedented: The means are new and the carnage horrifying, but terrorism on U.S. soil was not unknown in the early years of the twentieth century.

But whereas in our reiterated invocation and abuse of the idea of "evil" we have imprudently trivialized the concept, with terrorism we have made the opposite mistake. We have raised an otherwise mundane act of politically motivated murder into a moral category, an ideological abstraction, and a global foe. We should not be surprised to find that this has once again been achieved by the ill-informed invocation of inappropriate twentieth-century analogies. "We" are not merely at war with terrorists; we are engaged in a worldwide civilizational struggle—"a global enterprise of uncertain duration," according to the Bush administration's 2002 National Security Strategy—with "Islamo-Fascism."

There is a double confusion here. The first, of course, consists of simplifying the motives of the anti-Fascist movements of the 1930s, while lumping together the widely varying Fascisms of early-twentieth-century Europe with the very different resentments, demands, and strategies of the (equally varied) Muslim movements and insurgencies of our own time. Familiarity with recent history might help correct these errors. But the more serious mistake consists of taking the form for the content: defining all the various terrorists and terrorisms, with their contrasting and often conflicting objectives, by their actions alone. It would be rather as though one were to lump together Italian Red Brigades, the German Baader-Meinhof gang, the Provisional IRA, the Basque ETA, Switzerland's Jura Separatists, and the National Front for the Liberation of Corsica, call the resulting amalgam "European Extremism" . . . and then declare war against the phenomenon of political violence in Europe.

The danger of abstracting "terrorism" from its different contexts, setting it upon a pedestal as the greatest threat to Western civilization, or democracy, or "our way of life," and targeting it for an indefinite war is that we shall neglect the many other challenges of the age. On this, too, the illusions and errors of the cold war years might have something to teach us about ideological tunnel vision. Hannah Arendt, once again: "The greatest danger of recognizing totalitarianism as the curse of the century would be an obsession with it to the extent of becoming blind to the numerous small and not so small evils with which the road to hell is paved."[7]

But of all our contemporary illusions, the most dangerous is the one that underpins and accounts for all the others. And that is the idea that we live in a time without precedent: that what is happening to us is new and irreversible and that the past has nothing to teach us . . . except when it comes to ransacking it for serviceable precedents. To take but one example: Only a quite astonishing indifference to the past could lead an American secretary of state to discourage outside efforts to end Israel's calamitous 2006 war in Lebanon (itself an ill-fated replay of an equally calamitous invasion twenty-five years before) by describing the unfolding disaster as "the birth-pangs of a new Middle East." The modern history of the Middle East is drenched in the blood of serial political miscarriages. The last thing the region needs is yet another incompetent foreign midwife.[8]

Such foolhardiness is perhaps easier to sell in a country like the United States—which venerates its own past but pays the history of the rest of humankind insufficient attention—than in Europe, where the cost of past mistakes and the visible evidence of their consequences were until recently quite hard to miss. But even in Europe a younger generation of citizens and politicians is increasingly oblivious to history: Ironically, this is especially the case in the former Communist lands of Central Europe, where "building capitalism" and "getting rich" are the new collective goals, while democracy is taken for granted and even regarded in some quarters as an impediment.[9]

But even "capitalism" has a history. The last time the capitalist world passed through a period of unprecedented expansion and great private wealth creation, during the "globalization" *avant le mot* of the world economy in the decades preceding World War I, there was a widespread assumption in imperial Britain—much as there is in the U.S. and Western Europe today—that this was the threshold of a truly unprecedented age of indefinite peace and prosperity. Anyone seeking an account of this confidence—and what became of it—can do no better than read the magisterial opening paragraphs of John Maynard Keynes's *Economic Consequences of the Peace*: a summary of the hubristic illusions of a world on the edge of catastrophe, written in the aftermath of the war that was to put an end to all such irenic fancies for the next fifty years.[10]

It was Keynes, too, who anticipated and helped prepare for the "craving for security" that Europeans would feel after three decades of war and economic collapse. As I have suggested above, it was in large measure thanks to the precautionary services and safety nets incorporated into their postwar systems of governance that the citizens of the advanced countries lost the gnawing sentiment of insecurity and fear which had dominated political life between 1914 and 1945.

Until now. For there are reasons to believe that this may be about to change. Fear is reemerging as an active ingredient of political life in Western democracies. Fear of terrorism, of course; but also, and perhaps more insidiously, fear of the uncontrollable speed of change, fear of the loss of employment, fear of losing ground to others in an increasingly unequal distribution of resources, fear of losing control of the circumstances and routines of one's daily life. And, perhaps above all, fear that it is not just we who can no longer shape our lives but that those in authority have lost control as well, to forces beyond their reach.

Few democratic governments can resist the temptation to turn this sentiment of fear to political advantage. Some have already done so. In which case we should not be surprised to see the revival of pressure groups, political parties, and political programs based upon fear: fear of foreigners; fear of change; fear of open frontiers and open communications; fear of the free exchange of unwelcome opinions. In recent years such people and parties have done well in a number of impeccably democratic countries—Belgium, Switzerland, and Israel, as well as more vulnerable republics like Russia, Poland, and Venezuela—and the challenge they present has tempted mainstream parties in the U.S., Denmark, Holland, France, and the United Kingdom to take a harsher line with visitors, "aliens," illegal immigrants, and cultural or religious minorities. We can expect more along these lines in years to come, probably aimed at restricting the flow of "threatening" goods and ideas as well as people. The politics of insecurity are contagious.

In that case we might do well to take a second glance at the way our twentieth-century predecessors responded to what were, in many respects, comparable dilemmas. We may discover, as they did, that the collective provision of social services and some restriction upon inequalities of income and wealth are important economic variables in themselves, furnishing the necessary public cohesion and political confidence for a sustained prosperity—and that only the state has the resources and the authority actively to underwrite those services and provisions and limitations in our collective name.

We may find that a healthy democracy, far from being threatened by the regulatory state, actually depends upon it: that in a world increasingly polarized between isolated, insecure individuals and unregulated global forces, the legitimate authority of the democratic state may be the best kind of intermediate institution we can devise. What, after all, is the alternative? Our contemporary cult of economic freedom, combined with a heightened sense of fear and insecurity, could lead to reduced social provision and minimal economic regulation, but accompanied by extensive governmental oversight of communication, movement, and opinion. "Chinese" capitalism, as it were, Western-style.

What, then, are the limits of the democratic state? What is the proper balance of private initiative and public interest, of liberty and equality? What are the manageable objectives of social policy, and what constitutes interference and overreach? Where exactly should we situate the inevitable compromise between maximized private wealth and minimized social friction? What are the appropriate boundaries of political and religious communities, and how best should we minimize frictions across them? How should we police those conflicts (both within states and between them) that cannot be negotiated? And so forth.

These are the challenges of the coming century. They were also the challenges that faced the last century, which is why they will sound at least a little familiar to some. They are a reminder that the simple nostrums of today's ideologues of "freedom" are no more help to us in a complex world than were those of their predecessors on the other side of the twentieth-century ideological chasm; a reminder, too, that yesterday's Left and today's Right share among other things an overconfident propensity to deny the relevance of past experience to present problems. We think we have learned enough from the past to know that many of the old answers don't work, and that may be true. But what the past can truly help us understand is the perennial complexity of the questions.

NOTES

[1] "Never such innocence,
    Never before or since,
    As changed itself to past
    Without a word—the men
    Leaving the gardens tidy,
    The thousands of marriages
    Lasting a little while longer:
    Never such innocence again."
        Philip Larkin, *MCMXIV*

[2] See, classically, Lytton Strachey's *Eminent Victorians,* first published in 1918.

[3] See, e.g., my discussion of the writings of John Gaddis in Chapter XXI.

[4] Thomas Friedman, "Living Hand to Mouth," *New York Times,* October 26, 2005.

[5] In substance this point applies even to China, for all the formal "Communist" attributes of the governing apparatus.

[6] For this view of the matter see, e.g., Michael Mandelbaum, *The Ideas That Conquered the World: Peace, Democracy, and Free Markets in the Twenty-first Century* (NY, Public Affairs, 2003)

[7] Hannah Arendt, *Essays in Understanding, 1930–1954* (New York: Harcourt Brace, 1995), 271–272.

[8] Condoleezza Rice, in a briefing at the State Department, July 21, 2006. *http://www.state.gov/ secretary/rm/2006/69331.htm*

[9] I am grateful to Ivan Krastev of the Central European University for allowing me to read his unpublished paper on "The Strange Death of Liberal Central Europe," which contains a stimulating discussion of this topic.

[10] John Maynard Keynes, *The Economic Consequences of the Peace* (New York: Harcourt, Brace, Jovanovich, 1920) Chapter II: "Europe Before The War."

Part One

THE HEART OF DARKNESS

his best he was one of the greatest reporters of the century. His early enthusiasm for Vladimir Jabotinsky and Revisionist Zionism led him to an extended stay in Palestine in 1926–27, and he returned there for eight months in 1945. One product of these sojourns was *Promise and Fulfillment: Palestine 1917–1949*, still one of the best pieces of writing on its subject, despite its author's prejudices and because of them. *Spanish Testament* (1937) ranks with the Civil War reporting of Orwell. *The Scum of the Earth* (1941) is not just a riveting description of Koestler's experience in the French internment camps of Gurs and Le Vernet, it is also one of the most convincing and thoughtful accounts of the rotting, vengeful atmosphere in France as it entered the abyss. And Koestler's autobiographies *Arrow in the Blue* and *The Invisible Writing*—together with his classic memoir of Communist faith and disillusion *The God That Failed* (1949)—afford an insight into the life and the opinions of a true child of the century. One day they will be required reading for every historian of our age.

The strengths of Koestler's journalism derive from the same characteristics that marred his later forays into science and philosophy. Those books—notably *Insight & Outlook, The Sleepwalkers, The Act of Creation, The Ghost in the Machine, The Case of the Midwife Toad,* and *The Roots of Coincidence*, most of them published in the 1960s—were panned by specialists for their idiosyncratic speculation, their searching for coherence and meaning in every little coincidence and detail, their abuse of analogy, and the overconfident intrusion of their author into matters of which he was comparatively ignorant.

But those same Koestlerian traits give his essays and his reportage a bite and a freshness that time has not softened. In "The Yogi and the Commissar" and "The Trail of the Dinosaur," Koestler's engaged invective and his mordant and bitter commentaries on the illusions and the venality of his contemporaries are not just a pleasure to read. (His description of Simone de Beauvoir as "a planet shining with reflected light" has certainly stood the test of time.) They are also a sure guide to some of the opinions, the quarrels, and the beliefs that shaped the era. And they were hugely influential in shaping contemporary opinion.

In David Cesarani's words, "By the force of his arguments and his personal example, Koestler emancipated thousands of people from thralldom to Marx, Lenin and Stalin."* For this reason alone, the author of *Darkness at Noon* (of which more later) would merit a major biography. It is a task much facilitated by the copious written record—in addition to the books already mentioned and a half dozen novels, Koestler kept detailed diaries and conducted a sustained correspondence with his many wives, lovers, friends, and enemies. Cesarani has put all this material to very good use; the result is a lively narrative of Koestler's life, works, and opinions. Cesarani's descriptions and summaries of the published works are conventional, but then it is not easy to do justice at second hand to writings whose virtue lies in their vivacity and their immediacy. About the later writings, certainly, it would take an inordinately sympathetic biographer to avoid remarking upon the likelihood that they will soon be justly forgotten; even so, Cesarani is kind enough to suggest that some of Koestler's parascientific aperçus "may yet have the last laugh on the grey beards of Academe." It is not clear why he thinks so. If it proves true, it will only be as a result of the sort of coincidence that Koestler set out so resolutely to deny.

About Koestler the man, Cesarani has rather more to say, and much of it is to the point. Arthur Koestler seems to have suffered from what Cesarani, following many of Koestler's own friends, calls "a crippling deficit of self-regard." He was a smallish man, an outsider for most of his life, who wanted very much to please and to be liked, but who succeeded in arguing, breaking with, and sometimes brawling with almost everyone he met. Like Sartre, he took Benzedrine to sustain him during his spells of writing, and he drank like a fish. His drinking led to bouts of quarrelsome violence and an extraordinary series of smashed cars; and when he wasn't drinking, fighting, or writing he was often depressed and consumed with self-doubt. He was strikingly generous to strangers with the riches he earned from *Darkness at Noon* and his later writings, but he was selfish and narcissistic in his private life. According to his biographer, he was inordinately attracted to powerful men and weak women.

Of all these traits, it is Koestler's status as an outsider that seems to me the most salient and interesting. Like many Central European intellectuals of his generation, Koestler had no fixed abode. He wandered

---

* David Cesarani, *Arthur Koestler: The Homeless Mind* (New York: Free Press, 1999).

from country to country, from language to language, from one commitment to the next. He knew and socialized with all the significant writers
and thinkers of his age in Berlin, Paris, Jerusalem, London, and New
York, but he was never "one of them." It was perhaps a misfortune that
he should have ended up in England: Of all his transitory homes, this
was the place where belonging came hardest for the foreigner.

Koestler's accent, his intensity, his experience, and his sense of the
tragic all put him at odds with the distinctive English preference for
understatement and irony. In New York, he was taken Very Seriously. In
Paris, his friends quarreled with him over the Great Issues of the day. But
in London, where he tried very hard to become English and strove for
acceptance and membership, Koestler was sometimes an object of amuse-
ment and even ridicule. His English contemporaries admired him, certainly. They respected him and they acknowledged his influence. But on
the whole they did not understand him.

David Cesarani is English—he is professor of modern Jewish history
at the University of Southampton—and it seems to me that he, too, does
not always understand Arthur Koestler. He certainly finds him a bit annoying. His new book frequently second-guesses Koestler's own memoirs
and questions their credibility. It takes Koestler to task for his opinions
and raps him over the knuckles for his shortcomings. This seems all a bit
harsh. Koestler's memoirs certainly retell his life story from his own distinctive perspective (how else would they tell it?), and the story itself
occasionally changes from one version to the next, in keeping with his
evolving interests. Still, Koestler is actually a rather good source of information about his own weaknesses. He admits to his false toughness, his
insecurities, his constant unfulfilled search for the perfect Cause and the
perfect woman, and his many personal failings. He faithfully recorded
and castigated his "complexes": his guilt, his dissipation, his womanizing,
and his bad manners.

Cesarani acknowledges this, but then he admonishes Koestler for
failing to pull his socks up and improve himself. Even when Koestler does
correct a failing, Cesarani finds fault in his motives. In his Spanish jail,
awaiting execution, Koestler came to the firm and abiding conviction
that no abstract ideal can justify individual suffering. Cesarani disapproves: "It is perturbing and hard to accept in one who was so critical of

others for their lack of imagination, that Koestler only realised that nothing, not even the most rationally compelling cause, was worth the sacrifice of a single life when it was his life that was at stake." Once released, Koestler went on to devote his energies to dismantling the myth of dialectical materialism. But his rationalist critique of Marxism-Leninism's fake science falls short of his biographer's expectations, and Cesarani rebukes him for the "heuristic gaffe" of deploying a "materialist" criticism against a materialist illusion.

A biographer is entitled to censure his subject on occasion. More serious is Cesarani's distance from Koestler's European world. There are some minor but revealing errors: Otto Katz, another displaced Central European Jew, who was executed in Prague in December 1952 as a "fellow conspirator" in the trial of Rudolf Slánský, was not the cover name of André Simone (not "Simon"); it was the other way around. The Italian essayist and onetime colleague of Koestler's was Nicolà Chiaromonte, not Nicholas Chiaromonte. Ernest Gellner was decidedly not a "Viennese-born philosopher." *France-Observateur* (not "Observateur") was not a Communist sheet, but a neutralist journal of the non-Communist Parisian Left, which gives its attacks on Koestler in 1950 a significance quite different from the one suggested by Cesarani. And if André Gide was recording opinions about Koestler in his diary "in the 1960s," then Cesarani has had access to some very privileged information: Gide died in 1951.

Minor gaffes such as these help explain deeper misunderstandings. Cesarani has a soft spot for Simone de Beauvoir and cites her more than once as a guide to Koestler's failings. Commenting on Koestler's anti-Communism in February 1948 (at the time of the Prague coup), de Beauvoir opines: "He is remorseful not to be any longer a Communist, because now they are going to win and he wants to be on the winning side." This tells us quite a lot about de Beauvoir, but not much about Koestler. In a similar vein we are informed approvingly that she thought Koestler had "a mediocre Marxist education." That is true—though coming from this source it is a bit ripe. But it is irrelevant. Men and women did not become Communists in interwar Europe owing to the close study of Marxist texts. In Koestler's own words (not cited by Cesarani), "What an enormous longing for a new human order there was in the era between the world wars, and what a miserable failure to live up to it."

That is why people joined the Communist Party, and it is also why they were so reluctant to abandon it. Cesarani cannot fathom why Koestler did not make a clean and early break with the party—after all, his disillusion began with his firsthand observations of the Soviet Union just a year after he became a Communist. According to his biographer, Koestler's claims of early disillusionment should therefore be treated with suspicion—it "took a long time to have much effect." It was only (!) in 1938 that Koestler broke with the German Communists in Parisian exile, and even then he promised not to attack or "break fealty with" the Soviet Union. Cesarani finds this odd and describes it as a very "late" break with Communism. But it is absolutely at one with the experience of many ex-Communists of the time. It was not easy to leave the party, with all the fellowship and the security that it offered; and 1938 was hardly a time to hand hostages to Fascist fortune by embarrassing your former comrades and discounting their illusions and their suffering. It is easy for Cesarani now to castigate Koestler and his contemporaries for not seeing the light right away and behaving accordingly. At the time, in continental Europe, matters were a little more complicated.

The distance separating Cesarani from Koestler when it comes to understanding the mood of Europe before (and after) the war is chiefly one of space: the space that separates Britain from Europe. Obviously Cesarani understands the turbulent background to intellectual and emotional choices in the first half of the century: the Central European catastrophe of 1918–33 (revolution-inflation-dictatorship), the threat of Hitler, the promise of Communism, Spain, wartime collaboration, and the Soviet occupation of half the continent. But none of these calamities happened in Britain, to its eternal good fortune; and a historian of Britain may too readily underestimate their significance when accounting for attitudes and actions across the Channel.

Still, if there is a real difficulty with Cesarani's approach, it results from an unbridgeable distance not in space but in time. For in two crucial respects, Cesarani's book is deeply anachronistic. In the first place, he takes Koestler severely to task for his attitude to women. There is no doubt that the way Arthur Koestler treated women was, to say the least, disrespectful. It is not so much that he had serial affairs and wives—that might plausibly be interpreted as evidence that he rather liked women, even if he failed to like any one woman for very long. But there is a lot of evidence that Koestler did not so much seduce women as accost them and expect them to sleep with him; and when they demurred, he was pushy and demanding.

Most of the women whom Koestler tried to bed were younger than him, and were often impressed by his fame. However badly he treated them, they tended, in Sidney Hook's words, to "make allowances" for him. He indulged his sexual whims with little regard for the feelings of others, and he could be as violent and reckless at home as he was in cafés or at the wheel. On at least one occasion (according to Cesarani) Koestler forced someone to have sex against her will. That is quite a rap sheet. It should be sufficient to introduce a degree of shadow into any portrait of the man. Yet Cesarani goes much, much further. Koestler, he writes, had a sustained record of "beating and raping" women. In Cesarani's intemperate words, Koestler was nothing less than "a serial rapist."

If Koestler were alive, he would surely sue for libel, and he would surely win. Even on Cesarani's own evidence, there is only one unambiguously attested charge of rape: In 1952 Koestler assaulted Jill Craigie, the wife of English politician and future Labour Party leader Michael Foot, in her own home during her husband's absence. Much of the rest consists of circumstantial evidence and a strong dose of present-minded interpretation. Thus both Koestler and Simone de Beauvoir acknowledged that they had one night of bad sex, a mutual mistake. De Beauvoir attributed it to Koestler's persistence—she finally gave in under the pressure of his importuning. Is this rape? A number of other women attest that Koestler pestered them for sex—some conceded, some didn't. Whether they did or they didn't, many women seem to have remained fond of Koestler after the experience. For Cesarani, this is inexplicable: "Perhaps he attracted a certain kind of masochistic personality for whom he fulfilled a particular need?" As for those who had sex with Arthur Koestler and went back for more, they presumably had a "compulsion to re-enact that wounding process."

Maybe. Or maybe they just enjoyed themselves. Cesarani, like Koestler at his most polemical, sees everything in black or white. Either you are making consensual, mutually initiated, monogamous, nonaggressive, amorous love, or else something very dark and unpleasant is taking place: rape—or, more commonly, "date-rape,"—a term that occurs with disarming frequency in this book. As for the notion that someone might indeed be disposed to sexual domination, and even occasionally to force, and yet be appealing to women—well, this has apparently never occurred to Cesarani, even as a hypothesis. As a consequence, there is something tedious and "sexually correct" about his account of Koestler's adventures. Cesarani doesn't like the younger Koestler's multitude of relationships, his "relentless pursuit of women." Koestler himself explained reasonably enough that he habitually sought female companionship and comfort, but for Cesarani, "there comes a point when his rationalizations for sleeping around ring hollow."

Worse for poor Koestler, he preferred women. If he had bisexual leanings, he suppressed them: "To him, heterosexuality was the norm, men were dominant partners and women were submissive." Worse still, Koestler was not always faithful to one woman at a time: nor, indeed, were his women always faithful to him. Celia Paget briefly abandoned Koestler for a weeklong fling with Albert Camus, prompting an outburst from Cesarani, who finds it "extraordinary" that "people who constantly talked about friendship and loyalty" spent so much time in bed with their friends. Describing Koestler's occasional taste for threesomes, Cesarani writes of "another gruesome triangular encounter." The reader is constantly aware of the author's presence, hovering pruriently and commenting sniffily upon the copulations of his protagonists. "Conventional morality seems to have had little purchase in these circles." Quite.

Why should it? Even if we exclude as special pleading the claim (advanced by Koestler's fellow Hungarian George Mikes) that if Koestler did not take no for an answer he was only practicing the sexual mores of his birthplace, the fact remains that sleeping around, "betraying" one's lover or one's spouse, treating women as submissive, and behaving in a generally "sexist" manner was hardly a trait peculiar to Arthur Koestler. Cesarani may not be old enough to remember the world before the sexual revolutions of the 1960s, and he may lack personal experience of the conventions and the morals of the European intelligentsia. But as a historian he should surely hesitate before chastising his subject for attitudes and assumptions that were widely shared in his cultural and social milieu. To the best of my knowledge, the overwhelming majority of the Hungarian, Austrian, Russian, German, and French intellectuals who pass through the pages of Cesarani's book shared most of Koestler's views on such matters, even if they were not always so assiduous or so successful in practice. You have only to read their memoirs. Even the English were a lot less conventionally well behaved back then; but since *their* misdemeanors often involved partners of the same sex, Cesarani would probably find less to reprove.

The present-minded primness of Cesarani's tone is often unintentionally funny and self-revealing. What sounds like a rather entertaining luncheon gathering of Koestler and some women friends becomes a "grisly assembly of ex-lovers." When poor Cynthia Jeffries (Koestler's last wife) takes up German and cooking, she earns Cesarani's lasting disapproval for these "strikingly submissive gestures." And Cesarani wholly deplores "Koestler's assumption that a life of promiscuity and deception is normal and should be pleasurable, were it not for the inconvenience of a bad conscience." If Koestler was ever made uncomfortable by his conscience—and there is not much evidence that he was—it was surely as nothing to the discomfort that he has caused his biographer by so obviously enjoying bodily pleasures and indulging them to the full. You can almost feel Cesarani's relief when Koestler gets too old for extramarital sex and settles into respectable middle age.

Reviewers of the English edition of this book have been much taken with the issue of Koestler's sideline in rape, and have asked how far this should alter posterity's view of him. But Koestler's attitude toward women has never been in doubt—you have only to read his memoirs or some of the novels, notably *Arrival and Departure*. We now know that he raped the wife of a friend and forced his attentions on some reluctant women. This is deeply unattractive behavior. But Koestler was no moralist. He did not preach about human goodness or pose himself as an exemplar of anything. If it turned out that he was a closet racist, or had remained all his life a secret member of the Communist Party, or had privately financed violent terrorist organizations, then some of his publications would indeed seem very odd, and we should have to ask how far he wrote in good faith. But nothing he wrote about sex is in contradiction with his actions. And nothing he wrote about politics, or intellectuals, or the death penalty, depends for its credibility upon his sexual behavior. Koestler was a great journalist who exercised great influence; no more, no less. And neither of those claims is hostage to our views about his private life, after the fact.

THE SECOND ANACHRONISM in Cesarani's book concerns Koestler's Jewishness. On this score it is easier to sympathize with the biographer. Arthur Koestler was a Jew, born of Jewish parents into early-twentieth-century Budapest's large and thriving Jewish community. He was drawn into Zionism while at university in Vienna: By 1924, at the age of nineteen, he was chairman of the Association of Jewish Nationalist Students in Austria. He spent much of the late twenties in Mandate Palestine, learning a passable café Hebrew, and he would return there in 1945. In addition to *Promise and Fulfillment*, his Palestine stints resulted in *Thieves in the Night* (1946), a novel about a Jewish settlement marked by the writer's sympathy for the politics of Menachem Begin's Irgun. *Arrival and Departure*, published in 1943, was another novel shaped by Koestler's interest in the fate of the Jews, this time in occupied wartime Europe. After the declaration of the State of Israel, Koestler left the Middle East, never to return; but he remained sufficiently involved with the Jewish dilemma to write *The Thirteenth Tribe*, which appeared in 1976. It is a bizarre, misguided attempt to demonstrate that the Ashkenazi Jews of Europe are descended from Khazar tribesmen in the Caucasus—and thus need feel no special affinity for, nor obligation toward, Israel and the traditional Jewish heritage.

From all this, it would seem reasonable to infer that being Jewish was rather important to Arthur Koestler. Yet Koestler himself tended to downplay its significance. When he was not writing about Israel, Jews did not figure prominently in his work, and the autobiography goes to some lengths to understate the influence of his Jewish heritage upon his education or his opinions. Cesarani finds this a little odd, and his suspicions are probably justified, if only in part. Koestler's efforts to be what Isaac Deutscher called "a non-Jewish Jew" only serve to remind us just how very Jewish his story is, not least (for non-practicing Central

Europeans of his generation) in the effort to deny that being Jewish did or should matter. Koestler was too intelligent to claim that being Jewish was an elective affinity and that he could just choose not to be: History (that is, Hitler) had deprived him of that choice. In later years, though, he certainly behaved as though he wished it were otherwise.

Cesarani is right to note all this. But in his determination to show that Koestler was in denial, he inverts Koestler's own emphasis and finds, or claims to find, a Jewish dimension in almost everything Koestler wrote or did. When Koestler joins the German Communist Party, he is seeking an alternative way to "resolve the Jewish Question": His Communist activities, his political engagements in Popular Front Paris, and his adventures in Spain only make sense to Cesarani when seen through the prism of Jewishness. How else to account for Koestler's decision to leave Palestine in 1929 and engage in European politics? "A passionate involvement of seven years' duration in Jewish affairs could not be dropped instantly, even less when events thrust the fate of the Jews into prominence. On the contrary, Koestler's ideological, political and geographical peregrinations make more sense if they are seen in the light of his complex Jewish identity."

This is reductionist. it is perfectly possible to turn away from seven years of youthful involvement in a political or national movement, and to redirect one's attentions to an entirely different set of causes. Many of us have made precisely such a change. In the last, turbulent years of Weimar Germany, a switch from Jabotinsky to Stalin might seem unusual, but it was readily explicable—and Koestler was still only twenty-six years old when he joined the party.

According to Cesarani, however, it just doesn't make sense: "Although he explained his dive into the Communist Party in a variety of more or less convincing ways, it appears most logical when it is seen as having a significant Jewish dimension." Does it really? And what does logic have to do with it? Political choices in that time and in that place were made out of optimism, pessimism, fear, longing, illusion, calculation. Even if it were somehow "logical" for a Jew to become a Communist, that would not explain why any one Jew in fact did so. There were many non-Jewish Communists, and even more Jewish non-Communists, in interwar Europe; the isomorphic relationship between Communism and non-

Zionist, nonpracticing Jews may seem evident to Cesarani, but it was less obvious at the time.

In a similar vein, Cesarani is not well pleased with Koestler's attitude to Israel after 1948. Koestler left Israel in that year and did not return; his memoirs, written shortly afterward, do indeed play down his earlier involvement in Jewish affairs, something that Cesarani calls "repression." In later years, in keeping with his rather Manichaean intellectual style, Koestler claimed that the existence of a national state offered Jews a clear and unavoidable choice between aliyah and assimilation, between Zionism and the abandonment of a redundant tradition. His insistence on the impossibility of any middle path provoked a famous correspondence in 1952 with Isaiah Berlin, who suggested that there were many ways to be Jewish, and that a certain untidiness and incoherence in one's way of life might be preferable to the uncompromising options proposed by Koestler.

Cesarani goes further. He finds fault with Koestler's etiolated account of Jewishness ("His version of Judaism was nonsensical . . . Judaism does have a national dimension, but it also has a universal message") and rather disapproves of Koestler's "un-Jewish" admiration for the civilization of Christian Europe. He censures Koestler's decision to live for a while in the Austrian Alps, and cannot fathom his envy for the village communities that he saw around him in Alpbach ("until quite recently those very same Tyroleans had been shooting and gassing his ilk wherever they found them"). When Koestler suggests that the existence of Israel will help Jews overcome those characteristics that were shaped by and encouraged anti-Semitism, Cesarani interprets him as "blaming the victims of Nazi persecution for their appalling fate." There is much more in this vein.

But Cesarani has missed something in his haste to hold Koestler up to contemporary standards of Jewish consciousness and find him sorely lacking. Koestler was as much an outsider in Palestine and Israel as he was everywhere else. This may have made him an unsuccessful Zionist, but it sharpened his observer's antennae. As he wrote to Celia Paget, "This country is only bearable for people who have very strong emotional ties with it—otherwise the climate is hell and the provincialism of life would bore you to death." He deeply believed in the need for a Jewish "dwarf state" to exist, and he thought it both inevitable and on the whole a good thing that Israel would over time transform Jews into Israelis. He just didn't particularly want to be there when it happened.

In other words, Koestler was reluctant to abandon precisely that sense of ambivalence and rootlessness which he so criticized in European Jewry—and which Cesarani correctly identifies as central to his personality and his writing. He was uncomfortable in Israel; he could hardly take refuge in religion or community; and the option of a Holocaust-driven sense of Jewish affirmation was simply not open to him. This is Cesarani's biggest mistake, to suppose that the sensibilities and the concerns of Jews today should have been those of a Jew of Koestler's generation.

Koestler thought and wrote about the Nazi destruction of the Jews of Europe, and his sense of the necessity of Israel was deeply informed by that experience. But—and in this respect he was representative of most Jewish intellectuals of his time—the Holocaust was not and could not be a consideration in his own identity. That would come later, much later. In the two decades following 1945, the years of Koestler's greatest prominence and public engagement, Jews and non-Jews alike paid only occasional attention to Auschwitz and its implications.

It makes no sense to write of a twentieth-century Hungarian Jew—whose formative experiences were the secularized Jewish worlds of Budapest and Vienna; who passed through all the major political upheavals of the interwar years; whose overwhelming postwar preoccupation was the Communist threat and whose elective milieu was the urban intelligentsia of continental Western Europe—as though he should have shaped his life and works by the light of the Shoah, and to suggest that if he failed to do so he was engaging in a massive exercise in denial and repression. For it is surely not his Jewishness, nor even his failure to live up to other people's expectations for a Jew, that makes Arthur Koestler interesting or significant.

WHAT DOES MATTER, of course, is *Darkness at Noon*, first published in 1940. This was Koestler's most enduring book and his most influential contribution to the century. In France alone it sold 420,000 copies in the first decade after the war. It has never been out of print in half a dozen languages, and it is widely credited with having made a singular and unequaled contribution to exploding the Soviet myth. It made Koestler a rich and famous man, and if he had not written it we would not now be reading his biography. Any assessment of Arthur Koestler's standing must rest on our reading of this book and its impact.

The story is well known. Koestler mixed his own experience of the death cell in Spain with his personal knowledge of Karl Radek and Nikolai Bukharin (both of whom he had met in Moscow) and produced the story of Nicholas Salmanovitch Rubashov, an old Bolshevik who has fallen victim to the Stalinist purges. The book was written between 1938 and 1940, and Koestler could draw on wide public awareness of the recent Moscow trials, the setting for his study of the dilemma of Communist fealty and disillusion. Rubashov is an amalgam, but also a type: the Bolshevik activist who has suppressed his own opinions and judgment in favor of those of the Party and the Leader, only to find that he now stands accused of having "objectively" opposed the party line, and thus the Grand Narrative of History.

There is no plot as such—the outcome is inevitable. But before he is executed, Rubashov engages in introspective reflections upon his loyalties and his motives. More important, he takes part in a series of exchanges with his interrogators. In these conversations Koestler reproduces not just the official charges made against the accused at the show trials, but also the moral and political logic behind them. History and Necessity, Means and Ends, intuitive reason and dialectical logic: These are all invoked and explicated in the great disputations in the novel, as first Ivanov and then Gletkin seeks to convince Rubashov that he should confess for the higher good of the party.

A part of the novel's appeal was that it captured and confirmed a popular understanding of how Communism worked and what was wrong with it. Even a neo-Trotskyist critic such as Irving Howe, who thought the book paid insufficient attention to the social context of Stalinism, conceded that it was an unimpeachable and terrifying depiction of the workings of the Communist mind. Above all, *Darkness at Noon* functioned with extraordinary effectiveness at two quite distinct levels. For a mass audience, it presented Communism as a lie and a fraud, where facts, arguments, and trials were rigged to achieve the ends sought by a ruthless dictatorial regime. But for a more discriminating intellectual readership, the book portrayed Communism not just unforgivingly, but also with a curiously human face.

Despite its obvious debt to nineteenth-century Russian literature, as well as to older accounts of witch trials and the Inquisition, *Darkness at Noon* is remarkably benign as a depiction of prison and interrogation. There are no scenes of torture. There is hardly any violence at all. The message is clear and explicitly stated: Unlike the Nazis and the Fascists, the Communists do not use physical torture to extract the curious confessions people make in court. Instead they convince their victims of their own guilt. The whole exercise operates at a rather rarefied level of dialectical conversation, especially between Ivanov and Rubashov. Even Gletkin, the "new" man, uses threats and force only out of necessity.

Whether Koestler knew that this was utterly false is unclear. But there has long been copious evidence that Communist regimes—in the Soviet Union, in the satellite states of Eastern Europe, and elsewhere— were as brutal and bloodthirsty as other modern tyrannies. Communist dictators resorted to violence and torture no less than any other dictators. Koestler's emphasis upon dialectics rather than nightsticks suggests an almost reassuring picture of the essential rationality of Communism, for all its crimes. Yet there is no doubt that he was not in the least interested in drawing a veil over Communism's worst features. So what was going on?

The answer is that *Darkness at Noon* is not a book about the victims of Communism. It is a book about Communists. The victims— Rubashov and his fellow prisoners—are Communists. Koestler is all but silent on the famines, the expropriations, the wholesale deportations of peoples authorized by Stalin. As he would write a decade later in *The God That Failed*, "How our voices boomed with righteous indignation, denouncing flaws in the procedure of justice in our comfortable democracies; and how silent we were when our comrades, without trial or conviction, were liquidated in the Socialist sixth of the earth. Each of us carries a skeleton in the cupboard of his conscience; added together they would form galleries of bones more labyrinthine than the Paris catacombs." But the skeletons are those of Communists, mostly of Communist intellectuals. And Koestler's novel is a magnificent effort by an intellectual former Communist to explain to other intellectuals why Communism persecuted its own intellectuals and why they conspired in their own humiliation.

It is also, for related reasons, an indirect apologia for Koestler's own passage through Communism. The crimes and errors of Communism are not denied. Quite the contrary. But they are presented as essentially intellectual deformations: logical derivations from legitimate starting points rendered fatal by the failure to take into account the individual and his capacity for independent judgment. In short, they are the sort of mistakes, however tragic and terrible, that intelligent and well-intentioned men can make when they are in thrall to great ideals. To adapt Shane's reassuring words in Jack Schaeffer's great eponymous novel, "No one need feel ashamed to be beaten by History."

For this reason, *Darkness at Noon* seems curiously dated today. It operates entirely within its protagonists' schema. Like Rubashov, Koestler believed that "for once History had taken a run, which at last promised a more dignified form of life for mankind; now it was over." He also gives quite a lot of credit to the interrogators, who are presumed to be acting in good faith. In Gletkin's parting words, "The Party promises only one thing: after the victory, one day when it can do no more harm, the material of the secret archives will be published. Then the world will learn what was in the background of this Punch & Judy show as you called it, which we had to act to them according to history's textbook. . . . And then you, and some of your friends of the younger generation, will be given the sympathy and pity which we denied you today." Koestler, of course, believes no such thing. But he believed that the Gletkins believe it. And that assumption renders the book, today, altogether less convincing as an insight into the Communist mind.

It follows from this—and this is not intended to diminish his significance—that Arthur Koestler has ceased to be a living source of ideas and has become a historical object. His greatest book is not the infallible account of its subject for which it was once taken; but it does offer a revealing insight into the limits of even the most devastating criticism of Communism at midcentury. *Darkness at Noon* may have undermined the plausibility of the Soviet state, but at the price of confirming the conventional intellectual assumption that Communism was nevertheless quite unlike other authoritarian regimes, and fundamentally better (or at least more interesting). This was not Koestler's intention, but he might not have disagreed.

Koestler's genius lay not in his analysis of Communism, but in his polemical brilliance when engaging with Communists (or Fascists) and their admirers. This, together with his journalism, is why he mattered then and matters now. He was witty—his essay on "The Little Flirts of St. Germain des Prés" and his vision of Parisian intellectual life under a Soviet occupation ("Les Temps héroïques," published in Paris in 1948) are not just devastating and appropriately sexually inflected accounts of the Left Bank fellow-traveling milieu of Sartre and his friends; they are also very funny (or "scabrous" and "malicious," in Cesarani's words).

Koestler got a lot of things right and saw some things long before most other people. As early as 1969, reporting for the London *Sunday Times* on his travels through the postcolonial islands of the western Pacific, he foresaw both the unanticipated consequences of decolonization and the paradox of what we are now pleased to call "globalization": "mass-produced uniform culture" and ever-more-acute "venomous local conflicts of religion, language and race." Above all, Koestler was rather brave—he had no hesitation in facing down hostile audiences or speaking unpopular truths.

This did not endear him to many people. At the founding meeting of the Congress for Cultural Freedom in Berlin in 1950, many delegates—notably A. J. Ayer and Hugh Trevor-Roper—were quite put off by Koestler's intensity and his uncompromising tactics. His obsession with the fight against Communism (like all his other obsessions) brooked no compromise and seemed to lack all proportion. But then Sidney Hook, a fellow organizer of the Congress, rightly observed that "Koestler was capable of reciting the truths of the multiplication table in a way to make some people indignant with him."

This made Koestler an uncomfortable presence, someone who brought disruption and conflict in his train. But that is what intellectuals are for. Arthur Koestler's nonconformism—which makes him as mysterious to his biographer as he was annoying to his contemporaries and precious to his friends—is what has assured him his place in history. Below the rages and the polemics, beyond the violence and the predatory sexuality, the eccentricities and the changes of direction, there seems to have been a steady current of moral concern and political insight that charges his best writing with a lasting glow. As Thomas Fowler says of Alden Pyle in *The Quiet American*, "I never knew a man who had better motives for all the trouble he caused."

This essay first appeared in the New Republic *in 2000 as a review of* Arthur Koestler: The Homeless Mind *by David Cesarani.*

CHAPTER II

The Elementary Truths
of Primo Levi

P rimo Levi was born in Turin in 1919, in the apartment where he would live for most of his life and where he killed himself in April 1987.[1] Like many Jewish families in the region, the Levis had moved from the Piedmontese countryside to Turin in the previous generation and were culturally assimilated. Primo grew up under Fascism, but it was only with the imposition of the Race Laws, in 1938, that this had any direct impact upon him. He studied chemistry at the university in Turin, with the help of a sympathetic professor who took him on notwithstanding the regulations excluding Jews, and afterward found work of a sort in various establishments willing to take on a Jewish chemist in spite of his "race."

With the fall of Mussolini in July 1943, everything changed. For a brief, confusing interlude Italy lay suspended between the Allies, who had occupied Sicily and the far south, and the Germans, who had not yet invaded from the north. But in September the Italian occupying army in France straggled back through Turin, "a defeated flock," in Levi's words, followed shortly after by the inevitable Germans, "the gray-green serpent of Nazi divisions on the streets of Milan and Turin." Many of Levi's Jewish contemporaries from Turin were already involved in the resistance movement Giustizia e Libertà (whose local leadership, until his arrest, had included "my illustrious namesake" Carlo Levi, the future author of *Christ Stopped at Eboli*), and after the German invasion Primo Levi joined them. He spent three months with the armed resistance in the foothills of the Alps before his group was betrayed to the Fascist militia and captured on December 13, 1943.[2]

Levi, who declared his Jewish identity, was sent to the transit camp at Fossoli di Carpi and thence, on February 22, 1944, he was transported to Auschwitz with 649 other Jews, of whom 23 would survive. Upon arrival Levi was stamped number 174517 and selected for Auschwitz III–Monowitz, where he worked at the synthetic rubber plant owned by I. G. Farben and operated for them by the SS. He stayed at Auschwitz until the camp was abandoned by the Germans in January 1945 and liberated by the advancing Red Army on January 27. For the next nine months he was swept from Katowice, in Galicia, through Belorussia, Ukraine, Romania, Hungary, Austria, Germany, and finally home to Turin in a picaresque, involuntary odyssey described in *La tregua* (*The Reawakening*).

Once back in Turin he took up the reins of his "monochrome" life, following the twenty-month "Technicolor" interlude of Auschwitz and after. Driven by an "absolute, pathological narrative charge,"[3] he wrote *Se questo è un uomo* (*If This Is a Man*), a record of his experiences in Auschwitz. The book found hardly any readers when it appeared in 1947. Primo Levi then abandoned writing, married, and began work for SIVA, a local paint company where he became a specialist, and international authority, on synthetic wire enamels. In 1958 the prestigious Turin publishing house Einaudi republished his book, and—encouraged by its relative success—Levi wrote *La tregua*, its sequel, which appeared in 1963. Over the next decades Levi gained increasing success and visibility as a writer, publishing *Il sistema periodico* (*The Periodic Table*) and *La chiave a stella* (*The Monkey's Wrench*), two collections of short pieces; *Se non ora, quando?* (*If Not Now, When?*), a novel about Jewish resistance in wartime Europe; *Lilìt e altri racconti* (*Moments of Reprieve*), further recollections and vignettes of his camp experience; a variety of essays and poems; and regular contributions to the culture pages of *La Stampa*, the Turin daily. In 1975 he left SIVA and devoted himself to writing full-time. His last book, *I sommersi e i salvati* (*The Drowned and the*

Saved), was published in 1986, the year before his death. A small esplanade in front of the Turin synagogue on Via Pio V was named after him in April 1996.[4]

The fate of Levi's books, in Italian and in translation, is instructive. When he took *Se questo è un uomo* to Einaudi in 1946, it was rejected out of hand by the publisher's (anonymous) reader, Natalia Ginzburg, herself from a prominent Turinese Jewish family. Many years later Giulio Einaudi claimed to have no knowledge of the reasons for the book's rejection; Levi himself laconically ascribed it to "an inattentive reader."[5] At that time, and for some years to come, it was Bergen-Belsen and Dachau, not Auschwitz, that stood for the horror of Nazism; the emphasis on political deportees rather than racial ones conformed better to reassuring postwar accounts of wartime national resistance. Levi's book was published in just 2,500 copies by a small press owned by a former local resistance leader (ironically, in a series dedicated to the Jewish resistance hero and martyr Leone Ginzburg, Natalia Ginzburg's husband). Many copies of the book were remaindered in a warehouse in Florence and destroyed in the great flood there twenty years later.

La tregua did better. Published in April 1963, it came in third in the national Strega Prize competition that year (behind Natalia Ginzburg's *Lessico famigliare* . . .), brought renewed attention to his first book, and began Levi's rise to national prominence and, eventually, critical acclaim. But his foreign audience was slow in coming. Stuart Woolf's translation of *Se questo è un uomo* was published in Britain in 1959 as *If This Is a Man*, but sold only a few hundred copies. The U.S. version, with the title *Survival in Auschwitz* (which captures the subject but misses the point), did not begin to sell well until the success of *The Periodic Table* twenty years later. *La tregua* was published here under the misleadingly optimistic title *The Reawakening*, whereas the original Italian suggests "truce" or "respite"; it is clear as the book ends that for Levi his months of wandering in the eastern marches of Europe were a kind of "time out" between Auschwitz-as-experience and Auschwitz-as-memory. The book closes with the dawn command of Auschwitz, "Get up!"—"Wstawach!"

German translations followed in time, and Levi eventually gained an audience in the Federal Republic. French publishers, however, avoided Levi for many years. When *Les Temps Modernes* published extracts from

Se questo è un uomo, in May 1961, it was under the title "J'étais un homme" ("I was a man"), which comes close to inverting the sense of the book. Gallimard, the most prestigious of the French publishing houses, for a long time resisted buying anything by Levi; only after his death did his work, and his significance, begin to gain recognition in France. There, as elsewhere, the importance of Levi's first book only came clearly into focus with the (in some countries posthumous) appearance of his last, *The Drowned and the Saved.* Like his subject, Primo Levi remained at least partially inaudible for many years.

IN ONE SENSE, Primo Levi has little to offer a biographer. He lived an unremarkable professional and private life, save for twenty months, and he used his many books and essays to narrate and depict the life that he did lead. If you want to know what he did, what he thought, and how he felt, you have only to read him. As a result, any retelling of his "life and works" risks ending in a self-defeating effort to reorder and paraphrase Levi's own writings. And that is just what Myriam Anissimov has done in her new account of Levi, which has already appeared in French and Italian to mixed reviews. Some mistakes of fact in the Italian and French editions have been cleared up, and the English translation, while unexciting, is readable and contains much information.*

But Anissimov's prose is uninspired and mechanical. Her lengthy narrative of his life is a choppy mix of long excerpts and rewordings from Levi himself interspersed with clunky and inadequate summaries of "context": Italian Jewry, Fascist race laws, the postwar Italian boom, 1968 in Turin, and the publishing history of his books. Some of the background material seems to have been inserted at random, as though the author had come upon a misplaced file card and inserted its contents, then and there, into the text.

Worse, the author somehow fails to explain to the reader just why Primo Levi is so very interesting. She alludes to the distinctive quality of his prose style and is rightly critical of reviewers and specialists for their failure to appreciate him; but she has little feel for just those

---

* Myriam Anissimov, *Primo Levi: Tragedy of an Optimist* (Woodstock, NY: Overlook, 1999).

features of Levi's writings that make him stand out, both in contemporary Italian literature and in Holocaust memoirs. An ironist and a humorist who travels playfully back and forward across an extended keyboard of themes, tones, and topics, Primo Levi is presented in this account as an optimistic, assimilated Italian Jew brought low by the tragedy of Auschwitz. This is roughly comparable to describing Ulysses, Levi's favorite literary figure and alter ego, as an old soldier on his way back from the wars who encounters a few problems en route. Not false, but hopelessly inadequate.[6]

Primo Levi had various identities and allegiances. Their overlapping multiplicity did not trouble him—though it frustrated his Italian critics and perplexes some of his readers in the American Jewish community— and he felt no conflict among them. In the first place, he was Italian, and proud of it. Despite the country's embarrassing faults, he took pride in it: "It often happens these days that you hear people say they're ashamed of being Italian. In fact we have good reasons to be ashamed: first and foremost, of not having been able to produce a political class that represents us and, on the contrary, tolerating for thirty years one that does not. On the other hand, we have virtues of which we are unaware, and we do not realize how rare they are in Europe and in the world."[7]

Like most Italians, though, Levi was first of all from somewhere more circumscribed—in his case, Piedmont. This is a curious place, a small corner of northwest Italy squeezed up against the Alps; the homeland of the Savoy royal family, Italian laicism, and, in Turin, its austere, serious capital city, the headquarters of Fiat. Parts of what used to be Piedmontese territory are now French, and the local dialect is permeated with French or almost French words and phrases. Levi, like most Piedmontese, was immensely proud of his region of origin, and that sentiment suffuses his writings. The "dazzling beauty" of its mountains, lakes, and woods is referred to more than once—for Levi was an enthusiastic amateur climber and much of Piedmont is Alpine or pre-Alpine terrain. The distinctive dialect of the region plays a part in Levi's writing—as it did in his life, for Lorenzo Perrone, the bricklayer from Fossano who saved him in Auschwitz, was recognized there by Levi thanks to his Piedmontese speech. A number of the characters in Levi's writings use local dialect, and in both *The Monkey's Wrench* and *The Periodic Table* he apologizes for the difficulty of capturing the cadences of their conversation in the written word.[8]

The Piedmontese are famously reserved, restrained, private: in short, "un-Italian." Italo Calvino wrote of the "Piedmontese eccentricity" in Levi's "science fiction" tales; Levi, who thought that he was credited with altogether too much wisdom by his readers, was nonetheless willing to concede that he did possess the distinctive quality of "moderation . . . that is a Piedmontese virtue." And his roots in Turin, "a mysterious city for the rest of Italy," played a part in his fate, too. The Turinese, he writes, don't leave: "It is well known that people from Turin transplanted to Milan do not strike root, or at least do it badly." Should his family have got away while they could—to somewhere else in Italy, to Switzerland, to the Americas? Not only would it have been difficult and expensive, and required more initiative than he or his family possessed, but the very idea of leaving home did not cross their minds: "Piedmont was our true country, the one in which we recognized ourselves."[9]

The constraint and correctness of Primo Levi's Piedmont are dupli-cated and reinforced by his vocation, the "sober rigor" of chemistry. The decision to study science was shaped in part, under Fascism, by the fact that it "smelled" good—in contrast to history or literary criticism, warped and degraded by ideological or nationalist pressure. But Levi the student was also drawn to the chemist's calling: "The nobility of Man, acquired in a hundred centuries of trial and error, lay in making himself the con-queror of matter. . . . I had enrolled in chemistry because I wanted to remain faithful to this nobility."

Moreover, the chemist must perforce describe the world as it *is*, and the precision and simplicity of this requirement seems to have conformed closely to Levi's own distaste for gloss, for commentary, for excess of any kind. "I still remember Professor Ponzio's first chemistry lesson, from which I got clear, precise, verifiable information, without useless words, expressed in a language that I liked enormously, also from a literary point of view: a definite language, essential."[10]

In chemistry, moreover (as in climbing), a mistake matters—a point made with casual emphasis in the story "Potassium," where the young ap-prentice chemist Levi mistakes potassium for its near neighbor sodium and sets off an unexpected reaction: "One must distrust the almost-the-same (sodium is almost the same as potassium but with sodium nothing would have happened), the practically identical, the approximate, the or-even, all surrogates, and all patchwork. The differences can be small but they lead to radically different consequences, like a railroad's switch points; the chemist's trade consists in good part in being aware of these differences, knowing them close up and foreseeing their effects. *And not only the chemist's trade.*" (Emphasis added.)[11]

Chemicals appear frequently in Levi's writing, and not just in *The Periodic Table.* Sometimes they are subjects in their own right, sometimes they serve as metaphors for human behavior, occasionally as illuminating analogies. Dr. Gottlieb, in *The Reawakening,* is described as emanating intelligence and cunning "like energy from radium." But the impact of his training upon his writing is most obvious in Levi's distinctive style. It has a taut, tight, distilled quality; contrasted with the florid, experimental, syntactically involuted writing of some of his contemporaries and commentators, it has the appeal of medieval plainsong. This was no accident—"I have always made an effort to move from dark to clear, like a filtration pump that sucks in cloudy water and expels it clarified, if not sterile."[12]

In an essay "On Obscure Writing," Levi castigates those who can't write in a straightforward way: "It is not true that disorder is required in order to describe disorder; it is not true that chaos on the written page is the best symbol of the extreme chaos to which we are fated: I hold this to be a characteristic error of our insecure century." And in an open letter, "To a Young Reader," Levi reminds his audience that textual clarity should never be mistaken for unsophisticated thinking. Levi's style did not endear him to professional critics; until the late seventies "in the eyes of critics he remained an appealing, worthy, but un-influential outsider in the world of literature."[13]

Levi's style is not just simple, it is unerringly precise; he modeled *Survival in Auschwitz* on the weekly production report used in factories. All of that book and some of his other writing is in an urgent, imperative present tense, telling the reader what must be known: "It has to be realized that cloth is lacking in the Lager." The force of Levi's testimony, like the appeal of his stories, comes from this earthy, concrete specificity. When men left Ka-Be (the "infirmary" of Auschwitz III) their pants fell down, they had no buttons, their shoes hurt: "Death begins with the shoes. . . . " The very density of the detail, the point-by-point reconstruction of how men worked and how they died—this is what gives the narrative its power and its credibility.[14]

The same is true of Levi's many accounts of individuals, which glide imperceptibly forward from description to analogy, from analogy to juxtaposition and thence to judgment. Of "the Moor," one of the Italians at Auschwitz, he writes: "It was quite clear that he was possessed by a desperate senile madness; but there was a greatness in his madness, a force and a barbaric dignity, the trampled dignity of beasts in a cage, the dignity that redeemed Capaneus and Caliban." Of ruined Munich, where Levi wandered the streets when his train stopped on its interminable journey back to Italy: "I felt I was moving among throngs of insolvent debtors, as if everybody owed me something, and refused to pay." Of "Cesare" (Lello Perugia, his Italian companion on the journey home): "Very ignorant, very innocent and very civilized." In *The Periodic Table* Levi writes that "today I know that it is a hopeless task to try to dress a man in words, make him live again on the printed page." But he does.[15]

It is the detail in Levi's writing that is doing the narrative work, and the moral work too. Like Albert Camus, he has a feel for the "thingness" of experience. He was well aware that this could cause discomfort to some modern readers. In *The Monkey's Wrench* he is gently ironic as he heaps on the technical description: Since there just are no synonyms, the reader "must be brave, use his imagination or consult a dictionary. It may be useful for him anyway, since we live in a world of molecules and ball-bearings." The emphasis on work in many of his stories was no accident—a number of the writers and novels he most admired deal explicitly with the honor and autonomy that come from skilled labor; "Faussone," the composite protagonist of *The Monkey's Wrench*, is a Conradian character drawn in part on Renaud, the skipper in Roger Vercel's novel *Remorques*, which Levi openly acknowledged as one of his influences. Levi himself identified with skilled work, saying, "I've always been a rigger-chemist." In "The Bridge" he goes further and explicitly states that being good at your job and taking pleasure from it constitutes if not the highest, then at least "the most accessible form of freedom."[16]

The cynical inscription over the gates of Auschwitz held a special resonance for Primo Levi: He truly believed that work makes you free.

PRIMO LEVI WAS PIEDMONTESE, a chemist, a writer—and a Jew. Were
it not for Hitler, this last would have been a matter of near indifference
to him. Jews in Italy had been present since before the destruction of the
Second Temple (in AD 70); and with the exception of the Roman Jews,
whose ghetto had only been abolished upon the liberation of Rome in
1870, they were virtually assimilated into the general population. Even
the Sephardic Jews of Piedmont, relatively "recent" arrivals, could trace
their origins to the fifteenth-century expulsions from Spain (as their
names, often drawn from the towns in France where they had lived en
route to Italy, suggest), while the earliest recorded permission for Jews to
settle in Turin dates from 1424.

There had indeed been a ghetto system in Piedmont, established in
the early eighteenth century (rather late by European standards), and the
Savoyard monarchy was not always benevolent toward the Jews. But following the emancipation decrees of March 1848 their situation rapidly
improved, and with the coming of liberal Italy Jews entered without difficulty into the mainstream of Turinese and Italian life. The country had
a Jewish prime minister, and Rome a Jewish mayor, before 1914. There
were Jewish generals in the army, fifty of them during World War I. Even
the Fascist Party had a significant share of the Jewish population among
its members (and a Jewish finance minister as late as 1932).

To be sure, there was anti-Semitism—especially in Trieste, where it
was inherited from Austrian rule. And however cynical or even ambivalent Mussolini himself felt about the Race Laws, these cut deep into the
self-confidence of the Italian Jews. But the significant Jewish presence
in the Italian anti-Fascist resistance owed more to deep traditions of
free-thinking liberalism than to any sense of Jewish victimhood. In any
case, there were not many Jews. Even by West European standards the
Jewish population of Italy was small: just 33,000 in a population of
nearly 35 million in 1911, increased to 57,000 by 1938, thanks to the
annexation of Trieste, new "racial" definitions, and the presence of some
10,000 foreign Jewish refugees from Nazism. The largest concentration

of Jews was to be found in Rome (about 12,000 in the 1931 census); there were fewer than 4,000 in Turin, where they made up about 0.5 percent of the local population.[17]

The Jews of Italy suffered badly during the eighteen months of German occupation, though not as badly as Jews elsewhere. Nearly seven thousand Italian Jews died in deportation; but the rest survived the war, a better rate than in most of the rest of Europe. In part this is because the Holocaust came late to Italy (not that this helped the Jews of Hungary); in part because the Jews of Italy were so scattered and well integrated; and in some measure because they found support and sustenance among their fellow Italians, with the usual dishonorable exceptions. From Turin, just 245 Jews were deported, most to Auschwitz; 21 returned after the war, Primo Levi among them.[18]

Thanks to the war, Primo Levi's Jewishness moved to the center of his being: "This dual experience, the racial laws and the extermination camp, stamped me the way you stamp a steel plate. At this point I'm a Jew, they've sewn the star of David on me and not only on my clothes." This was in part a result of his encounter for the first time with other Jews—the Libyan Jews at Fossoli (exhibiting "a grief that was new for us") and the Ashkenazim in Auschwitz. Jewishness posed difficulties for Levi, and not just because he had no religion; his concern with work, with *Homo faber*—man the maker—made him peculiarly sensitive to the etiolated, over-intellectual qualities of Jewish life: "If man is a maker, we were not men: we knew this and suffered from it." It also explains his initial enthusiasm for the Zionist project in its innocent, agrarian incarnation. But the very difference of Jews was also their virtue. In "Zinc" he sang the praises of "impurity," in metals and in life, the impurity that the Fascists so abhorred with their longing for sameness, that impurity "which gives rise to changes, in other words, to life. . . . I too am Jewish. . . . I am the impurity that makes the zinc react."[19]

Levi found it embarrassing and constricting to be treated "just as a Jew," as he was by many in the U.S.; predictably he has been criticized by some in the American Jewish community for the insufficiencies and partial quality of his Jewish identity.[20] But he was not inhibited about writing and speaking as a survivor, bearing witness and obeying the distinctively Jewish exhortation to remember. All of his writing is shadowed by his experience in Auschwitz—you cannot read anything by Levi without prior knowledge of that experience, for he assumes it in the reader and expects it. His first and last books are devoted to it. In *The Periodic Table* it is omnipresent, even in stories unrelated to that past, but which at unexpected moments suddenly twist back to it. In *The Monkey's Wrench* the point is made explicitly, following his explanation to Faussone of the story of Tiresias: "In distant times I, too, had got involved with Gods quarreling among themselves; I, too, had encountered snakes in my path, and that encounter had changed my condition, giving me a strange power of speech."[21]

As a survivor, Levi's trajectory was quite representative. At first, people didn't want to listen to him—Italians "felt purified by the great wave of the anti-Fascist crusade, by participation in the Resistance and its victorious outcome."[22] Giuliana Tedeschi, another Italian survivor of Auschwitz, had a comparable experience: "I encountered people who didn't want to know anything, because the Italians, too, had suffered, after all, even those who didn't go to the camps. . . . They used to say, 'For heaven's sake, it's all over,' and so I remained quiet for a long time." In 1955 Levi noted that it had become "indelicate" to speak of the camps—"One risks being accused of setting up as a victim, or of indecent exposure." Thus was confirmed the terrible, anticipatory dream of the victims, during and after the camps: that no one would listen, and if they listened they wouldn't believe.[23]

Once people did start to listen, and believe, the other obsession of the survivor began to eat away at Levi—the shame, and guilt, of survival itself, made worse in his case by the embarrassment of fame. Why should he, Levi, have survived? Had he made compromises that others had refused? Had others died in his place? The questions are absurd, but they crowd in upon Levi's later writings, obscurely at first, openly toward the end. In the poem "Il superstite" ("The Survivor," February 1984), their implications are explicit:

> *Stand back, leave me alone, submerged people,*
> Go away. I haven't dispossessed anyone,
> *Haven't usurped anyone's bread.*
> *No one died in my place. No one.*

Go back into your mist.
It's not my fault if I live and breathe,
Eat, drink, sleep and put on clothes.

The guilt of the survivor—for surviving, for failing to convey the depths of others' suffering, for not devoting every waking hour to testimony and recall—is the triumphant legacy of the SS, the reason why, in Nedo Fiano's words, "At bottom I would say that I never completely left the camp."[24]

The shame of not being dead, "thanks to a privilege you haven't earned," is tied to Levi's central concern and the title of his first book: What does it mean to reduce a person to "an emaciated man, with head drooped and shoulders curved, on whose face and in whose eyes not a trace of thought is to be seen"? Levi, like other surviving witnesses, was ashamed of what he had seen, of what others had done; he felt "the shame the Germans did not know, that the just man experiences at another man's crime; the feeling of guilt that such a crime should exist. . . . " That, too, is how he explained the death of Lorenzo Perrone, the bricklayer working outside Auschwitz who had saved him but had been unable to live, as the years passed, with the memory of what he had seen: "He, who was not a survivor, had died of the survivors' disease."[25]

As a survivor, then, Levi was tragically typical; as a witness to the Holocaust he was not. Like all such witnesses, of course, he wrote both to record what had happened and to free himself from it (and was driven forward by the sense that he was doomed to fail on both counts). And like all survivors, his testimony is by definition partial: "We, the survivors, are not the true witnesses. . . . We are . . . an anomalous minority: we are those who by their prevarications, or their attributes or their good luck did not touch bottom. Those who did so, those who saw the Gorgon, have not returned to tell about it, or they returned mute."[26] In Levi's case he survived Auschwitz through good health (until the end, when his fortuitous sickness kept him in the infirmary and off the final death march), some knowledge of German, his qualifications as a chemist, which gave him indoor work during the final winter, and simple luck. Others have similar stories.

Levi knew little of the political organization among some of the prisoners. He did not benefit from *protekcja*, privileges and favor from other prisoners. His view of the camp as an accumulation of isolated "monads," rather than a community of victims, is contested by others (though not by all). But it is not for these reasons that Levi is a distinctive and unique witness to the Holocaust, perhaps the most important. It is because he writes in a different key from the rest; his testimony has a fourth dimension lacking in anything else I have read on this subject. Tadeusz Borowski is cynical, despairing. Jean Améry is angry, vengeful. Elie Wiesel is spiritual and reflective. Jorge Semprún is alternately analytical and literary. Levi's account is complex, sensitive, composed. It is usually "cooler" than the other memoirs—which is why, when it does suddenly grow warm and glow with the energy of suppressed anger, it is the most devastating of them all.[27]

Where some have tried to draw meaning from the Holocaust, and others have denied there is any, Levi is more subtle. On the one hand, he saw no special "meaning" in the camps, no lesson to be learned, no moral to be drawn. He was revolted at the notion, suggested to him by a friend, that he had survived for some transcendental purpose, been "chosen" to testify. The romantic idea that suffering ennobles, that the very extremeness of the camp experience casts light on quotidian existence by stripping away illusion and convention, struck him as an empty obscenity; he was too clearheaded to be seduced by the thought that the Final Solution represented the logical or necessary outcome of modernity, or rationality, or technology.

Indeed, he was increasingly drawn to pessimism. The revival of "revisionism," the denial of the gas chambers, depressed him intensely, and toward the end of his life he began to doubt the use of testimony, feeling the "weariness of a man who kept on having to repeat the same thing." The near-pornographic exploitation of human suffering—in Liliana Cavani's film *The Night Porter*, for example—brought him close to despair. His only resource to ward off the enemies of memory was words. But "the trade of clothing facts in words," he wrote, "is bound by its very nature to fail."[28]

And yet there was something to be gleaned from the camps: "No human experience is without meaning or unworthy of analysis. . . ." The offense against humanity was ineradicable and could return—indeed, it

is never absent. But in his first book and his last, Levi has something—
not redemptive, but essential—to say about the human condition. In
"The Gray Zone," the most important chapter of *The Drowned and the
Saved*, Levi brings into focus a theme he has intimated in various earlier
works: the infinite gradations of responsibility, human weakness, and
moral ambivalence that have to be understood if we are to avoid the
pitfall of dividing everything and everybody into tidy poles: resisters and
collaborators, guilty and innocent, good and evil. Chaim Rumkowski,
the "king" of the Lodz ghetto, was part of "a vast zone of gray consciences
that stands between the great men of evil and the pure victims." So was
"Dr. Müller," Levi's overseer in the Auschwitz chemical laboratory and
future correspondent: "Neither infamous nor a hero: after filtering off
the rhetoric and the lies in good or bad faith there remained a typically
gray human specimen, one of the not so few one-eyed men in the kingdom of the blind."[29]

Just as it is too reassuringly simple to treat the camps as a metaphor
for life, thereby according to the SS a posthumous victory, so we should
not compartmentalize Auschwitz as a black hole from which no human
light can emerge. The importance of language—that we can communicate and we must communicate, that language is vital to humanity and
the deprivation of language the first step to the destruction of a man—
was enforced within the camp (words were replaced by blows—"that was
how we knew we were no longer men"); but it can be applied outside.
For life outside is beautiful, as Levi notes in *Survival in Auschwitz*, and
human identity is multifold, and evil does exist and goodness too, and
much in between. There is no meaning in all this, but it is true and has
to be known and made known.[30]

Levi's dispassionate capacity to contain and acknowledge apparently
contradictory propositions frustrated some of his critics, who accused
him of failing to condemn his tormentors, of remaining altogether too
detached and composed. And the idea of a "gray zone" worried some who
saw in it a failure to exercise judgment, to draw an absolute moral distinction between the murderers and their victims. Levi resisted this criticism.
It is true that his early writings were deliberately cool and analytical,
avoiding the worst horrors lest readers prove incredulous—"I thought
that my account would be all the more credible and useful the more it

appeared objective and the less it sounded overly emotional." And Levi certainly preferred the role of witness to that of judge, as he would write many years later. But the judgments, albeit implicit, are always there.[31]

To Jean Améry, who suggested that Levi was a "forgiver," he replied that "forgiveness is not a word of mine." But then, as he acknowledged, his experience had been different from that of Améry, an Austrian Jew in the Belgian resistance who was captured and tortured before being sent to Auschwitz (and who would take his own life in 1978). Levi was no less obsessed with the Germans but sought, he insisted, to understand them, to ask how they could do what they had done. Yet Améry's suggestion was pertinent, and it speaks to the astonishing exercise of self-control in Levi's writings; for there can be no doubt that he had very, very strong feelings indeed about Germans, and these began to come out toward the end of his life. In *Survival in Auschwitz* there are already references to "the curt, barbaric barking of Germans in command which seems to give vent to a millennial anger." Germans are addressed in the vocative—"You Germans you have succeeded." And there are hints of collective condemnation: "What else could they do? They are Germans. This way of behaviour is not meditated and deliberate, but follows from their nature and from the destiny they have chosen."[32]

By the time he came to write *The Drowned and the Saved*, Levi was less inhibited. *Survival* achieved its goal, he claims, when it was finally translated into German. "Its true recipients, those against whom the book was aimed like a gun, were they, the Germans. Now the gun was loaded." Later he writes that the "true crime, the collective, general crime of almost all Germans of that time, was that of lacking the courage to speak." And the book ends with an unambiguous accusation of collective responsibility against those Germans, "the great majority" who followed Hitler, who were swept away in his defeat, and who have "been rehabilitated a few years later as the result of an unprincipled political game." And while he was careful to insist that blanket stereotyping of Germans was unjust and explained nothing, Levi took pains to emphasize again and again the specificity of the Holocaust, even when compared to the crimes of other dictators or the Soviet camps.[33]

Primo Levi, then, could judge and he could hate. But he resisted both temptations; the very space that he preserved between the horrors he had witnessed and the tone he used to describe them substitutes for moral evaluation. And, as Czesław Miłosz wrote of Albert Camus, "he had the courage to make the elementary points." The clarity with which he stripped down his account of the essence of evil, and the reasons why that account will endure and why, in spite of Levi's fears, the SS will not be the ones to dictate the history of the Lagers, are exemplified in this excerpt from *The Reawakening*, where Levi is describing the last days of a child who had somehow survived in Auschwitz until the Russians arrived:

Hurbinek was a nobody, a child of death, a child of Auschwitz. He looked about three years old, no one knew anything of him, he could not speak and he had no name; that curious name, Hurbinek, had been given to him by us, perhaps by one of the women who had interpreted with those syllables one of the inarticulate sounds that the baby let out now and again. He was paralysed from the waist down, with atrophied legs, thin as sticks; but his eyes, lost in his triangular and wasted face, flashed terribly alive, full of demand, assertion, of the will to break loose, to shatter the tomb of his dumbness. The speech he lacked, which no one had bothered to teach him, the need of speech charged his stare with explosive urgency: it was a stare both savage and human, even mature, a judgement, which none of us could support, so heavy was it with force and anguish. . . .

During the night we listened carefully: . . . from Hurbinek's corner there occasionally came a sound, a word. It was not, admittedly, always exactly the same word, but it was certainly an articulated word; or better, several slightly different articulated words, experimental variations on a theme, on a root, perhaps on a name.

Hurbinek, who was three years old and perhaps had been born in Auschwitz and had never seen a tree; Hurbinek, who had fought like a man, to the last breath, to gain his entry into the world of men, from which a bestial power had excluded him; Hurbinek, the nameless, whose tiny forearm—even his—bore the tattoo of Auschwitz; Hurbinek died in the first days of March

1945, free but not redeemed. Nothing remains of him: he bears witness through these words of mine."[34]

This essay first appeared in the **New York Review of Books** *in 1999 as a review of* Primo Levi: Tragedy of an Optimist *by Myriam Anissimov. Ms. Anissimov took offense at some of my comments on her book: Her response—and my reply—were published in the* **New York Review of Books,** *vol. 46, no. xiii, August 1999.*

NOTES TO CHAPTER II

[1] Levi left no suicide note, but he was known to be depressed. His death is widely regarded as deliberate, but some uncertainty remains.

[2] "*I soldati passavano come un gregge disfatto,*" Levi in *La Repubblica*, September 7, 1983, quoted in Claudio Pavone, *Una Guerra Civile: Saggio storico sulla moralità nella Resistenza* (Turin: Bollati Boringhieri, 1991), 16. See also "Gold," in Primo Levi, *The Periodic Table* (New York: Schocken Books, 1984), 130; "Arsenic," in *The Periodic Table*, 170.

[3] See Levi's interview with Risa Sodi in *Partisan Review* 54, no. 3 (1987), 356; and Giuseppe Grassano, *Primo Levi, Il Castoro* (Florence: La Nuova Italia, 1981), quoted in Myriam Anissimov, *Primo Levi* (Woodstock, NY: Overlook, 1999), 257.

[4] The main works by Levi in English are *Survival in Auschwitz* (first published by the Orion Press, 1959); *The Reawakening* (New York: Touchstone, 1995); *The Periodic Table* (New York: Schocken Books, 1984); *The Monkey's Wrench* (New York: Penguin, 1995); *If Not Now, When?* (New York: Penguin, 1995); *Moments of Reprieve: A Memoir of Auschwitz* (New York: Penguin, 1995); *The Mirror Maker* (London: Abacus, 1997); *The Drowned and the Saved* (New York: Vintage, 1989); *Other People's Trades* (New York: Summit, 1989).

[5] See Giulio Einaudi, "Primo Levi e la casa editrice Einaudi," in *Primo Levi as Witness*, ed. Pietro Frassica (Florence: Casalini Libri, 1990), 31–43; and Levi in Ferdinando Camon, *Conversations with Primo Levi* (Marlboro, VT: Marlboro, 1989), published in Italian as *Autoritratto di Primo Levi* (Padua: Edizioni Nord-Est, 1987), 51.

[6] The only sustained element of metaphor, or at least of literary indulgence, in Levi's writing is the repeated allusion to the odyssey of Ulysses. The mnemonic significance in *Survival in Auschwitz* of the Canto of Ulysses from Dante's *Inferno* is famous: "Think of your breed: for brutish ignorance / Your mettle was not made; you were made men, / To follow after knowledge and excellence." But Ulysses is everywhere—after the showers, when the *Blockälteste*, "like Polyphemus," touches everyone to see if they are wet; in the Katowice camp, where Russian soldiers "took pleasure in food and wine, like Ulysses' companions after the ship had been pulled ashore"; in the "cyclopean, cone-shaped gorge" where Levi searched for nickel; and in an infinity of allusions of style and form, notably in the invocation of lost companions, drowned and saved alike. See *Survival in Auschwitz*, pp. 103, 133; *The Reawakening*, p. 60; "Nickel," in *The Periodic Table*, p. 64. See also the thoughtful chapter by Victor Brombert, "Primo Levi and the Canto of Ulysses," in *In Praise of Antiheroes: Figures and Themes in Modern European Literature 1830–1980* (Chicago: University of Chicago Press, 1999), 115–138.

[7] "The Story of Avrom," in *Moments of Reprieve*, 81. Among the Italian virtues that Levi prized highly was a relative unconcern for national or ethnic difference: "'Italy is an odd country,'

Chaim said . . . 'but one thing is certain, in Italy foreigners aren't enemies. You'd think the Italians are more enemies to one another than to foreigners . . . it's strange, but it's true.'" (*If Not Now, When?*, p. 323).

[8] In the story "Arsenic" Levi is quite specific about one character, the client who comes to seek chemical analysis of some poisoned sugar: He spoke "excellent Piedmontese with witty Astian tones" (*The Periodic Table*, p. 170). Asti is a small town just forty miles from Turin, distant enough to give its speech a multitude of subtle local identifying marks of its own.

[9] Calvino is quoted by Anissimov, *Primo Levi*, p. 300; for moderation as a Piedmontese virtue, see Primo Levi's interview with Roberto di Caro in *L'Espresso*, April 26, 1987, also cited by Anissimov, p. 401. See also "Gold" and "Potassium" in *The Periodic Table*, pp. 51, 127; for "a mysterious city," see Camon, *Conversations with Primo Levi*, p. 75 (afterword to U.S. edition).

[10] See "Iron," in *The Periodic Table*, p. 41; Primo Levi and Tullio Regge, *Dialogo* (Princeton, NJ: Princeton University Press, 1989), 19.

[11] "Potassium," *The Periodic Table*, p. 60.

[12] *The Reawakening*, p. 97; Primo Levi, interview in *La Stampa*, June 5, 1983, quoted by Anissimov, *Primo Levi*, p. 357.

[13] Primo Levi, "Dello scrivere oscuro," *Opere* (Turin: Giulio Einaudi, 1997), vol. 2, p. 677; "A un giovane lettore," *Opere*, vol. 2, p. 847. See also his troubled comments on Paul Celan's "Todesfuge" in "La ricerca delle radici," *Opere*, vol. 2, p. 1513: "Scrivere è un trasmettere; che dire se il messagio è cifrato e nessuno conosce la chiave?" ("To write is to transmit; but what if the message is coded and no one knows the key?") On Levi's critics see Domenico Scarpa, "Un anno di Primo Levi" in *La Rivista dei Libri*, May 1998, p. 35.

[14] See *Survival in Auschwitz*, pp. 29–30, 51.

[15] See *The Reawakening*, pp. 99, 204; "Iron," *The Periodic Table*, p. 48.

[16] See *The Monkey's Wrench*, pp. 139, 143, 146. See also Levi, "L'avventura tecnologica," in *Opere*, vol. 2, pp. 1444–1452.

[17] Contrast the contemporary Jewish population of Greece, 76,000; of the Netherlands, 140,000; or of France, 350,000. For Mussolini's motives in introducing the Race Laws, see Gene Bernardini, "The Origins and Development of Racial Anti-Semitism in Fascist Italy," *Journal of Modern History*, no. 3 (September 1977): 431–453.

[18] On the history of Italian Jews under Fascism see Susan Zuccotti, *The Italians and the Holocaust: Persecution, Rescue, and Survival* (Lincoln, NE: University of Nebraska Press, 1996); for details of deportations from Turin, see Liliana Picciotto Fargion, "Gli ebrei di Torino deportati: notizie statistiche (1938–1945)," in *L'ebreo in oggetto: L'applicazione della normativa antiebreica a Torino, 1938–1943,* ed. Fabio Levi (Turin: Silvio Zamorani, 1991), 159–190.

[19] See Camon, *Conversations with Primo Levi*, p. 68; *Survival in Auschwitz*, p. 12; "Hydrogen" and "Zinc" in *The Periodic Table*, pp. 24, 34–35.

[20] See, e.g., Fernanda Eberstadt, "Reading Primo Levi," in *Commentary* 80, no. 4 (October 1985), who finds much of his work "fastidious" and "insubstantial" (p. 47); also Levi's comments to Risa Sodi in "An Interview with Primo Levi," pp. 355–366.

[21] *The Monkey's Wrench*, p. 52. On the concept of "shadowing," and the problem of reading literature "backshadowed" by the Holocaust, see the sensitive and insightful remarks of Michael André Bernstein, notably in *Foregone Conclusions: Against Apocalyptic History* (Berkeley: University of California Press, 1994).

[22] Furio Colombo, "Introduction," in Zuccotti, *The Italians and the Holocaust*, p. x.

[23] Giuliana Tedeschi in Nicola Caracciolo, *Uncertain Refuge: Italy and the Jews During the Holocaust* (Urbana: University of Illinois Press, 1995), 121. Levi is quoted from *L'Eco dell'educazione ebraica*, in Anissimov, *Primo Levi*, p. 273.

24 *Moments of Reprieve*, prologue. For the Italian original see Levi, *Opere*, vol. 2, p. 576. Nedo Fiano is in Caracciolo, *Uncertain Refuge*, p. 69.

25 See *If Not Now, When?*, p. 295; *Survival in Auschwitz*, p. 82; *The Reawakening*, p. 16; *Moments of Reprieve*, p. 118.

26 *The Drowned and the Saved*, pp. 83–84.

27 Tadeusz Borowski, *This Way for the Gas, Ladies and Gentlemen* (New York: Penguin, 1976); Jean Améry, *Par-delà le crime et le châtiment: Essai pour surmonter l'insurmontable* (Arles: Actes Sud, 1995); Elie Wiesel, *Night* (New York: Hill and Wang, 1960); Jorge Semprún, *Literature or Life* (Viking, 1997).

28 Anissimov, *Primo Levi*, p. 5; "Carbon," in *The Periodic Table*, p. 232.

29 For Rumkowski, see *Moments of Reprieve*, p. 127; for Dr. Müller, see "Vanadium," in *The Periodic Table*, pp. 221–222.

30 "*Io pensavo che la vita fuori era bella . . .* " ("I was thinking that life outside was beautiful"), *Opere*, vol. 1, p. 160. Contrast the testimony of Franco Schönheit, in Alexander Stille, *Benevolence and Betrayal: Five Italian Jewish Families Under Fascism* (New York: Summit, 1991), p. 347: "Certainly these are experiences, but always absurd experiences. How can you learn something from an experience of this kind? That's part of the reason I never talk with my children about it; those experiences teach nothing. They belong to a world of the impossible, totally outside the sphere of ordinary humanity."

31 *The Reawakening*, "Afterword," pp. 210, 222; contrast the report that Levi and Leonardo de Benedetti drew up in 1945 at the request of the Soviet authorities in Katowice, which describes gas chambers, crematoria, and disease in unadorned detail. It was later published in Italy in the journal *Minerva Medica*. See *Opere*, vol. 1, pp. 1331–1361.

32 See Anissimov, *Primo Levi*, p. 288; *Survival in Auschwitz*, pp. 15, 128, 135–136.

33 *The Drowned and the Saved*, pp. 168, 182, 203; *Primo Levi*, "Buco Nero di Auschwitz," *La Stampa*, January 22, 1987.

34 *The Reawakening*, pp. 25–26.

CHAPTER III

The Jewish Europe
of Manès Sperber

The conventional history of Europe in the twentieth century
begins with the collapse of continental empires in the course
of World War I. From Lenin's revolution in 1917 there arose a
vision that in time came to seem the only alternative to the descent into
Fascism of much of the civilized world. Following the heroic struggles
of World War II and the defeat of Fascism, the choice for thinking
people seemed to lie between Communism and liberal democracy; but
the latter was polluted for many by its imperialist ambitions, by the
self-serving character of its democratic proclamations. Only at the end
of the century, in our own day, has Communism, too, lost its last shreds
of credibility, leaving the field to an uncertain liberalism shorn of confidence and purpose.

That is the history of our century, as it seemed, and seems, to many
in its time; and only in retrospect, and slowly, have its deeper and more
convoluted patterns and meanings been unraveled and acknowledged, by
scholars and participants alike. But there is another history of our era, a
"virtual history" of the twentieth century, and it is the story of those men
and women who lived through the century and also saw through it, who
understood its meaning as it unfolded. There were not many of them.
They did not need to wait for 1945, or 1989, to know what had hap-

pened and what it had meant, to see beyond the illusions. For various reasons, they saw across the veil earlier. Most of them are now dead. Some of them died young, paying dearly for their disquieting perspicacity. A strikingly large number of these clear-sighted voyagers through the century were Jews, many from East-Central Europe.

Manès Sperber was one of them. He is not very well known in the English-reading world; he wrote mainly in German, occasionally in French. His major work of fiction, *Like a Tear in the Ocean*, which appeared in 1949, is a very long, semiautobiographical roman à clef and not widely read. Its subject matter is a little like that of the early novels of André Malraux: It dissects the thoughts and the actions of small groups of intellectuals, revolutionaries, and conspirators adrift in the century. Unlike Malraux, however, Sperber was never attracted to "historic personalities" of the Left or the Right. Indeed, the elegiac mood of his book, and its intellectual tone, is more reminiscent of Arthur Koestler in *Darkness at Noon* or Victor Serge in *The Case of Comrade Tulayev*, two other ex-Communists obsessed with their former allegiance.

But Sperber was an influential man in his day. He was a member of that brilliant fellowship of exile in postwar Paris that included Czesław Miłosz, Kot Jelenski, Ignazio Silone, Boris Souvarine, François Fejtö, and Arthur Koestler. From 1946 he held a strategic editorial position at Calmann-Levy, the French publishing house, where he published in French some of the most significant writing from German-speaking Central Europe. He was also, with Koestler, Raymond Aron, Michael Polanyi, Edward Shils, and Stephen Spender, one of the animators of the Congress for Cultural Freedom in the 1950s. It has been suggested that he and Koestler drew on their Comintern experience at the Berlin meeting of 1950, when the official justification and description of the Congress for Cultural Freedom was being drawn up. While others discussed and argued interminably, Sperber and Koestler put forward a preprepared text and got it voted through. If so, this would make Sperber one of the founding fathers of cold war liberalism, which is a bit misleading, since he also remained a lifelong friend of the non-Communist left. He even served with Raymond Aron and André Malraux, in 1945, in the latter's short-lived Ministry of Information, a "ministry of all the talents" intended to assist in the postwar recovery of French cultural and intellectual life; and he co-wrote, with Koestler and Albert Camus, an influential pamphlet against the death penalty.

Sperber's memoirs, which were published in German in the 1970s and have now appeared in English, have little to say about all that.* They take us from his birth in Austrian Galicia in 1905 to the end of World War II and his decision to settle in Paris, where he stayed until his death in 1984. Even for the period they cover, the memoirs are sketchy and selective. Sperber was an enthusiastic practitioner of Adlerian psychology between the wars, and wrote two books about its founder; but we learn little of this, and nothing at all of his reasons for breaking with Adler and his ideas. This is a pity, since Sperber was deeply and permanently influenced by Adler's categories: His book is full of sometimes heavy-handed psychological "insights," describing men whose lives were framed by a commitment to Communism as "suffering from the superpersonal reference compulsion," digressing into a clinical consideration upon "disactualized memory," and so on. Sperber even admits to some community of ideas with Wilhelm Reich (another Galician Jew who went to Berlin by way of Vienna); and he concedes that the rabbinical emphasis upon interpretation makes psychology a Jewish science par excellence.

The memoirs suffer a little, too, from Sperber's need to write them from memory. His early life, as we shall see, hardly lent itself to the peaceful accumulation of a private archive. Sometimes, when at a loss, he recycles material from his novel as though it were a primary source—quoting Doino Faber, his fictional alter ego, as evidence for a contemporary event or attitude. But none of this matters once he gets down to his story, a narrative of the first half of his life told as a tale of five cities.

The first of those cities was Zablotow, an undistinguished shtetl in Galicia on the eastern edge of the Austro-Hungarian empire. Here Sperber, raised among impoverished *luftmenschen* who had no visible means of support and lived for the coming of the Messiah, learned to be a Jew. Not only did he study Hebrew and Jewish texts, but he imbibed also the historical essence of Jewish identity, becoming aware of Christian

---

* Manès Sperber, *All Our Yesterdays.* Vol. 1: *God's Water Carriers;* Vol. 2: *The Unheeded Warning;* Vol. 3: *Until My Eyes Are Closed with Shards* (Holmes & Meier, 1991–94).

hostility by the time he was four, partaking in and observing the rituals of remembrance and celebration that conflated past and present, distance and proximity. He learned the word *Yerushalayim*, or Jerusalem, before being told the name of his own village; and "I knew the name of Captain Dreyfus before I knew my own." The pogrom in Kishinev in 1903 and the pogrom in Blois in 1171 formed, from his earliest days, an undifferentiated element in his own sense of identity and vulnerability. A good student, Sperber was expected by his learned father and grandfather to follow in their ways.

World War I tore up Sperber's world—quite literally, since the Austrian-Russian battles took place in the region of Zablotow—and deposited him, a solitary, frightened adolescent, already rootless, in Vienna. He stayed in Vienna for nine years, forging the love-hate relationship with the place that was so common in his generation. It was during this time that Sperber lost his faith, though not his sense of identity. Like many Jewish adolescents, then and since, he turned for a while to a radical left-wing Zionist movement, Hashomer Hatzair, or the Young Guard, as a sort of halfway house between Judaism and assimilation. In the process, he acquired that curious anticonventional moral fervor borrowed by some of the Zionist youth movements from the pre-1914 German *Wandervogel* clubs: from the echoes of which, Sperber says, he never rid himself completely.

It was in Vienna that he discovered and embraced Alfred Adler and his ideas, but in other ways the Vienna years were for Sperber a time of frustration, a period of "antitheses," when he was caught between faith and skepticism, community and individual, bond and fracture. Like others, he blamed Vienna for these dilemmas, though he confesses to having embraced the place all the more with each disappointment. In contrast to the novelist Joseph Roth, another Galician Jew, Sperber kept his distance from Austria, the reality and the myth. Roth went further in his search for assimilation, attributing to the defunct monarchy a supercosmopolitanism that would compensate for his own and others' lost Jewishness, making of Austria-Hungary a place for people without a place. As Roth would observe in *The Emperor's Tomb*, the true Austria was not the Austro-Germans in Graz or Salzburg; it was the Slavs, the Muslims, and the Jews at the imperial peripheries: Only they bore true allegiance to the crown. And he was right. For the shtetl Jews especially, as Sperber notes, the Emperor Franz Josef I meant more than he did for anyone else. He was the guarantor of their civil rights, their only shield against the coming of hatred and despotism. As Sperber's own father lamented in 1916, upon hearing of the old emperor's death, "Austria has died with him. He was a good emperor for us. Now everything will be uncertain! It is a great misfortune for us Jews." It was.

Sperber's solution to Roth's dilemma was not to reinvent Vienna, but to leave it. In 1927 he went to Berlin, where he became a member of the German Communist Party. This was characteristic of many Eastern European Jewish radicals, who joined the party in the 1920s and left it in disgust a few years later (in contrast to Western European intellectuals, Jewish and non-Jewish, who joined later but stayed through the mid-1950s and beyond). Sperber did not so much abandon radical Zionism as transpose its goals. He overcame his feeling of failure at not joining the pioneers in Palestine by reasoning that the fate of Jews would be decided by the coming victory of socialism.

His descriptions of the years between his arrival in Berlin and the rise of Hitler are among the best in his memoirs, full of acute observation of the Communist world and powerful first-person accounts of encounters with Nazis. Like Arthur Koestler, Hans Sahl, and other contemporaries, Sperber was immunized against later ideological illusion by firsthand experience of the disastrous mistakes of the German Communists in the face of Nazism—although he also claims that observation of courageous German working-class demonstrators in January 1933, misled and then abandoned by their party leaders, kept him committed to the cause of working people for the rest of his life, despite the glaring unreality of Communist paeans to proletarian strength and unity.

In 1933, at twenty-eight already politically experienced and ideo-logically disabused, Sperber nearly took his insights with him to the grave. He was arrested and interrogated by the SS during a sweep in March and spent some weeks in prison, a Jewish Communist awaiting either death or transfer to a camp. For reasons that he was unable to explain, he was instead released back into the streets of Berlin, whence he immediately escaped, after some adventures, to Paris. Here, as in Vienna and Berlin, he settled in and made a life for himself. Reflecting on his relationship to all these cities, he asks, "Am I not like a fatherless child who says 'Papa' to every friendly man?"

His main contacts in Paris, a city full of émigrés and refugees from Nazism, were still the German-speaking Communists and ex-Communists. He would not formally leave the party until 1937, and much of the third volume of his memoirs is taken up with asking why he waited so long. "No man in his right mind," after all, could believe the Moscow Trials. According to Sperber, his doubts about the Radiant Future had begun as early as 1931, after a revealing journey to Moscow and subsequent insights into the daily life of "Socialist Man." His answer to his question is familiarly jesuitical (talmudic?). He felt entitled to remain silent, not for the sake of opportunism, but "if my contradiction was bound to be useless." Moreover, he did not want to know uncomfortable things, and thus managed to avoid them as long as possible: "I certainly did not want to be burdened with useless secrets, but beyond this I shrank from knowledge that would cause me both political and emotional difficulties."

In the thirties mood of anti-Fascist unity this was enough to keep Sperber at odds with his own instincts for much of the decade. In his own memoirs, Hans Sahl, another German-speaking Jewish émigré, remembers Sperber, a little unflatteringly, as a man who at the time did not hesitate to "politically neutralize" critics of Stalin even among his own friends. The truth is probably that Sperber, like many others, was halfway out of Communism when the rise of Hitler stopped him in his path, trapping him between his loathing for Nazism and his disillusion with Communism and pushing him into a silence that only a few (Arthur Koestler and Boris Souvarine were among them) had the moral courage to break.

In other respects, though, the early Paris years brought some relief. "The radical indifference of Parisians, and their decided disinclination to be drawn into the lives of foreigners or let such persons into their lives guarantees every individual a personal freedom that is hardly known elsewhere." By 1939, Sperber was ready to be alone, even lonely. His joining years were behind him, and his various identities had all been sloughed off. Psychology was set aside for a life of writing. With the outbreak of war, however, the French ceased to be indifferent to the foreigners in their midst (if they ever really were), and Sperber's progress out of his past was stopped dead in its tracks.

The fifth town in Sperber's European odyssey is one he never visited. By good fortune, he avoided falling into the hands of the Vichy police and so, unlike the majority of Central European Jewish refugees caught in France after the German victory, he was not interned for later dispatch to Auschwitz. But Auschwitz is the key to the rest of his life. It sets the tone for his recollection in tranquillity of all that went before.

Sperber divides human history into what came before the Shoah and what remains. Before 1933, and in some ways even until 1943 (when he first learned of the death camps), he had shared some of the illusions of his Marxist contemporaries: "Like almost all leftists, I was led astray by my belief that no matter what the Nazis professed and whatever promises they made as social demagogues, they would never act against the interests of capitalism and question its principle of the inviolability of private property." What the Nazis (and their collaborators in the Ukraine and in Croatia especially) subsequently did to Jews, "to my people," haunted him evermore, casting a film of pain across his memory.

When he returned to Germany and to Vienna after the war, nothing remained. It was as though all the links in the chain of his life had been snapped. The significance of this realization, for the reader of these memoirs, is considerable. The memoirs themselves do not directly discuss the impact of Auschwitz, which is the theme of a number of postwar essays by Sperber collected in a volume called *Être Juif.* But if one reads Sperber's "recovered" awareness of Jewishness back into his story of the years 1905–46, the narrative acquires a forceful new dimension. In what looks like just another twentieth-century European life, we find a distinctively Jewish story.

That story is told in a variety of keys. In the first place, Sperber's various institutional and ideological affiliations and defections conflate into a single, repeated experience: his loss of certainty at the moment of breaking with the religion of his forefathers. Thenceforth he is constantly tempted by "knowledge," only to shrink away from it, wary of its illusory quality, skeptical about its philosophical and historical adequacy. And always his father and grandfather are there at his shoulder—a reminder that if you must believe in just one truth, then let it be the first. There is an image somewhere in his novel of a rabbi's son hiding Hegel's *Phenomenology of Mind* inside a Hebrew Bible. It is an image that accounts for Sperber's own trajectory at more than one level.

As with the loss of faith, so with the decision to "engage." Sperber makes the point that secularized Jews readily transfer the religious imperative to make a better world—and the belief that this can be done, and therefore must be done—into some form of secular millenarianism. This is a rather familiar idea. But his more telling observation derives from his gloss on a comment made by Karl Kraus, that Jews in Western and Central Europe had, "in their unsuccessful flight from their Jewishness, sought a refuge in self-hatred." Sperber seems to have believed that whereas Western European Jews not only threw themselves into the secular fray as a substitute for faith, but also set aside the internal Jewish constraints upon extremism—the distaste for the inauthentic, the obsession with justice, and so forth—it was his Eastern European Jewish roots that provided him with the anchor that kept him from drifting into revolutionary amoralism, opportunism, and the like. This is hardly a testable proposition. Indeed, one could just as well reverse the theme, and understand Sperber's failure to criticize Stalin publicly as an echo of his ancestors' refusal to transgress their own taboos. What matters, however, is that this is how Sperber came to see the dilemmas of engagement and duty. We are very far from Sartre.

Sperber's emphasis upon specifically Jewish forms of engagement casts light upon another recurring theme in his writings, the theme of messianism. Sperber asks, "Why should a very young Jew from the Eastern Galician shtetl Zablotow have concerned himself with the struggle of the German proletariat?" Why, indeed. Well, like Leninism, Judaism has its intuitively absurd side: If it seems odd to claim that a tiny political faction in Russia had the authority of history to speak for the workers of the world, how much odder to suppose that a universal God should have attached himself for eternity to one tiny itinerant people. The only thing that could possibly satisfy both claims was vindication in the future: world revolution in the one case, the coming of the Messiah in the other.

Sperber remarks upon this similarity, and admits that when he turned away from Judaism to Hegel and Marx, "I knew myself to be in the lineage of my messianic great-grandfather." But he goes further. There is also a difference between these worldviews, and the difference is this: The messiah of his great-grandfather did not come (and therefore, one might add, was real); but Sperber's messiah came, and proved false. In later essays Sperber wrote about Sabbatai Zevi, the false messiah of the seventeenth century, and his misguided Jewish followers. This, surely, was no casual interest. Sperber and his fellow Communists, whether they knew it or not, sat squarely in a tradition of Jewish error. They were benighted adherents to false idols and mistaken messiahs, wanderers from the path of truth. In the end, he suggests, it is wiser to abandon all heartwarming certainties in favor of a lonely skepticism.

The pain of Auschwitz, for Sperber, had an extra sharpness owing to his relation to things German, especially the German language. American, British, French, Russian, and Sephardic Jews cannot enter into this pain—which Sperber shared with Walter Benjamin, Stefan Zweig, Paul Celan, Hannah Arendt, and many others—because the love of German language and literature was a peculiarity of assimilated or near-assimilated Central European Jews. What Sperber says of his own refusal to see all the way into Nazism, before and after Hitler's seizure of power, is true of many others: "I was resisting a break with Germany." Once the damage was done, however, these same German-speaking Jews had, for this very reason, a special understanding of the true havoc wreaked by Hitler—a deeper understanding, indeed, than many Germans themselves.

But Sperber, unlike Arendt or Zweig, was also a shtetl Jew from Galicia. Thus he lived in many languages, growing up amid Hebrew, Yiddish, German, Polish, and Ukrainian. He is insistent that the Jews of Eastern Europe, in contrast with their Western cousins, never lived in ghettos. They lived in towns of their own; they were not homeless, but rooted in an authentic autonomous culture of their own. Living athwart the frontier of Eastern European and Central European Jewry, Sperber understood the cosmopolitan centrality of Germanness but also the power—familial, linguistic, ceremonial—of an original, local culture. Writ larger, this meant that Sperber was in an unusually good position to understand the Europe of our time, past and present.

Whatever insights Jewishness affords into recent history, however,

Jews were always marginal to that history. The specific forms of Jewish marginality—prejudice, exile, persecution—fit Jews well enough for twentieth-century life, just as the twentieth century could be made to fit all too easily into the shape of Jewish memory. As Sperber observes, he was taught to think of Egypt, Babylon, the Diaspora, the Crusades, the expulsion from Spain, and the pogroms of the seventeenth-century Ukraine as a single moment in time, or rather out of time, a simultaneity of suffering which it was incumbent upon Jews to remember. When he left Zablotow, he thought to leave all that: "If Jewish shtetls still existed today they would belong, for me, only to a remote past." Owing to Hitler, however, Zablotow is joined to the present and to the past, and bound to the roll of horrors by Sperber's reawakened duty to bear witness.

It is this belated return to an abandoned ancestral duty—to the obligation to remember, drilled into him in early childhood in three languages: Gedenk! Errinere dich! Tizkor!—that drives Sperber, shapes his memoirs, justifies them; and it is this same particularism that lifts his memoirs, paradoxically, beyond their Jewish frame of reference. Sperber's achievement was partly the fulfillment of a personal responsibility "we are become the walking cemeteries of our murdered friends"—but it was something more general, too. Like Koestler, Zweig, and so many others, Sperber put his best work into his memoirs, offering testimony to a lost world: "I must speak of it as though I am the last to have known it. And in effect I am one of the last, one of the walking coffins of an exterminated world." The extermination of the past—by design, by neglect, by good intention—is what characterizes the history of our time. That is why the ahistorical memory of a marginal community that found itself in the whirlwind may yet be the best guide to our era. You don't have to be Jewish to understand the history of Europe in the twentieth century, but it helps.

This essay first appeared in the New Republic *in 1996 as a discussion of the recently republished, three-volume autobiography of Manès Sperber.*

CHAPTER IV

Hannah Arendt and Evil

H annah Arendt died in 1975, leaving a curious and divided legacy. To some she represented the worst of "Continental" philosophizing: metaphysical musings upon modernity and its ills unconstrained by any institutional or intellectual discipline and often cavalierly unconcerned with empirical confirmation. They note her weakness for a phrase or an aperçu, often at the expense of accuracy. For such critics her insights into the woes of the century are at best derivative, at worst plain wrong. Others, including the many young American scholars who continue to study and discuss her work, find her a stimulating intellectual presence; her refusal to acknowledge academic norms and conventional categories of explanation, which so frustrates and irritates her critics, is precisely what most appeals to her admirers. Twenty years after her death they see her desire for a "new politics" of collective public action vindicated by the revolutions of 1989, and her account of modern society in general and totalitarianism in particular confirmed by the course of contemporary history. Both sides have a point, though it is sometimes difficult to remember that they are talking about the same person.

In fact, and despite the broad range of topics covered in her writings, Hannah Arendt was throughout her adult life concerned above all with two closely related issues: the problem of political evil in the twentieth century and the dilemma of the Jew in the contemporary world. If we add to this the special difficulty she experienced in acknowledging the distinctive place of Germany in the story she tried to tell—a difficulty of which she was not, it seems to me, always fully aware—we have grasped the central threads of all her writings, even those that seem at first reading most abstracted from such concerns. It does not follow from this that Arendt's various works can be reread in this light as a single, continuous, coherent theoretical undertaking—she is every bit as diffuse and muddled as her critics claim; but if we understand her main historical concerns against the background of her own obsessions, it becomes a little easier to see just what holds together the various parts of her oeuvre and why they provoke such diverse and powerful responses.

The central place in all of Arendt's thinking of the problem of totalitarianism seems obvious.[1] In a 1954 piece, "Understanding and Politics," reprinted in Jerome Kohn's useful and very well-edited collection of her early essays,* she stakes out her territory without ambiguity: "If we want to be at home on this earth, even at the price of being at home in this century, we must try to take part in the interminable dialogue with the essence of totalitarianism." As she would later express it in her "Thoughts about Lessing," the "pillars of the best-known truths" lie shattered today, and the first task of the survivors is to ask how this happened and what can be done.[2] That her own attempt to make sense of the age would not endear her to everyone was something she anticipated as early as 1946, well before the appearance of *The Origins of Totalitarianism*: "Those few students," she wrote in "The Nation," ". . . who have left the field of surface descriptions behind them, who are no longer interested in any particular aspect nor in any particular new discovery because they know that the whole is at stake, are forced into the adventure of structural analyses and can hardly be expected to come forward with perfect books."

Origins is, indeed, not a perfect book. Nor is it particularly original. The sections on imperialism lean heavily on the classic work *Imperialism*, by J. L. Hobson, published in 1905, and on Rosa Luxemburg's Marxist

---

* Hannah Arendt, *Essays in Understanding, 1930–1954* (New York: Harcourt Brace, 1995).

account in *The Accumulation of Capital* (1913). Luxemburg's version was particularly appealing to Arendt because of its emphasis on the self-perpetuating (and self-defeating) nature of capitalist expansion, a characteristic which Arendt then transposed onto totalitarianism; but she also found the general Marxist approach congenial, less for its broader historical claims, which she dismissed and indeed associated with the totalitarian phenomenon itself, than for Marxism's attack on bourgeois philistinism and its adulation of the proletariat. She felt some affinity with both of these prejudices. She borrowed widely, and with rather less acknowledgment, from the works of Franz Neumann and Franz Borkenau, exiles like herself who had in large measure anticipated her account of the Nazi and Soviet states. Her debt to Boris Souvarine, a disillusioned French Trotskyist who published in 1935 a brilliant and prescient study of Stalin, is, however, openly and generously recognized, though her enduring nostalgia for a certain lost innocence of the Left prevented her from endorsing Souvarine's root-and-branch inclusion of Lenin in his condemnation of the Soviet enterprise.[3]

The lasting importance of Arendt's major work thus rests not upon the originality of its contribution but on the quality of its central intuition. What Arendt understood best, and what binds together her account of Nazism and her otherwise unconnected and underdeveloped discussion of the Soviet experience, were the psychological and moral features of what she called totalitarianism.

By breaking up and taking over all of society, including the whole governing apparatus itself, totalitarian regimes dominate and terrorize individuals from within. The arbitrary and apparently irrational, antiutilitarian nature of life under such regimes destroys the texture of shared experience, of reality, upon which normal life depends and disarms all attempts by reasonable men to understand and explain the course of events. Hence the tragic failure of outsiders to perceive the danger posed by totalitarian movements, and the lasting inability of commentators to grasp the enormity of the events they were witnessing. Instead of admitting what Arendt called the "utter lunacy" of Stalinism or Nazism, scholarly and other analysts looked for some firm ground of "interest" or "rationality" from which to reinsert these developments into the familiar political and moral landscape.[4]

In the case of Nazism they thus missed the central place of genocide. Far from being just another exercise in mass violence, the plot to eliminate whole peoples and categories of people represented the ultimate in the control and dismantling of the human person and was thus not extraneous to the meaning of the regime but the very basis of it. Similarly, the Stalinist era was not a perversion of the logic of Historical Progress but its very acme—evidence of the infinite malleability of all experience and reality at the service of an idea.

It is not necessary to endorse this account in all its detail to understand that Arendt had it essentially right. At the time and for many years afterward she was assailed by historians, political scientists, and others for the excessively moral, even metaphysical quality of her approach, for her conflation of very different social experiences into a single story, and for her neglect of a variety of factors and (in the Soviet case) "achievements" that might moderate her interpretation. As Eric Hobsbawm remarked in a review of *On Revolution*, historians and others would be "irritated, as the author plainly is not, by a certain lack of interest in mere fact, a preference for metaphysical construct or poetic feeling . . . over reality."[5]

Most of all, of course, many of her readers could not understand, much less endorse, the merging of German and Russian regimes into a single type. They quite correctly noted her annoying habit of attributing to totalitarian regimes, even to Hitler and Stalin themselves, a sort of ideological self-awareness, as though they themselves knew that they were engaged in making their own ideological predictions (about the Jewish "problem" or the inevitability of class conflict) come true; Arendt admitted as much many years later in a September 1963 letter to Mary McCarthy, where she concedes that "the impact of ideology upon the individual may have been overrated by me [in the *Origins*]."[6]

Since then, however, historians, essayists, and dissidents have done much to illustrate and confirm her account.[7] Her emphasis upon the centrality of terror, which seemed disproportionate when she first proposed it, now sounds almost commonplace. As Arendt expressed it, terror executes on the spot the death sentence supposedly pronounced by Nature upon races and persons, or else by History upon classes, thus speeding up "natural" or "historical" processes.[8] Her criticism of the

Jacobins, in *On Revolution*, for aiming at a Republic of Virtue and installing instead a reign of terror, offended many at the time for its cavalier
unconcern with the classic accounts and interpretations of the French
Revolution, Marxist and liberal alike. It now sounds like a benign anticipation of the historical consensus espoused by François Furet and
other scholars, notably in their appreciation of terror not as an extraneous
political device but as the primary motor and logic of modern tyranny.

If Hannah Arendt understood something that so many others missed,
it was because she was more concerned with the moral problem of "evil"
than with the structures of any given political system; as she put it in
"Nightmare and Flight," first published in 1945 and reprinted in the
Essays, "The problem of evil will be the fundamental question of postwar
intellectual life in Europe—as death became the fundamental question
after the last war."

It is telling to discover from Kohn's collection that she was an avid
and careful reader of some of the great antimodern Catholic writers—in
a 1945 essay on "Christianity and Revolution" she discusses not only
Charles Péguy and Georges Bernanos but also, and less predictably,
G. K. Chesterton. In our post-Christian world, discussion of evil has a
curious, anachronistic feel, rather like invoking the devil; even when
modern students of murderous regimes acknowledge the value of describing them as evil, they have been reluctant to invoke the term in any ex-
planatory capacity. But Arendt suffered no such inhibitions, which is
why, long before her controversial essay on Eichmann, she engaged the
matter of evil head-on. It was not sufficient, she wrote in a 1953 response
to Eric Voegelin's criticism of *Origins*, to treat the totalitarian criminals
as "murderers" and punish them accordingly. In a world where murder
had been accorded the status of a civic duty, the usual moral (and legal)
categories will not suffice.[9] The following year she developed the point
further in "Understanding and Politics": "The trouble with the wisdom
of the past is that it dies, so to speak, in our hands as soon as we try to
apply it honestly to the central political experiences of our time.
Everything we know of totalitarianism demonstrates a horrible originality which no far-fetched historical parallels can alleviate."

This observation isn't very helpful for lawyers (Arendt was trying to
account for what she saw as the failure of the Nuremberg Trials), but it

does account for her resort to the notion of "banality" when she came to address the problem of Eichmann. Her earlier inclination had been to describe the evil quality of totalitarianism as something utterly "radical"; but Karl Jaspers and others had noted the risk entailed here of making Nazism in particular seem somehow unique and thus, in an awful way, "great." As she thought about the matter more, she developed a rather different line of reasoning: In various essays and later in *The Human Condition* and *The Life of the Mind* she argues that evil comes from a simple failure to *think*.

If this implies that evil is a function of stupidity, then Arendt is merely indulging a tautology of her own making. Moreover, since she nowhere suggests that goodness is a product (or description) of intelligence, she probably did not mean to be taken too seriously. After all, as Mary McCarthy pointed out in a letter of June 1971, if, e.g., Eichmann truly "cannot think" then he is just a monster. But if he has a "wicked heart" then he is exercising some freedom of choice and is thus open to moral condemnation in the usual way. Here, as elsewhere, we do well not to make of Arendt too consistent a thinker.

However, as an account of a certain sort of evil person Arendt's idea was suggestive. In a 1945 essay, "Organized Guilt and Universal Responsibility," she quotes an interview with a camp official at Majdanek. The man admits to having gassed and buried people alive. Then: Q. "Do you know the Russians will hang you?" A. "(Bursting into tears) Why should they? What have I done?"[10] As she commented, such people were just ordinary job-holders and good family men. Their deeds may be monstrous, evidence in Arendt's words of "the bankruptcy of common sense," but the officials themselves are quite simply stupid, ordinary, everyday persons—in short, banal. There is something frustratingly, terrifyingly plausible about this observation.[11] It rings true not just for Eichmann, but for other more recently prominent characters as well— Klaus Barbie or Paul Touvier—and thus suggests something important about the totalitarian state and its servants.

When Arendt came under attack for proposing this characterization it was in part because she did so too soon, as it were, but also because she attached it to a series of provocative and controversial remarks on the other subject that obsessed her, Jews. In order to understand the complexities of Arendt's relationship to her own, and other people's, Jewishness, it is crucial to remember that she was, after all, a German Jew. Like the German-speaking Jews of Prague, Vienna, and other cities of the old Empire, the Jews of Germany were different from the Jews of the East, and they knew it and felt it.

They were educated and cultivated in German, steeped in German *Bildung*, and quite lacked the difficult and frequently distant relationship to the dominant language and culture that shaped Jewish experience in Russia, Poland, and elsewhere in East-Central Europe. They certainly knew that they were Jews and that their non-Jewish German neighbors and fellow citizens knew they were Jewish; but this did not diminish their identification with the idea of Germanness. In the words of Moritz Goldstein, writing in 1912 and quoted with approval by Arendt in her essay on Walter Benjamin, "our relationship to Germany is one of unrequited love."[12] As she wrote of Rahel Varnhagen, the subject of one of her first books, "Abroad, her place of origin was called Berlin; in Berlin it was called Judengasse."[13]

This deep sense of her own Germanness is invoked by Margaret Canovan, among others, to account for the care Arendt took in her study of totalitarianism to divert attention away from the distinctively *German* sources of Nazism and make of it a general "Western" or "modern" deviation. This seems likely; Arendt never really confronted the fact that the worst persecutions, of Jews in particular, in the modern era took place in Germany. As late as 1964, while enjoying herself with some German interviewers, she admitted to Mary McCarthy that "in my youth, I used to be rather lucky with German *goiim* (never, incidentally, with German Jews) and I was amused to see that some of my luck still holds."

She also had some of the characteristic German prejudices of her youth, notably with respect to the less fortunate peoples to the south and east; in a piece dating from 1944 she scornfully dismissed the European émigré press in the U.S., "worrying their heads off over the pettiest boundary disputes in a Europe thousands and thousands of miles away— such as whether Teschen belongs to Poland or Czechoslovakia, or Vilna to Lithuania instead of to Poland!" No "Ost-Jud" would have missed the significance of these disputes. Of the Ost-Juden themselves, Arendt wrote dismissively in *The Origins of Totalitarianism:* "These East European conditions, however, although they constituted the essence of the Jewish mass question, are of little importance in our context. Their political significance was limited to backward countries where the ubiquitous hatred of Jews made it almost useless as a weapon for specific purposes."

This almost snobbish, High German quality also contributed to her troubled relations with American Jewry; as William Barrett put it, "one part of her never quite assimilated to America." With her classical education and memories of youth in Königsberg and student days in Marburg and Heidelberg, she probably found many of the American Jews she met, intellectuals included, rather philistine if not positively autodidacts.[14] They in turn could not grasp how one might be so assertively and proudly Jewish and yet (and above all) German at the same time. For she most certainly was Jewish. The titles of the closing chapters of *Rahel Varnhagen* give the clue: "Between Pariah and Parvenu" and "One Does Not Escape Jewishness."

This unambiguous identity did not of course preclude a certain distance from Jewishness—far from it; Arendt was always most critical of her own world and its tragic political myopia. In *Rahel Varnhagen* she notes that "the Berlin Jews considered themselves exceptions. And just as every anti-Semite knew his personal exceptional Jews in Berlin, so every Berlin Jew knew at least two eastern Jews in comparison with whom he felt himself to be an exception."[15] In her essay on Rosa Luxemburg, another exceptional Jewish woman with whom she felt a close affinity, she makes the same point in a different key: "While the self-deception of assimilated Jews consisted in the mistaken belief that they were just as German as the Germans, just as French as the French, the self-deception of the intellectual Jews consisted in thinking that they had no 'fatherland,' for their fatherland actually was Europe."[16]

Her critical distance from official Zionism was consistent with such attitudes. Hannah Arendt had become Zionist in Germany, had passed through a neo-Zionist phase in which she was drawn to binationalism in Palestine, and was never anti-Israel; as she wrote to Mary McCarthy in December 1968, "Any real catastrophe in Israel would affect me more deeply than almost anything else." But she was quite firmly antinationalist, Jewish or any other kind; hence the impossibility of her position for many American Jews, who could not readily imagine a strong secular Jewish consciousness divorced from any sympathy for the "national solution." Moreover her deeply held belief, as much aesthetic as political, in the need to separate the private from the public meant that she found something distasteful (and perhaps a little "oriental"?) in the confident political style and self-promotion of many of the leading figures in North American Jewry, including certain intellectuals of her own acquaintance.

It was this cultural abyss, as much as the substance of the work, that explains the otherwise absurd furor over *Eichmann in Jerusalem*. At thirty years' distance the book seems much less controversial. Copious research on the *Judenräte*, the Jewish councils of Nazi-dominated Europe, suggests what should have been obvious at the time: Arendt knew little about the subject, and some of her remarks about Jewish "responsibility" were insensitive and excessive,[17] but there is a troubling moral question mark hanging over the prominent Jews who took on the task of administering the ghettos. She was not wrong to raise the matter, nor was she mistaken in some of her judgments; but she was indifferent, perhaps callously so, to the dilemmas Jews faced at the time, and was characteristically provocative, even "perverse" (as the historian Henry Feingold put it) in insisting on the powers of the Jewish leaders and neglecting to call due attention to their utter helplessness and, in many cases, their real ignorance of the fate that awaited the Jews.

If the councils were in one sense the heirs to older self-governing bodies of existing Jewish communities and thus responsible for eliding the distinction between running Jewish life and administering Jewish death, they were also the chosen device of the Nazis for pursuing their own policies.[18] Here as elsewhere it was Nazi policy to make others do their work for them, and while it is almost certainly the case that utter noncooperation would have made things infinitely harder for the Germans, the same observation applies all the more forcibly to the relative compliance of locally appointed non-Jewish authorities in occupied France, Belgium, the Netherlands, and elsewhere.

Arendt made things worse for herself by inserting her controversial but brief comments on this subject into a text that not only introduced the notion of "banality"—such that Jews seemed to become "responsible," Germans merely "banal"—but also criticized Israel for having staged a "show trial" and chosen to emphasize "crimes against the Jewish people" instead of "crimes against humanity." The irony is that the Eichmann trial *was* a show trial—much as the more recent Barbie and Touvier trials in France were show trials, not in the sense of being rigged but in their primarily pedagogical function. The guilt of the accused in all these cases was never in question. Ben-Gurion was less interested in establishing Eichmann's responsibility, or even in exacting revenge, than in educating a new generation about the past sufferings of the Jews, and thereby further strengthening the foundations of the still fragile Jewish state.

Arendt was thus raising fundamental questions about memory, myth, and justice in the postwar world. Her critics, like Lionel Abel and Norman Podhoretz, could score "debater's points" as Mary McCarthy scornfully put it in a sympathetic letter, but they had not a clue about what she was trying to accomplish, and probably still don't. Like so many others in the initial postwar decades, they were dependent on what Karl Jaspers called "life-sustaining lies," though he too could not help chiding his former student for her naïveté in failing to notice "that the act of putting a book like this into the world is an act of aggression" against just such lies.[19] Today, with much of Europe taken up with issues of guilt, memory, past responsibility, "gray zones" of compliance and collaboration, and the problem of individual and collective retribution, Arendt's concerns are once again central.

Compared with these matters, Arendt's properly philosophical and theoretical legacy is light indeed. This might have come as no surprise to her—in a conversation with Günter Gaus, reprinted in the *Essays*, she renounced any claim to being a "philosopher." Her critics would agree; Stuart Hampshire once wrote, "She seems to me to be inaccurate in argument and to make a parade of learned allusion without any detailed inquiry into texts."[20] One senses a constant tension between a residual duty on Arendt's part to undertake philosophy and a natural preference (and gift) for political and moral commentary and what she called intellectual *action*. It is tempting to see this as a tension between Heidegger and Jaspers, the dominant intellectual influences upon her. At her worst she could lapse considerably toward Heidegger; in Judith Shklar's words, "Philosophy was for both of them an act of dramatizing through word play, textual associations, bits of poetry, and other phrases from their direct experiences." It was "passionate thinking."[21] She would slip into phrases like "world alienation," and even in a letter to McCarthy from February 1968 could write like this: "I have a feeling of futility in everything I do. Compared to what is at stake everything looks frivolous. I know this feeling disappears once I let myself fall into that gap between past and future which is the proper temporal *locus* of thought. . . ."[22]

In many of Arendt's ventures into theory, the dominant impression is one of confusion. Categories tumble over one another, their meaning unclear and variable. "She rambles on in the style of an essayist who freely associates one remembered quotation, or fragment of an idea with another until it becomes time to stop" (Hampshire again). Her habit of tracing concepts genetically, which in the case of political ideas takes her back to Plato, is particularly unhelpful when applied to abstractions and mental categories like "thinking" and "willing." One is not surprised to learn, in a 1954 letter to Mary McCarthy, that she finds Hume "not so interesting." McCarthy herself, an affectionate and admiring friend and reader, chided Arendt over the rather misty quality of the argument in her essay on Lessing: "There are wonderful thoughts in the Lessing speech but sometimes they have to be sensed, rather than clearly perceived, through a fog of approximate translation, e.g., 'humanity,' 'humaneness,' 'humanitarianism,' which are occasionally treated as synonymous and occasionally not."

It was not the translator's fault. Arendt may or may not have been confused, but she is certainly confusing and it does her little service to pretend otherwise. At times she seems to be evincing an innocent nostalgia for the lost world of the ancient polis, at others she is displaying sympathy for a sort of syndicalist collectivism (while finding its nearest contemporary incarnation, the Israeli kibbutz, "rule by your neighbors" and not very appealing). She invokes the distinction between ancient (participatory) liberty and the modern (private) kind with an apparent preference for the former; yet she was unshakably against conflating the private and the public and thought that modern American "social" legislation—for example desegregation of schools—could be dangerous just because it sought to blur the distinction.

The Human Condition, her most finished piece of theoretical writing, boils down to a single, albeit powerful, idea: that we have lost the sense of public space, of acting in concert, and have instead become slaves to a vision of human life that consists of a curious combination of "making"—the error of placing *Homo faber* at the center of political theory—and "History," the dangerous belief in fate and determined outcomes to which she attributed so many of the woes of our age. These are worthy insights, albeit a touch unreflectively communitarian, and it isn't difficult to see why each new generation of students thinks it has found in Hannah Arendt a trenchant critic of its times. But taken together they are in some conflict, and in any case offer neither a conceptually all-embracing nor a historically rich account of how we got where we are. They also propose no practically applicable solution to any particular political or social problem.

That is because Arendt herself was not setting out to construct any such all-embracing accounts or solutions. Most of her writings were initially conceived as separate lectures, essays, or articles, the forms at which she excelled. They are nearly all, in the proper sense of the word, occasional pieces, designed to respond to a particular event or to address a crisis or problem. And since most of the events in Arendt's world, and all of the crises and problems, returned in due course to the issue of totalitarianism, its causes and consequences, her contributions to modern thought have to be understood as variations on a single theme: We live in the midst of a political crisis whose extent we have yet fully to grasp, and we must act (by thought and by deed) so as to minimize the risk of repeating the experiences of our century. The first need is to recapture—or at least see the virtue of trying to recapture—the old republican qualities of civility, moderation, public discourse, and the like. This isn't a bad starting point for modern political theory—and once again Arendt came early to a position since adopted by many others. But it is, after all, only a starting point.

I HAVE SUGGESTED THAT Hannah Arendt was at her best in short bursts, when she was commenting, appraising, criticizing, or merely thinking aloud on some issue of contemporary significance. Indeed some of the essays in the Kohn collection, notably an unpublished paper from 1950 or 1951 called "The Eggs Speak Up," seem to me among the best pieces she ever wrote and should put an end to a certain image of Arendt as a "theorist" of the cold war, or even an intellectual precursor of "neo-conservatism."[23] It thus comes as no surprise that her long correspondence with Mary McCarthy, published for the first time in its entirety, should be such a pleasure.[24] The letters are not particularly intimate or self-revelatory on Arendt's part, but they do show a relaxed and warm side of her; she seemed to feel that McCarthy was one of the few people who saw what she was about (of *Eichmann in Jerusalem* she tells McCarthy that "you were the only reader to understand what otherwise I have never admitted—namely that I wrote this book in a curious state of euphoria").

She also demonstrates rather more human feeling than her correspondent could sometimes muster; following a series of highly emotional letters from Mary McCarthy in 1960 about the new love in her life (her future husband, James West) and the irritating difficulties posed by various ex-spouses and children from past marriages, it is left to Arendt to bring her friend down to earth with a gentle bump: "Please don't fool yourself: nobody ever was cured of anything, trait or habit, by a mere woman, though this is precisely what all girls think they can do. Either you are willing to take him 'as is' or you better leave well enough alone. What is going to happen to these poor children? To add to the shock of parental separation the shock of separating them from each other seems a bit unwise. But how can one judge without knowing anything[?]."

When Mary McCarthy seemed vexed that Hannah Arendt continued to maintain friendly relations with Bowden Broadwater, the husband whom McCarthy was abandoning, Arendt chided her: "The fact is that you brought him into my life, that without you he never would have become—not a personal friend which, of course, he is not—but a friend of the house, so to speak. But once you placed him there you cannot simply take him away from where he is now. As long as he does not do something really outrageous which he has not done so far and really turns against you which he has not done either, I am not going to sit in judgment. . . . You say you cannot trust him. Perhaps you are right, perhaps you are wrong, I have no idea. But it strikes me that you can forget so easily that you trusted him enough to be married to him for fifteen years." The age difference between them was not great (Arendt was born in 1906, McCarthy in 1912), but one is never in any doubt who was the mature woman, who the precocious girl.

The tone of the correspondence is not always serious. Predictably, there is much gossip, some of it funny. Arendt had no time for most French intellectuals, notably those in fashion. In 1964 she wrote to McCarthy, "I have just finished reading *Les Mots*—and was so disgusted that I was almost tempted to review this piece of highly complicated lying. . . . I am going to read les confessions of Simone—for their gossip value, but also because this kind of bad faith becomes rather fascinating." A few months later she provides a follow-up report: "This [de Beauvoir's *Force of Circumstance*] is one of the funniest books I read in years. Incredible that no one has taken that apart. Much as I dislike Sartre, it seems he is punished for all his sins by this kind of a cross. Especially since her unwavering true love for him is the only mitigating circumstance in the 'case against her,' really quite touching."

McCarthy, of course, was past mistress at this sort of thing; when in 1966 the Parisian *Nouvel Observateur* ran the headline "Est Elle Nazie?" over its excerpts from *Eichmann in Jerusalem*, she described it as "a sales promotion stunt, coated over with 'anti-fascist' piety," which is about right. A couple of years later the editor, Jean Daniel, sought unsuccessfully to make amends: "Daniel opposed it, I gather. But then he ought to have resigned. To say that here [Paris] is of course ludicrous. No French intellectual would ever resign on a point of principle unless to associate himself with another clique."

If the pair were prejudiced against French intellectuals, others come off little better. McCarthy gives a wonderfully acerbic report of a London dinner party in 1970, full of "silly zombies," from which she reports a remark by Sonia Orwell, as recalled by Stephen Spender, to illustrate the depths of British snobbery: "Auschwitz, oh dear, *no*! That person was never in Auschwitz. Only in some very *minor* death camp." Arendt's prejudices come into play at a rather more rarefied level. Of Vladimir Nabokov she writes in 1962: "There is something in [him] which I greatly dislike. As though he wanted to show you all the time how intelligent he is. And as though he thinks of himself in terms of 'more intelligent than.' There is something vulgar in his refinement." In the same letter she replies to McCarthy's request for her views on *The Tin Drum*:

"I know the Grass book but could never finish it. In my opinion, mostly secondhand, derivative, *outré* but with some very good parts in it."

The most savage comments are, however, reserved for the New York intellectual scene. Philip Rahv's "Marxist assurance" is compared by McCarthy to conversation with "some fossilized mammoth"; the "PR [*Partisan Review*] boys" in general get short shrift, except "Danny Bell," whom Arendt grudgingly concedes "is the only one who has got a conscience that bothers him once in a while. He is also a bit more intelligent than the others." Of the editor of the *New Yorker*, whose office in 1956 had pressed her for more details in a piece she had written, Mary McCarthy comments: "Shawn is really a curious person; he's a self-educated man and he assumes that everybody, like his own former untaught self, is eager to be crammed with information. A sentence larded with dates and proper names fills him with gluttonous delight—like a *boeuf à la mode*."[25]

McCarthy could be serious; her intermittent comments on Richard Nixon, from the 1959 "kitchen debate" with Khrushchev to a timely reminder from 1974 that the much eulogized late president was also a crook, are well taken, and she was a gifted scene setter, whether traveling in Sicily or describing a European dinner party with the wives of dead writers ("We had a party yesterday. . . . It was full of widows, like *Richard III*"). But in the later correspondence there enters a morbid, even mildly paranoid tone. She doesn't understand why her books get such a poor reception and feels abandoned by her friends. After one attack on her in 1974 she wrote to Arendt: "I can't help feeling, though I shouldn't, that if one of my friends had been in *my* place *I* would [have] raised my voice. This leads to the conclusion that I am peculiar, in some way that I cannot make out; *indefensible*, at least for my friends" (all emphases in original). Even Arendt comes under suspicion—"Something is happening or has happened to our friendship. . . . The least I can conjecture is that I have got on your nerves." Whether or not this was the case is unclear—Arendt was much too well bred to say anything in reply. But the somewhat brittle texture of McCarthy's gifts and her fundamentally narcissistic personality may have begun to grate a little. There is a distinctly cooler tone in Arendt's last letters, many of which were dictated.

Whereas there is something ultimately rather monotonous in

McCarthy's end of the correspondence, caustic and self-regarding, Arendt's letters have a more measured and cosmopolitan tone. She never tells McCarthy of her own personal dilemmas, for example her frustrations in continuing her long relationship with Heidegger. But a long description from August 1972 of the ambiance at the Rockefeller Center for writers and artists in Bellagio, Italy, not only captures brilliantly the luxuriant, sybaritic, unworldly mood of the retreat, but also nails down some of its comic contradictions, which appear to have changed not at all: "Now imagine this place filled, but by no means crowded, with a bunch of scholars, or rather professors, from all countries, . . . almost all of them rather mediocre (and this is putting it charitably) with their wives, some of them are plain nuts, others play the piano or type busily the non-masterworks of their husbands."

She writes perceptive and balanced comments on the student events of 1968 (in France and the U.S.), in contrast to McCarthy, who completely misread what was happening and assured Arendt in June of that year that de Gaulle had "made a mistake in his rapid veer to the Right; he will scare the middle voter whom he was *hoping* to scare with his anti-Communist rhetoric." (In fact de Gaulle and his party scored a huge electoral victory two weeks later by virtue of that very rhetoric.) On the whole it seems fair to conclude that whereas Mary McCarthy's letters, however entertaining, are rather ephemeral, the contributions by Arendt have a weightier texture and can still be read with profit as a commentary on her times.

Like the *Essays*, moreover, they also help us understand Hannah Arendt herself a little better. While she may indeed have been, in McCarthy's words, "a solitary passenger on her train of thought,"[26] she was not altogether alone on her journey through the twentieth century. Her elective affinity might have been with the great Germans, past and present, but her true community lay elsewhere, as her friendships and acquaintances suggest. She was born in Königsberg, a city on the geographical periphery of the culture of which it was at the same time a center. This gives her more in common than she may have realized with contemporary writers born in other vulnerable cities at once central and peripheral—Vilna, Trieste, Danzig, Alexandria, Algiers, even Dublin—and accounts for her membership in a very special and transient community, that twentieth-century republic of letters formed against their will by the survivors of the great upheavals of the century.

These lost cosmopolitan communities, in which Germans, Jews, Greeks, Italians, Poles, French, and others lived in productive disharmony, were torn from their roots in World War I and obliterated in World War II and during its aftermath. This shared experience accounts for Arendt's understanding of Moritz Goldstein's "unrequited love" (the very phrase also used by Miłosz in his account in *The Captive Mind* of Polish intellectuals' longing for a disappearing West), and for her instinctive affinity with Albert Camus.[27] They were all "chance survivors of a deluge," as she put it in a 1947 dedication to Jaspers, and wherever they ended up, in New York, Paris, or Rome, they were constrained, like Camus's Sisyphus, to push the boulder of memory and understanding up the thankless hill of public forgetting for the rest of their lives.

In Arendt's case the responsibility, as she felt it, was made heavier by a conscientious, and perhaps distinctively Jewish, refusal to condemn modernity completely or to pass a curse upon the Enlightenment and all its works. She certainly understood the temptation, but she also saw the danger. The tendency to treat Western liberal democracy as somehow "shallow," already present in the appeal of "Eastern" solutions before 1914,[28] has revived twice over in our own time. On the first occasion, in the sixties, Arendt's response was unambiguous: The struggle against the deceptive charms of what we would now call cultural relativism was for her a matter of moral courage, of exercising what she called judgment. In a letter to Jaspers in December 1963 she reflected that "even good and, at bottom, worthy people have, in our time, the most extraordinary fear about making judgments. This confusion about judgment can go hand in hand with fine and strong intelligence, just as good judgment can be found in those not remarkable for their intelligence."[29] Hannah Arendt was not afraid to judge, and be counted.

For the recent resurfacing of the critical attitude toward the Enlightenment, notably in certain Central European circles seduced by the post-Heideggerian notion that the soulless, technological, "fabricating" society of our century is an outgrowth of the Godless hubris of the French Enlightenment and its successors, Arendt herself bears some indirect responsibility. It is the very woolliness of her thoughts on these matters that has lent them to just such interpretations, and her reluctance to distance herself definitively from her former lover and mentor did not help. But she would never have made the mistake of supposing that the end of Communism promised some sort of definitive success for its opponents, or that the responsibilities of various strands in Western thought for the woes of our time thereby disqualified the Western tradition as a whole. She made a good many little errors, for which her many critics will never forgive her. But she got the big things right, and for this she deserves to be remembered.

This essay first appeared in the New York Review of Books *in 1995, reviewing a new collection of Hannah Arendt's essays and her recently published correspondence with Mary McCarthy. It provoked an angry response from some readers still furious with Hannah Arendt for her comments thirty years previously in* Eichmann in Jerusalem *concerning the "banality of evil." The ensuing exchanges were published in the* New York Review of Books, *vol. 42, no. viii, May 1995, and vol. 42, no. xiv, September 1995.*

NOTES TO CHAPTER IV

[1] The recent analysis by Margaret Canovan, *Hannah Arendt: A Reinterpretation of Her Political Thought* (Cambridge: Cambridge University Press, 1992; 1994) has the unusual virtue of emphasizing this point, and is now the best general discussion of Arendt's work. The new study by Maurizio Passerin d'Entrèves, *The Political Philosophy of Hannah Arendt* (New York: Routledge, 1993), is subtle and thorough but makes everything a bit tidy.

[2] "On Humanity in Dark Times: Thoughts about Lessing," in *Men in Dark Times* (New York: Harcourt Brace Jovanovich, 1968), 10.

[3] For perhaps related reasons, her work lacks the interpretive elegance of the work of Jacob Talmon, whose *Origins of Totalitarian Democracy* (London: Secker and Warburg, 1952) presents a more fully worked-out critical theory of the intellectual origins of Communism.

[4] "It is precisely because the utilitarian core of ideologies was taken for granted that the antiutilitarian behavior of totalitarian governments, their complete indifference to mass interests, has been such a shock." *The Origins of Totalitarianism* (first published by Harcourt Brace, 1951; all citations from the 1961 edition), p. 347.

[5] E. J. Hobsbawm in *History and Theory*, vol. 4, no. 2 (1965), quoted by Elizabeth Young-Bruehl, *Hannah Arendt: For Love of the World* (New Haven, CT: Yale University Press, 1982), 403.

[6] She had a surer touch when dealing with intellectuals themselves. Of fin de siècle French essayists like Léon Daudet, Charles Maurras, and Maurice Barrès she wrote, "It was their philosophy of pessimism and their delight in doom that was the first sign of the imminent collapse of the European intelligentsia." *The Origins of Totalitarianism*, p. 112.

[7] For a truly original account of Soviet *Gleichschaltung* at work, see Jan T. Gross, *Revolution from Abroad: The Soviet Conquest of Poland's Western Ukraine and Western Belorussia* (Princeton, NJ: Princeton University Press, 1987).

8 See *Origins of Totalitarianism*, p. 466.

9 Hannah Arendt, "A Reply," *The Review of Politics*, January 1953, vol. 15, no. i, pp. 76–84.

10 One is reminded of the admission by Hoess, the Auschwitz commandant: "We were all so trained to obey orders without even thinking that the thought of disobeying an order would never have occurred to anybody." Quoted by Telford Taylor, *Anatomy of the Nuremberg Trials: A Personal Memoir* (New York: Knopf, 1992), 363.

11 It, too, has since received impressive confirmation in studies of "ordinary" torturers, murderers, and genocidal criminals. See in particular Christopher Browning, *Ordinary Men: Reserve Police Battalion 101 and the Final Solution in Poland* (New York: HarperCollins, 1992).

12 "Walter Benjamin, 1892–1940," in *Men in Dark Times*, p. 184.

13 *Rahel Varnhagen: The Life of a Jewish Woman* (New York: Harcourt Brace Jovanovich, 1974), 219.

14 See William Barrett, *The Truants: Adventures Among the Intellectuals* (Garden City, NY: Anchor/Doubleday, 1982), 99.

15 *Rahel Varnhagen*, p. 85.

16 "Rosa Luxemburg: 1871–1919," in *Men in Dark Times*, p. 42.

17 E.g., "The whole truth is that if the Jewish people had really been unorganized and leaderless, there would have been chaos and plenty of misery but the total number of victims would hardly have been between four and a half and six million people." *Eichmann in Jerusalem: A Report on the Banality of Evil* (New York: Viking Penguin, 1963), 125.

18 See Henry Feingold's remarks on "The Judenrat and the Jewish Response" in Yehuda Bauer and Nathan Rotenstreich, eds., *The Holocaust as Historical Experience* (New York: Holmes and Meier, 1981), 223. I am grateful to Professor Steven Zipperstein for this and other references. The complexities of this subject, notably the very wide range of Jewish responses at the time, are well summarized in Michael Marrus, *The Holocaust in History* (Hanover, NH: University Press of New England, 1987), notably in chapter 6, "The Victims."

19 Quoted by Gordon Craig in his review of the Arendt-Jaspers *Correspondence*, in *The New York Review of Books*, May 13, 1993, p. 12.

20 Stuart Hampshire, review of *The Life of the Mind*, in *The* (London) *Observer*, July 30, 1978. Curious about why Arendt is taken seriously in the U.S. as a political theorist and public philosopher, Hampshire asks: "Is this difference merely a clash between analytical philosophy in the British manner and the post-Hegelian, German tradition of thought which has a foothold in the USA, is entrenched in France and has been rejected here?"

21 Judith Shklar, "Hannah Arendt as Pariah," *Partisan Review*, vol. 50, no. 1 (1983): 67.

22 The letter is dated February 9, 1968, a week after the beginning of the Tet offensive, and should of course be understood in context. Arendt was deeply troubled by the Vietnam War and its destructive impact upon American public life, as well as by the domestic conflicts of the era; she was not the only contemporary intellectual to give vent to occasional feelings of frustration and helplessness in the face of these developments.

23 Discussing the emerging idea that exploitation, dictatorship, and corruption were somehow lesser evils, she writes: "Some anti-totalitarians have already started even to praise certain 'lesser evils' because the not-so-far-away time when these evils ruled in a world still ignorant of the worst of all evils looks like the good old days by comparison . . . The greatest danger of recognizing totalitarianism as the curse of the century would be an obsession with it to the extent of becoming blind to the numerous small and not so small evils with which the road to hell is paved." *Essays in Understanding*, pp. 271–272.

24 *Between Friends: The Correspondence of Hannah Arendt and Mary McCarthy, 1949–1975*, edited and with an introduction by Carol Brightman (New York: Harcourt Brace Jovanovich, 1995). According to the editor, the only cuts concern actionable remarks, mostly by McCarthy.

25 Publishers' copy editors get the usual incandescent authorial rebukes. Thus Arendt in 1971 on some minor dispute with the editors at Harcourt Brace: "This whole nonsense comes from

their zeal to show how necessary they are, how well they worked and how much, etc; plus, of course, sheer undiluted stupidity with more than a bit of méchanceté. The outrage is that they make us *work* to undo what they did, and each time they put one of their idiotic queries in the margin one rushes back to reference and God knows what. If we were compensated by the hour by the publisher for unnecessary work they would begin to be a bit more careful. . . . These people are not 'professionals,' they are actually unemployable people who have succeeded in landing a job which hardly exists to begin with."

[26] See Mary McCarthy, "Saying Goodbye to Hannah," in *Occasional Prose* (New York: Harcourt Brace Jovanovich, 1985), 37, quoted by Carol Brightman in her introduction to the letters, p. xvi.

[27] For a suggestive interpretation of the underappreciated similarities of outlook between Camus and Arendt, see Jeffrey C. Isaac, *Arendt, Camus, and Modern Rebellion* (New Haven, CT: Yale University Press, 1992). The heading of the last chapter of Arendt's *On Revolution*, "The Revolutionary Tradition and Its Lost Treasure," could have been the title of any number of works by Camus.

[28] See her remarks on this in *Origins of Totalitarianism*, p. 245.

[29] Quoted by Elizabeth Young-Bruehl from a letter to Jaspers not included in the published Correspondence. See *Hannah Arendt: For Love of the World*, p. 338.

Part Two

THE POLITICS OF INTELLECTUAL ENGAGEMENT

CHAPTER V

Albert Camus:
"The best man in France"

Albert Camus died in a car accident in France, on January 4, 1960, at the age of forty-six. Despite the Nobel Prize for Literature, awarded him just three years before, his reputation was in decline. At the time of the award, critics fell over one another to bury its recipient; from the right, Jacques Laurent announcing that in awarding the prize to Camus *"le Nobel couronne une oeuvre terminée,"* while in the left-leaning *France-Observateur* it was suggested that the Swedish Academy may have believed it was picking out a young writer, but it had in fact confirmed a "premature sclerosis." Camus's best work, it seemed, lay far behind him; it had been many years since he had published anything of real note.

For this decline in critical esteem, Camus himself was at least partly to blame. Responding to the fashions of the day, he had engaged in philosophical speculations of a kind to which he was ill-suited and for which he was only moderately gifted—*The Myth of Sisyphus* (1942) has not worn well, for all its resonating aphorisms. In *L'Homme Révolté* (1951) Camus offered some important observations about the dangers of lyrical revolutionary illusions; but Raymond Aron said much the same thing to vastly more devastating effect in *L'Opium des intellectuels*, while Camus's naive, almost autodidactic philosophical speculations exposed him to a cruel and painful riposte from Sartre that severely damaged his credibility with the *bien-pensant* intellectual Left and permanently undermined his public self-confidence.

If his literary reputation, as the author of *L'Étranger* and *La Peste*, was thus unfairly diminished in contemporary opinion by Camus's unsuccessful forays into philosophical debate, it was his role as France's leading public intellectual, the moral voice of his era, that weighed most heavily upon him in his last decade. His editorials in the postwar paper *Combat* had given him, in Aron's words, a singular prestige;[1] it was Camus whose maxims set the moral tone of the Resistance generation as it faced the dilemmas and disappointments of the Fourth Republic. By the late fifties this burden became intolerable, a source of constant discomfort in Camus's writing and speeches. In earlier years he had accepted the responsibility: "One must submit," as he put it in 1950.[2] But in the last interview he ever gave, in December 1959, his resentful frustration is audible: "I speak for no one: I have enough difficulty speaking for myself. I am no one's guide. I don't know, or I know only dimly, where I am headed (*"Je ne sais pas, ou je sais mal, où je vais"*).[3]

Worst of all, for Camus and his audience, was the dilemma posed by the tragedy of French Algeria. Like most intellectuals of his generation, Camus was bitterly critical of French policy; he condemned the use of torture and terror in the government's "dirty war" against the Arab nationalists, and he had been a vocal and well-informed critic of colonial discrimination against the indigenous Arab population ever since the thirties (at a time when many of the Parisian intellectuals who would later distinguish themselves in the anticolonial struggle knew little and cared less about the condition and needs of France's overseas subjects). But Camus was born in Algeria, the son of impoverished European immigrants. He grew up in Algiers and drew on his experiences there for much of his best work. Unable to imagine an Algeria without Europeans, or to imagine indigenous Europeans of his milieu torn from their roots, he struggled to describe a middle way; in his words, *"Une grande, une éclatante réparation doit être faite . . . au peuple Arabe. Mais par la France toute entière et non avec le sang des Français d'Algérie."*[4] As France and Algeria alike grew ever more polarized over the issue, Camus's search for a liberal compromise came to seem forlorn and irrelevant. He withdrew into silence.[5]

In the years following his death Camus's standing continued to fall. Most people living in metropolitan France were unconcerned by the fate of Algeria and its various communities, Arab or European; as for the intellectuals, their interests in the sixties and seventies were so far from those which had moved Camus as to make him an object of scorn, condescension, and, finally, neglect. He was overtaken by the radical and increasingly intolerant politicization of a younger generation, by the self-lacerating *tiers-mondisme* of the later Sartre and his followers, by the "anti-humanist" vogue among scholars, by new fashions in literature, and, most of all, by a decline in the status of the writer. Looking back on his own time in the sixties as founder/editor of the *Nouvel Observateur,* Jean Daniel would recall "quickly discovering that it was among the human sciences—history, sociology, ethnology, philosophy—that one had to look for the equivalent of the *littérateurs* who, in my youth, had served as *maîtres à penser*."[6] In the world of Barthes, Robbe-Grillet, Lévi-Strauss, and Foucault, Camus was *dépassé*. Not that he was unread: *L'Étranger, La Peste,* and *Caligula* were established texts of the lycée and university curricula, as they were (and are) on the reading lists of millions of students abroad. Albert Camus had become, in his own lifetime or very shortly thereafter, a worldwide "classic." And this, too, was held against him.

It was thus at first sight rather curious to find him once again in the headlines, his last, unfinished novel a major publishing coup upon its belated appearance in 1994, thirty years after it was written.* Over 200,000 copies of *Le premier homme* have now been sold. To be sure, this renewal of interest does not come out of the blue. In the seedy, corrupt public atmosphere of the dying Mitterrand era, a clear moral voice has been sorely lacking, as more than one French commentator has glumly observed. Moreover, the French have become grimly aware of the decayed and neglected condition of their literary heritage; Albert Camus was one of the last of an era of great French writers, a link to the world of Roger Martin du Gard, Jules Romains, Gide, Mauriac, and Malraux. One re-

---

* *Le premier homme* (Gallimard, Paris, 1994).

viewer, musing on the success of *Le premier homme*, wondered whether the French weren't "celebrating the myth of a brilliant life, transformed by accidental death into a destiny, a sign from beyond the grave, a reproach from the days when French literature counted for something. . . ."[7] There is truth in this view, but to appreciate the contemporary impact of Camus we need to look a little further.

Camus's rejection of violence, of terror in all its forms, reduced him to impotent silence at the height of the Algerian civil war and rendered him inaccessible to the generation that followed. But by the late seventies, with nothing but blood and ashes to show for their support of revolutionary repression in Europe, in China, in Cuba, and in Cambodia, French thinkers had swung around to a point of view remarkably close to that of Camus—though usually without acknowledgment: It was one thing to repeat Camus's warning that "*il est des moyens qui ne s'excusent pas*,"[8] quite another to admit he had been correct all along. The so-called New Philosophers, such as André Glucksmann or Bernard-Henri Lévy, did not rehabilitate Camus, but they contributed significantly to the process whereby those who once scorned him for his "moralizing" obsession with responsibility have themselves now lost all favor. They have been discredited by their casual resort to future history to justify present crimes, and by the ease with which they asserted that others must suffer for the sins of their own fathers. The lucidity and moral courage of Camus's stand shine through today in a way that was not possible in the polarized world of 1958: "As for me, I find it disgusting to beat the other man's breast, in the manner of our judge-penitents."[9]

Perhaps most important of all, the French-Algerian trauma is now behind us, and as it recedes into memory (and forgetting) it takes with it the confidence and the anger that shaped the attitudes of both sides. Thirty years after gaining its independence, Algeria is again in trouble, divided and bloodied by a fundamentalist movement temporarily held in check by a military dictatorship. However hopelessly naive Camus's appeal for a compromise between assimilationist colonialism and militant nationalism, his prognosis for the future of a country born of terror and civil war was all too accurate: "Tomorrow Algeria will be a land of ruins and of corpses that no force, no power in the world, will be able to restore in our century."[10] What Camus understood perhaps better and earlier than any of his (metropolitan) contemporaries was not Arab nationalism—though as early as 1945 he had predicted that the Arabs could not much longer be expected to tolerate the conditions under which they were governed—but the particular culture of Algeria's European inhabitants, and the price that would be paid should anyone attempt to shatter it. The lost world of French Algeria is at the center of his last, unfinished novel, and it is a subject to which French readers are open now in a way that would have been unthinkable in 1960, when the manuscript was found in Camus's briefcase at the scene of his death.

Le premier homme was to have been Camus's bildungsroman, a trip-tych of his life and times. Although he had been at work on it for some time (it is first mentioned in his *Carnets* in 1951), we have only the open-ing section, dealing with his childhood and the search for his dead father. The work is unmistakably, unambiguously autobiographical; as published it contains all his notes and corrections, and one finds Camus occasionally interpolating the first person singular, as though this were indeed the story of young Albert Camus and not of "Jacques Cormery" (from the family name of his paternal grandmother). Like Camus's father Lucien, "Henri Cormery" was mortally wounded at the Battle of the Marne, in October 1914, and is buried at a cemetery in Saint-Brieuc, the small Breton town to which Lucien Camus was evacuated and where he died from his wounds. His widow, her two sons (of whom the younger, Albert/Jacques, was not yet one year old), and their maternal grandmother are left in Belcourt, a poor European district of Algiers, living penuriously from the mother's earnings as a domestic servant. The book is organized around two intersecting narratives: the quest of Jacques, now entering middle age, for the father he never knew, and the story of his childhood in a world dominated by his mother and grandmother.

Reading the inscription on his father's tombstone, Jacques is caught up short by the realization that when he died in 1914, Henri Cormery was just twenty-nine years old, younger than the son now standing by his grave. The anonymity, the poverty, the brevity of his life echo through the book, a coda to the world of the European immigrants (Camus/Cormery was born into a family of immigrants from German-occupied Alsace, thus doubly exiled), to the unremembered past of the community, of the fam-ily, and of his own son, to the alienated manner of his dying—"*Il n'avait jamais vu la France. Il la vit et il fut tué.*"[11] Jacques, "who hated conventional gestures of this kind," had long avoided visiting the grave. As an older Frenchman reminds him, "You don't need a father—you raised yourself all alone." The visit sets off a search for roots and creates in the story of young Cormery an oscillation and tension between the absent father and the second dominant theme of the work, the author's troubling mother.

Catherine Camus, who was descended from Minorcan immigrants (a Spanish connection in which her son took great pride), was illiterate, partly deaf, and hardly spoke at all. In life and in the novel this silence, and her virtual inability to express herself in word or gesture, produced in her son a desperate confusion. As Camus put it in a much earlier work, "He pities his mother, is this the same as loving her? She never caressed him—she would not have known how."[12] In *Le premier homme* Jacques Cormery loves his mother "hopelessly," but in his silent observations of the mute, exhausted woman he is "filled with vague anxiety in the face of a misfortune (*malheur*) he could not understand." Like Camus, Cormery concludes that there is something magnificently dignified and even honorable about his mother's silence in the face of such adversity, but it leaves him silent, too, unable to find a way through to this parent as well and frustrated at his inadequacy.[13]

What saves Cormery, from his despair and his past, is education. Here Camus writes from the heart, not only of the primary-school teacher who entered his life as a partial surrogate father, but also of the almost inexpressible importance of the French system of free primary education and competitive secondary-school scholarships for poor children of his generation. One of the most moving passages in the book comes when the teacher visits Cormery's house for the first time and convinces his mother and grandmother to allow him to sit for the scholarship, even though success (and acceptance into the lycée) would deprive them of his earning capacity for years to come. This same chapter ends on the book's only elegiac note—young Jacques passes the exam, says goodbye to his primary-school teacher, and enters, with mixed feelings, upon a new world. It is a reminder that Camus, more than any of his fellow postwar literati, was a pure product of the Third Republic, and that its ethical and pedagogical ideals meant more to him than to most of his contemporaries. When his Nobel Prize acceptance speech was published in 1958, it was to that same schoolteacher, M. Louis Germain, that Camus dedicated it.

Beyond the attention paid to the father, to the mother, and to its young protagonist's schooling, *Le premier homme* addresses three topics already to be found in Camus's early essays and stories: sensuality, poverty, and the special meaning, for him, of Algeria. No reader of Camus could have missed the importance of physical sensations and the world of the flesh throughout his work, from *L'Étranger*, where the omnipresent sun plays out its fateful role, to the Nobel Prize speech, where he spoke of never having been able to do without the light, the sense of well-being, the life of freedom in which he grew up.[14] His last novel luxuriates in the sheer sensuality of the sun, of the sea, of youthful bodies in the water and at the beach. Nowhere else in Camus's writing is one so aware of his pleasure in such things, and of his ambivalence toward the other, cerebral world in which he had chosen to dwell. In *Le premier homme* Camus has recaptured something he tried to explain in a much earlier story, "Noces à Tipasa," the appeal of "a life that tastes of warm stone."[15] The marginal notes reveal his intentions: "the book must be heavy with objects and with physicality."[16]

Algeria, too, is physically present, its smells, its sounds, the topography of Algiers itself on its magnificent bay, the adventures of Jacques and his friends through the streets and the docks, hunting expeditions with his uncle into the backcountry. And there are the Arabs, "this attractive, disturbing people, at once close and separate." In the childhood chapters Arabs come and go fleetingly, part of the natural streetscape of a mixed community, but when the older Jacques visits his birthplace and gets into conversation with a *colon*, the latter explains to him that it is inevitable that Europeans and Arabs will now fight each other, brutally. And then they will once again live together. Why? "Because that is what this land desires." As for Camus/Cormery, his own feelings are made explicit: "So it was each time he left Paris for Africa, a quiet jubilation, his spirit opening wide, the satisfaction of someone who has just made a neat escape and who laughs when he thinks of the faces of the guards." Yet Algeria is also a realm of doubts, a problem-filled place for Camus/Cormery, "the land of forgetting where everyone was the first man."[17]

This is but one of the uses made of the book's title. Like the others
it concerns identity—that of the European in Algeria, that of the self-
created Camus/Cormery born into a fatherless family of silent women,
that of the orphaned father himself. And across all of these meanings
there falls the shadow of poverty, the book's pervasive theme and the occasion for some of Camus's sharpest observations. The truly poor, he
notes, speak little of the past—they are too obsessively concerned with
surviving in the present; hence Jacques Cormery's inability to find his
own roots through his family, who seemed to him to have none—to have
come from everywhere and to be living nowhere—"fatherless, with no
transmitted tradition . . . one had to create one's own inheritance. He was
born on a land without ancestors and without memory." The very purpose of the novel, according to Camus's own notes, was to "tear this
impoverished family from the destiny of the poor which is to disappear
from history without trace. The Voiceless." But like all scholarship boys,
Camus/Cormery's success in breaking clear of his background is dearly
bought: When he first enters the lycée Cormery is asked by a school official to list his parent's occupation. He has no idea what it is—his mother
cleans other people's houses and does their laundry. A friend advises him
that she is therefore a *domestique.* He writes it down, and is overcome
with "shame—and the shame of having felt shame."[18] Like everything
else in this book—the magnificent passages of recollections, the alterna-
tion between Camus's characteristic classical brevity and less familiar,
lyrical, paragraph-long descriptions, the absence of ironic restraint or
distance—this has the ring of absolute authenticity.

   Le premier homme is not only a recapitulation and development of
Camus's earlier stories and essays—many of which are echoed here,
down to a phrase—but also an invaluable reminder of what was central
to his concerns and what, contemporary opinion notwithstanding,
merely peripheral. Much of the idea of the "absurd," to which he owed
his early fame, can now be understood as Camus's way of trying to express the importance for him of place and sensation. Thus there is a
passage in *Sisyphus* where he writes as follows: "In a universe suddenly
divested of illusions and lights, man feels an alien, a stranger. His exile
is without remedy since he is deprived of the memory of a lost home or
the hope of a promised land. This divorce between a man and his life,

the actor and his setting, is properly the feeling of absurdity."[19] Just as Camus is known to have felt that critics missed the point of the Algerian settings in *La Peste* and (especially) in *L'Étranger*, so his critics and admirers alike often both overinterpreted and lost the message of his non-literary writings.

In reading *Le premier homme* we are also reminded, forcibly, that one of the most enduring messages in Camus's oeuvre was of discomfort; he was an outsider in Paris, *étranger* in something of the sense used in his most famous novel. It was not that he felt out of place in the role of the intellectual, rather that there were two conflicting personalities in play, only one of which was understood and appreciated by his colleagues. When, during the Algerian conflict, he tried to explain the other part and hence his own pained ambivalence, few understood; "the Mediterranean separated within me two universes, one where memories and names were conserved in measured spaces, the other where the traces of man were swept across great distances by the sandy wind." This separation of worlds had always troubled Camus; in an early (1939) review of *Bread and Wine* he picked out for comment the passage where Silone's hero reflects on the risk of theorizing too much about the peasants and thereby coming to know them ever less.[20] Camus, too, worried (and continues to worry in his last work) about the risk of losing touch, of severing one's roots before one has even found them. And it was this essentially psychological intuition into the condition of the rudderless intellectual that helped give to Camus's ethics of limits and of responsibility their peculiar authority.

It is this moral authority that is lacking in contemporary France, and that partly accounts for the enthusiasm with which *Le premier homme* has been met. The book itself is wonderful in many ways, incomplete and unpolished though it may be. But that is not why many people buy it. Camus's own heirs and his publisher, Gallimard, were wary in their presentation of it, having withheld it for many decades for fear it would only further harm its author's already dented reputation. The situation today could not be more different. After two decades of painful and incomplete inquiry into their troubled history, with Vichy a still-festering sore and the intellectual giants of the recent past reduced to a rubble of embarrassing citations, Camus the Just remains, in the prescient words of one critic, "the most noble witness of a rather ignoble age."[21] In an era of self-promoting media intellectuals, vacantly preening before the admiring mirror of their electronic audience, Camus's patent honesty, what his former schoolteacher called "*ta pudeur instinctive*,"[22] has the appeal of the genuine article, a hand-crafted masterwork in a world of plastic reproductions. Jean-Paul Sartre, who did so much to tarnish his old friend's reputation, and whose own advocacy of violence and terror would have truly shocked Camus had he lived to read it, went a long way toward making amends in the obituary he contributed to *France-Observateur*. Camus, he wrote, "represented in this century . . . the contemporary heir to that long line of moralists whose work perhaps constitutes whatever is most distinctive in French letters."[23] Sartre was surely right, and the belated publication of Albert Camus's last novel is a sharp reminder that the French have been missing his distinctive voice these past thirty years. They miss it still.

This review of Le premier homme, *Albert Camus's posthumous novel, first appeared in the* New York Review of Books *in October 1994. It was Hannah Arendt who, writing to her husband from Paris in 1951, described Albert Camus as "the best man in France."*

NOTES TO CHAPTER V

[1] See Raymond Aron, *Mémoires* (Paris: Julliard, 1983), 208.

[2] See Albert Camus's "L'Enigme" in *Essais,* ed. by Roger Quilliot (Paris: Gallimard, 1965), 863.

[3] See "Dernière Interview d'Albert Camus" (December 20, 1959) in *Essais,* p. 1925.

[4] "Major and conspicuous amends have to be made . . . to the Arab people. But by all of France and not with the blood of the French of Algeria."

[5] "L'Algérie déchirée," in *Actuelles III (Chroniques algériennes 1939–1958)* (Paris: Gallimard, 1958), p. 143 (written in 1956). In 1958, in his last published thoughts on the subject, he complained that "on attend trop d'un écrivain en ces matières. Même, et peut-être surtout, lorsque sa naissance et son coeur le vouent au destin d'une terre comme l'Algérie, il est vain de le croire détenteur d'une vérité révélée." ("too much is asked of the writer in these matters. Even, and perhaps especially, when his origins and his heart tie him to the fate of a land like Algeria it is fruitless to think him possessed of a revealed truth.") (*Actuelles III,* "Avant-propos," 27.)

[6] Jean Daniel, *L'Ère des Ruptures* (Paris: Grasset, 1979), 29–30.

[7] Bernard Fauconnier, *Magazine Littéraire,* No. 322 (June 1994), p. 60.

[8] Albert Camus, *Lettres à un ami Allemand* (Paris: Gallimard, 1948, 1972) No. 1 (July 1943), p. 19.

[9] "Avant-propos," *Actuelles III,* p. 23. "En ce qui me concerne, il me paraît dégoûtant de battre sa coulpe, comme nos juges-pénitents, sur la poitrine d'autrui."

[10] Albert Camus, "Lettre à un militant Algérien" (October 1955) in *Actuelles III,* p. 128.

[11] "He had never seen France. He saw it and was killed."

[12] "Entre Oui et Non," from *L'Envers et l'Endroit*, originally published in Algiers in 1937, republished in *Essais;* see p. 25.

[13] "Et ce qu'il désirait le plus au monde, qui était que sa mère lût tout ce qui était sa vie et sa chair, cela était impossible. Son amour, son seul amour serait à jamais muet." ("And what he desired more than anything in the world, that his mother might read that which constituted his life and very being, this was impossible. His love, his only love, would be forever mute.") See *Le premier homme,* Annexes (Camus's own notes), p. 292.

[14] *Discours de Suède*, December 12, 1957 (Paris: Gallimard, 1958), 20.

[15] "Noces à Tipasa" (first published in 1939) in *Essais,* p. 58.

[16] "Il faudrait que le livre pèse un gros poids d'objets et de chair."

[17] "La terre d'oubli où chacun était le premier homme."

[18] "Et d'un seul coup [il] connut la honte et la honte d'avoir eu honte."

[19] *Le mythe de Sisyphe, essai sur l'absurde* (first published in 1942) in *Essais, p. 101.*

[20] In *Alger Républicain*, May 23, 1939.

[21] Pierre de Boisdeffre, "Camus et son destin," in *Camus* (Paris: Hachette, 1964), pp. 265-279 (see p. 277).

[22] In a letter from Louis Germain to Camus, dated April 30, 1959, and published as an annex to *Le premier homme,* p. 328.

[23] "Il représentait en ce siècle, et contre l'Histoire, l'héritier actuel de cette longue lignée de moralistes dont les oeuvres constituent peut-être ce qu'il y a de plus original dans les lettres françaises." J.-P. Sartre, "Albert Camus" in *France-Observateur,* January 7, 1960 [reprinted in *Situations IV* (Paris: Gallimard, 1964), 126–129].

CHAPTER VI

Elucubrations: The "Marxism" of Louis Althusser

I was brought up a Marxist. Nowadays that is not much of a boast, but it had its advantages. Parents and grandparents were imbued with all of the assumptions and some of the faith that shaped the European Socialist movement in its heyday. Coming from that branch of East European Jewry that had embraced social democracy and the Bund (the Jewish Labor organization of early-twentieth-century Russia and Poland), my own family was viscerally anti-Communist. In its eyes, Bolshevism was not only a dictatorship, it was also—and this, too, was a serious charge—a travesty of Marxism. By the time I went to university, I had been thoroughly inoculated with all the classical nineteenth-century texts; and as a result I was immune to the wide-eyed enthusiasm with which Marxist revelations were greeted by those of my freshman peers who were discovering them for the first time.

Thus, when I arrived in Paris as a graduate student in the late sixties, I was skeptically curious to see and to hear Louis Althusser. In charge of the teaching of philosophy at the École Normale Supérieure, the French elite academy for future teachers and leaders, Althusser was touted by everyone I met as a man of extraordinary gifts, who was transforming our understanding of Marx and reshaping revolutionary theory. His name, his ideas, his books were everywhere. But listening to him, at a crowded and sycophantic seminar, I was utterly bemused. For Althusser's account of Marxism, to the extent that I could make any sense of it, bore no relation to anything I had ever heard. It chopped Marx into little bits, selected those texts or parts of texts that suited the master's interpretation, and then proceeded to construct the most astonishingly abstruse, self-regarding, and ahistorical version of Marxist philosophy imaginable. The exercise bore no discernible relationship to Marxism, to philosophy, or to pedagogy. After a couple of painful attempts to adapt myself to the experience and to derive some benefit from it, I abandoned the seminar and never went back.

Returning to the subject many years later, and constrained for professional reasons to read Althusser's mercifully few published works, I understood a little better what had been going on, intellectually and sociologically. Althusser was engaged in what he and his acolytes called a "symptomatic reading" of Marx, which is to say that they took from him what they needed and ignored the rest. Where they wished Marx to have said or meant something that they could not find in his writings, they interpreted the "silences," thereby constructing an entity of their own imagination. This thing they called a science, one that Marx was said to have invented and that could be applied, gridlike, to all social phenomena.

Why invent a Marxist "science" when so much was already at hand, the Marxist "theory of history," "historical materialism," "dialectical materialism," and the rest? The answer is that Althusser, like so many others in the sixties, was trying to save Marxism from the two major threats to its credibility: the grim record of Stalinism and the failure of Marx's revolutionary forecasts. Althusser's special contribution was to remove Marxism altogether from the realm of history, politics, and experience, and thereby to render it invulnerable to any criticism of the empirical sort.

In Althusser-speak, Marxism was a theory of structural practices: economic, ideological, political, theoretical. It had nothing to do with human volition or agency, and thus it was unaffected by human frailty or inadequacy. These "practices" determined history. Their respective importance, and their relationship to one another, varied with circumstances; the "dominant structure" was sometimes "economic practice" and sometimes "political practice," and so on. Of particular significance was the notion of "theoretical practice." This oxymoronic phrase, which came to be chanted, mantralike, all over Europe in those years, had the special charm of placing intellectuals and intellectual activity on the same plane as the economic organizations and the political strategies that had preoccupied earlier generations of Marxists.

This subjectless theory of everything had a further virtue. By emphasizing the importance of theory, it diverted attention from the embarrassing defects of recent practice. In such an account, Stalin's crime was not that he had murdered millions of human beings, it was that he had perverted the self-understanding of Marxism. Stalinism, in short, was just another mistake in theory, albeit an especially egregious one, whose major sin consisted of its refusal to acknowledge its own errors. This was important to Althusser, who was a member of the French Communist Party and who sought to admit the embarrassing history of that organization without undermining whatever remained of its claim to revolutionary omniscience. The party's leadership itself had responded to this conundrum by belatedly treating Stalin as an unfortunate but parenthetical episode in the otherwise unblemished record of Communism. His crimes were a mere deviation born of the cult of personality. But Althusser went one better by showing that "Stalin" and his works constituted only a collective analytical error. This performed the double service of keeping personalities out of the matter and reiterating the centrality of concepts.

It is hard, now, to recapture the mood of the sixties, in which this absurd dialectical joust seemed appealing. But Althusser unquestionably filled a crucial niche. He gave young Maoists an impressively high-flown language in which to be "anti-humanist" Communists, dismissive of the "Italian road" to Socialism. At the time this was a matter of some importance: The early works of Marx, notably the Economic and Philosophical Manuscripts, had only recently entered the canon, having for many years languished unknown and untranslated. Placed alongside his other youthful writings, they suggested a rather different Marx from the conventional image passed down from Engels via the popularizers of the early European Socialist movements; a man more interested in Romantic-era philosophy than in classical economics, an idealist whose agenda was not simply social revolution but the moral transformation of mankind. The interest in this "humanist" Marx had been aroused both by the recent French rediscovery of Hegel and by a new generation of radical intellectuals seeking to locate Marx in something other than the lineage imposed upon the European left by the doctrinaire positivism of Leninism.

Taking his cue from the growing fashion for "structuralism" (initially confined to linguistics and anthropology, but by the early sixties seeping into sociology and philosophy), Althusser worked hard to excommunicate this humanist and understandably more appealing Marx as "unscientific." In his view, to emphasize the moral condition and responsibilities of individual men was to detract from an appreciation of the larger, impersonal forces at work in history, and thus to delude the workers, or anyone else, into believing they could act on their own behalf, instead of accepting the authority of those who spoke and thought for them. In his words, "only theoretical anti-humanism justifies general practical humanism."

To flesh out his structuralist account, Althusser invented something that he and his followers called "Ideological State Apparatuses." In his heyday these were confined to the public and political world. In his memoirs, however, his attention was diverted to more personal matters.* Althusser informs us that "it is an irrefutable fact that the Family is the most powerful State Ideological Apparatus" (obligatory capitals), and in reflecting upon his experience in a mental hospital he wonders "what can now be done to free the mentally ill from the Hell created for them by the combined operations of all the Ideological State Apparatuses." In Althusserian dogma the presence of these repressive and all-embracing ogres was held particularly responsible for the inconvenient stability and durability of liberal democracy. Of special note was the announcement that the university was, of all of these, the dominant one for our era. "Theoretical practice" in the academic arena was thus the site of ideological battle; and philosophy was absolutely vital as the "class struggle

---

* Louis Althusser, *L'Avenir dure longtemps* (Paris: Stock, 1993); trans: *The Future Lasts Forever* (New York: New Press, 1993).

in theory." Scholars in their seminars were on the front line, and need feel guilty no more.

Althusser borrowed a term from the philosopher Gaston Bachelard and announced that an "epistemological break" in Marx's writings had occurred somewhere in the mid-1840s. Everything he wrote before the break was neo-Hegelian humanist flannel and could be ignored. Henceforth left-wing students and lecturers were free to jettison those bits of (the early) Marx that seemed to speak of alienation, reconciliation, human agency, and moral judgment.

This was hard for many people in the sixties to swallow. In Italy and in the English-speaking world, most young left-wingers were more attracted to the idea of a gentler, kinder Marx. In France, however, where the sordid political compromises of the Socialists and Communists during the battle over decolonization had left a sour taste among some of their younger supporters, this static, structuralist Marx sounded analytically pure and politically uncompromising.

By the end of the seventies however, Althusser's star was on the wane. He had been absent during the events of May 1968, and had showed little interest in the political developments of that year. His only direct comment on the "failed revolution" of 1968 was characteristic and revealing: "When revolt ends in defeat without the workers being massacred, it is not necessarily a good thing for the working class which has no martyrs to mourn or commemorate." Even his erstwhile followers admitted that he had nothing new to offer, and his rigid stance in defense of Marxism, Communism, and "the revolution" made him appear irrelevant in a decade that saw the publication in France of *The Gulag Archipelago*, the tragedy in Cambodia, the eclipse of Mao, and the steady loss of radical faith among a generation of French intellectuals. Had matters been left there, Althusser could have looked forward to a peaceful and obscure old age, a curious relic of a bizarre but forgotten era.

But then, on November 16, 1980, he murdered his wife Hélène in their apartment at the École Normale. Or, as the jacket copy of The New Press's translation of his memoir coyly puts it, "while massaging his wife's neck [he] discovered he had strangled her." (To be fair, this is how Althusser himself explained the event; but it is curious to find the claim reproduced unattributed on the book.) Althusser was examined by doctors, found to be mentally unfit to stand trial, and locked away in a psychiatric hospital. Three years later he was released and spent his last years in a dreary flat in north Paris, emerging occasionally to startle passers-by with "Je suis le grand Althusser!" It was in these years that he drafted two versions of an autobiography. They were found after his death in 1990 and first published in French, as a single book, in 1992.

These "memoirs" are curious. Althusser would have us read them as Rousseau-like confessions, but that is hard to do, and the comparison is embarrassingly unflattering to their author. They are clearly an attempt on Althusser's part to make sense of his madness, and to that extent they are indeed revealing; by his own account he wrote them "to free myself from the murder and above all from the dubious effects of having been declared unfit to plead" (it is ironic that their posthumous impact on any unprejudiced reader will surely be to confirm the original forensic diagnosis). As a genre, however, they really come closer to magical realism. The book, especially a short early draft incongruously titled "The Facts," is full of fantasies and imagined achievements, so much so that it is sometimes hard to disentangle the fictive Althusser from the rather mundane creature whose sad story emerges in these pages.

That story is soon told. Althusser was born in 1918, the eldest child of middle-class French parents in Algeria. His father was a banker whose career took him back to Marseilles in Louis's adolescent years. The young Althusser had an utterly uneventful early career. Academically promising, he was sent to the lycée in Lyon to prepare for the entrance exam to the École Normale. He passed the exam, but had to postpone his higher education when he was drafted into the army in 1939. Like many French soldiers, he had a futile war; his company was rounded up by the Germans in 1940, and he spent the next five years in a prisoner of war camp. About the only interesting thing that seems to have happened to him there was that he learned, somewhat belatedly, the pleasures of masturbation (he was not to make love for the first time until he was twenty-nine).

Finally admitted to the École upon his return to France, Althusser did well there, coming in second in the national philosophy examinations. Having spent his adolescence and his youth as an active young Catholic, he discovered left-wing politics at the École and joined the

Communist Party in 1948, which was about the time when other young intellectuals, nauseated and shocked by its Stalinist culture and tactics, were beginning to leave it. Shortly after graduating, Althusser obtained a teaching post at the École and settled into the quiet, secure life of an academic philosopher. He was to stay in the same post until being forcibly retired in the aftermath of the scandal that ended his career.

It was during his student years that Althusser met his future wife, Hélène Légotien (she had abandoned her family name, Rytmann, during the war), a woman nine years his senior who had played an active part in the Communist Resistance. As he acknowledges in his memoir, it was a troubled relationship. They were held together by bonds of mutual destructiveness. By 1980, he writes, "the two of us were shut up together in our own private hell." Hélène seems to have been an unhappy woman, insecure, tormented, and bitter—and with good reason. The Communist Party abandoned her after the war, falsely accusing her of some obscure act of betrayal during the Resistance. Uneasy with her own immigrant Jewish background, and desperate for the love and attention of her husband, she put up with his moods, his women friends, and his colleagues, most of whom looked down on her from the very great height of their own vaunted intellectual standing. She was clearly not a person comfortable with herself or others; and Althusser's own bizarre personality can only have made matters worse.

For what emerges clearly from his own account is that Althusser was always a deeply troubled person. This memoir is warped and curdled by his morbid self-pity, by his insecurity and the repeated invocation of Lacanian clichés to account for his troubles. Indeed, the book's main theme is his own psychological and social inadequacy, a defect for which he naturally holds his parents responsible, in equal parts. His mother's insistence on naming him for a dead uncle is blamed for his lifelong sense of "not existing": Louis being homonymic with the word "lui," meaning "him," the young Althusser's name rendered him impersonal and anonymous. (He seems not to have given much thought to the millions of happy Louis among his fellow countrymen.) According to Althusser, his mother "castrated" him with her excessive care and attention; hence his belated discovery of women and his inability to form satisfactory relations with them. And so it goes, for page after page.

Small wonder that when Louis does away with his wife, after forty years of manic-depressive bouts, hospitalization, treatment, and analysis, we learn that he was taking his revenge on the older woman who not only brought him to Communism but substituted, as he admits, for mother and father alike.

There is a human tragedy here, but it is presented in a breathtakingly narcissistic key. Althusser wrote this memoir not in order to comprehend why he killed his wife, but to show himself and others that he was sane. He had been, as he puts it, "deprived of his status as a philosopher" by being declared unfit to plead, and this final loss of identity, this fear that once again he would "not exist," seems to have been the driving compulsion behind his autobiography. If we take him at his word, this fear of "not existing" was the very engine that propelled his life's work. By elaborating a doctrine in which human volition and human action counted for naught, in which theoretical speculation was the supreme practice, Althusser could compensate for a life of gloomy, introspective inaction by asserting and legitimizing his existence in the arena of the text. As he says, "I . . . emerged as the victor, in the realm of pure thought."

This much, at least, we can learn from the memoir, and it casts interesting new light on the otherwise inexplicably murky and self-referential quality of the earlier philosophical writings. Althusser was reconstructing Marx to give his own life a shape with which he could live, and one that could stand respectable comparison with those of his father (a successful banker) and his wife (a Resistance fighter). We thus learn from this book that Althusser was conscious, in every sphere of his life, of "having practiced a great deception," though it never seems to have occurred to him that this insight bodes ill for the credibility of his intellectual legacy. Unfortunately for its author, however, the book reveals much more. We are presented not only with a man who is on the edge of insanity, obsessed with sexual imagery (a stick of asparagus is "stiff as a man's penis" and so on), dreams of grandeur, and his own psychoanalytical history but also with a man who is quite remarkably ignorant.

He seems to know nothing of recent history (among his howlers is an indictment of the "Polish fascist" Pilsudski for starting World War II). He appears only late in life to have discovered Machiavelli and other classics of Western philosophy, and he even admits to a skimpy and partial acquaintance with Marx's texts (something one might have inferred from his published work). He is also unsophisticated to the point of crudity in his political analysis. He seems to have learned nothing and to have forgotten nothing in the last twenty years of his life. Thus there is much talk of "the hegemony of bourgeois, imperialist capitalism"; and he is dismissive of the dissidents of the Soviet bloc ("cut off from their own people") and contemptuous of writers like André Glucksmann for "putting around unbelievable horror stories of the Gulag." Those words were written in 1985!

One puts down this depressing book with an overwhelming sense of bewilderment. How could it be that so many intelligent and educated people were taken in by this man? Even if we allow that his manic fancies met some widespread need in the sixties, how are we to account for the continuing fascination that he exercises in certain circles today? In France he is largely forgotten, though the jacket blurb by Didier Eribon describes the autobiography as "magnificent" and explains that "madness [is] the inevitable price of philosophy." It is a conclusion whose deductive logic and historical accuracy are truly in the Althusserian tradition; but Eribon is a French journalist who has made a career of playing the fawning hyena to the preening lions of Parisian intellectual life, and he is not representative.

In the United States, however, there are still university research centers that devote time and money to the study of Althusser's thought, and mount expensive conferences at which professors lecture one another earnestly about "Althusserianism" in everything from linguistics to hermeneutics. Meanwhile respectable English-language publishers continue to market books with titles like *The Althusserian Legacy, Althusser and the Detour of Theory, Reading Althusser; Althusser and the Renewal of Marxist Social Theory,* and (inevitably) *Althusser and Feminism:* most of them unreadable excursions into the Higher Drivel.

Althusser was not a charlatan. He himself really believed that he had discovered something significant—or was about to discover something significant—when his illness struck. It is not because he was mad that he was a mediocre philosopher; indeed, the recognition of his own intellectual mediocrity may have contributed to his depressions, and thence to his loss of sanity. If there is something humiliating about the

Althusserian episode in intellectual history then, the humiliation is not his alone. He was a guru, complete with texts, a cult, and true believers; and he showed occasional insight into the pathos of his followers, noting that they imitated his "smallest gestures and inflections."

Althusser's work and his life, with his drugs, his analysts, his self-pity, his illusions, and his moods, take on a curiously hermetic quality. He comes to resemble some minor medieval scholastic, desperately scrabbling around in categories of his own imagining. But even the most obscure theological speculation usually had as its goal something of significance. From Althusser's musings, however, nothing followed. They were not subject to proof and they had no intelligible worldly application, except as abstruse political apologetics. What does it say about modern academic life that such a figure can have trapped teachers and students for so long in the cage of his insane fictions, and traps them still?

This review of Louis Althusser's memoirs first appeared in the New Republic *in March 1994. As a footnote to my comments on the curious cult of Althusser in British and American academia, readers may be interested to learn that courses devoted to his thought are still on offer in many universities, my own included.*

CHAPTER VII

Eric Hobsbawm and the Romance of Communism

Eric Hobsbawm is the best-known historian in the world. *The Age of Extremes* (published in 1994) was translated into dozens of languages, from Chinese to Czech. His memoirs were a best seller in New Delhi; in parts of South America—Brazil especially—he is a cultural folk hero. His fame is well deserved. He controls vast continents of information with confident ease—his Cambridge college supervisor, after telling me once that Eric Hobsbawm was the cleverest undergraduate he had ever taught, added: "Of course, you couldn't say I taught him—he was unteachable. Eric already knew everything."

Hobsbawm doesn't just know more than other historians. He writes better, too: There is none of the fussy "theorizing" or grandiloquent rhetorical narcissism of some of his younger British colleagues (none of the busy teams of graduate researchers, either—he does his own reading). His style is clean and clear. Like E. P. Thompson, Raymond Williams, and Christopher Hill, his erstwhile companions in the British Communist Historians' Group, Hobsbawm is a master of English prose. He writes intelligible history for literate readers.

The early pages of his autobiography are perhaps the finest Hobsbawm has ever written.* They are certainly the most intensely personal. His Jewish parents—he from the East End of London, she from Habsburg Austria—met and married in neutral Zurich during World War I. Eric, the older of their two children, was born in Alexandria in 1917—though his recollections begin in Vienna, where the family settled after the war. They struggled with little success to make ends meet in impoverished, truncated post-Habsburg Austria. When Eric was eleven, his father, returning "from another of his increasingly desperate visits to town in search of money to earn or borrow," collapsed and died on their doorstep one frozen February night in 1929. Within a year his mother was diagnosed with lung disease; after months of unsuccessful treatment in hospitals and sanatoriums, she died, in July 1931. Her son was just fourteen.

Eric was sent to Berlin to live with an aunt. His account of the death throes of German democracy is fascinating—"We were on the *Titanic,* and everyone knew it was hitting the iceberg." A Jewish orphan swept up in the desperate politics of the Weimar Republic, the young Hobsbawm joined the German Communist Party (KPD) at his *Gymnasium* (high school). He experienced at close quarters the suicidal, divisive strategy imposed by Stalin on the KPD, which was ordered to attack the Social Democrats, not the Nazis; he took part in the courageous illusions and hopeless marches of Berlin's Communists. In January 1933 he learned of Hitler's appointment as chancellor from the newsstands as he walked his sister home from school. Like the narrative of his Viennese childhood, his Berlin stories seamlessly interweave moving personal recollections with a historian's reflections upon life in interwar Central Europe: "It is difficult for those who have not experienced the "Age of Catastrophe" of the twentieth century in central Europe to see what it meant to live in a world that was simply not expected to last, in something that could not really even be described as a world, but merely as a provisional way-station between a dead past and a future not yet born." These first hundred pages alone are worth the price of the book.

The Hobsbawm children were moved to England (they had British

---

* *Interesting Times: A Twentieth-Century Life* (New York: Pantheon, 2004).

passports and relatives in London). Within two years the precociously gifted Eric had mastered the transition to English-language education and won an Open Scholarship to read history at King's College, Cambridge. There he began his lifelong ascent into the British elite, beginning with remarkable performances in his undergraduate examinations and election to the Apostles, the self-selecting "secret society" of Cambridge (whose members before him included Wittgenstein, Moore, Whitehead, Russell, Keynes, E. M. Forster, and the "Cambridge spies" Guy Burgess and Anthony Blunt). Noel Annan, his King's contemporary, described the undergraduate Hobsbawm as "astonishingly mature, armed cap-a-pie with the Party's interpretation of current politics, as erudite as he was fluent, and equipped to have a view on whatever obscure topic one of his contemporaries might have chosen to write a paper."[1]

After the war, Hobsbawm's politics slowed his formal progress up the English academic career ladder; but for his Communist Party membership he would probably have held distinguished chairs at a young age. Nevertheless, with each new book—from *Primitive Rebels* to *The Age of Capital*, from *Industry and Empire* to *The Invention of Tradition*—his national and international celebrity steadily grew. In retirement, Hobsbawm's career has been capped with all manner of glories: He has lectured everywhere, holds a multitude of honorary degrees, and is a Companion of Honor to the Queen of England.

His travels over the years have placed Hobsbawm in some intriguing circumstances: He rode on a Socialist Party newsreel truck during the 1936 Bastille Day celebrations in Paris at the height of the Popular Front (there is a photograph of him there, uncannily recognizable across a span of nearly seven decades); he crossed briefly into Catalonia during the early stages of the Spanish Civil War. In Havana he once translated—ad lib—for Che Guevara. In his autobiography he writes with unforced enthusiasm of journeys and friendships in Latin America, Spain, France, and—especially—Italy. Unlike most other British historians—and historians of Britain, which was his first calling—he is not only polylingual but also instinctively cosmopolitan in his references. His memoirs are refreshingly reticent about immediate family and loves; they are filled instead with the men and women who composed his public world. They record a long and fruitful twentieth-century life.

But something is missing. Eric Hobsbawm was not just a Communist—there have been quite a lot of those, even in Britain. He *stayed* a Communist, for sixty years. He let his membership in Britain's tiny Communist Party lapse only when the cause for which it stood had been definitively buried by History. And unlike almost every other intellectual to fall under the Communist spell, Hobsbawm evinces no regrets. Indeed, though he concedes the utter defeat of everything Communism stood for, he unblinkingly insists that, halfway through his ninth decade, "The dream of the October Revolution is still there somewhere inside me."

Predictably, it is this unrelenting refusal to "renege" on a lifelong commitment to Communism that has attracted public comment. Why, Hobsbawm has been asked in countless interviews, did you not leave the party in 1956, like most of your friends, when Soviet tanks crushed the Hungarian uprisings? Why not in 1968, after the Red Army invaded Prague? Why do you still appear to believe—as Hobsbawm has suggested on more than one occasion in recent years—that the price in human lives and suffering under Stalin would have been worth paying if the outcomes had been better?

Hobsbawm responds dutifully if a little wearily to all such interrogations, sometimes conveying a touch of disdainful impatience at this obsession with his Communist past; he has, after all, done a lot of other things too. But he invites the question. By his own account, Communism has absorbed most of his life. Many of the people he writes about so engagingly in his autobiography were Communists. For many decades he wrote for Communist publications and attended party functions. When others left the party, he stayed. He devotes a lot of time to describing his loyalties; but he never really explains them.

Hobsbawm's attachment to Communism has very little to do with Marxism. For him, being a "Marxist historian" just means having what he calls a "historical" or interpretative approach. When Hobsbawm was young, the movement to favor broad explanations over political narrative, to emphasize economic causation and social consequences, was radical and iconoclastic—Marc Bloch's Annales group was pressing similar changes upon the French historical profession. In today's historiographical landscape these concerns appear self-evident, even conservative. Moreover— unlike the Gramscian epigones at the *New Left Review*—Hobsbawm has a very English unconcern with continental-style, intra-Marxist debates and theory, to which he pays little attention in his writings.

In Hobsbawm's version, even Communism itself is hard to pin down. There is little in his account about what it felt like to be a Communist. Communists, in Britain as elsewhere, spent most of their time in agit-prop—selling the party publications, canvassing for the party candidates at elections, spreading the "general line" at cell meetings and in public debates, organizing meetings, planning demonstrations, fomenting (or preventing) strikes, manipulating front organizations, and so on: mundane, routine, often grindingly tedious work undertaken out of faith or duty. Virtually every Communist or ex-Communist memoir I can recall devotes considerable space to such matters—indeed, this is often the most interesting part of such books, because these routines took up so much time and because, in the end, they were the very life of the party.[2]

But as Eric Hobsbawm makes clear, he had no taste for such local branch work—except as a high school student, when he braved SA brown-shirts and undertook the truly dangerous job of canvassing for the doomed KPD in the March 1933 elections. In later years, however, he devoted himself entirely to working in "academic or intellectual groups." After 1956, "convinced that, since the Party had not reformed itself, it had no long-term political future in the country," Hobsbawm dropped out of Communist activism (though not out of the party itself). So we learn nothing from his memoir about Communism as a way of life, or even as a politics.

This detachment from the party as a micro-society is entirely in character, however. It would be idle to speculate on the link between the traumas of Hobsbawm's youth and the affinities of the man, though he himself concedes that "I have no doubt at all that I must also bear the emotional scars of those sombre years somewhere on me." But it is clear that he always kept the world at a certain distance, shielding himself against tragedy, as he explains, by "my intellectualism and lack of interest in the world of people." This has not prevented Eric Hobsbawm from being very good company and enjoying it too. But it may account for a certain deficiency in empathy: He is not much moved either by his former comrades' enthusiasms or by their crimes. Others left the party in despair because it had meant so much to them; Hobsbawm was able to remain because, in his daily life at least, it meant so little.

In a rather different key, however, Eric Hobsbawm fitted much better into the Communist mold than many of his more wholeheartedly engaged contemporaries. There have been numerous all-consuming micro-societies in the history of the modern European Left. In Britain alone there were the Socialist Party of Great Britain, the Independent Labour Party, the Fabians, assorted Social Democratic and anarchist federations, not to speak of Trotskyists and other latter-day Old Believers.[3] But what distinguished the Communist Party, in Britain as elsewhere, was the principle of authority, the acceptance of hierarchy, and the addiction to order.

Eric Hobsbawm is decidedly a man of order, a "Tory communist," as he puts it. Communist intellectuals were never "cultural dissidents"; and Hobsbawm's scorn for self-indulgent, post-anything "leftism" has a long Leninist pedigree. But in his case there is another tradition at work. When Hobsbawm scornfully dismisses Thatcherism as "the anarchism of the lower middle class," he is neatly combining two anathemas: the old Marxist abhorrence of disorderly, unregulated self-indulgence; and the even older disdain of the English administrative elite for the uncultivated, socially insecure but economically ambitious service class of clerks and salesmen, formerly Mr. Pooter, now Essex Man.[4] Eric Hobsbawm, in short, is a mandarin—a Communist mandarin—with all the confidence and prejudices of his caste.

This comes as no surprise: As Hobsbawm writes of his ascent into the Apostles back in 1939, "even revolutionaries like to be in a suitable tradition." The British mandarin class, in universities as in the civil service, were frequently attracted to the Soviet Union (albeit at a distance): What they saw there was planned improvement from above by those who know best—a familiar conceit. The Fabians especially (Shaw, Wells, the Webbs) understood Communism in this light, and they were not alone. This, I think, is why reviewers of Hobsbawm in Britain are often bemused when critics fuss over his Communism: not just because it is bad form to invoke a man's private opinions; or because Soviet Communism happened to other people far away (and quite long ago) and has no echo in local experience or history; but because engineering human souls is tempting to elites of every stripe.

But Eric Hobsbawm is not just a very senior and rather proud "member of the official British cultural establishment" (his words); if he were, he must surely long since have set aside his attachment to an institutional corpse. He is also a romantic. He has romanticized rural bandits, brilliantly if implausibly shifting the moral authority of industrial proletarians onto rural rebels. He romanticizes Palmiro Togliatti's Italian Communist Party—which in the light of recent revelations sits ill with Hobsbawm's insistence upon "not deluding oneself even about the people or things one cared about most in life."[5]

Eric Hobsbawm still romanticizes the Soviet Union—"Whatever its weaknesses, its very existence proved that socialism was more than a dream," a claim that can only make sense today if intended as bitterly ironic, which I doubt. And he even romanticizes the much-vaunted "hardness" of Communists, their purportedly clear-eyed grasp of political reality. To say the least, this sits uncomfortably with the litany of disastrous strategic errors committed by Lenin, Stalin, and every single one of their successors. At times Hobsbawm's rueful nostalgia sounds curiously like that of Rubashev in Koestler's *Darkness at Noon*—"For once History had taken a run, which at last promised a dignified form of life for mankind; now it was over."

In *Interesting Times* Hobsbawm reveals a distinctly soft spot for the German Democratic Republic, hinting more than once at a certain lack of moral fiber in those intellectuals who abandoned it for the sirens of the West ("Those who could not stand the heat got out of the kitchen"). He tends, I suspect, to confuse the shabby authoritarianism of the GDR with the remembered charms of Weimar Berlin. And this, in turn, leads to the romantic core of his lifetime commitment to Communism: an enduring fidelity both to a singular historical moment—Berlin in the last months of the Weimar Republic—and to the alert, receptive youth who encountered it. He says as much in a recent interview: "I didn't want to break with the tradition that was my life and with what I thought when I first got into it."[6]

In his memoirs he is explicit: "I came to Berlin in the late summer of 1931, as the world economy collapsed. . . . [It was] the historic moment that decided the shape both of the twentieth century and of my life." It is not a coincidence that Eric Hobsbawm's description of those months is the most intense, charged—even sexually charged— prose he has ever written. He was certainly not the only sensitive ob- server to grasp immediately what was at stake. Writing home from Cologne, where he was studying, the twenty-six-year-old Raymond Aron described the "abyss" into which Germany was slipping. He, too, understood intuitively that the *Titanic* had hit the iceberg; that the future of Europe now hinged on the political lessons one drew from this defining moment. What Aron saw in Germany between 1931 and 1933 would become the central moral and political reference for the rest of his life and work.[7]

One can't help but admire Hobsbawm's uncompromising decision to keep faith with his adolescent self, navigating alone at the dark heart of the twentieth century. But he pays a high price for that loyalty, far higher than he realizes. "There are certain clubs," he has said, "of which I would not wish to be a member."[8] By this he means ex-Communists. But ex-Communists—Jorge Semprún, Wolfgang Leonhard, Margarete Buber-Neumann, Claude Roy, Albert Camus, Ignazio Silone, Manès Sperber, and Arthur Koestler—have written some of the best accounts of our terrible times.[9] Like Solzhenitsyn, Sakharov, and Havel (whom Hobsbawm revealingly never mentions), they are the twentieth century's Republic of Letters. By excluding himself from such company, Eric Hobsbawm, of all people, has provincialized himself.

The most obvious damage is to his prose. Whenever Hobsbawm enters a politically sensitive zone, he retreats into hooded, wooden lan- guage, redolent of Party-speak. "The possibility of dictatorship," he writes in *The Age of Extremes*, "is implicit in any regime based in a single, irremovable party." The "possibility"? "Implicit"? As Rosa Luxemburg could have told him, a single irremovable party *is* a dictatorship. Describing the Comintern's requirement in 1932 that German Communists fight the Socialists and ignore the Nazis, Hobsbawm in his memoirs writes that "it is now generally accepted that the policy . . . was one of suicidal idiocy." *Now?* Everyone thought it criminally stupid at the time and has thought so ever since—everyone, that is, except the Communists.

Hobsbawm is sufficiently tone-deaf in such matters that he can still cite with approval the nauseating sentiments in Bertolt Brecht's poem "To Those Born After Us":

> *We, who wanted to prepare the ground for kindness*
> *Could not be kind ourselves.*

After that it comes as less of a surprise to read Hobsbawm's curious description of Khrushchev's famous "secret speech" in 1956 as "the brutally ruthless denunciation of Stalin's misdeeds." Note that it is the denunciation of Stalin that attracts the epithets ("brutal," "ruthless"), not his "misdeeds." In his enthusiasm for the Communist omelet, Hobsbawm has clearly lost little sleep over the millions of broken eggs in unmarked graves from Wroclaw to Vladivostok. As he says, History doesn't cry over spilled milk.

At most, he evinces regret at the injustices committed by Communists on Communists: recalling that the trial of Traicho Kostov in Sofia in 1949 "left me unhappy," he describes it as the first of the "show trials which disfigured the last years of Stalin." But it wasn't. In Bulgaria itself there had been an earlier show trial, that of the Agrarian leader Nikola Petkov, who was tried and executed in September 1947 by Kostov's own party. However, Petkov passes unmentioned. *His* judicial murder does not reflect ill on Stalin.

As Hobsbawm half concedes, he might have been wiser to stick to the nineteenth century—"given," as he puts it, "the strong official Party and Soviet views about the twentieth century."[10] He still seems to be writing in the shadow of an invisible censor. When describing the survival into the 1920s of Habsburg-era links between independent Austria and Czechoslovakia, he concludes: "The frontiers were not yet impenetrable, as they became after the war destroyed the Pressburg tram's bridge across the Danube." Younger readers might reasonably infer that a fractured tram line was the only obstacle to Czechs and Slovaks seeking to visit postwar Austria after 1948; Hobsbawm avoids mention of any other impediment.

These are not atavistic slips of the pen, occasional Homeric nods. British commentators who tiptoe politely around them in homage to the author's accomplishments are simply patronizing an old friend.

Hobsbawm deserves better. François Furet once said that leaving the French Communist Party in protest at the Soviet invasion of Hungary "was the most intelligent thing I have ever done." Eric Hobsbawm chose to remain, and that choice has hobbled his historical instincts. He can acknowledge his mistakes readily enough—his underestimation of the sixties, his failure to anticipate the precipitate decline of Eurocommunism after the mid-seventies, even his high hopes for the Soviet Union, which, "as I now know, was bound to fail."

But he doesn't seem to understand why he made them—even the concession that the USSR was "bound" to fail is simply an inversion of the previous assumption that it was "bound" to succeed. Either way the responsibility lies with History, not men, and old Communists can sleep easy. This retroactive determinism is nothing but Whig History plus dialectics; and dialectics, as a veteran Communist explained to the young Jorge Semprún in Buchenwald, "is the art and technique of always landing on your feet."[11] Hobsbawm has landed on his feet, but from where he stands much of the rest of the world is upside down. Even the significance of 1989 is obscure to him. Of the consequences of the victory of the "free world" (his scare quotes) over the Soviet Union he merely warns: "The world may yet regret that, faced with Rosa Luxemburg's alternative of socialism or barbarism, it decided against socialism."

But Red Rosa wrote that nearly one hundred years ago. The socialism of which Eric Hobsbawm dreamed is no longer an option, and the barbaric dictatorial deviation to which he devoted his life is very largely to blame. Communism defiled and despoiled the radical heritage. If today we face a world in which there is no grand narrative of social progress, no politically plausible project of social justice, it is in large measure because Lenin and his heirs poisoned the well.

Hobsbawm closes his memoirs with a rousing coda: "Let us not disarm, even in unsatisfactory times. Social injustice still needs to be denounced and fought. The world will not get better on its own." He is right, on every count. But to do any good in the new century we must start by telling the truth about the old. Hobsbawm refuses to stare evil in the face and call it by its name; he never engages the moral as well as the political heritage of Stalin and his works. If he seriously wishes to pass a radical baton to future generations, this is no way to proceed.

he Left has long shied away from confronting the Communist
.on in its family closet. Anti-anticommunism—the wish to avoid
ing aid and comfort to cold warriors before 1989, and End-of-History
.iumphalists since—has crippled political thinking in the Labor and
Social Democratic movements for decades; in some circles it still does.
But as Arthur Koestler pointed out in Carnegie Hall in March 1948:
"You can't help people being right for the wrong reasons. . . . This fear of
finding oneself in bad company is not an expression of political purity;
it is an expression of a lack of self-confidence."[12]

If the Left is to recover that self-confidence and get up off its knees,
we must stop telling reassuring stories about the past. *Pace* Hobsbawm,
who blandly denies it, there was a "fundamental affinity" between
extremes of left and right in the twentieth century, self-evident to anyone
who experienced them. Millions of well-meaning Western progressives
sold their souls to an oriental despot—"The ludicrous surprise," wrote
Raymond Aron in 1950, "is that the European Left has taken a pyramid
builder for its God."[13] The values and institutions that have mattered to
the Left—from equality before the law to the provision of public services
as a matter of right—and that are now under assault—owed nothing to
Communism. Seventy years of "real existing Socialism" contributed
nothing to the sum of human welfare. Nothing.

Perhaps Hobsbawm understands this. Perhaps, as he writes of James
Klugmann, the British Communist Party's house historian, "he knew what
was right, but shied away from saying it in public." If so, it isn't a very proud
epitaph. Evgenia Ginzburg, who knew something about the twentieth century, tells of blotting out the screams from the torture cells in Moscow's
Butyrki prison by reciting over and over to herself Michelangelo's poem:

> *Sweet is't to sleep, sweeter to be a stone.*
> *In this dread age of terror and of shame,*
> *Thrice blest is he who neither sees nor feels.*
> *Leave me then here, and trouble not my rest.*[14]

Eric Hobsbawm is the most naturally gifted historian of our time; but
rested and untroubled, he has somehow slept through the terror and
shame of the age.

This review of Eric Hobsbawm's autobiography first appeared in the New York Review of Books *in November 2003.*

NOTES TO CHAPTER VII

[1] Noel Annan, *Our Age: English Intellectuals Between the World Wars—A Group Portrait* (New York: Random House, 1991), 189.

[2] See, for example, Raphael Samuel, "The Lost World of British Communism" (Part I), *New Left Review*, no. 154 (November–December 1985): 3–53, where he sketches a marvelous portrait of "an organization under siege, . . . [maintaining] the simulacrum of a complete society, insulated from alien influences, belligerent towards outsiders, protective of those within"; "a visible church," as Samuel tells it, tracing "an unbroken line of descent from the founding fathers, claiming scriptural precedent for our policies, adopting patristic labels for our anathemas."

[3] For an illustration of life in a hundred-year-old party sustained by a happy marriage of doctrinal purity and political irrelevance, see Robert Barltrop, *The Monument: The Story of the Socialist Party of Great Britain* (London: Pluto, 1975).

[4] See George and Weedon Grossmith, *Diary of a Nobody* (London, 1892).

[5] In April 1963, shortly before his death, Togliatti wrote to Antonin Novotny, general secretary of the Czechoslovak Communist Party, begging him to postpone the forthcoming public "rehabilitation" of the victims of the December 1952 trial of Rudolph Slánský. Such an announcement, he wrote (implicitly acknowledging the PCI's complicity in defending the show trials of the early fifties), "would unleash a furious campaign against us, bringing to the fore all the most idiotic and provocative anti-Communist themes [i temi più stupidi e provocatori dell'anticommunismo] and hurting us in the forthcoming elections." See Karel Bartošek, *Les Aveux des Archives: Prague-Paris-Prague, 1948–1968* (Paris: Seuil, 1996), 372, Appendix 28; and more generally, Elena Aga-Rossi and Victor Zaslavsky, *Togliatti e Stalin: Il PCI e la politica estera staliniana negli archivi di Mosca* (Bologna: Il Mulino, 1997), especially 263ff.

[6] Sarah Lyall, "A Communist Life with No Apology," *New York Times*, August 23, 2003.

[7] See my "The Peripheral Insider: Raymond Aron and the Wages of Reason," in *The Burden of Responsibility: Blum, Camus, Aron, and the French Twentieth Century* (Chicago: University of Chicago Press, 1998), 137–183.

[8] See Neal Ascherson, "The Age of Hobsbawm," *The Independent on Sunday*, October 2, 1994.

[9] For example, Jorge Semprún, *The Autobiography of Federico Sánchez and the Communist Underground in Spain* (New York: Karz, 1979), first published in Barcelona in 1977 as *Autobiografía de Federico Sánchez*; Wolfgang Leonhard; *Child of the Revolution* (New York: Pathfinder Press, 1979), first published in Cologne in 1955 as *Die Revolution entlässt ihre Kinder*; Claude Roy, *Nous* (Paris: Gallimard, 1972); Margarete Buber-Neumann, *Von Potsdam nach Moskau: Stationen eines Irrweges* (Stuttgart: Deutsche Verlags-Anstalt, 1957).

[10] Note the implied separation between "Soviet" and "Party," as though local Communists were quite distinct from those in Moscow (and thus not responsible for the latter's crimes). Eric Hobsbawm knows better than anyone else that this is humbug. The whole point of Lenin's break with the old Socialist International was to centralize revolutionary organizations into a single unit on the Bolshevik model, taking instructions from Moscow. That was the purpose of the famous "Twenty-one Conditions" of Comintern membership with which Lenin split Europe's Socialist parties in 1919–1922—not to mention the unwritten Twenty-second Condition, according to the French Socialist leader Paul Faure, which authorized the Bolsheviks to ignore all the other twenty-one when it suited them.

[11] "Mais c'est quoi, la dialectique?" "C'est l'art et la manière de toujours retomber sur ses pattes, mon vieux!" Jorge Semprún, *Quel Beau Dimanche* (Paris: Grasset, 1980), 100.

[12] Arthur Koestler, "The Seven Deadly Fallacies," in *The Trail of the Dinosaur and Other Essays* (New York: Macmillan, 1955), 50.

[13] Raymond Aron, *Polémiques* (Paris: Gallimard, 1955), 81.

[14] Evgenia Ginzburg, *Journey into the Whirlwind* (New York: Harcourt Brace Jovanovich, 1967), 162.

CHAPTER VIII

Goodbye to All That? Leszek Kołakowski and the Marxist Legacy

L eszek Kołakowski is a philosopher from Poland. But it does not seem quite right—or sufficient—to define him that way. Like Czesław Miłosz and others before him, Kołakowski forged his intellectual and political career in opposition to certain deep-rooted features of traditional Polish culture: clericalism, chauvinism, anti-Semitism. Forced to leave his native land in 1968, Kołakowski could neither return home nor be published there: Between 1968 and 1981 his name was on Poland's index of forbidden authors, and much of the work for which he is best known today was written and published abroad.

In exile Kołakowski lived mostly in England, where he has been a Fellow of All Souls College, Oxford, since 1970. But as he explained in an interview last year, Britain is an island; Oxford is an island in Britain; All Souls (a college without students) is an island in Oxford; and Dr. Leszek Kołakowski is an island within All Souls, a "quadruple island."[1] There was indeed once a place in British cultural life for intellectual émigrés from Russia and Central Europe—think of Ludwig Wittgenstein, Arthur Koestler, or Isaiah Berlin. But an ex-Marxist Catholic philosopher from Poland is more exotic, and despite his international renown Leszek Kołakowski is largely unknown—and curiously underappreciated—in his adoptive land.

Elsewhere, however, he is famous. Like many Central European scholars of his generation Kołakowski is multilingual—at ease in Russian, French, and German as well as Polish and his adopted English—and he has received accolades and prizes galore in Italy, Germany, and France especially. In the United States, where Kołakowski taught for many years in the Committee on Social Thought at the University of Chicago, his achievements have been generously acknowledged, culminating in 2003 in the award of the first Kluge Prize from the Library of Congress— bestowed for lifetime achievement in those fields of scholarship (the humanities above all) for which there is no Nobel Prize. But Kołakowski, who has more than once declared himself most at home in Paris, is no more American than he is English. Perhaps he is properly thought of as the last illustrious citizen of the Twentieth-Century Republic of Letters.

In most of his adoptive countries, Leszek Kołakowski is best known (and in some places only known) for *Main Currents of Marxism*, his remarkable three-volume history of Marxism: published in Polish (in Paris) in 1976, in England by Oxford University Press two years later, and now reprinted in a single volume by Norton here in the U.S.[2] No doubt this is as it should be; *Main Currents* is a monument of modern humanistic scholarship. But there is a certain irony in its prominence among Kołakowski's writings, for its author is anything but a "Marxologist." He is a philosopher, a historian of philosophy, and a Catholic thinker. He spent years studying early modern Christian sects and heresies and for most of the past quarter-century has devoted himself to the history of European religion and philosophy and to what might best be described as philosophical-theological speculations.[3]

Kołakowski's "Marxist" period, from his early prominence in postwar Poland as the most sophisticated Marxist philosopher of his generation through his departure in 1968, was actually quite brief. And for most of that time he was already a dissident: As early as 1954, aged twenty-seven, he was being accused of "straying from Marxist-Leninist ideology." In 1966 he delivered a famously critical lecture at Warsaw University on the tenth anniversary of the "Polish October" and was officially reprimanded by party leader Władysław Gomułka as the "main ideologue of the so-called revisionist movement." When Kołakowski was duly expelled from his university chair it was for "forming the views of the youth in a man-

ner contrary to the official tendency of the country." By the time he arrived in the West, he was no longer a Marxist (to the confusion, as we
shall see, of some of his admirers); a few years later, having written the
most important book on Marxism of the past half-century, Kołakowski
had what another Polish scholar politely terms a "declining interest in the
subject."[4]

This trajectory helps explain the distinctive qualities of *Main Currents
of Marxism*. The first volume, "The Founders," is conventionally arranged as a history of ideas: from the Christian origins of the dialectic
and the project of total salvation through German Romantic philosophy
and its impact on the young Karl Marx, and on to the mature writings
of Marx and his colleague Friedrich Engels. The second volume is revealingly (and not, I think, ironically) entitled "The Golden Age." It carries
the story from the Second International, founded in 1889, to the Russian
Revolution of 1917. Here, too, Kołakowski is concerned above all with
ideas and debates, conducted at a sophisticated level by a remarkable
generation of European radical thinkers.

The leading Marxists of the age—Karl Kautsky, Rosa Luxemburg,
Eduard Bernstein, Jean Jaurès, and V. I. Lenin—are all given their due,
each accorded a chapter that summarizes with unflagging efficiency and
clarity their main arguments and their place in the story. But of greater
interest, because they don't usually figure so prominently in such general
accounts, are chapters on the Italian philosopher Antonio Labriola, the
Poles Ludwik Krzywicki, Kazimierz Kelles-Krauz, and Stanisław
Brzozowski, together with Max Adler, Otto Bauer, and Rudolf Hilferding:
the "Austro-Marxists." The relative abundance of Poles in Kołakowski's
account of Marxism is doubtless owed in part to local perspective and
some compensation for past neglect. But like the Austro-Marxists (accorded one of the longest chapters in the whole book) they represent an
ever-timely reminder of the intellectual riches of Central Europe's fin de
siècle, forgotten and then expunged from a narrative long dominated by
Germans and Russians.[5]

The third volume of *Main Currents*—the part that addresses what
many readers will think of as "Marxism," that is to say the history of
Soviet Communism and Western Marxist thought since 1917—is bluntly
labeled "The Breakdown." Rather less than half of this section is devoted

to Soviet Marxism, from Stalin to Trotsky; the rest deals with assorted twentieth-century theorists in other lands. A few of these, notably Antonio Gramsci and György Lukács, are of continuing interest to students of twentieth-century thought. Some, such as Ernst Bloch and Karl Korsch (Lukács's German contemporary), have a more antiquarian appeal. Others, notably Lucien Goldmann and Herbert Marcuse, seem even less interesting now than they did in the mid-seventies when Kołakowski dismissed them in a few pages.

The book ends with an essay on "Developments in Marxism Since Stalin's Death," in which Kołakowski passes briefly over his own "revisionist" past before going on to record in a tone of almost unremitting contempt the passing fashions of the age, from the higher foolishness of Sartre's *Critique de la raison dialectique* and its "superfluous neologisms" to Mao Zedong, his "peasant Marxism," and its irresponsible Western admirers. Readers of this section are forewarned in the original preface to the third volume of the work: While recognizing that the material addressed in the last chapter "could be expanded into a further volume," the author concludes, "I am not convinced that the subject is intrinsically worthy of treatment at such length." It is perhaps worth recording here that whereas the first two parts of *Main Currents* appeared in France in 1987, this third and final volume of Kołakowski's masterwork has still not been published there.

It is quite impossible to convey in a short review the astonishing range of Kołakowski's history of Marxist doctrine. It will surely not be superseded: Who will ever again know—or care—enough to go back over this ground in such detail and with such analytical sophistication? *Main Currents of Marxism* is not a history of socialism; its author pays only passing attention to political contexts or social organizations. It is unashamedly a narrative of ideas, a sort of bildungsroman of the rise and fall of a once-mighty family of theory and theorists, related in skeptical, disabused old age by one of its last surviving children.

Kołakowski's thesis, driven through 1,200 pages of exposition, is straightforward and unambiguous. Marxism, in his view, should be taken seriously: not for its propositions about class struggle (which were sometimes true but never news); nor for its promise of the inevitable collapse of capitalism and a proletarian-led transition to socialism (which failed entirely as prediction); but because Marxism delivered a unique—and truly original—blend of Promethean Romantic illusion and uncompromising historical determinism.

The attraction of Marxism thus understood is obvious. It offered an explanation of how the world works—the economic analysis of capitalism and of social class relations. It proposed a way in which the world ought to work—an ethics of human relations as suggested in Marx's youthful, idealistic speculations (and in György Lukács's interpretation of him, with which Kołakowski, for all his disdain for Lukács's own compromised career, largely concurs[6]). And it announced incontrovertible grounds for believing that things *will* work that way in the future, thanks to a set of assertions about historical necessity derived by Marx's Russian disciples from his (and Engels's) own writings. This combination of economic description, moral prescription, and political prediction proved intensely seductive—and serviceable. As Kołakowski has observed, Marx is still worth reading—if only to help us understand the sheer versatility of his theories when invoked by others to justify the political systems to which they gave rise.[7]

On the link between Marxism and Communism—which three generations of Western Marxists tried valiantly to minimize, "saving" Marx from his "distortion" at the hands of Stalin (and Lenin)—Kołakowski is explicit. To be sure, Karl Marx was a German writer living in mid-Victorian London.[8] He can hardly be held responsible in any intelligible sense for twentieth-century Russian or Chinese history and there is thus something redundant as well as futile about the decades-long efforts of Marxist purists to establish the founders' true intent, to ascertain what Marx and Engels would have thought about future sins committed in their name—though this reiterated emphasis on getting back to the truth of the sacred texts illustrates the sectarian dimension of Marxism to which Kołakowski pays special attention.

Nevertheless, Marxism as a doctrine cannot be separated from the history of the political movements and systems to which it led. There really is a core of determinism in the reasoning of Marx and Engels: their claim that "in the last analysis" things are as they have to be, for reasons over which men have no final control. This insistence was born of Marx's desire to turn old Hegel "on his head" and insert incontrovertibly material causes (the class struggle, the laws of capitalist development) at the heart of historical explanation. It was against this convenient epistemological backstop that Plekhanov, Lenin, and their heirs were to lean the whole edifice of historical "necessity" and its accompanying machinery of enforcement.

Moreover, Marx's other youthful intuition—that the proletariat has a privileged insight into the final purposes of history thanks to its special role as an exploited class whose own liberation will signal the liberation of all humankind—is intimately attached to the ultimate Communist outcome, thanks to the subordination of proletarian interests to a dictatorial party claiming to incarnate them. The strength of these logical chains binding Marxist analysis to Communist tyranny may be judged from the many observers and critics—from Mikhail Bakunin to Rosa Luxemburg—who anticipated Communism's totalitarian outcome, and warned against it, long before Lenin got anywhere near the Finland Station. Of course Marxism might have gone in other directions: It might also have gone nowhere. But "the Leninist version of Marxism, though not the only possible one, was quite plausible."[9]

To be sure, neither Marx nor the theorists who followed him intended or anticipated that a doctrine that preached the overthrow of capitalism by an industrial proletariat would seize power in a backward and largely rural society. But for Kołakowski this paradox merely underscores the power of Marxism as a system of belief: If Lenin and his followers had not insisted upon (and retroactively justified in theory) the ineluctable necessity of their own success, their voluntaristic endeavors would never have succeeded. Nor would they have been so convincing a prototype to millions of outside admirers. To turn an opportunistic coup, facilitated by the German government's transport of Lenin to Russia in a sealed train, into an "inevitable" revolution required not just tactical genius but also an extended exercise of ideological faith. Kołakowski is surely right: Political Marxism was above all a secular religion.

Main Currents of Marxism is not the only first-rate account of Marxism, though it is by far the most ambitious.[10] What distinguishes it is Kołakowski's Polish perspective. This probably explains the emphasis in his account on Marxism as an eschatology—"a modern variant of apocalyptic expectations which have been continuous in European history." And it licenses an uncompromisingly moral, even religious reading of twentieth-century history: "The Devil is part of our experience. Our generation has seen enough of it for the message to be taken extremely seriously. Evil, I contend, is not contingent, it is not the absence, or deformation, or the subversion of virtue (or whatever else we may think of as its opposite), but a stubborn and unredeemable fact."[11] No Western commentator on Marxism, however critical, ever wrote like that.

But then Kołakowski writes as someone who has lived not just inside Marxism but under Communism. He was witness to Marxism's transformation from an intellectual theorem to a political way of life. Thus observed and experienced from within, Marxism becomes difficult to distinguish from Communism—which was, after all, not only its most important practical outcome but its only one. And the daily deployment of Marxist categories for the vulgar purpose of suppressing freedom—which was their primary use value to Communists in power—detracts over time from the charms of the theorem itself.

This cynical application of dialectics to the twisting of minds and the breaking of bodies was usually lost on Western scholars of Marxism, absorbed in the contemplation of past ideals or future prospects and unmoved by inconvenient news from the Soviet present, particularly when relayed by victims or witnesses.[12] His encounters with such people doubtless explain Kołakowski's caustic disdain for much of "Western" Marxism and its progressive acolytes: "One of the causes of the popularity of Marxism among educated people was the fact that in its simple form it was very easy; even [*sic*] Sartre noticed that Marxists are lazy. . . . [Marxism was] an instrument that made it possible to master all of history and economics without actually having to study either."[13]

It was just one such encounter that gave rise to the sardonic title essay in the newly published collection of Kołakowski's writings.* In 1973, in *The Socialist Register*, the English historian E. P. Thompson published "An Open Letter to Leszek Kołakowski" in which he took the erstwhile Marxist to task for having let down his Western admirers by abjuring the

---

* *My Correct Views on Everything* (South Bend, IN: St. Augustine's, 2006).

revisionist Communism of his youth. The "Open Letter" was Thompson at his priggish, Little-Englander worst: garrulous (the letter runs to one hundred pages of printed text), patronizing, and sanctimonious. In a pompous, demagogic tone, with more than half an eye to his worshipful progressive audience, Thompson shook his rhetorical finger at the exiled Kołakowski, admonishing him for apostasy: "We were both voices of the Communist revisionism of 1956. . . . We both passed from a frontal critique of Stalinism to a stance of Marxist revisionism. . . . There was a time when you, and the causes for which you stood, were present in our innermost thoughts." How dare you, Thompson suggested from the safety of his leafy perch in middle England, betray us by letting your inconvenient experiences in Communist Poland obstruct the view of our common Marxist ideal?

Kołakowski's response, "My Correct Views on Everything," may be the most perfectly executed intellectual demolition in the history of political argument: No one who reads it will ever take E. P. Thompson seriously again. The essay explicates (and symptomatically illustrates) the huge moral gulf that was opened up between "Eastern" and "Western" intellectuals by the history and experience of Communism, and which remains with us today. Kołakowski mercilessly dissects Thompson's strenuous, self-serving efforts to save socialism from the shortcomings of Marxism, to save Marxism from the failures of Communism, and to save Communism from its own crimes: all in the name of an ideal ostensibly grounded in "materialist" reality—but whose credibility depended on remaining untainted by real-world experience or human shortcomings. "You say," Kołakowski writes to Thompson, "that to think in terms of a 'system' yields excellent results. I am quite sure it does, not only excellent, but miraculous; it simply solves all the problems of mankind in one stroke."

Solving the problems of mankind in one stroke; seeking out an all-embracing theory that can simultaneously explain the present and guarantee the future; resorting to the crutch of intellectual or historical "systems" to navigate the irritating complexity and contradictions of real experience; saving the "pure" seed of an idea or an ideal from its rotten fruit: Such shortcuts have a timeless allure and are certainly not the monopoly of Marxists (or indeed the Left). But it is understandably tempting to dismiss at least the Marxist variant of such human follies: Between the disabused insights of former Communists like Kołakowski and the self-righteous provincialism of "Western" Marxists like Thompson, not to speak of the verdict of history itself, the subject would appear to have self-destructed.

Maybe so. But before consigning the curious story of the rise and fall of Marxism to a fast-receding and no-longer-relevant past, we would do well to recall the remarkable strength of Marxism's grip upon the twentieth-century imagination. Karl Marx may have been a failed prophet and his most successful disciples a clique of tyrants, but Marxist thought and the Socialist project exercised an unparalleled hold on some of the best minds of the last century. Even in those countries that were to fall victim to Communist rule, the intellectual and cultural history of the age is inseparable from the magnetic attraction of Marxist ideas and their revolutionary promise. At one time or another many of the twentieth century's most interesting thinkers would unhesitatingly have endorsed Maurice Merleau-Ponty's encomium: "Marxism is not a philosophy of history, it is *the* philosophy of history and to renounce it is to dig the grave of Reason in history. After that there can be only dreams or adventures."[14]

Marxism is thus inextricably intertwined with the intellectual history of the modern world. To ignore or dismiss it is willfully to misinterpret the recent past. Ex-Communists and former Marxists—François Furet, Sidney Hook, Arthur Koestler, Leszek Kołakowski, Wolfgang Leonhard, Jorge Semprún, Victor Serge, Ignazio Silone, Boris Souvarine, Manès Sperber, Alexander Wat, and dozens of others—have written some of the best accounts of twentieth-century intellectual and political life. Even a lifelong anti-Communist like Raymond Aron was not embarrassed to acknowledge his undiminished interest in the "secular religion" of Marxism (to the point of recognizing that his obsession with combating it amounted to a sort of transposed anticlericalism). And it is indicative that a liberal like Aron took particular pride in being far better read in Marx and Marxism than many of his self-styled "Marxist" contemporaries.[15]

As the example of the fiercely independent Aron suggests, the attraction of Marxism goes well beyond the familiar story, from ancient Rome to contemporary Washington, of scribblers and flatterers drawn to despots. There are three reasons why Marxism lasted so long and exerted such magnetism upon the best and the brightest. In the first place, Marxism is a very big idea. Its sheer epistemological cheek—its Promethean commitment to understanding and explaining *everything*—appeals to those who deal in ideas, just as it appealed for that reason to Marx himself. Moreover, once you substitute for the proletariat a party that promises to think in its name, you have created a collective organic intellectual (in the sense coined by Gramsci) which aspires not just to speak for the revolutionary class but to replace the old ruling class as well. In such a universe, ideas are not merely instrumental: They exercise a kind of institutional control. They are deployed for the purpose of rescripting reality on approved lines. Ideas, in Kołakowski's words, are Communism's "respiratory system" (which, incidentally, is what distinguishes it from otherwise similar tyrannies of Fascist origin, which have no comparable need of intelligent-sounding dogmatic fictions). In such circumstances, intellectuals—Communist intellectuals—are no longer confined to speaking truth to power. They *have* power—or at least, in the words of one Hungarian account of this process, they are on the road to power. This is an intoxicating notion.[16]

The second source of Marxism's appeal is that Marx and his Communist progeny were not a historical aberration, Clio's genetic error. The Marxist project, like the older Socialist dream which it displaced and absorbed, was one strand in the great progressive narrative of our time: It shares with classical liberalism, its antithetical historical twin, that narrative's optimistic, rationalistic account of modern society and its possibilities. Marxism's distinctive twist—the assertion that the good society to come would be a classless, post-capitalist product of economic processes and social upheaval—was already hard to credit by 1920. But social movements deriving from the initial Marxian analytical impulse continued for many decades to talk and behave as though they still believed in the transformative project.

Thus, to take an example: The German Social Democratic Party effectively abandoned "revolution" well before World War I; but only in 1959, at the Congress of Bad Godesberg, did it officially lift the mortgage of Marxist theory that lay upon its language and goals. In the intervening years, and indeed for some time afterward, German Social Democrats—like British Labourites, Italian Socialists, and many others—continued to speak and write of class conflict, the struggle against capitalism, and so forth: as though, notwithstanding their mild and reformist daily practice, they were still living out the grand Romantic narrative of Marxism. As recently as May 1981, following François Mitterrand's election to the presidency, eminently respectable French Socialist politicians—who would not have described themselves as "Marxist," much less "Communist"—talked excitedly of a revolutionary "grand soir" and the coming transition to socialism, as though they were back in 1936, or even 1848.

Marxism, in short, was the deep "structure" of much progressive politics. Marxist language, or a language parasitic upon Marxist categories, gave form and an implicit coherence to many kinds of modern political protest: from social democracy to radical feminism. In this sense Merleau-Ponty was correct: The loss of Marxism as a way of relating critically to the present really has left an empty space. With Marxism have gone not just dysfunctional Communist regimes and their deluded foreign apologists but also the whole schema of assumptions, categories, and explanations created over the past 150 years that we had come to think of as "the Left." Anyone who has observed the confusion of the political Left in North America or Europe over the past twenty years and asked themselves "But what does it stand for? What does it want?" will appreciate the point.

But there was a third reason why Marxism had appeal, and those who in recent years have been quick to pounce upon its corpse and proclaim the "end of History," or the final victory of peace, democracy, and the free market, might be wise to reflect upon it. If generations of intelligent men and women of good faith were willing to throw in their lot with the Communist project, it was not just because they were lulled into an ideological stupor by a seductive tale of revolution and redemption. It was because they were irresistibly drawn to the underlying ethical message: to the power of an idea and a movement uncompromisingly attached to representing and defending the interests of the wretched of the earth. From first to last, Marxism's strongest suit was what one of Marx's biographers calls "the moral seriousness of Marx's conviction that the destiny of our world as a whole is tied up with the condition of its poorest and most disadvantaged members."[17]

Marxism, as the Polish historian Andrzej Walicki—one of its more acerbic critics—openly acknowledges, was the most influential "reaction to the multiple shortcomings of capitalist societies and the liberal tradition." If Marxism fell from favor in the last third of the twentieth century, it was in large measure because the worst shortcomings of capitalism appeared at last to have been overcome. The liberal tradition—thanks to its unexpected success in adapting to the challenge of depression and war and bestowing upon Western democracies the stabilizing institutions of the New Deal and the welfare state—had palpably triumphed over its antidemocratic critics of Left and Right alike. A political doctrine that had been perfectly positioned to explain and exploit the crises and injustices of another age now appeared beside the point.

Today, however, things are changing once again. What Marx's nineteenth-century contemporaries called the "Social Question"—how to address and overcome huge disparities of wealth and poverty and shameful inequalities of health, education, and opportunity—may have been answered in the West (though the gulf between poor and rich, which seemed once to be steadily closing, has for some years been opening again, in Britain and above all in the U.S.). But the Social Question is back on the *international* agenda with a vengeance. What appears to its prosperous beneficiaries as worldwide economic growth and the opening of national and international markets to investment and trade is increasingly perceived and resented by millions of others as the redistribution of global wealth for the benefit of a handful of corporations and holders of capital.

In recent years respectable critics have been dusting off nineteenth-century radical language and applying it with disturbing success to twenty-first-century social relations. One hardly needs to be a Marxist to recognize that what Marx and others called a "reserve army of labor" is now resurfacing, not in the back streets of European industrial towns but worldwide. By holding down the cost of labor—thanks to the threat of outsourcing, factory relocation, or disinvestment[18]—this global pool of cheap workers helps maintain profits and promote growth: just as it did in nineteenth-century industrial Europe, at least until organized trade unions and mass labor parties were powerful enough to bring about improved wages, redistributive taxation, and a decisive twentieth-century shift in the balance of political power—thereby confounding the revolutionary predictions of their own leaders.

In short, the world appears to be entering upon a new cycle, one with which our nineteenth-century forebears were familiar but of which we in the West have no recent experience. In the coming years, as visible disparities of wealth increase and struggles over the terms of trade, the location of employment, and the control of scarce natural resources all become more acute, we are likely to hear more, not less, about inequality, injustice, unfairness, and exploitation—at home but especially abroad. And thus, as we lose sight of Communism (already in Eastern Europe you have to be thirty-five years old to have any adult memory of a Communist regime), the moral appeal of some refurbished version of Marxism is likely to grow.

If that sounds crazy, remember this: The attraction of one or another version of Marxism to intellectuals and radical politicians in Latin America, for example, or in the Middle East, never really faded; as a plausible account of local experience Marxism in such places retains much of its appeal, just as it does to contemporary antiglobalizers everywhere. The latter see in the tensions and shortcomings of today's international capitalist economy precisely the same injustices and opportunities that led observers of the first economic "globalization" of the 1890s to apply Marx's critique of capitalism to new theories of "imperialism."

And since no one else seems to have anything very convincing to offer by way of a strategy for rectifying the inequities of modern capitalism, the field is once again left to those with the tidiest story to tell and the angriest prescription to offer. Recall Heine's prophetic observations about Marx and his friends at the midpoint of the nineteenth century, in the high years of Victorian growth and prosperity: "These revolutionary doctors and their pitilessly determined disciples are the only men in Germany who have any life; and it is to them, I fear, that the future belongs."[19]

I don't know whether the future of radical politics belongs to a new generation of Marxists, unmoved by (and perhaps unaware of) the crimes and failures of their Communist predecessors. I hope not, but I wouldn't bet against it. Jacques Attali, onetime political adviser to President Mitterrand, last year published a large, hastily penned book on Karl Marx. In it he argues that the fall of the Soviet Union has liberated Marx from his heirs and freed us to see in him the insightful prophet of capitalism who anticipated contemporary dilemmas, notably the global inequalities generated by unrestrained competition. Attali's book has sold well. His thesis has been widely discussed: in France, but also in Britain (where in a 2005 BBC Radio poll listeners voted Karl Marx "the greatest philosopher of all time"[20]).

Of course one could respond to Attali as Kołakowski responded to Thompson's analogous claim that the good ideas of Communism might be saved from its embarrassing actuality: "For many years I have not expected anything from attempts to mend, to renovate, to clean up or to correct the Communist idea. Alas, poor idea. I knew it, Edward. This skull will never smile again." But Jacques Attali, unlike Edward Thompson and the recently resurfaced Antonio Negri, is a man with sharp political antennae, finely tuned to changes in the mood of the hour. If he thinks that the skull might smile again, that moribund, system-building explanations of the Left may indeed be due for revival—if only as a counterpoint to the irritating overconfidence of contemporary free-marketeers of the Right—then he is probably not wholly mistaken. He is certainly not alone.

In the early years of this new century we thus find ourselves facing two opposite and yet curiously similar fantasies. The first fantasy, most familiar to Americans but on offer in every advanced country, is the smug, irenic insistence by commentators, politicians, and experts that today's policy consensus—lacking any clear alternative—is the condition of every well-managed modern democracy and will last indefinitely; that those who oppose it are either misinformed or else malevolent and in either case doomed to irrelevance. The second fantasy is the belief that Marxism has an intellectual and political future: not merely in spite of Communism's collapse but because of it. Hitherto found only at the international "periphery" and in the margins of academia, this renewed faith in Marxism—at least as an analytical tool if not as a political prognostication—is now once again, largely for want of competition, the common currency of international protest movements.

The similarity, of course, consists in a common failure to learn from the past—and a symbiotic interdependence, since it is the myopia of the first that lends spurious credibility to the arguments of the second. Those who cheer the triumph of the market and the retreat of the state, who would have us celebrate the unregulated scope for economic initiative in today's "flat" world, have forgotten what happened the last time we passed this way. They are in for a rude shock (though, if the past is a reliable guide, probably at someone else's expense). As for those who dream of rerunning the Marxist tape, digitally remastered and free of irritating Communist scratches, they would be well advised to ask sooner rather than later just what it is about all-embracing "systems" of thought that leads inexorably to all-embracing "systems" of rule. On this, as we have seen, Leszek Kołakowski can be read with much profit. But history records that there is nothing so powerful as a fantasy whose time has come.

This essay, published on the occasion of Norton's praiseworthy decision to republish in one volume Leszek Kołakowski's Main Currents of Marxism, *first appeared in the* New York Review of Books *in September 2006. My brief allusion to E. P. Thompson provoked a spirited retort from Mr. Edward Countryman. His letter and my reply were published in the* New York Review of Books, *vol. 54, no. ii, February 2007.*

NOTES TO CHAPTER VIII

[1] "On Exile, Philosophy & Tottering Insecurely on the Edge of an Unknown Abyss," dialogue between Leszek Kołakowski and Danny Postel, *Daedalus* (Summer 2005): 82.

[2] *Glowne Nurty Marksizmu* (Paris: Instytut Literacki, 1976); *Main Currents of Marxism* (Oxford: Clarendon Press/Oxford University Press, 1978; New York: Norton, 2006).

[3] See, e.g., his *Chrétiens sans église: la conscience réligieuse et le lien confessional au XVIIe siècle* (Paris: Gallimard, 1969); *God Owes Us Nothing: A Brief Remark on Pascal's Religion and on the Spirit of Jansenism* (Chicago: University of Chicago Press, 1995); and the essays collected in *My Correct Views on Everything*, notably "The Devil in History" and "Concern with God in an Apparently Godless Era."

[4] Andrzej Walicki, *Marxism and the Leap to the Kingdom of Freedom: The Rise and Fall of the*

Communist Utopia (Stanford, CA: Stanford University Press, 1995), vii. Of his own journey from confident orthodoxy to skeptical opposition, Kołakowski has just this to say: "True, I was almost omniscient (yet not entirely) when I was twenty years old, but, as you know, people grow stupid when they grow older. I was much less omniscient when I was twenty-eight, and still less now." See "My Correct Views on Everything: A Rejoinder to E. P. Thompson," originally published in *The Socialist Register*, 1974; reprinted in *My Correct Views on Everything*, p. 19.

5 Kelles-Krauz, at least, has been retrieved from neglect by Timothy Snyder, whose *Nationalism, Marxism and Modern Central Europe: A Biography of Kazimierz Kelles-Krauz, 1872–1905* was published by Harvard University Press in 1997.

6 Elsewhere Kołakowski writes of Lukács—who served briefly as cultural commissar in Béla Kun's Hungarian Soviet Republic of 1919 and later, at Stalin's behest, abjured every interesting word he ever penned—that he was a great talent who "put his intellect at the service of a tyrant." As a result, "his books inspire no interesting thought and are considered 'things of the past' even in Hungary, his native country." See "Communism as a Cultural Formation," *Survey* 29, no. 2 (Summer 1985); reprinted in *My Correct Views on Everything* as "Communism as a Cultural Force," p. 81.

7 See "What Is Left of Socialism," first published as "Po co nam pojecie sprawiedliwosci spolec-znej?" in *Gazeta Wyborcza*, May 6–8, 1995; republished in *My Correct Views on Everything*.

8 In *Main Currents* Marx is firmly placed in the German philosophical world that dominated his mental landscape. Marx the social theorist receives short shrift. As for Marx's contributions to economics—whether the labor theory of value or the predicted fall in the rate of profit under advanced capitalism—these get little sustained attention. Considering that Marx himself was unhappy with the outcome of his economic investigations (one reason why *Das Kapital* remained unfinished), this should perhaps be thought a mercy: The predictive powers of Marxian economics have long been discounted even by the Left, at least since Joseph A. Schumpeter's *Capitalism, Socialism, and Democracy* (New York, London: Harper and Brothers, 1942). Twenty years later, Paul Samuelson condescended to allow that Karl Marx was at best "a minor post-Ricardian."

Even for some of his own disciples, Marxist economics were rendered moot by history within a few years of their first appearance. In *Evolutionary Socialism* (first published in 1899), Engels's friend Eduard Bernstein decisively dismantled the prediction that the contradictions of capitalist competition must lead to worsening conditions for workers and a crisis that could only be resolved by revolution. The best English-language discussion of this subject is still Carl E. Schorske, *German Social Democracy, 1905–1917: The Development of the Great Schism* (Cambridge, MA: Harvard University Press, 1955).

9 Kołakowski, "The Devil in History," *Encounter*, January 1981; reprinted in *My Correct Views on Everything*, p. 125.

10 The best single-volume study of Marxism, brilliantly compressed but embracing politics and social history as well as men and ideas, remains George Lichtheim's *Marxism: An Historical and Critical Study*, first published in London in 1961. Of Marx himself, two very different biographies from the seventies, by David McLellan (*Karl Marx: His Life and Thought*, New York: Harper and Row, 1974) and Jerrold Seigel (*Marx's Fate: The Shape of a Life*, Princeton, NJ: Princeton University Press, 2004), remain the best modern accounts, but should be supplemented with Isaiah Berlin's remarkable essay *Karl Marx: His Life and Environment*, which first appeared in 1939.

11 "The Devil in History," in *My Correct Views*, p. 133. A little later in the same interview Kołakowski emphasizes again the eschatological structure of political messianism: descent into hell, absolute break with past sins, the arrival of a New Time. But in the absence of God,

such undertakings are condemned to incoherence; faith pretending to be knowledge doesn't work. See pp. 136–137.

[12] The unreliability of such witnesses was a long-standing theme of Western progressive apologetics for Stalinism. In much the same way, American Sovietologists used to discount evidence or testimony from Soviet bloc exiles or émigrés—too much personal experience, it was widely agreed, can distort a person's perspective and inhibit objective analysis.

[13] Kołakowski's scorn for *bien-pensant* Western progressives was widely shared by fellow Poles and other "Easterners." In 1976 the poet Antonin Słonimski recalled Jean-Paul Sartre's encouragement to Soviet bloc writers twenty years earlier not to abandon Socialist Realism lest this weaken the "Socialist Camp" vis-à-vis the Americans: "Freedom for him, every limitation for us!" See "L'Ordre règne à Varsovie," *Kultura* 3 (1976): 26– 27, quoted in Marci Shore, *Caviar and Ashes: A Warsaw Generation's Life and Death in Marxism, 1918–1968* (New Haven, CT: Yale University Press, 2006), 362.

[14] See Maurice Merleau-Ponty, *Humanisme et terreur: essai sur le problème communiste* (Paris: Gallimard, 1947). The quotation is from the 1969 American edition, *Humanism and Terror* (Boston: Beacon), p. 153. For an exemplary account of the founding generation of Polish Communist intellectuals (a startlingly gifted group of artists and writers born around 1900, the last to be educated in the old polyglot empires and the first to come of age in independent Poland), see Marci Shore's recently published *Caviar and Ashes,* a scholarly elegy to a lost world.

[15] Raymond Aron, "Un philosophe libéral dans l'histoire" (1973), in *Essais sur la condition juive contemporaine* (Paris: Éditions de la Fallois, 1989), 222. See also Aron, *D'une sainte famille à l'autre: essais sur les marxismes imaginaries* (Paris: Gallimard, 1969), 11: "Like the friends of my youth I never separated philosophy from politics, nor thought from commitment; but I devoted rather more time than them to the study of economics and social mechanisms. In this sense I believe I was more faithful to Marx than they were." A full quarter century after his death, Aron's lectures on Marx at the Collège de France were reconstituted and published by his former students and colleagues under the revealing title *Le Marxisme de Marx* (Paris: Éditions de Fallois, 2002).

[16] György Konrád and Ivan Szelényi, *The Intellectuals on the Road to Class Power* (New York: Harcourt, Brace, Jovanovich, 1979). Waclaw Machajski, an early-twentieth-century Polish anarchist, anticipated just this aspect of Marxism in his criticism of the implicit privileges that Marxist social democracy would accord the intelligentsia. See Marshal Shatz, *Jan Waclaw Machajski: A Radical Critic of the Russian Intelligentsia and Socialism* (Pittsburgh, PA: University of Pittsburgh Press, 1989). Kołakowski discusses Machajski briefly in *Main Currents* (pp. 493, 917) and in "The Myth of Human Self-Identity," in *The Socialist Idea: A Reappraisal,* edited by Leszek Kołakowski and Stuart Hampshire (New York: Basic Books, 1974), reprinted in *My Correct Views on Everything.*

[17] Seigel, *Marx's Fate,* p. x.

[18] Intelligent proponents of globalization, like Jagdish Bhagwati, insist that free trade and international competition have not directly reduced the real wages of workers in advanced countries. But it is the threat of outsourcing, job loss, or factory relocation that restrains pressure for higher wages, not the fact of competition per se—and it applies with equal effect in unionized, "Rhineland" economies like Germany and more competitive societies like the U.S. But even Bhagwati concedes that there has been a steady depression of real wages in advanced countries, though in his optimistic account globalization has at least helped slow the process somewhat. See Jagdish Bhagwati, *In Defense of Globalization* (New York: Oxford University Press, 2004), 123–124. See also the remarks by Paul Donovan, an economist at UBS, quoted in the *Financial Times,* June 5, 2006, p. 1: "The US labour market may be tightening but there is still an ample

supply of workers worldwide, and this may be capping what domestic workers can demand."

[19] Quoted in S. S. Prawer's *Karl Marx and World Literature* (Oxford: Oxford University Press/ Clarendon Press, 1976), 151.

[20] Marx received 28 percent of the votes cast, more than Socrates, Plato, Aristotle, Aquinas, and Kant combined. David Hume came second with 13 percent. For Attali see Jacques Attali, *Karl Marx ou l'esprit du monde* (Paris: Fayard, 2005).

CHAPTER IX

A *"Pope of Ideas"? John Paul II and the Modern World*

The glossy publicity material for *His Holiness,* a book published simultaneously in eight countries and in excerpted form by *Reader's Digest,* contains a list of nineteen "Possible Questions" for the authors.* Designed for anticipated press conferences and interviews, these questions are anything but probing and do not suggest that the authors, both investigative journalists, hold their colleagues in high esteem. Nevertheless, such "puff" questions are revealing in their way: More than half of them are invitations to the authors to boast of their discoveries, and they show that Bernstein and Politi (who writes for the Italian daily *La Repubblica*) mean their subtitle to be taken seriously. They do believe that they have brought to light the hidden history of our time.

Their book is written in a style appropriate to such a claim, rhetorically inflated and awash in hints of secret conversations, confidential informants, and unrevealable sources. In their chatty descriptions of people, places, and events, the authors miss few opportunities to reproduce a cliché. A Jewish attorney in the pope's birthplace is said to have

---

* Carl Bernstein and Marco Politi, *His Holiness: John Paul II and the Hidden History of Our Time* (New York: Doubleday, 1996).

been held "in the highest esteem both by his co-religionists and by most of the Gentile movers and shakers of Wadowice." As a substitute for an account of Karol Wojtyła's debt to Polish literature, we are told that "Adam Mickiewicz, the Romantic bard, in particular set strings resonating in Karol." At audiences with the new pope, we learn, "nuns went crazy." *His Holiness* is simultaneously urgent and soggy, with gobbets of interesting information adrift in a tumbling onrush of breathless, "colorful" prose.[1]

What have our authors discovered that lay hidden before? According to their own claim, two things. First, a hitherto unknown alliance during the 1980s between Pope John Paul II and the Reagan administration, whose aim was to bring down Communism in Europe and prevent its appearance in Central America. Second, that the role of the pope in engineering the downfall of Communism in Europe was vastly more important than anyone had hitherto suspected. They also claim to have revealed for the first time the nature and extent of U.S. (covert) support for Solidarity after the imposition of martial law in Poland in December 1981, and to have shown that it was papal influence that shaped U.S. policy in other matters—notably the opposition of the Reagan and Bush administrations to international agencies that support and practice family planning.

Since the authors are cagey about some sources—"secret," "confidential," and "private" appear frequently in the rather unhelpful endnotes—and heavily dependent on interviews (over three hundred by their account), it is impossible to check or corroborate much of the information.[2] But it seems reasonable to believe them when they tell us that William Casey (director of the CIA) and Vernon Walters ("Presidential ambassador-at-large") met regularly with the pope, briefing him on U.S. satellite information about Soviet troop movements and the like. It seems plausible to infer that the U.S. administration came to think of the Polish pope as a natural and powerful ally, treated him as such, and were in their turn favored by a pope whose objectives dovetailed well enough with those of the U.S. governments of the era—as they put it, "Wojtyła's Church became the administration's principal ideological ally in the struggle against the Sandinistas." In the same way, the authors are probably right when they say that the minutes of the Soviet Politburo in the early eighties reveal a lot of nervousness over Poland and its friend in the Vatican. As the Polish Communists well knew, a change in the position of the Catholic Church, from compromise to resistance, could have a destabilizing impact on th e local regime and region.

Bernstein and Politi may therefore be said, giving them maximum credit, to have demonstrated convincingly the existence of mutual U.S.-Vatican interests and support as well as the fears aroused in Soviet circles by actual or anticipated papal initiatives.[3] But they can hardly be said to have discovered things previously unknown. Thus the authors claim to have uncovered a "covert CIA operation, secretly authorized by Carter, to smuggle anti-Communist books and literature into Eastern Europe." I am interested, though not surprised, to learn that these smuggling operations had CIA financial backing; but that books were being taken clandestinely into Communist countries during the decade prior to their liberation is old news, and not only to those of us who had a walk-on part in that drama. The same is true of American backing for Solidarity in its underground years; all that this book adds to our knowledge of that support is an estimate, based on confidential sources, of the amounts involved ($50 million) and the supposition that this support was part of a secret agreement with the Vatican. In neither case will this information come as a shock to contemporary observers, scholars, or other journalists.

It is thus absurd to describe as "essentially accurate" Richard Allen's puerile and self-serving description of the Reagan-Vatican relationship as "one of the greatest secret alliances of all time." It is a gross overstatement to suggest that the Vatican and Warsaw joined Moscow and Washington as the "essential coordinates" of the cold war. These and other hyperbolic claims reflect the authors' own blinkered perspective, as well as their rather charitable attitude toward their sources, whose information is rarely questioned and whose motives pass uninvestigated. In any history of the last years of the cold war, or of the collapse and fall of the Soviet Union, the pope will obviously figure prominently, not least for the part played by Solidarity and the Polish opposition in the undermining of Communist credibility. In a similar vein, the story of the struggle for the soul of Latin America unavoidably entails consideration of the motives and interests of the Vatican at a time when those interests dovetailed with the overt and covert undertakings of conservative U.S. governments. But that is not the full story, and the incapacitating defect of this book is that it takes the part for the whole and believes that it has uncovered the hidden narrative of our time when it has in practice confirmed and fleshed out just one interesting chapter.

It is tempting to suppose that this might have been a better book had there been less Bernstein and more Politi. For Marco Politi is an expert on the Vatican, and it is the story of this pope and the hopes and disappointments surrounding him that offers a far more interesting clue to the history of our time than any number of energetic attempts to uncover secret alliances and hidden plots. The expectations aroused by the election of Cardinal Karol Wojtyła were unprecedented in modern times. In the Catholic Church he was regarded by some as a likely radical—open, imaginative, and young (just fifty-eight when elected pope in 1978), but already a veteran of Vatican II. Energetic, charismatic, and seemingly modern, this was the man who would complete the work of Popes John XXIII and Paul VI and who would lead the Church into a new era, a pastor rather than a Curial bureaucrat.

Many "liberation theologists" favored his election, and liberal cardinals and archbishops in South America and elsewhere campaigned for him. His conservative supporters took comfort in his reputation for unbending theological firmness and the moral and political absolutism deriving from his experience as a priest and prelate under Communism. This was a man who would not compromise with the Church's enemies. Others still saw in him an "intellectual" pope, at ease in the company of scholars and himself well versed in at least some aspects of modern thought, notably the philosophy of Husserl. All supposed that at the very least they would have a pope of the center, modern enough to handle the Church's new dilemmas, traditional enough to hold the line against too much innovation.

In some sense they were all wrong. Karol Wojtyła is not a man whose strong views cancel each other out or tend to equilibrium. He is, rather, a man of many extremes. He may have been the first non-Italian pope in half a millennium, but he was no outsider—perennially reelected to the Synodal Council of Bishops and a participant in Vatican II at the age of forty-two, he was a particular favorite of Paul VI and almost certainly that pope's private choice to succeed him. Like Cardinal Joseph Ratzinger, the powerful head of the Congregation for the Doctrine of the Faith* Wojtyła had been startled out of his early reforming enthusiasm by the radical aftershock of John XXIII's reforms and was already an instinctive administrative as well as a doctrinal conservative at the time of his election. But his style belied his message.

From the outset, this was a pope devoted to *Reconquista,* to breaking with his predecessors' Roman acquiescence in modernity, secularism, and compromise. His campaign of international appearances—complete with carefully staged performances in huge open arenas with oversized crucifixes and a paraphernalia of light, sound, and theatrical timing—was not undertaken without design. This was a Big pope, taking himself and his faith to the world; not the old, shrinking Western Catholic world of Italy, France, and Spain, but to Brazil, Mexico, the U.S., and the Philippines. There was something strikingly immodest about the ambitions of this new pope, visiting thirty-six countries in the first six years of his incumbency and openly proclaiming his goal, as the authors of this book rightly put it, of shaking "the Church out of its inferiority complex vis-à-vis the world." Intuitively grasping a central feature of Catholicism's popular appeal, John Paul II beatified and sanctified as no modern pope had done before him, virtually recasting the history of his Church in a hagiographic and martyrological vein.

The initial appeal of this energetic, messianic papal style was not confined to the non-European world. In Central Europe, too, the first Polish pontiff was no less adept at fulfilling his admirers' expectations. Breaking with the "Ostpolitik" of his predecessors, he visited Poland in the year following his elevation to the papacy, attracting huge gatherings of the faithful and the admiring and definitively throwing in the Church's lot with the forces for change that would soon thereafter coalesce into the Solidarity movement. He also discouraged Catholics everywhere in Central and Eastern Europe from negotiating, compromising, or debating with Marxism, and thereby offered his Church not merely as a silent sanctuary but as an alternative pole of moral and social authority, a crucial if temporary ally for the political opposition in Communist lands.

---

* His successor as Pope Benedict XVI.

The same charismatic self-confidence that was used to such public effect in the Philippines or Central America thus became a political weapon in Communist Europe, neutralizing the efforts of "reforming" Communist leaders to negotiate civic compromises with the newly emboldened local spiritual leadership. In the decade following his first visit to Poland, there can be no question but that John Paul II played a central part in the reduction and defeat of Soviet domination in Central and Eastern Europe. It was only after the initial wave of enthusiasm in Asia and the Americas had subsided, and Communism in Europe had been overthrown, that the contradictions of the new papacy began to emerge.

These can perhaps be seen most clearly in his misleading reputation as a "pope of ideas." From his early days as Archbishop of Kraków (a position to which he was appointed in 1958), Wojtyła had evinced a taste for intellectual companionship, inviting theologians and other scholars for frequent discussions and showing a disarming capacity to listen to views very different from his own. During his papacy he has been the host of a regular series of "conversations" at his summer residence in Castelgandolfo, where sociologists, philosophers, and historians have been invited to discuss problems of the modern world in the papal presence. The participants tend to be predominantly Polish or German, with a generous sprinkling of North Americans, but they have included some of the best-known names among contemporary scholars—Leszek Kołakowski, Edward Shils, Hans-Georg Gadamer, Ernest Gellner, Ralf Dahrendorf, Charles Taylor, Bernard Lewis, Emmanuel Le Roy Ladurie, and Paul Ricoeur, among others. Topics for discussion have included "Europe and Civil Society," "On Crisis," "Europe and its Offspring," "Man in the Modern Sciences," "Liberal Society," and so forth.[4]

To judge from the most recent of these conversations—on "The Enlightenment Today," held at Castelgandolfo in August—intellectual exchange with the pope is not the main object of the encounter. The pontiff listens for three days to a series of papers of varying quality. He takes no direct part in the ensuing discussion, but "summarizes" the proceedings at their completion. His summary is not so much a contribution to the subject as an occasion for accommodating the broader theme of the meeting to his own concerns. It is not clear how it could be otherwise. This is a man whose central contention about the modern world, as expounded in his many writings, is that it has undertaken for three hundred years a war against God and Christian values, a conflict in which he has now sought to engage himself and his Church to the full. The dilemmas and paradoxes of Liberalism, Enlightenment, Science, and secular philosophical speculation interest most of his guests at these meetings for their own sake. For the pope, however, while discussion of such matters may variously inform, depress, or even on occasion divert him, they serve above all to confirm what he already knows and believes.[5]

As a committed Thomist the pope derives his understanding of basic moral truths from his Faith.[6] The labors of Reason need to be heard and understood, but they have their place and must be kept in it. Bernstein and Politi are wrong to suppose that when he invoked words like "alienation" to describe the condition of working people, Wojtyła was, as they put it, "using Marxist language." The papal vocabulary of moral interrogation and condemnation has its own sources, and if modern social theories have adopted or adapted similar language this does not suggest that they mean the same thing, much less that a conversation is taking place. If we are to understand this pope and his practices we must first take him seriously on his own terms. His notions of absolute truth, of the unacceptability of "relativism"—whether in values or explanations of behavior, of good and evil, right and wrong—are founded upon the rock of Catholic fundamentalism, and it is upon that rock that the waves of ecumenicalism, "liberation theology," and modernization of Church liturgy, government, and practice have crashed in angry disappointment.

Karol Wojtyła is Polish. His Christian vision is not only rooted in the peculiarly messianic style of Polish Catholicism, but Poland itself is for him part of that Christian story.[7] He sees (or saw) in Poland not only the embattled eastern frontier of the True Faith, but also a land and a people chosen to serve as the example and sword of the Church in the struggle against Western materialism—the authors of this book quote a wartime colleague of Wojtyła who recalls him announcing that Poland's sufferings, like those of ancient Israel, were the price of its failure to realize its own ideal, to bear witness for Christ. This outlook, and his decades-long isolation from Western theological and political currents, probably account for his insensitive tendency to baptize anything and everything into a very particular Polish-Christian vision—witness his initial enthusiastic support for the projected Carmelite convent at Auschwitz, later withdrawn in the face of international protest. His thoughtless description of Poland under martial law as a "vast concentration camp" reflects a similar limitation.[8]

His Polish origins and his tragic early life also help to explain a marked inclination to Mariolatry—which in turn offers an indirect clue to his obsession with marriage and abortion. Karol Wojtyła lost his mother when he was eight (he would lose his only sibling, his older brother Edmund, three years later; his last surviving close relative, his father, died during the war when Wojtyła was nineteen). Following his mother's death he was taken by his father to the Marian sanctuary at Kalwaria Zebrzydowska and made frequent pilgrimages there in following years—Zebrzydowska, like Częstochowa, is an important center of the cult of the Virgin Mary in modern Poland. By the age of fifteen he was already the president of the Marian sodality in Wadowice, his hometown. He has always placed great store in apparitions of the Virgin and has visited sites all over the globe—in Guadeloupe (the Black Madonna), Argentina (Virgin of the Apparition), the Philippines (Virgin of Perpetual Help), Lourdes, and elsewhere. He has brought to the Vatican statues, icons, and depictions of Mary from all over the world. That Mehmet Ali Ağca should have shot (but failed to kill) him in Rome on May 13, 1981, merely confirmed his commitment—May 13 being the date of the Virgin Mary's reported appearance in Fátima (Portugal) in 1917. The pope's response was to have the bullet that was removed from his body installed in a golden crown and placed on the head of the Shrine of Our Lady of the Rosary at Fátima.[9]

This devotion to Marian symbols makes many Western Catholics, and not only among the laity, distinctly uneasy, and has generated resentment at pope John Paul II's imposition of a Polish partiality upon the universal Church. His mysticism, while also marked, is less characteristically Polish and has occasioned less debate. For all his bulk and energy and charisma, this is not a worldly pope. Wojtyła wrote his thesis on Saint John of the Cross, the sixteenth-century Spanish contemplative, and shares many of his subject's propensities—a taste for deep meditation, an unconcern verging on contempt for the things of this world, and an attraction to the "dark night of the soul," in which some hear a laudable call to Catholic soul-searching but which others find morbid. Wojtyła at first wished to become a monk (he was discouraged by his priest), and his longtime lack of interest in political resistance, whether against Nazis or Communists, reflects a remoteness that is echoed today in his utter unconcern with the widespread offense given by his moral pronouncements.

The combination of the Pole and the mystic in this pope may help explain why he has taken so aggressive a stand against "Western materialism and individualism," and thus against much of contemporary capitalism. It is of course the business of the Catholic Church to inveigh against material idols and the sin of pride. But Karol Wojtyła has gone much further. In his 1975 Lenten Exercises at the Vatican, three years before becoming pope, he explicitly announced that of the two threats to the Church, consumerism and persecution, the former was by far the greater danger and thus the worse enemy. Indeed, his criticisms of Marxism, both as a system of thought and as a political practice, derive from his broader condemnation of the worship of material progress, capitalist profit, and secular self-indulgence. Like Václav Havel and other opponents of Communism during the seventies and eighties, he believes that it is modernity, and the modern faithless West, that have been the source of our present crisis. Communism and its attendant evils, including environmental pollution, are but a secondary symptom and were anyway exported east from their Western sources.

It should be said that one consequence of this way of thinking is that pope John Paul II, like Havel, has an instinctive grasp of some of our current dilemmas—and he is, after all, as the authors of this book conclude, the only surviving international spokesman for *some* sort of system of universal values. There is much agreement today that we lack not only a broadly acknowledged moral compass but also any vision of the public space in which shared ideas of good and bad might have an effect. Lacking a common "community of destiny," so to speak, we are all too frequently tempted to fall back on communities of origin, the besetting sin of nationalism and "multiculturalism" alike. But the pope, characteristically, goes further. His own origins and trajectory have afforded him virtually no experience of life in a democracy, and he is given to conflating "soulless capitalism" with "selfish liberalism" in ways that suggest that he is insensitive to the complexities and costs of open societies. In his last years he has given way to the temptation to believe the worst of what he hears of post-Communist societies (Poland in particular)—hence the newly authoritarian note in his pronouncements, where attacks on selfish hedonism have merged with a dislike of freedom in many other forms as well.

All these habits of mind have now come together in the pope's crusade for "family values" in general and against abortion in particular. Here, too, the pope has the makings of a case—you don't have to be a conservative Catholic to worry about the texture of family life today, or to recognize that abortion or genetic engineering raises troubling ethical questions. But a genuine papal concern for our moral condition in these matters is vitiated for many by the insensitive way in which absolute authority is invoked in what are truly contested and painful debates. For this pope, marriage is not just a sacrament but a vocation. Condoms are not a "lesser evil" (an option with respectable antecedents in Christian theology) but forbidden. Abortion is a "holocaust." Men and, especially, women who slip from the path of righteousness stand utterly condemned—the Bishop of Łowicz in Poland, Monsignor Alojzy Orszulik, announced in September of this year that anyone in his diocese "guilty of the crime of abortion" would be excommunicated. Karol Wojtyła has turned his back not only on "modernity" and on compassion, but even on the recommendations of a 1966 Vatican commission on contraception, which gingerly suggested that there was nothing in the scriptures to justify root-and-branch condemnation of birth control.

The pope's obsession with sex—a subject on which he has written much, and in considerable graphic detail—curiously mirrors the concerns of those Americans whose culture he so scorns. And just as the abortion issue distorts large tracts of U.S. public life, so Wojtyła's fixation has damaged both his image and his impact elsewhere, notably in South America. His reiterated condemnation of the abuse of private property, and his reassertion of the natural right of all to share in the use and benefit of worldly resources, had raised hopes that this pope would be a resolute foe of what a British Conservative prime minister once called "the unacceptable face of capitalism." It was anticipated that even if he was not himself a committed proponent of social reform he would be consistently sympathetic to the victims of social and political repression. In a speech in Puebla, Mexico, in 1979 he reiterated the demands of the 1969 Medellín Conference, notably a "preferential love for the poor." In recent speeches in El Salvador and in France he has placed a growing emphasis on his opposition to wars and conflicts of all kinds, civil and international, and only this year, in San Salvador, he visited the tomb of Óscar Arnulfo Romero, the Salvadoran archbishop killed during Mass in 1980 by a rightist death squad.

But the same Archbishop Romero, a year before his death, had expressed private disappointment at the pope's lack of sympathy for the work of the Church in Latin dictatorships—"He recommended great balance and prudence, especially when denouncing specific situations. . . . I left, pleased by the meeting, but worried to see how much the negative reports of my pastoral work had influenced him."[10] By the end of the eighties the view seems to have become widespread among disappointed audiences and priests in Central and South America that papal sympathies for the victims of political repression were more easily aroused in the countries of Communist Europe. In Chile and Argentina, during visits in 1987, he devoted many hours of public speaking to attacks on proposals to liberalize the divorce laws, but refused to meet victims of Pinochet's repression or the Mothers of the Disappeared in Argentina. His compassion for the unborn, it seemed, could on occasion exceed his sympathy for the living—or the dead.[11]

This makes a little more sense when we recall that the pope is not just a would-be universal pastor. He is also the head of a huge, ancient institution and carries three distinctive responsibilities. First, he has the duty of preserving and transmitting the Church's doctrine. Where central doctrinal issues are not at stake, Wojtyła has been innovative and adventurous: He has visited synagogues, something no previous pope ever did, thereby acknowledging the legitimacy of other faiths; under his direction the Vatican has ceased to hold Jews responsible for the Crucifixion; and Wojtyła has been the first Catholic leader to offer some amends for the Church's silence during the Shoah. In fundamental matters, however, Karol Wojtyła has a marked taste for what in another context might be called "Founder's Intent": If Jesus did not choose women to be his priests, nor should John Paul II. Accidental disputes may come and go, but fundamental propositions must be retained and enforced, whether they concern the perpetual virginity of Mary, the Real Presence of Christ in the Eucharist, or the timeless validity of the properly doctrinal pronouncements of past councils and popes.

Secondly, the pope as head of the Church has administrative responsibilities which he, like many of his predecessors, sees primarily as issues of institutional discipline. In this respect, at least, there is a suggestive comparison between the Catholic Church and the erstwhile Secretariat of the Communist Party of the Soviet Union (though it has been many centuries since the Catholic Church had the capacity or desire to engage in the physical persecution of heretics). John Paul II is at the center of a worldwide apparatus always at risk of splitting into heretical segmentation. "Eurocommunism," "Socialism with a Human Face," "Local Roads to Socialism," and the like have their precise analogues in the modern Catholic Church.

In both instances reformers have occasionally harbored the illusion that they had a friend at the center who sympathized with their efforts to update ideology and governance—only to discover that the men at the top were in the end more concerned with power than popularity, more worried about preserving authority than discovering or disseminating justice. Under John Paul II the powers of local bishops have been contained and, like any local Communist Party secretary, they have been pressed to explain and justify their past actions, their present failures, and their future efforts. The bitter conclusion of Leonardo Boff, a Brazilian priest who left the service of the Church in 1992 after being condemned for deviations, echoes the disabused sentiments of countless former Communists: "Ecclesiastical power is cruel and merciless. It forgets nothing. It forgives nothing. It demands everything."[12]

Thirdly, the pope is only a temporary incumbent of the permanent chair of Saint Peter. He is above all responsible for ensuring continuity and the survival of his Church. Whatever his gestures to others—encounters with Jewish and Muslim communities, recognition of the State of Israel, ecumenical outreach to other Christians—the pope is not engaged in their concerns. The Catholic Church, as an institution about to enter its third millennium, plays for different stakes, and its concessions to any passing worldly considerations are at best tactical. Its overwhelming strategic objective is self-preservation. Much of what preoccupies contemporaries is thus of only contingent significance to the pope. That is why, from his own perspective, he is very properly deaf to the pain and anger aroused by the pronouncements of his pontificate. If he is right, and he is not a man given to doubt on that score, then not only is it good that he should pursue his chosen path, but he has no choice.

It has become commonplace to compare Karol Wojtyła, in the twilight of his reign, to Pius IX, the liberal cardinal who ascended to the papacy in 1846 at the young age of fifty-four. Disillusioned with liberalism after the experience of the revolutions of 1848, he retreated into deep conservatism and promulgated the doctrine of the Immaculate Conception of the Blessed Mary in 1854 and the doctrine of Papal Infallibility at the Vatican Council of 1869–70. In his Syllabus of Errors of 1864 he listed eighty errors of modernity, the last of which reads "that the Roman Pontiff can and should reconcile himself to and agree with progress, liberalism, and modern civilisation." By the end of his papacy, which lasted over thirty years, Pio Nono had made the Catholic Church synonymous with obscurantism and reaction.

Yet the very opposition that the hard-line Church aroused among the secular authorities of Europe helped save it. As a contemporary British diplomat noted: "The pope had made his Church ridiculous by the proclamation of the Immaculate Conception, of the Syllabus and of his own Infallibility, but these dogmas were of interest only to the faithful and in no way concerned or stood in the way of those who chose to ignore them. . . . Bismarck's anti-Church policy has compelled the German bishops to rally around the pope and suffer martyrdom for discipline's, obedience's and example's sake, and the Church that was ridiculous is becoming interesting to the religious and conservative population of Europe."[13]

Wojtyła's tragedy, of course, is that he began by benefiting from the popularity born of resilience in the face of persecution, and only later proceeded to expose his Church to ridicule for its moral intransigence. But there is an earlier comparison which is more to the point. In 1198, at the even younger age of thirty-eight, an Italian, Lotario de' Conti di Segni, became pope Innocent III. Energetic and authoritarian, Innocent set about centralizing power in the medieval Church. He proclaimed himself the Vicar of Christ (the title was not used before then), preached and organized an unsuccessful Fourth Crusade against the Infidel in 1204 and a brutal and utterly effective crusade against the Albigensian heretics of southwest France. At the Fourth Lateran Council of 1215, in the year before his death, he defined the modern doctrine of the Eucharist and the subordination of the bishops and the congregations to papal authority.

In between these professional duties he found time to bring down one medieval German emperor (Otto IV), raise up another (Frederick II), and give the French king his vital support in a conflict with the German Empire that resulted in the first great French military success (at Bouvines in 1214) and the definitive establishment of France as a power in Europe. With Innocent III the medieval papacy attained the zenith of its secular influence and theological authority. Yet the same man, by the very extent of his claims and rulings, was also the last of the great medieval popes and contributed to setting in motion those forces—secular and spiritual—that would lead to the downfall of the universal Church.

Karol Wojtyła's Church is no longer universal even in name. But the logic of his origins, his thought, and his circumstances has led him to stake out claims that no pope since Pius IX has asserted so aggressively, and no pope since Innocent III has ever been able to secure. Like Innocent, he has been a powerful but uncomfortable ally to a succession of secular partners, all of whom have some cause to regret their dealings with him. His successes are now behind him. The problems that he has bequeathed to his Church lie ahead.

This review of His Holiness, *by Carl Bernstein and Marco Politi, first appeared in the* New York Review of Books *in October 1996. My (one) reference to Karol Wojtyła's "Mariolatry" provoked a certain discomfort among some Polish correspondents.*

NOTES TO CHAPTER IX

[1] The book resembles nothing so much as a five-hundred-page *Time* magazine piece—as well it might, since it was in *Time* that Carl Bernstein, in 1992, first revealed the hitherto secret material on which the present book is based.

[2] Especially when the authors appear to be engaged in mind reading, as on page 487, where we are told what the pope was purportedly thinking while addressing an unappreciative audience in Kielce, Poland. Nothing in the sources for that speech suggest privileged authorial access to papal thoughts on the podium.

[3] There is some discussion of the hypothesis that it was the Soviet secret services who set up the unsuccessful attempt to kill the pope in 1981, but the authors of this book are no better informed than previous investigators and conclude rather lamely that the charge is credible but "not proven."

[4] The papers given at these encounters have been published in German, edited by Professor Krzysztof Michalski, the director of the Institute for Human Sciences in Vienna, which organizes the discussions.

[5] Things were probably a little different in earlier days, before the pontiff's present illness. But according to Czesław Miłosz, no hostile witness, matters were much the same at a Castelgandolfo "conversation" he attended in 1987. See Czesław Miłosz, *A Year of the Hunter* (New York: Farrar, Straus and Giroux, 1994), 21-27.

[6] On the pope's Thomism, and his theological leanings more generally, see George Huntston Williams, *The Mind of John Paul II* (New York: Seabury Press, 1981), especially chapter 4, "Mystic, Underground Seminarian, and Thomist."

[7] Nearly all Poles today are at least nominally Catholic. But it doesn't hurt to recall that this convenient conjunction of religious and secular identity, which served the Church so well in its struggle with Communism, is partly the work of the devil—or at least of his servants. It was Hitler and Stalin who gave Poland its present shape—until 1939 some 30 percent of Polish citizens practiced other faiths, and of those one third were Jews. His untroubled, innocent Polishness is a side of the pope that has always disturbed some of his more thoughtful compatriots and admirers, notably Miłosz.

[8] It may be that a gap has opened up between the Poles and their pope, a gap of which he has only recently become aware. Until the overthrow of Communism, the mere act of collective Catholic worship in Poland represented not only an expression of faith but also a widespread form of passive resistance to the authorities—hence the pope's own sense, shared by many outside observers in the time of Solidarity, that the country was solid in its obedient Catholicism. In the years since 1989 Polish citizens have gone their own way, increasingly deaf to the moral requirements and criticisms of the Catholic hierarchy—in recent opinion polls well over half those questioned favored legalized abortions. The image of Poland that Wojtyła shared with so many of his countrymen in times past, that of a land imbued with a collective Christian mission, may be on the wane.

The Poles were not alone in their national messianic complex. There are comparable strains in Russian nationalist thought, where there is a particular emphasis on an "alternative" Russian path. But although this strain in Russian thought is similarly imbued with symbolic religiosity, it is of course distinctly non-Catholic.

[9] The pope's first engagement on his recent visit to France was to pay homage to Saint Louis Grignion de Montfort, the eighteenth-century missionary author of *A Treatise on True Devotion to the Holy Virgin.*

[10] From Archbishop Romero's *Diary,* quoted in Tad Szulc, *Pope John Paul II: The Biography* (New York: Scribner, 1995), 326.

[11] Liberation theologists in particular were soon disillusioned with the new pope, for whom salvation can come from but one source, and who, in his own words, regards social questions as best left to sociologists. See *His Holiness,* p. 201.

[12] John Paul II is an ardent supporter of Opus Dei, the secretive society of influential lay Catholics founded in Spain before World War II and committed to a combination of modern secular influence and traditional conservative religion. He would probably not dissent from the claim

of Opus Dei's founder, Monsignor Escrivá y Balaguer, that God asks of his servants "holy intransigence, holy coercion and holy shamelessness." See Joan Estruch, *Saints and Schemers: Opus Dei and its Paradoxes* (New York: Oxford University Press, 1995), 262. The latest study of the administrative and institutional practices of the Vatican is by Thomas J. Reese *(Inside the Vatican: The Politics and Organization of the Catholic Church,* Harvard University Press Cambridge, MA, 1998).

[13] Odo Russell to Lord Derby, April 1, 1874, in *The Roman Question: Extracts from the Despatches of Odo Russell from Rome, 1858–1870,* ed. Noel Blakiston (London: Chapman & Hall, 1962), xxxvii. A few weeks earlier, on March 4, 1871, Russell had observed to his correspondent that "the Roman Church has always derived strength from persecution, but is impotent against the power of freedom and its blessings."

CHAPTER X

Edward Said:
The Rootless Cosmopolitan

When Edward Said died in September 2003, after a decade-long battle against leukemia, he was probably the best-known intellectual in the world. *Orientalism*, his controversial account of the appropriation of the East in modern European thought and literature, has spawned an academic subdiscipline in its own right: A quarter of a century after its first publication it continues to generate irritation, veneration, and imitation. Even if its author had done nothing else, confining himself to teaching at Columbia University in New York—where he was employed from 1963 until his death—he would still have been one of the most influential scholars of the late twentieth century.

But he did not confine himself. From 1967, and with mounting urgency and passion as the years passed, Edward Said was also an eloquent, ubiquitous commentator on the crisis in the Middle East and an advocate for the cause of the Palestinians. This moral and political engagement was not really a displacement of Said's intellectual attention—his critique of the West's failure to understand Palestinian humiliation closely echoes, after all, his reading of nineteenth-century scholarship and fiction in *Orientalism* and subsequent books (notably *Culture and Imperialism*, published in 1993). But it transformed the professor of comparative literature at Columbia into a very public intellectual, adored or execrated with equal intensity by many millions of readers.

This was an ironic fate for a man who fitted almost none of the molds to which his admirers and enemies so confidently assigned him. Edward Said lived all his life at a tangent to the various causes with which he was associated. The involuntary "spokesman" for the overwhelmingly Muslim Arabs of Palestine was an Episcopalian Christian, born in 1935 to a Baptist from Nazareth. The uncompromising critic of imperial condescension was educated in some of the last of the colonial schools that had trained the indigenous elite of the European empires; for many years he was more at ease in English and French than in Arabic and an outstanding exemplar of a Western education with which he could never fully identify.

Edward Said was the idolized hero of a generation of cultural relativists in universities from Berkeley to Bombay, for whom "orientalism" underwrote everything from career-building exercises in "postcolonial" obscurantism ("writing the other") to denunciations of "Western Culture" in the academic curriculum. But Said himself had no time for such nonsense. Radical antifoundationalism, the notion that everything is just a linguistic effect, struck him as shallow and "facile": Human rights, as he observed on more than one occasion, "are not cultural or grammatical things, and when violated they are as real as anything we can encounter."[1]

As for the popular account of his thought that has Edward Said reading (Western) writers as mere by-products of colonial privilege, he was quite explicit: "I do not believe that authors are mechanistically determined by ideology, class, or economic history." Indeed, when it came to the business of reading and writing, Said was an unabashedly traditional humanist, "despite the scornful dismissal of the term by sophisticated post-modern critics."[2] If there was anything that depressed him about younger literary scholars it was their overfamiliarity with "theory" at the expense of the art of close textual reading. Moreover, he enjoyed intellectual disagreement, seeing the toleration of dissent and even discord within the scholarly community as the necessary condition for the latter's survival—my own expressed doubts about the core thesis of *Orientalism* were no impediment to our friendship. This was a stance that many of his admirers from afar, for whom academic freedom is at best a contingent value, were at a loss to comprehend.

This same, deeply felt humanistic impulse put Edward Said at odds with another occasional tic of engaged intellectuals, the enthusiastic endorsement of violence—usually at a safe distance and always at someone else's expense. The "Professor of Terror," as his enemies were wont to characterize Said, was in fact a consistent critic of political violence in all its forms. Unlike Jean-Paul Sartre, a comparably influential intellectual for the previous generation, Said had some firsthand experience of physical force—his university office was vandalized and sacked, and both he and his family received death threats. But whereas Sartre did not hesitate to advocate political murder as both efficacious and cleansing, Said never identified with terrorism, however much he sympathized with the motives and sentiments that drove it. The weak, he wrote, should use means that render their oppressors uncomfortable—something that indiscriminate murder of civilians can never achieve.[3]

The reason for this was not that Edward Said was placid or a pacifist, much less someone lacking in strong commitments. Notwithstanding his professional success, his passion for music (he was an accomplished pianist, a close friend and sometime collaborator of Daniel Barenboim), and his gift for friendship, he was in certain ways a deeply angry man—as the essays in his posthumous book frequently suggest.* But despite his identification with the Palestinian cause and his inexhaustible efforts to promote and explain it, Said quite lacked the sort of uninterrogated affiliation to a country or an idea that allows the activist or the ideologue to subsume any means to a single end.

Instead he was, as I suggested, always at a slight tangent to his affinities. In this age of displaced persons he was not even a typical exile, since most men and women forced to leave their country in our time have a place to which they can look back (or forward): a remembered—more often misremembered—homeland that anchors the transported individual or community in time if not in space. Palestinians don't even have this. There never was a formally con-

---

* *From Oslo to Iraq* (New York: Pantheon, 2004). The present essay was first published as an introduction to this collection of Said's essays.

stituted Palestine, and Palestinian identity thus lacks that conventional anterior reference.

In consequence, as Said tellingly observed just a few months before his death, "I still have not been able to understand what it means to love a country." That, of course, is the characteristic condition of the rootless cosmopolitan. It is not very comfortable or safe to be without a country to love: It can bring down upon your head the anxious hostility of those for whom such rootlessness suggests a corrosive independence of spirit. But it *is* liberating: The world you look out upon may not be as reassuring as the vista enjoyed by patriots and nationalists, but you see farther. As Said wrote in 1993, "I have no patience with the position that 'we' should only or mainly be concerned with what is 'ours.'"[4]

This is the authentic voice of the independent critic, speaking the truth to power . . . and supplying a dissenting voice in conflicts with authority: As Said wrote in *Al-Ahram* in May 2001, "whether Israeli intellectuals have failed or not in their mission is not for us to decide. What concerns us is the shabby state of discourse and analysis in the Arab world." It is also the voice of the freestanding "New York intellectual," a species now fast approaching extinction—thanks in large measure to the same Middle Eastern conflict in which so many have opted to take up sides and identify with "us" and "ours."[5] Edward Said, as the reader of these essays will discover, was by no means a conventional "spokesman" for one party in that conflict.

The Munich daily *Die Süddeutscher Zeitung* headed its obituary of Said "Der Unbequeme"—the Uncomfortable Man. But if anything his lasting achievement was to make *others* uncomfortable. For the Palestinians Edward Said was an underappreciated and frequently irritating Cassandra, berating their leaders for incompetence—and worse. To his critics Said was a lightning rod, attracting fear and vituperation. Implausibly, this witty and cultivated man was cast as the very devil: the corporeal incarnation of every threat—real or imagined—to Israel and Jews alike. To an American Jewish community suffused with symbols of victimhood, he was a provocatively articulate remembrancer of Israel's very own victims. And by his mere presence here in New York, Edward Said was an ironic, cosmopolitan, *Arab* reminder of the parochialism of his critics.

The essays in this book cover the period December 2000 through

March 2003. They thus take us from end of the Oslo decade, the onset of the Second Intifada and the final breakdown of the "peace process," through the Israeli reoccupation of the West Bank and Gaza, the massacres of September 11, 2001, the American retaliation in Afghanistan, and the long run-up to the U.S. attack on Iraq—a distinctly turbulent and murderous twenty-eight months. During this time Edward Said wrote copiously and urgently about the alarming state of affairs in the Middle East, contributing at least one article a month, often more, despite his worsening medical condition (to which there is no reference in these writings until August 2002, and then only a casual, passing allusion).

All but one of the pieces collected here were contributed to an Arab-language outlet, the Cairo newspaper *Al-Ahram*. These writings are thus an opportunity for Edward Said's Western readers to see what he had to say to an Arab audience. What they show is that Said in his final years was consistently pursuing three themes: the urgent need to tell the world (above all Americans) the truth about Israel's treatment of the Palestinians; the parallel urgency of getting Palestinians and other Arabs to recognize and accept the reality of Israel and engage with Israelis, especially the Israeli opposition; and the duty to speak openly about the failings of Arab leadership.

Indeed, Said was above all concerned with addressing and excoriating his fellow Arabs. It is the ruling Arab regimes, especially that of the Palestinian Liberation Organization, that come in for the strongest criticism here: for their cupidity, their corruption, their malevolence and incredulity. This may seem almost unfair—it is, after all, the U.S. that has effective power, and Israel that was and is wreaking havoc among Edward Said's fellow Palestinians—but Said seems to have felt it important to tell the truth to and about his *own* people, rather than risk indulging "the fawning elasticity with regard to one's own side that has disfigured the history of intellectuals since time immemorial" (December 2000).

In the course of these essays Said recounts checklists of Israeli abuses (see, e.g., "Palestinians Under Siege" in December 2000; "Slow Death: Punishment by Detail" in August 2002; or "A Monument to Hypocrisy" in February 2003), a grim, depressing reminder of how Ariel Sharon's government is squeezing the lifeblood from the quarantined Palestinian communities: Abuses against civilians that were once regarded as criminal acts even in wartime are now accepted behavior by a government ostensibly at peace. But in Edward Said's account these abuses are not the accidental, unfortunate by-product of the return to power of a belligerent, irredentist general, but rather the predictable—and in Said's case, predicted—consequence of the Palestinians' engagement in the late, unlamented "peace process" itself.

For those of us who welcomed the Oslo process and watched hopefully as it developed over the course of the nineties, Said's disenchanted critique is depressing. But in retrospect it is difficult to deny that he got it right and we were wrong. As imagined by the Israeli peace party and welcomed by many others—Palestinians included—the Oslo process was supposed to build confidence and trust between the two sides. Contentious issues—the governance of Jerusalem, the right of return for Palestinian refugees, the problem of the Jewish settlements—would be dealt with "later," in "final status negotiations." Meanwhile the PLO would gain experience and credibility in the administration of autonomous Palestinian territory, and Israelis would live in peace. Eventually, two states—one Jewish, one Palestinian—would live in stable proximity, their security underwritten by the international community.

This was the premise behind the Declaration of Principles signed on the White House Lawn in September 1993. But the whole thing was deeply flawed. As Said reminds us, there were not two "sides" to these negotiations: There was Israel, an established modern state with an awesome military apparatus (by some estimates the fourth strongest in the world today), occupying land and people seized thirty years earlier in war. And there were the Palestinians, a dispersed, displaced, disinherited community with neither an army nor a territory of its own. There was an occupier and there were the occupied. In Said's view, the only leverage that the Palestinians had was their annoying *facticity:* They were there, they wouldn't go away, and they wouldn't let the Israelis forget what they had done to them.

Having nothing to give up, the Palestinians had nothing to negotiate. To "deal" with the occupier, after all, is to surrender—or collaborate. That is why Said described the 1993 Declaration as "a Palestinian Versailles"[6] and why he resigned in anticipation from the Palestinian

National Council. If the Israelis needed something from the Palestinians, Said reasoned, then the things that the Palestinians wanted—full sovereignty, a return to 1967 frontiers, the "right of return," a share of Jerusalem—should be on the table at the outset, not at some undetermined final stage. And then there was the question of Israel's "good faith."

When the initial Declaration was signed in 1993 there were just 32,750 Jewish housing units in settlements on the West Bank and in Gaza. By October 2001 there were 53,121—a 62 percent increase, with more to come. From 1992 to 1996, under the Labor governments of Yitzhak Rabin and Shimon Peres, the settler population of the West Bank grew by 48 percent, that of Gaza by 61 percent. To put it no stronger, this steady Israeli takeover of Palestinian land and resources hardly conformed to the spirit of the Oslo Declaration, whose Article 31 (Clause 7) explicitly states that "Neither side shall initiate or take any step that will change the status of the West Bank and the Gaza Strip pending the outcome of the permanent status negotiations."

Meanwhile, even as the PLO was authorized to administer the remaining Palestinian districts, Israel was constructing a network of "Jewish" roads crisscrossing those same regions and giving settlers and other Israelis exclusive access to far-flung housing units (and scarce aquifers) protected by permanent military installations.[7] The whole exercise was driven forward partly by an anachronistic Israeli conflation of land with security; partly by a post-'67 irredentist eschatology (with the Old Testament invoked as a sort of real estate contract with a partisan God); and partly by long-standing Zionist enthusiasm for territorial enlargement as an end in itself. From the Palestinian point of view the effect was to make the "Oslo process" an agonizing exercise in slow strangulation, with Gaza in particular transformed into a virtual prison under Palestinian warders, the Israeli army standing guard just outside the perimeter fence.

And then, in 2000, came the long-postponed "permanent status negotiations" themselves: first at Camp David and then, desperately, at Taba in the Sinai. Edward Said, of course, has no time for the conventional American view that President Clinton and Prime Minister Ehud Barak virtually gave away the farm and that even then the ungrateful PLO and its leader Yassir Arafat refused the gift. This is not because Said has any sympathy for Arafat but because the original Camp David offer was—as Tanya Reinhart described it in the Israeli daily *Yediot Aharonot* on July 8, 2000—so palpably a "fraud." The Palestinians were to get 50 percent of their own land, chopped into separate and often noncontiguous cantons; Israel was to annex 10 percent of the land; and the remaining 40 percent was to be left "undecided"—but under indefinite Israeli rule.

Five months later, at Taba, the Palestinians were offered an improved territorial deal, certainly the best they could ever have hoped for from an Israeli government. But the resulting Palestinian state would still have been utterly dependent on Israel and vulnerable to its whims; the grievances of Palestinian refugees were never fully addressed; and on the contentious issue of sovereignty over Jerusalem the Israelis would not budge. Indeed, even the last-minute Israeli concessions were still encumbered with what Said nicely terms "conditions and qualifications and entailments (like one of the endlessly deferred and physically unattainable estates in a Jane Austen novel). . . ."

Meanwhile Barak had continued to expand the population of the very settlements that his own negotiators recognized as a major impediment to agreement. Even if the PLO leaders had wanted to sell the Taba agreements to their constituents, they might have had difficulty doing so—the second intifada that burst out following Sharon's meticulously timed visit to the Temple Mount has been a disaster for the Palestinians, but it was born out of years—the Oslo years—of frustration and humiliation. On these grounds, as well as for reasons of his own, Arafat instructed the Palestinians not to sign.

Taba, and especially Camp David, were the bitter fruits of Oslo, and in Edward Said's view the PLO's error in engaging the process in the first place was well illustrated by its inevitable rejection of the outcome, retroactively discrediting the whole strategy of negotiations. In an *Al-Ahram* article of June 2002 Said is scathingly unforgiving of the PLO apparatchiks and their leader, who for a while did rather well out of the power they exercised as the "Vichyite" governors of occupied Palestine under Israel's benign oversight. They were and are "a byword for brutality, autocracy and unimaginable corruption" ("Palestinian Elections Now," *Al-Ahram* June 2002).

In other contributions to the same newspaper Said writes that Arafat and his circle "have made our situation worse, much worse." "Palestinians (and by extension other Arabs) have been traduced and hopelessly misled by their leaders," who have neither high principles nor practical, pragmatic strategies. "It has been years since Arafat represented his people, their sufferings and cause, and like his other Arab counterparts, he hangs on like a much too-ripe fruit without real purpose or position" ("Arab Disunity and Factionalism," *Al-Ahram*, August 2002).

What, then, is to be done? If the Palestinian leadership is corrupt and incompetent; if Israeli governments won't even keep faith with their own stated commitments, much less the desires of their interlocutors; if there is so much fear and loathing on all sides, how should the two-state solution be implemented, now that Israelis, Palestinians, and the international community—even the Americans—all at last accept it in principle? Here, once again, Edward Said was at odds with almost everyone.

In 1980, when he first publicly pressed for a two-state solution, Said was attacked and abused from all sides, not least by Arafat's own Al Fatah movement. Then, in 1988, the Palestinian National Council belatedly conceded that the best possible outcome was indeed the division of Palestine into two states—one Israeli, one Palestinian—echoing Said's insistence that there was no alternative to reciprocal territorial self-determination for Jews and Arabs alike.[8] But as the years went by, with half of the occupied territories expropriated; with the Palestinian community in shambles and the putative Palestinian territory a blighted landscape of isolated enclaves, flattened olive groves, and ruined houses, where humiliated adults were fast losing the initiative to angry, alienated adolescents, Said drew the increasingly irresistible conclusion.

Israel was never going to quit the West Bank, at least not in any way that would leave it in a coherent, governable condition. What kind of a state could the West Bank and Gaza ever constitute? Who but a criminal mafia would ever *want* to take on the task of "governing" it? The "Palestine" of PLO imaginings was a fantasy—and a rather unappealing one at that. For good or ill there was only going to be one real state in the lands of historic Palestine: Israel. This was not utopia; it was merely hardheaded pragmatism shorn of illusion. The genuinely realistic approach lay in accepting this fact and thinking seriously about how to make the best of it. "Much more important than having a state is the kind of state it is."[9] For the last decade of his life Edward Said was an unbending advocate of a single, secular state for Israelis and Palestinians.

What grounds did Edward Said have for his faith in a single-state solution, a nonexclusive, secular, democratic alternative to the present impasse? In the first place, the status quo is awful and getting worse: Two peoples, each sustained by its exclusive victim narrative, competing indefinitely across the dead bodies of their children for the same tiny piece of land. One of them is an armed state, the other a stateless people, but otherwise they are depressingly similar: What, after all, is the Palestinian national story if not a reproachful mirror to Zionism, a tale of expulsion, diaspora, resurrection, and return? There is no way to divide the disputed "homeland" to mutual satisfaction and benefit. Little good can come of *two* such statelets, mutually resentful, each with an influential domestic constituency committed to the destruction and absorption of its neighbor.

In the second place, something fundamental has changed in the Palestinian condition. For four decades millions of Palestinian Arabs—in Israel, in the occupied territories, in refugee camps across the Arab world, and in exile everywhere—had been all but invisible. Their very existence was long denied by Israeli politicians; their memory of expulsion had been removed from the official record and passed unmentioned in history books; the record of their homes, their villages, and their land was expunged from the very soil itself. That, as Said, noted, was why he kept on telling the same story: "There seems to be nothing in the world that sustains it; unless you go on telling it, it will just drop and disappear." And yet "it is very hard to espouse for five decades, a continually losing cause." It was as though Palestinians had no existence except when someone committed a terrorist atrocity—at which point that is *all* they were, their provenance uncertain, their violence inexplicable.[10]

That is why the "right of return" had so central a place in all Palestinian demands—not because any serious person supposed that Israel could take "back" millions of refugees and their descendants, but from the deeply felt need for *acknowledgment*: a recognition that the initial expulsion took place, that a primordial wrong was committed.

That is what so annoyed Said about Oslo: It seemed to excuse or forgive the Israelis for the occupation and everything else. But "Israel cannot be excused and allowed to walk away from the table with not even a *rhetorical demand* [my emphasis] that it needs to atone for what it did." ("What Price Oslo?" *Al-Ahram*, March 2002). Attention must be paid.

But attention, of course, *is* now being paid. An overwhelming majority of world opinion outside of the United States sees the Palestinian tragedy today much as the Palestinians themselves see it. They are the natives of Israel, an indigenous community excluded from nationhood in its own homeland: dispossessed and expelled, illegally expropriated, confined to "Bantustans," denied many fundamental rights, and exposed on a daily basis to injustice and violence. Today there is no longer the slightest pretence by well-informed Israelis that the Arabs left in 1948 of their own free will or at the behest of foreign despots, as we were once taught. Benny Morris, one of the leading Israeli scholars on the subject, recently reminded readers of the Israeli daily newspaper *Ha'aretz* that Israeli soldiers did not merely expel Palestinians in 1948–49, in an early, incomplete attempt at ethnic cleansing; they committed war crimes along the way, including the rape and murder of women and children.[11]

Of course Morris notoriously sees nothing wrong in this record—he treats it as the collateral damage that accompanies state building.[12] But this brings us to the third ground for thinking Said may be right about the chances for a single state. Just as the Palestinian cause has begun to find favor in public opinion, and is gaining the moral upper hand, so Israel's international standing has precipitately collapsed. For many years the insuperable problem for Palestinians was that they were being expelled, colonized, occupied, and generally mistreated not by French *colons* or Dutch Afrikaaners but, in Edward Said's words, by "the Jewish citizens of Israel, remnants of the Nazi Holocaust, with a tragic history of genocide and persecution."

The victim of victims is in an impossible situation—not made any better, as Said pointed out, by the Arab propensity to squeeze out from under the shadow of the Holocaust by minimizing or even denying it.[13] But when it comes to mistreating others, even victims don't get a free pass forever. The charge that Poles often persecuted Jews before, during, and after World War II can no longer be satisfactorily deflected by invoking Hitler's three million Polish victims. Mutatis mutandis, the same now applies to Israel. Until the military victory of 1967, and even for some years afterwards, the dominant international image of Israel was the one presented by its Left-Zionist founders and their many admirers in Europe and elsewhere: a courageous little country surrounded by enemies, where the desert had been made to bloom and the indigenous population airbrushed from the picture.

Following the invasion of Lebanon, and with gathering intensity since the first intifada of the late 1980s, the public impression of Israel has steadily darkened. Today it presents a ghastly image: a place where sneering eighteen-year-olds with M-16 carbines taunt helpless old men ("security measures"); where bulldozers regularly flatten whole apartment blocks ("collective punishment"); where helicopters fire rockets into residential streets ("targeted assassination"); where subsidized settlers frolic in grass-fringed swimming pools, oblivious of Arab children a few meters away who fester and rot in the worst slums on the planet; and where retired generals and cabinet ministers speak openly of bottling up the Palestinians "like drugged roaches in a bottle" (Rafael Eytan) and cleansing the land of its Arab cancer.[14]

Israel is utterly dependent on the United States for money, arms, and diplomatic support. One or two states share common enemies with Israel; a handful of countries buy its weapons; a few others are its de facto accomplices in ignoring international treaties and secretly manufacturing nuclear weapons. But outside Washington Israel has no *friends*—at the United Nations it cannot even count on the support of America's staunchest allies. Despite the political and diplomatic incompetence of the PLO (well documented in Said's writings); despite the manifest shortcomings of the Arab world at large—"lingering outside the main march of humanity";[15] despite Israel's own sophisticated efforts to publicize its case, the Jewish state today is widely regarded as a—*the*—leading threat to world peace. After thirty-seven years of military occupation, Israel has gained nothing in security; it has lost everything in domestic civility and international respectability; and it has forfeited the moral high ground forever.

The newfound acknowledgement of the Palestinians' claims and the steady discrediting of the Zionist project (not least among many profoundly troubled Israelis) might seem to make it harder rather than easier to envisage Jews and Arabs living harmoniously in a single state. And just as a minority of Palestinians may always resent their Jewish neighbors, there is a risk that some Israelis will never forgive the Palestinians for what the Israelis have done to them. But as Said understood, the Palestinians' aggrieved sense of neglect and the Israelis' insistence on the moral rectitude of their case were twin impediments to a resolution of their common dilemma. Neither side could, as it were, "see" the other. As Orwell observed in his *Notes on Nationalism*, "If one harbors anywhere in one's mind a nationalistic loyalty or hatred, certain facts, though in a sense known to be true, are inadmissible."

Today, in spite of everything, there is actually a better appreciation by some people on both sides of where—quite literally—the other is coming from. This, I think, arises from a growing awareness that Jews and Arabs occupy the same space and will continue to do so for the foreseeable future. Their fates are hopelessly entangled. Fence or no fence, the territory now ruled by Israel can only be "cleansed" of its Arab (or its Jewish) residents by an act of force that the international community could not countenance. As Said notes, "historic Palestine" is now a lost cause—but so, for the same reasons, is "historic Israel." Somehow or other, a single institutional entity capable of accommodating and respecting both communities will have to emerge, though when and in what form is still obscure.

The real impediment to new thinking in the Middle East, in Edward Said's view, was not Arafat, or Sharon, nor even the suicide bombers or the ultras of the settlements. It was the United States. The one place where official Israeli propaganda has succeeded beyond measure, and where Palestinian propaganda has utterly failed, is in America. American Jews (rather like Arab politicians) live in "extraordinary self-isolation in fantasy and myth" ("Crisis for American Jews," May 2002). Many Israelis are terribly aware of what occupation of the West Bank has done to their own society (if somewhat less sensitive to its effect on others): "Rule over another nation corrupts and distorts Israel's qualities, tears the nation apart, and shatters society" (Haim Guri).[16] But most Americans, including virtually every American politician, have no sense of any of this.

That is why Edward Said insists in these essays upon the need for

Palestinians to bring their case to the American public rather than just, as he puts it, imploring the American president to "give" them a state. American public opinion matters, and Said despaired of the uninformed anti-Americanism of Arab intellectuals and students: "It is not acceptable to sit in Beirut or Cairo meeting halls and denounce American imperialism (or Zionist colonialism for that matter) without a whit of understanding that these are complex societies not always truly represented by their governments' stupid or cruel policies." But as an American he was frustrated above all at his *own* country's political myopia: Only America can break the murderous deadlock in the Middle East, but "what the U.S. refuses to see clearly it can hardly hope to remedy."[17]

Whether the United States will awaken to its responsibilities and opportunities remains unclear. It will certainly not do so unless we engage a debate about Israel and the Palestinians that many people would prefer to avoid, even at the cost of isolating America—with Israel—from the rest of the world. In order to be effective, this debate has to happen in America itself, and it must be conducted by Americans. That is why Edward Said was so singularly important. Over three decades, virtually single-handed, he wedged open a conversation in America about Israel, Palestine, and the Palestinians. In so doing, he performed an inestimable public service at considerable personal risk. His death opens a yawning void in American public life. He is irreplaceable.

This essay was written as an introduction to Edward Said's posthumous essay collection From Oslo to Iraq and the Road Map, *published by Pantheon in 2004. It also appeared in the* Nation *in July of that same year.*

NOTES TO CHAPTER X

[1] See Edward Said, *Humanism and Democratic Criticism* (New York: Columbia University Press, 2004), 10, 136.

[2] See Edward Said, *Culture and Imperialism* (New York: Vintage Books, 1994), xxii; Edward Said, *Orientalism*, "Preface to the Twenty-fifth Anniversary Edition" (New York: Vintage Books, 1994), xxiii.

[3] In his 1961 preface to the French edition of Frantz Fanon's *The Wretched of the Earth*, Sartre described the violence of anticolonial revolutions as "man recreating himself . . . to shoot down a European is to kill two birds with one stone, to destroy an oppressor and the man he oppresses at the same time: there remain a dead man and a free man; the survivor, for the first time, feels a *national* soil under his foot." Jean-Paul Sartre, preface to *The Wretched of the*

Earth by Frantz Fanon (New York: Grove Press, 1968), 21–22. Contrast Said, whose models for Palestinian resistance are Gandhi's India, King's civil rights movement, and Nelson Mandela (see "The Tragedy Deepens," December 2000, in the *From Oslo to Iraq*).

⁴ See "Israel, Iraq and the United States," *Al-Ahram,* October 10–16, 2002, in ibid; Said, *Culture and Imperialism,* xxv.

⁵ To its lasting credit, Columbia University withstood considerable internal and public pressure to censure or even remove Said because of his public interventions on the Palestinian behalf.

⁶ Edward Said, *The Politics of Dispossession: The Struggle for Palestinian Self-Determination 1969–1994* (New York: Vintage Books, 1995), xxxiv.

⁷ This had the paradoxical consequence of segregating Jews and Arabs even as they became ever more economically interdependent: Israelis relying on cheap Palestinian labor, Palestinians dependent upon Israel for jobs and access to markets.

⁸ See, e.g., Edward Said, "Who Would Speak for Palestinians," *New York Times,* May 24, 1985.

⁹ Said, *The Politics of Dispossession,* p. xliii.

¹⁰ Said, *The Politics of Dispossession,* pp. xviii, 118. For the quite remarkable thoroughness with which Israeli archeologists and bureaucrats "cleansed" Israel of all evidence of its Palestinian past, see Meron Benvenisti, *Sacred Landscape: The Buried History of the Holy Land Since 1948* (Berkeley: University of California Press, 2000).

¹¹ Benny Morris, interviewed in *Ha'aretz,* January 8, 2004.

¹² "I don't think that the expulsions of 1948 were war crimes. You can't make an omelet without breaking eggs." *Ha'aretz,* January 8, 2004.

¹³ See Said, *The Politics of Dispossession,* p. xviii; and "Barenboim and the Wagner Taboo," *Al-Ahram,* August 16–22, 2001.

¹⁴ Already in 1975 the head of the housing department of Israel's Interior Ministry was reporting to Prime Minister Yitzhak Rabin that Israel's *own* Arabs were a "cancer in the Jewish body that has to be curbed and contained." See Ilan Pappe, *A History of Modern Palestine: One Land, Two Peoples* (New York: Cambridge University Press, 2004), 227. Thirty years on, only the metaphor has changed: "Something like a cage has to be built for them [Palestinians]. There is no choice—there is a wild animal there that has to be locked up." Benny Morris, *Ha'aretz,* January 8, 2004.

¹⁵ Said, *The Politics of Dispossession,* p. 371.

¹⁶ Quoted in Tom Segev, *Elvis in Jerusalem* (New York: Metropolitan Books, 2002), 125.

¹⁷ Edward Said, "Suicidal Ignorance," *Al-Ahram,* November 15–21, 2001, in *From Oslo to Iraq;* and "Blind Imperial Arrogance," *Los Angeles Times,* July 20, 2003.

Part Three

LOST IN TRANSITION: PLACES AND MEMORIES

CHAPTER XI

The Catastrophe:
The Fall of France, 1940

Europeans today live at peace with one another. They even like each other. In EU-sponsored "Eurobarometer" polls taken over the past decade, it is striking how far mutual suspicion has been diluted by closer acquaintance. There are exceptions, of course: Most of the small countries of Central and Eastern Europe retain some wariness of their immediate neighbors (thanks in part to forty years of enforced "fraternalism"); Italians esteem other Europeans but mistrust their fellow citizens (as do Greeks); the English popular press is alternately suspicious or contemptuous of the French, a sentiment warmly reciprocated. And then there are the Balkans. But by and large Europeans get on well together—the French and the Germans better than most.

The last of these is a very recent development. In 1946 in a speech in Zurich, Winston Churchill observed that "the first step in the re-creation of the European family must be a partnership between France and Germany." The auspices were not promising. Between 1800 and 1940 the French and the Germans fought five major wars: in 1806, when Napoléon crushed the Prussians at Jena; in 1813–15, when the Prussians got their revenge; in 1870–71, a Prussian victory that led to the declaration of a German Empire in occupied Versailles; in 1914–18; and again in 1940. In every case the military victory was followed by a settlement and an occupation deemed unjust and degrading by the losers. National memory on both sides of the Rhine was steeped in resentment. Prussians perceived the French after 1806 as harsh and humiliating victors, and the brutality of Prussian troops in occupied France after 1815 and again in 1871 was popularly regarded as just revenge—the wife of Otto von Bismarck, the German chancellor, notoriously suggested in the course of the Franco-Prussian War of 1870–71 that the French should be "shot and stabbed to death, down to the little babies" (her husband demurred).

In the course of World War I, when German troops once again occupied a segment of northern France, there were widespread rumors of atrocities against civilians. When the war ended and Germany was defeated, the French pressed more urgently than most for retribution. Alsace-Lorraine (annexed to the German Empire in 1871) was returned to the French, who also secured reparations considerably exceeding the large indemnity that the Germans had taken in the 1870s. When the Germans failed to pay up, the French premier Raymond Poincaré sent troops to occupy the Ruhr in 1923. This move secured little for France save widespread German antipathy and the long-remembered accusation that French soldiers had abused and mistreated unarmed civilians.

When Hitler's armies attacked France on May 10, 1940, both the conduct of the war and the apprehensions of civilians were thus shaped by seven generations of mutual antagonism. In their planning, the French high command thought exclusively of a war against Germany. When war broke out, millions of French civilians fled before not just the armies of the Third Reich but the remembered and recounted exploits of the Kaiser at Verdun, General Moltke at Sedan in 1870, and Marshal Blücher at Waterloo. German officers and their troops remembered the Ruhr, the Western Front, and Napoléon, preserved in cautionary tales for naughty children and hours of staff college lectures. Renewed hostilities between Germany and France would be a serious matter.

All of this was to be expected. What almost no one anticipated was the course of events in 1940 itself. It took the German armies just seven weeks to invade Luxembourg, break through the Ardennes forests into France, sweep the French before them, force the British, French, and Belgian armies into a pocket at Dunkirk, impose an armistice on the new French government of Marshal Pétain, occupy Paris, and stage a victory parade for Adolf Hitler on the Champs-Élysées. In six weeks of fighting, the French lost 124,000 dead, and a further 200,000 were wounded. At one point in the battle, on May 16–17, General Erwin Rommel took 10,000 French prisoners for the loss of one German officer and forty men. In the words of the historian Nicole Jordan, "The French military collapse in 1940 was one of the great military catastrophes in world history."[1]

Hitler's victory brought Mussolini into the war, seeking spoils before the dust settled. It shaped British and American attitudes toward France for the next generation. It precipitated the overthrow of France's Third Republic and the establishment of an authoritarian, collaborationist regime at Vichy. It confirmed Hitler's delusions of strategic genius, reinforced his dominion over his generals, and left him free to concentrate first on defeating Britain and then, when this proved awkward, to turn his attentions to southeast Europe and the Soviet Union. Most of all it led to profound soul-searching and self-questioning by the French. How could this have happened? Twenty years after Versailles, why had the most powerful army in continental Europe succumbed so utterly to its hereditary enemy?

This self-questioning produced at least one work of unsurpassed brilliance, Marc Bloch's *Étrange Défaite*. France's most distinguished historian, a reserve officer (the oldest in the French army) who volunteered for service in 1939, Bloch recorded his testimony in 1940; it was only published after the war, by which time its author, an active member of the Resistance, had been shot by the Germans. All subsequent commentators on 1940, including Ernest May, the most recent historian of the battle, pay due homage to Bloch's essay, describing their own efforts as a mere footnote or amendment to his penetrating analysis. They are right to do so, for Bloch sketched out what is still the conventional explanation of the French disaster.[2]

In this account France labored under two self-imposed handicaps. First, its military leadership was incompetent. In anticipation of war with Germany, the French had constructed from the Swiss border north to Luxembourg a defensive line named after the minister who oversaw its construction, André Maginot. The long frontier between France and Belgium was left unsecured. But French strategy, seeking to avoid war on

French soil, presumed that any fighting would take place in Belgium or farther east and was thus apparently geared to taking the offensive in spite of the Maginot forts. French foreign policy in turn reflected this wish to project a conflict with Germany away from the frontiers: Between the wars France had sought out alliances, especially in Eastern and Southern Europe. But since the French high command was determined to avoid war at all costs, France could offer nothing of substance to its allies—a weakness revealed in 1938 at Munich and again in 1939, when the French, like the British, let Hitler destroy Poland with his western borders unthreatened.

French generals were not just strategically confused; they were also tactically and administratively incompetent. As Bloch and many subsequent historians have shown, the French high command proved chronically unable to devolve responsibility, react to changed circumstances, organize transport, maintain communications, stockpile fuel, or even record the whereabouts of its arms depots. French commanders let their conscripted soldiers sit idly around from September 1939 until May 1940 (when they might have been better employed in arms factories) and then expected them to fight a fast-moving, confusing battle against an incomparably better-led foe.

When the Germans attacked, the French general staff did not know what was happening to them, and even if they had they could not have responded. The contrast with their opponents is illuminating. Both sides had tanks, but German generals like Rommel and Heinz Guderian knew how to exploit them. German officers were allowed to take the initiative when opportunities arose, and they did so. The French were trained to follow orders and detailed plans, but when circumstances changed they could not get new orders because there was no radio communication between General Maurice Gamelin, the overall commander, and his officers at the front.

The other French handicap was political. The country was divided between Left and Right, a public scar that lay athwart a deeper wound, the memory of World War I and the desire to avoid a repetition. For much of the 1930s it had proved impossible to form a stable government. The Popular Front government of 1936, the only one with a clear program and a workable parliamentary majority, was resented by the Right for its reformist projects and its Jewish socialist prime minister, Léon Blum, and by the Left for its failure to pursue a revolutionary transformation. Left and Right alike were too busy with internecine ideological quarrels to pay serious attention to the coming crisis, and even though the French built better tanks and aircraft than is sometimes thought, they didn't have enough of them.

Those few political leaders (Blum among them) who belatedly advocated a common front against the Nazi threat were accused of trying to drag France into a war for Danzig, for Britain, or for the Jews. The press, like the political parties, was venal and corrupt, often financed by foreign interests and governments. In such circumstances, the defeat of France might not have been anticipated, but it was all too readily explicable in retrospect. A rotting, divided polity collapsed unprotesting when its incompetent military caste caved in before a magnificent German war machine. For millions of Frenchmen, like Mathieu in Sartre's *La Mort dans l'âme*, the war ended before it had hardly begun.[3]

IN HIS IMPRESSIVE new book, Ernest May takes issue with this account.* In his view, the French defeat of 1940 was not just a shock; it need not have happened. Things might well have gone the other way, and they very nearly did. The French political situation was not as hopeless as later commentators have asserted, and anyway it played little part in the course of events. The French general staff was incompetent (here May brings new evidence in support of the conventional account), but it lost the battle through a handful of avoidable errors. Had things gone otherwise, history would have taken a very different path, and we would not now be rummaging around in the French past to seek the deeper roots of the country's debacle. According to May, it is not the French defeat but the German victory that needs explaining. What happened in May 1940, in his words, is "indicative of the condition of particular French military units, not of the French national soul."

It is hard to do justice to his book in a brief summary. May has done thorough research in German, French, British, and American archives;

---

* *Strange Victory: Hitler's Conquest of France* (New York: Hill & Wang, 2001).

he has examined a huge secondary literature, and he makes a strong case. His argument, in essence, is this: Hitler was convinced that he could beat the French, but his generals were not. Like most contemporary commentators, they took French military capacity at face value and wanted to avoid a confrontation as long as possible. As it turned out, Hitler was right; but had he been wrong, his (in May's view fragile) grip on Germany might well have been prized loose. And he was only right by a stroke of good fortune.

Hitler originally wanted to strike against France in the late fall of 1939, following the success of his Blitzkrieg in Poland. The weather proved unfavorable and the attack was postponed. But had it taken place as planned, it would not have been southwest, through the Ardennes, but west, through central Belgium and into the plains of northern France. This is significant, because Gamelin's own strategy for a war with Germany was also to push hard into Belgium, to meet the Germans as far north and east of France as possible; with France's borders with Germany and eastern Belgium secure, the army's premier divisions would take the offensive. In such a scenario the finest frontline units of both armies would thus have clashed in Flanders, and the French, backed by the British, the Belgians, and perhaps the Dutch, would have had a reasonable chance of success.

The German general staff anticipated the direction of French thinking, and it was this knowledge that made them skeptical of Hitler's plans, which they did their best to oppose. However, in January 1940, information about German invasion plans had fallen by chance into Belgian hands. This confirmed Gamelin in his already unshakable conviction that the Belgian route (the so-called Dyle-Breda variant, named after the Belgian river and Dutch town that were its initial objectives) was the one to take. But in view of the security breach, the Germans decided to make a crucial adjustment to their own scheme and strike down through the Ardennes instead, sending weaker troops into central Belgium as a decoy.

To the untutored eye the tightly forested Ardennes hills around Sedan, where the Germans broke through in May 1940, look quite impenetrable—an unpropitious place through which to advance a modern army. Even today, with more and better roads and bridges, the woods and the Meuse River form a significant impediment. The French general staff, from Pétain to Gamelin, was presumably far from untutored, but it had long since come to the same conclusion. When five Panzer divisions smashed through the forests and seized the bridges, they were faced by one of the weakest units in the French order of battle, General André Corap's Ninth Army, much of which consisted of elderly reserves and barely trained recruits.

No one seems to have noticed the long columns of German troops approaching Sedan from the north. No strategic reserve was moved up when the Meuse front collapsed and Corap's army disintegrated—there was none (it had been sent to Belgium with the rest of the French armies). General Charles Huntziger, whose Second Army was defending the unthreatened frontier to the east and who was in overall charge of the sector, refused to send reinforcements; he did not understand the extent of the disaster and had anyway fallen for Goebbels's bluff about an imminent attack near Switzerland.

By the time the French high command understood what was happening it was too late. Guderian and Rommel cut a swath through northern France, heading for the English Channel. Caught in a trap, the main French army and the British Expeditionary Force desperately retreated to the coast while on May 28 the Belgian king precipitately surrendered—a betrayal of his allies that would cost him his throne after the war. Gamelin and his officers gave up the struggle after some half-hearted and ill-coordinated efforts to engage the Germans, and France collapsed.[4]

In May's view, only once Hitler gained the initial advantage in the Ardennes did France's structural weaknesses come into play. Rigid and pessimistic—victims of their prewar overestimation of German prowess and resources—the French generals had no contingency plans for a German breakthrough. At best they could only imagine plugging holes to maintain a continuous front. The French could no more envisage a rapid war of maneuver than they could believe that the Maginot Line might prove irrelevant. Gamelin had been so deeply committed to a "cut-price war on the peripheries" that neither he nor his political masters had anything to offer when the war came to France itself.[5]

Above all, the French were desperately weak in intelligence. May is particularly strong on this and shows how and why French generals either did not know what the Germans were planning or else could make no sense of what knowledge they had. They discounted all evidence that should have led them to shift their focus from the Low Countries to the Ardennes, and unlike the Germans, they had no staff structure for analyzing, filtering, or sharing their data. In any case, the quality of that data left everything to be desired: In early October one report to the intelligence arm of the French air force advised, "According to intelligence from good sources, the Hitler regime will continue to hold power until the spring of 1940 [and] then will be replaced by communism."

In this context we can better appreciate Gamelin's disarming confession to a postwar commission of inquiry, when questioned about his incompetent disposition of French tanks: "Personally, I envisaged a group of four tank divisions around Chalons. How was I to know it would get broken up? We had no advance knowledge of where and how the Germans would attack."[6]

Professor May has written an accessible and impeccably scholarly account of a major moment of the century. There are some wonderful vignettes (e.g., of Neville Chamberlain writing to his sister on March 12, 1939, three days before Hitler seized Czechoslovakia: "Like Chatham, 'I know that I can save this country and I do not believe that anyone else can'"), and the detail, especially for Germany, is copious and illuminating.

The main direction of the argument is not perhaps altogether new: Donald Cameron Watt and others have described the diplomatic and domestic background to Hitler's attack on France; the French setting in 1940 was exhaustively charted by Jean-Louis Crémieux-Brilhac; and the story of the battle has already been told more than once.[7] But May gives his predecessors full and due credit, and his own interpretation would for the most part be accepted by them in turn. It is generally agreed that Hitler was a successful gambler who had to overcome the caution of his own staff, just as it is now thought that France could have forced and fought a long war had she had better generals. Nothing *needed* to be as it was.

Professor May's emphasis upon the element of chance in the outcome of the battle of France leads him to some rather ambitious counterfactual hypotheses. If the French had anticipated the Ardennes offensive, he writes in his introduction, "it is more than conceivable that the outcome would have been not France's defeat but Germany's and, possibly, a French victory parade on the Unter den Linden in Berlin." This is no casual aside. Four hundred pages later May stakes an even greater claim: "Absent defeats in battle in May 1940, France was in no more danger of moral collapse than Britain, it seems to me, and in less danger than Germany." If her armies had been set back in 1940, Nazi Germany "might have imploded." I think some of these claims are exaggerated and ill conceived, but the insistence upon contingency is salutary. It isn't enough to point to Vichy or even to interwar French domestic squabbling if one wants to explain the distinctively fortuitous actions of May 1940. And if things had gone differently, then much else would be changed too.

Here, however, the problems begin. May writes, "If the war had been fought where the French expected it to be fought, it would have gone much more as they expected it to go." Well, yes. As evidence he cites the brief success of one of France's better generals, Georges Blanchard. On May 13 at Hannut, southeast of Brussels, some of his armored units under General René Prioux met and briefly overcame their German opposite numbers. This leads May to speculate on what might have been if Blanchard's First Army had been in the right place at the right time: French tanks *could* beat German Panzer units.

But I can add "ifs" of my own. Blanchard's armored divisions were France's best soldiers, and in Belgium they overcame not Rommel's Panzer IVs but smaller, weaker Panzer Is and IIs. If they had faced more than a secondary German force, they might have fared a lot worse. And even if they had done well, all the other factors would still be in place. May asks what might have happened if Blanchard's forces had pressed ahead with their initial success. But they didn't. Would they have done so even if they had beaten the main German army? It wasn't part of Gamelin's "plan," and like the ill-fated Marshal Bazaine in 1870, he stuck to it unwaveringly. And if Prioux had been defeated, the French would still have had no strategic reserve, poor supplies, an inefficient chain of command, etc. A rout would probably have ensued.

It thus requires a long chain of one-directional "ifs" to reach a point at which a decisive French victory becomes not only possible but likely. One would have to unravel not just one or two chance outcomes but the complex sequence of decisions and personalities and practices that put chance on the side of the Germans and not the French. I have nothing against the Cleopatra's Nose approach to crucial historical choices: If Lenin had not been shipped across Germany to the Petrograd Finland Station in 1917, then twentieth-century history would indeed look very different. But although Germany's victory undoubtedly hinged on Hitler's insights into French weakness, the failings that he detected (and that his generals missed) can only be explained in their broader context. That is the trouble with much counterfactual speculation: It takes the last move in a sequence, correctly observes that it might have been very different, and then deduces either that all the other moves could also have been different or else that they don't count.

But for all the other moves to have been different in the required way, we need a parallel universe. And for them not to count, we need to distort the historical context. Professor May is intensely sensitive to the crosscurrents and pressures of German domestic affairs, which made Hitler vulnerable; he all but ignores political turbulence in France. This bolsters his assertion that Hitler could have been brought down by defeat and that France could easily have won, but it is hardly a balanced treatment. Whenever Nazi generals express doubts or dissent, May takes their anxiety at face value; when French generals show comparable apprehension or pessimism, he interprets it as instrumental rhetoric, designed to pad the military budget. When French generals or politicians are optimistic about their situation, however, he takes this for good coin. He emphasizes French technical strengths and downplays or dismisses talk of cynicism or social division.

This asymmetrical treatment sets the scene for a narrative in which the German victory is a surprise and the French defeat a chapter of accidents. But it misses much of the relevant story. Why, after all, were most French generals such bunglers? Why, for example, did Gamelin restore normal leave for the French army on May 7, 1940—a transcendently incompetent move? Why did Huntziger refuse air cover to his troops at Sedan, leaving an open target for the morale-destroying attacks of the Stukas? If good generals could have done better by their country, it is their absence that needs explaining.

A clue is to be found in a September 1940 photograph of the council of ministers at Vichy. There sits General Huntziger, two places away from Pétain and wearing the same self-satisfied look as his master.[8] Three months after the worst defeat in French history, the men directly responsible for it were comfortably ensconced in a regime that their defeat helped to install. General Maxime Weygand, who replaced Gamelin in command for the last days of the debacle, was the first minister of national defense at Vichy. His primary concern in the waning hours of the battle was not the German army but a possible Communist uprising in Paris upon the heels of a defeat. Such men may not have expected to lose the war, but they resigned themselves to defeat all the quicker because they did not regard the Germans as the greatest threat.

Weygand, like Pétain, was old enough to remember the Paris Commune of 1871, and it haunted his generation of reactionary and monarchist officers. The France that they were sworn to defend did not, in their eyes, include the political Left, successors to the Communards whose martyrdom was commemorated in eastern Paris every spring. Even Gamelin, an apolitical general by prevailing French standards, was not immune. As early as May 16, with the battle not yet lost, he was preparing his excuses. The army, he told the politicians, had collapsed because of Communist penetration.[9]

May misses this because he is unconcerned with domestic disputes, believing that by the late 1930s the corrosive hatreds of earlier years had been set aside and France was as stable and united as Britain, if not more so. But it was in October 1937 that the eminently respectable *Nouvelles économiques et financières* was sneering at the "Jew Blum," "our ex-prime minister whose real name is Karfunkelstein." In April 1938, after the Anschluss, Pierre Gaxotte (later of the Académie Française) was still describing Blum as "a disjointed un-French puppet with the sad head of a Palestinian mare. . . . Between France and this cursed man, we must choose. He is the very incarnation of everything that sickens our flesh and our blood. He is evil. He is death."[10]

In *Scum of the Earth* Arthur Koestler wrote of the vicious nationalist hatreds and threats swirling around France in the months preceding the battle of France. And from no less a source than Charles de Gaulle we have contemporary testimony to the partisan, paranoid, hate-filled atmosphere of the French parliament during the installation of Paul Reynaud's government on March 21, two months before the German invasion. If Ernest May believes that France in May 1940 was a nation resolute, united, and in a condition to face the German threat, he is deeply mistaken.[11]

The Communists had not forgiven Blum for his failure to intervene on behalf of the Spanish loyalists in 1936; for his insistence on compromise in the Popular Front legislation of that year; and perhaps above all for his success in preserving the French Socialist Party following the schism with the Communists in December 1920. In December 1940 they approached the Vichy authorities with an informal offer to testify against Blum at his forthcoming show trial. (Fortunately for the French Communist Party's future standing, their proposal was ignored.) The unions were still seething in resentment at Daladier's November 1938 laws abrogating the labor reforms of 1936. Anti-Fascism, which might once have been an effective motive for unity, had been undermined and corroded by successive governments' obsession with not alienating Mussolini, to whom France continued to look for support until the very eve of defeat. The army was riddled with conspirators—May makes no mention of the Cagoule, the shadowy officers' plot scotched by Interior Minister Marx Dormoy (for which he was later murdered by the Vichy Milice). Anti-foreign and anti-Communist legislation was in place by September 1939, long before Pétain came to office.

Above all, the French lacked confidence. For twenty years they had been reminded by politicians and generals of the failure of the French population to grow, of the trauma of the Great War, of the need to avoid another conflict. When it came time in 1940 to assure the French that they were as brave, as well equipped, as strong, and as confident as their foes, these same politicians and generals sounded understandably hollow. A collective fear and self-doubt had been instilled in the nation, adding an irrational dimension to the country's all-too-real shortage of men.

May himself quotes the British ambassador in Paris in September 1938 claiming "all that is best in France is against war, *almost* at any price." When war broke out a year later, Brigadier Edward Spears, bilingual and warmly Francophile, reported home that "many French people . . . argue . . . that . . . they have perhaps been duped and are fighting for England."[12] Did everything and everyone somehow come together in the next six months? Of course not.

None of this sufficiently explains what happened when the Panzers crashed through the woods at Sedan. But without it we don't have any explanation at all. Is it necessary to abandon the constraints of the political and cultural setting in order to engage in fruitful counterfactual speculation? I don't think so. Nor do I see why good military history need ignore the political and social background in order to keep faith with the fortunes of war. As it happens, there is a classic work of military history which encompasses all these concerns, and it is highly germane to Professor May's theme.

In Michael Howard's account of the Franco-Prussian War, first published in 1961, the events of 1870–71 closely anticipate those of May 1940.[13] On both occasions the French displayed strategic confusion, planning for an offensive but waiting to be attacked; as Friedrich Engels observed in July 1870, when the war began, if the French didn't take the offensive their declaration of war made no sense. Yet in 1870 as in 1939, the generals made a pointless advance into the neighboring Saarland, then retreated and waited upon events. The tactical and administrative failings were also strikingly similar: At seventy years' distance French generals twice failed to understand railway timetables, put men and supplies in the right place, concentrate troops effectively, organize retreats, or communicate among themselves—mistakes their predecessors had already made in Emperor Napoléon III's Italian campaign of 1859. Both Michael Howard and Marc Bloch write of the "chaos" of mobilization. And in 1870 as in 1940 German officers proved more flexible, took more initiative, and adapted better to changing circumstances.

On neither occasion were the French at a significant technical disadvantage. Indeed, in 1870 they had the new *chassepot* breech-loading rifles, superior to anything the Germans could field. But French soldiers weren't trained in the use of the new weapon (one is reminded of Sartre's description of the "respectful terror" with which French reservists in 1939 handled weapons they had never even seen before being mobilized). Thousands of the guns were left forgotten in obscure and poorly sited arms dumps. The French were as deficient in intelligence gathering in 1870 as they would be in 1940, with the result that they were constantly wrong-footed by German movements. Moltke, like his successors in Hitler's general staff, believed in bypassing French defensive positions whenever possible; together with the French habit of exaggerating enemy numbers, this led the static French armies to surrender even before giving battle.

The outcome of the Franco-Prussian War, when huge French armies were surrounded and captured at Sedan and Metz, was as much a shock to the French and the rest of Europe as was the battle of 1940: "The completeness of the Prussian success in 1870 thus astounded the world," Michael Howard writes. Meanwhile the nineteenth-century generals were as determined as their successors to avoid a social revolution even at the cost of national surrender. But some of them appreciated the scale of their humiliation and tried, like General Bourbaki, to salvage their honor by taking their lives (no comparable sense of shame is recorded for the men of 1940).

Howard is cuttingly dismissive of these failed generals, writing of their "incompetence and paralysis," and he shows time and again how they might have acted differently. But throughout the narrative he restrains his speculation about what might have been to the limits of what was plausible, in view of the broader context. Thus, of the demoralizing impact on soldiers of a badly organized mobilization he writes, "They might yet, with brilliant leadership, win victories; but they were in no condition to stand up to the shock of defeat."

Howard's general conclusion (which can be applied virtually unchanged to the collapse of 1940) is tellingly different from May's: "The incompetence of the French high command explained much: but the basic reasons for the catastrophe lay deeper, as the French themselves, in their humiliation, were to discern. The collapse at Sedan, like that of the Prussians at Jena sixty-four years earlier, was the result not simply of faulty command but of a faulty military system; and the military system of a nation is not an independent section of the social system but an aspect of it in its totality. The French had good reason to look on their disasters as a judgment."

Pace Ernest May, we should do likewise.

*This essay, a review of Ernest May's new study of the fall of France in 1940,
first appeared in the* **New York Review of Books** *in February 2001.*

NOTES TO CHAPTER XI

¹ Nicole Jordan, "Strategy and Scapegoatism: Reflections on the French National Catastrophe, 1940," in *The French Defeat of 1940: Reassessments*, ed. Joel Blatt (Providence, RI: Berghahn Books, 1998), 13.

² Marc Bloch, *Étrange Défaite: Témoignage écrit en 1940* (Paris: Société des Éditions Franc-tireurs, 1946).

³ Raymond Aron later wrote that "I lived through the thirties in the despair of French decline. . . . In essence, France no longer existed. It existed only in the hatred of the French for one another." See Tony Judt, *Past Imperfect: French Intellectuals, 1944–1956* (Berkeley: University of California Press, 1992), 15.

⁴ The Belgian government, which had declared its neutrality in 1936, was always reluctant to cooperate with the French and did not allow French and British troops to enter Belgian territory until 6:30 a.m. on May 10, the day the Germans attacked.

⁵ See Nicole Jordan, "The Cut-Price War on the Peripheries: The French General Staff, the Rhineland and Czechoslovakia," in *Paths to War: New Essays on the Origins of the Second World War*, ed. Robert Boyce and Esmonde M. Robertson (New York: St. Martin's, 1989), 128–166; see also Nicole Jordan, *The Popular Front and Central Europe: The Dilemmas of French Impotence, 1918–1940* (Cambridge, New York: Cambridge University Press, 1992).

⁶ *Les Événements survenus en France de 1933 à 1945: Témoignages et documents recueillis par la Commission d'Enquête Parlementaire* (Paris: Imprimerie de l'Assemblée Nationale, n.d.), 2:548. Gamelin's testimony was given on December 23, 1947.

⁷ Donald Cameron Watt, *How War Came: The Immediate Origins of the Second World War, 1938–1939* (New York: Pantheon, 1989); Jean-Louis Crémieux-Brilhac, *Les Français de l'an 40* (Paris: Gallimard, 1990); Alistair Horne, *To Lose a Battle: France 1940* (Boston: Little, Brown, 1969).

⁸ See *Collaboration and Resistance: Images of Life in Vichy France 1940–1944* (New York: Abrams, 2000), 24; French edition published by La Documentation Française, Paris, 1988.

⁹ People do not speak much of the 1871 Paris Commune today. But for over one hundred years it was the principal historical and symbolic reference of the French and European Left and a bogeyman for conservatives everywhere. From Lenin to Weygand and on into the streets of 1968, its memory and its shadow were constantly invoked, as both a model and a warning. For the most recent account in English see Robert Tombs, *The Paris Commune, 1871* (London, New York: Longman, 1999).

¹⁰ See Pierre Birnbaum, *Un Mythe politique: "La République juive"* (Paris: Fayard, 1988).

¹¹ Arthur Koestler, *Scum of the Earth* (New York: Macmillan, 1941); Charles de Gaulle, *Mémoires de guerre*, vol. 1: *L'Appel* (Paris: Plon, 1955), p. 25.

¹² Spears is quoted by John C. Cairns in "Reflections on France, Britain and the Winter War Prodrome, 1939– 1940" in Blatt, *The French Defeat of 1940*, p. 283. Spears's memoirs cast an unflattering light on the mood of the time: Edward L. Spears, *Assignment to Catastrophe*, vol. 1, *Prelude to Dunkirk, July 1939–May 1940*; vol. 2, *The Fall of France, June 1940* (A.A. Wyn, 1954 and 1955).

¹³ Michael Howard, *The Franco-Prussian War: The German Invasion of France, 1870–1871* (London: Rupert Hart-Davis, 1961; Collier, 1969).

CHAPTER XII

À la recherche du temps perdu:
France and Its Pasts

As you drive along the magnificently engineered, impeccably landscaped *autoroutes* of France, you cannot miss the unusual information panels set off to the right at frequent intervals. Conspicuous but somehow unobtrusive, in warm earth colors, these cluster in pairs. First comes a panel of two or three symbols—sufficiently simple and pointed to arouse the interest of the speeding motorist, but not immediately self-explanatory: a bunch of grapes, perhaps, or a stylized depiction of a building or a mountain.

Then, a kilometer or so farther on, allowing just enough time for the occupants of the car to ask one another what it meant, the panel explains itself in a second panel, similarly sited, telling you that you are now passing the vineyards of Burgundy, the cathedral at Reims, or the Mont Sainte-Victoire. And there, off to right or left (the second panel has a helpful arrow suggesting where you should look), a field of grapes, a Gothic spire, or Cézanne's favorite hill emerges on cue.

These panels are not necessarily accompanied or followed by an exit road. Their purpose is not to lead you to the thing depicted, much less tell you about it. They are there to alleviate the boredom of high-speed motoring, to tell the traveler on advanced modern highways what it is that he or she is passing through unawares. And there is an obvious irony in the fact that you need to be traveling on roads that rigorously separate you from the minutiae of the landscape in order to have that landscape interpreted for you.

Moreover, these panels are intentionally and unapologetically didactic: They tell you about the French past—or about present-day activities (wine-making, for example) that provide continuity with the past—in ways that reinforce a certain understanding of the country. Ah, we say, yes: The battlefield of Verdun; the amphitheater at Nîmes; the cornfields of the Beauce. And as we reflect upon the variety and the wealth of the country, the ancient roots and modern traumas of the nation, we share with others a certain memory of France. We are being led at seventy miles an hour through the Museum of France that is France itself.

France is unique. But it is not alone. We are living through an era of commemoration. Throughout Europe and the United States, memorials, monuments, commemorative plaques, and sites are being erected to remind us of our heritage. In itself, this is not a new development: At the battle site of Thermopylae in Greece, the Leonidas Monument (erected in 1955) reproduces an ancient text exhorting passersby to remember the heroic defeat of the Spartans at the hands of Xerxes in 480 bc. The English have long celebrated and commemorated defeats (from Hastings in 1066 to Dunkirk in 1940); Rome is a living memorial site of Western civilization; and the brief story of the U.S. is recounted, incarnated, represented, and monumentalized across the land, from Colonial Williamsburg to Mount Rushmore.

In our day, however, there is something new. We commemorate many more things; we disagree over what should be commemorated, and how; and whereas until recently (in Europe at least) the point of a museum, a memorial plaque, or a monument was to remind people of what they already knew or thought they knew, today these things serve a different end. They are there to tell people about things they may not know, things they have forgotten or never learned. We live in growing fear that we shall forget the past, that it will somehow get misplaced among the bric-a-brac of the present. We commemorate a world we have lost, sometimes even before we have lost it.

In erecting formal reminders or replicas of something we ought to remember, we risk further forgetfulness: By making symbols or remnants stand for the whole, we ease ourselves into an illusion. In James Young's words, "Once we assign monumental form to memory, we have to some degree divested ourselves of the obligation to remember. . . . Under the illusion that our memorial edifices will always be there to remind us, we take leave of them and return only at our convenience." Moreover, monuments—war memorials for example—blend imperceptibly over time into the landscape: They become part of the past, rather than a reminder of it.[1]

In the United States discussion of such matters usually takes place under the sign of "memory wars." Who has the right to design an exhibition, assign meaning to a battlefield, inscribe a plinth or a plaque? These are tactical skirmishes in the greater cultural conflict over identity: national, regional, linguistic, religious, racial, ethnic, sexual. In Germany (or Poland) arguments about how to remember or commemorate the recent past have been distilled into painful, compensatory attention to the extermination of the European Jews—planned in Germany, executed in Poland. Instead of recording and giving form to pride and nostalgia, commemoration in such circumstances rouses (and is intended to rouse) pain and even anger. Once a public device for evoking and encouraging feelings of communal or national unity, public commemoration of the past has become a leading occasion for civic division, as in the dispute over whether a Holocaust memorial should be built in Berlin.

The place of the historian in all this is crucial but obscure. The contrast between memory and history should not be overstated: Historians do more than just remember on behalf of the rest of the community, but we certainly do that too. Mere remembering, in Milan Kundera's words, is, after all, just a form of forgetting, and the historian is responsible, at the very least, for correcting mis-memory.[2] In Nice today, for example, the main shopping street has been relabeled with a plaque reading "Avengueda Jouan Medecin. Consou de Nissa 1928–1965." This is a politically correct attempt, in the French context, to remind passersby that the local inhabitants once spoke an Italianate Provençal patois and to invoke on behalf of the city's distinctive identity the memory of that language. But Jean Médecin, the mayor of Nice between 1928 and 1965, had no particular interest in local dialects or customs, did not use the old Niçois form of his name or title, and was as French, and French-speaking,

as they come—as were most of his constituents in his day. This one instance can stand for many where a false past has been substituted for the
real one for very present-minded reasons; here, at least, the historian can
help set memory back on its feet.

Historians do deal in memory, then. And we have long been in the
business of criticizing and correcting official or public memory, which
has ends of its own to serve. Moreover, in the writing of contemporary
or near-contemporary history, memory is a crucial resource: not just
because it adds detail and perspective, but because what people remember and forget, and the uses to which memory is put, are the building
blocks of history too. Saul Friedländer has put memory—his own and
others'—to exemplary use in his history of Nazi Germany and the Jews;
Henry Rousso very effectively turned an account of the way in which the
French successively remembered and forgot the Vichy years into a history
of postwar France itself. Memory here is made a subject of history, while
history resumes, at least in part, an older, mnemonic role.[3]

Thus, when the French historian Pierre Nora draws a clear distinction between "memory," which "wells up from groups that it welds together," and "history," which "belongs to everyone and to no one and
therefore has a universal vocation," he seems at first to be drawing too
stark a contrast. Surely we all agree today that such tidy lines separating
subjective and objective ways of understanding the past are blurred and
arbitrary, relics of an older, innocent approach to historical study? How
is it that the director of the most important and influential modern
project for the dissection of national historical memory should choose to
begin by insisting on so rigid a distinction?[4]

To understand Nora's approach, and the cultural significance of the
huge three-part, seven-volume, 5,600-page collective work on *Les Lieux
de mémoire* that he edited over the course of the years 1984–92, we must
return to France and to its unique experience.[5] France is not only the
oldest national state in Europe, with an unbroken history of central government, language, and public administration dating back at least to the
twelfth century; it was also, of all the countries of Western Europe, the
one which had changed the least until very recently. The landscape of
France, the rural community and its way of life, the occupations and
routines of daily existence in provincial towns and villages had been less

disrupted by industry, modern communications, or social and demographic change than was the case in Britain, Germany, Belgium, Italy, or any other comparable Western state.

Similarly, the political structure of the country—its forms of national and provincial administration, relations between center and locality, the hierarchy of legal, fiscal, cultural, and pedagogic authority reaching down from Paris to the smallest hamlet—had altered remarkably little over the centuries. The political form of Old Regime France was destroyed in the Revolution, of course. But its authoritarian content and style were faithfully reproduced by the imperial and republican heirs to the Bourbon monarchy, from Robespierre and Napoléon Bonaparte to Charles de Gaulle and François Mitterrand.

The serial political upheavals of the nineteenth century left relatively little mark upon the daily experience of most Frenchmen once the disturbances had subsided. Even the postrevolutionary political divisions of the country—Right/Left, monarchist/republican, Communist/Gaullist—settled over time into the national cultural topography, sedimented layers of political habit whose very schisms formed part of the shared French experience. In Philippe Burrin's words, "France has tended to conceive of its conflicts in historical terms, and to conceive of its history in terms of conflict."[6]

In the course of the 1970s and early 1980s, this whole edifice—variously and affectionately described and recalled as *la France profonde, la douce France, la bonne vieille France, la France éternelle*—seemed, to the French, to come crashing down around their heads. The agricultural modernization of the 1950s and 1960s, the migration of the sons and daughters of peasants to the cities, had been steadily depleting and depopulating the French countryside, even as it grew vastly more productive. The towns and cities themselves, long preserved in the dowdy urban aspic of decay and underinvestment, suddenly became crowded and energetic. The revitalized national economy effected a transformation in the jobs, travel patterns, and leisure time of a new class of city-dwellers. Roads and railways that had gathered weeds and grime for decades were rebuilt, relandscaped, or replaced by a virtually new network of national communications.

Much of this began almost unnoticed in the gloomy postwar era and accelerated through the years of high prosperity and optimism of the sixties. But its effect was only really appreciated a decade later—until then it was the changes and the gains, rather than the losses, that attracted commentary, if at all. And by the time the French did collectively begin to look back in anxiety and perplexity at a rapidly disappearing past that most adults could still recall from their own childhoods, this sense of loss coincided with the precipitous collapse of that other eternal fixture of French life, the political culture inherited from 1789. Thanks to the historian François Furet and his colleagues, the Revolution was displaced from its pedestal and ceased to determine, by projection forward across the centuries, the self-understanding of the French political community. In a related development, the Communist Party ceased during the course of the 1970s to be a fixed star in the ideological firmament, its prestige collapsing along with its vote; in the parallel political universe of the intelligentsia, Marxism, too, lost its appeal.

A Socialist president was elected by popular suffrage in 1981 and proceeded in less than two years to abandon all the tenets of traditional socialism, notably the promise of a *grand soir* of onetime revolutionary transformation that had marked the Left since 1792 and that had, in part, helped to propel him into power. The Right was no longer bound together by the person and aura of Charles de Gaulle, who had died in 1970, and the fundamental measure of political conservatism in France— the propensity of conservative voters to be practicing Catholics—was undermined by the collapse of public religious observance as the churches of village and small-town France lost their parishioners in the rush to the metropolitan centers. By the early eighties the ancient foundations of French public life appeared to be crumbling away.

Finally, and belatedly, the French—at least in Pierre Nora's account— awoke to their country's shriveled international status.[7] No longer a world player, France was not even the most significant regional power, thanks to the steady rise of West Germany. Fewer and fewer people in the world were speaking French, and between the economic and cultural dominance of the United States and the recent addition of the United Kingdom to the European Community, the universal hegemony of English was on the horizon. The colonies were almost gone, and one legacy of the sixties—the renewed interest in local and regional languages and culture—

seemed to threaten the very integrity and unity of France itself. At the same time another legacy of the sixties—the demand that light be cast on murky corners of the national past—was arousing interest in the wartime Vichy regime that de Gaulle and his contemporaries had sought so assiduously to put behind them for the sake of national reconciliation.

In what seemed to fearful local observers to be a single and somehow related process, France was thus modernizing, downsizing, and splitting apart all at once. Whereas the France of, say, 1956 had been in most important respects fundamentally similar to the France of 1856—even down to a remarkable continuity of geographical patterns of political and religious allegiance—the France of 1980 did not even much resemble the country just ten years earlier. There seemed to be nothing left to hold on to—no myths, no glory, no peasants. As Pascal Ory expressed it, with plaintive irony, in his entry on "Gastronomy" in *Realms of Memory*: "Will French cuisine be all that remains when everything else has been forgotten?"[8]

Pierre Nora's ambitious project was born in this time of doubt and lost confidence. It even had a certain urgency about it—all fixed reference points were disappearing, the "ancestral stability" had gone. What had once been daily life was on its way to becoming a historical object. The centuries-old structures of French life, from field patterns to religious parades, from local memories passed on across the generations to official national history enshrined in word and stone, all were going or gone. They were not yet history, but were no longer part of a common national experience.

There was a pressing need to capture the moment, to depict a France passing uneasily from an experienced past to a historical one, to fix historically a set of national traditions that was slipping beyond the realm of lived memory. *Lieux de mémoire*, as Nora puts it in his introductory essay, "exist because there are no longer any *milieux de mémoire*, settings in which memory is a real part of everyday experience." And what are *lieux de mémoire*? "[They] are fundamentally vestiges . . . the rituals of a ritual-less society; fleeting incursions of the sacred into a disenchanted world: vestiges of parochial loyalties in a society that is busily effacing all parochialisms."[9]

Les Lieux de mémoire is a splendid enterprise, and a very French one. Between 1984 and 1992 Pierre Nora brought together nearly 120 scholars, almost all of them French (all but a few professional historians), and set them the task of capturing, in 128 entries, what it is (or was) to be France. The criteria of inclusion changed over time. The first volume to be published dealt with *La République* and was concerned with the symbolic, monumental, commemorative, and pedagogic forms of republican life in modern France, the Pantheon in Paris being a notable example. The second volume—three times the size of its predecessor—took on *La Nation* and addressed everything from geography and historiography to symbols and embodiments of glory (Verdun, the Louvre), the importance of words (the Académie Française), and the image of the State (Versailles, the National Statistics, etc.). The third volume—*Les Frances*—is larger than the first two volumes combined and contains just about everything that one could conceivably associate with France and that was not already included in volumes one and two.

By 1992, therefore, the project had broken from its moorings and acquired encyclopedic aspirations. The methodological focus of the earlier volumes was gone, too. In Nora's preface to the English-language edition, the contrast with his introduction to the first French volume, published twelve years earlier, is revealing: "A *lieu de mémoire* is any significant entity, whether material or non-material in nature, which by dint of human will or the work of time has become a symbolic element of the memorial heritage of any community (in this case, the French community)." It is hard to think of anything—any word, place, name, event, or idea—that could not qualify. As one foreign commentator observed, "By the end, the foreign reader loses the thread. Is there anything that isn't a '*lieu de mémoire*'?"[10]

PIERRE NORA HAS always insisted that he intended his project to be a sort of counter-commemorative history, deconstructing, as it were, the myths and memories it records. But as he ruefully concedes in his concluding essay in the final volume, the work has had a strange destiny: Commemoration has overtaken it, and it is now a sort of scholarly *lieu de mémoire* in its own right. There are three reasons for this. First, Nora is a very powerful figure in French intellectual life and for his magnum opus he secured the services of some of France's best scholars; their essays are small masterpieces, classic contributions to their subject. Predictably, these volumes have acquired some of the status—and disadvantages—of a work of reference.[11]

Second, the long-standing national "canon" of historical memory—what counted as part of France's heritage or *patrimoine* and why—has fallen apart. That is Nora's theme. In his words: "The dissolution of the unifying framework of the nation-state has exploded the traditional system that was its concentrated symbolic expression. There is no commemorative superego: the canon has vanished." Accordingly, where the national heritage was once carefully controlled for pedagogic and aesthetic value, today anything and everything is material for memory and commemoration.[12]

This process was noticeably accelerated in 1988 by Mitterrand's Culture Minister Jack Lang, whose politically calculated additions to the list of protected items in the *patrimoine culturel* of France (previously limited to heirlooms like the Pont du Gard or Philip the Bold's ramparts at Aigues-Mortes) included a nineteenth-century Provençal crèche and the marble countertop of the Café du Croissant at which the Socialist leader Jean Jaurès drank his last cup of coffee before his assassination in July 1914. In a nice postmodern touch the crumbling façade of the Hôtel du Nord on Paris's Quai de Jemappes was added to the national *patrimoine* in nostalgic homage to Marcel Carné's popular film of that name—even though the film itself was entirely shot in a studio.

This recovery of randomly assorted items-for-commemoration is indeed testimony to the collapse of continuity of time and memory in a hitherto centralized culture, and Nora was surely right to invoke it in explaining the origin of his *Lieux de mémoire*. But what was new in the eighties is now commonplace, and a standard trope in studies of memory and tradition in changing societies. As a paradoxical result, Nora's own heroic recovery and recording of memories and commemorations is not so much a starting point for new thinking on this subject as itself a reverentially acknowledged object for admiration: "worth a journey."

The third reason for the odd career of these volumes is that despite the many brilliant insights in Nora's own essays, the work as a whole is uncertain about itself: What began as a melancholy exercise in national self-analysis ends on a curiously conventional, almost celebratory note—"In these symbols we truly discover 'realms of memory' at their most glorious."[13] That is probably a faithful reflection of the change of mood in France in the years since Nora first conceived his work—from a sense of loss to a sensation of nostalgic pride—but it seems odd that a work of history should become quite so emotionally engaged in its subject matter. Nora has firmly insisted that he did not want these volumes to be just a "promenade touristique dans le jardin du passé"[14] but that is what they risk becoming.

Inevitably, too, there are parts of the garden that suffer unexplained neglect, even under the editor's panoptic gaze. There is no entry in any of the volumes of *Les Lieux de mémoire* on either Napoléon Bonaparte or his nephew Louis-Napoléon, or even on the political tradition of *bonapartisme* that they bequeathed to the nation. This is bizarre. As Chateaubriand remarked in *Mémoires d'outre-tombe*, apropos the anachronistic coronation of Charles X in 1824: "Henceforth the figure of the Emperor overshadows everything else. It is behind every event and every idea: the pages of this low age shrivel at the sight of his eagles."[15] Chateaubriand was no neutral observer, and we are no longer in 1824, but his point still holds—for good and ill, France is suffused with the legacy of Bonaparte. From the Invalides to the Arc de Triomphe, from the *Code civil* to France's periodic dalliances with political generals, from the disabling republican suspicion of strong executive power to the organization of departmental archival collections, the spirit of Napoléon is with us still.

Similarly, every visitor to modern Paris is a beneficiary (or victim) of the ambitions of Louis-Napoléon and his Second Empire. The Louvre today is Louis-Napoléon's Louvre, for all Mitterrand's efforts. The Parisian road and transport network grew out of imperial ambitions, thwarted or otherwise. In Louis-Napoléon's case the lack of direct interest in him and his regime shown by Nora's collection may also reflect a broader lack of concern with towns, town planning, and urbanism in general: a perhaps excessive care to record France's love affair with its peasants and its land may account for this.[16]

No study of *lieux de mémoire* for Europe as a whole could possibly neglect Napoléon Bonaparte—his battles, his laws, his depredations, his unintended impact on resentful national sensibilities in the Low

Countries, Italy, and Germany. "Boney will get you if you don't eat your food/go to sleep" was a popular threat directed to recalcitrant children in many parts of England and Spain within living memory. And his absence from Nora's collection is thus an important reminder of just how very French-centered the work is, even down to its silences.[17] More than once Nora emphasizes that France is not just utterly unique, but indescribably special. "France," we learn, has "a history more burdensome than that of any other European country."[18] Really? Germans and Russians, at least, might wish to demur; Poles too.

Only France, we are encouraged to believe, has history and memory on a scale sufficient to justify and fulfill the ambitions of *Les Lieux de mémoire*. Furthermore, for Nora, "France is . . . a 'nation of memory' in the same sense in which the Jews, long landless and stateless, have survived throughout history as a people of memory." And—just to nail the point down—only in French, apparently, can one even speak of *lieux de mémoire*: "Neither in English, nor German, nor Spanish can one find a satisfactory equivalent. Doesn't this difficulty in moving into other languages already suggest a sort of singularity?"[19] According to Marc Fumaroli in "The Genius of the French Language," this linguistic distinction has something to do with the French tradition of rhetoric, inherited directly from the Latin. The Italians presumably have it too, then; but perhaps they lack the necessary historical burdens? As the Italians say (there is no satisfactory French equivalent): *magari*.

Are these distinctively French characteristics of *Les Lieux de mémoire*—the book and the things themselves—not an insuperable impediment to translation? No: The English-language version, whose third volume was published in June (the previous two volumes appeared in 1996 and 1997), is a major publishing event in its own right. It is as copiously and beautifully illustrated as the original, and the translation, by Arthur Goldhammer, is wonderful—sensitive to the different styles of the various contributors and superbly confident and learned in its grasp of a grand variety of technical and historical terms. The books are a pleasure to read, in English as in French.*

---

*The translation under review, *Realms of Memory: The Construction of the French Past*, is a three-volume abridgment published in 1998 by Columbia University Press.

Even the title is an imaginative leap across cultures. A *lieu*, in French, commonly translates into English as a place, or site. Thus for *lieux de mémoire* one might write "memory-sites," or "places of memory" (as in "places in the heart," perhaps). But Nora clearly intended his *lieux* to indicate concepts, words, and events as well as real places, and the concreteness of English means that "place" won't do. "Site" might have served, but there are so many actual sites studied in Nora's collection that the term could seem misleadingly spatial. "Realms of memory" has the opposite problems, of course—"realm" in modern English has retained only the loftiest of the uses of its French cousin, *royaume*, and is quite abstract, thereby diluting some of the emphasis on soil and territory that is so important in French memory. But as intercultural compromises go it is elegant and suggestive.

Inevitably, there is some loss. Nora has wisely reduced the overall number of articles from 128 to 44, though he mostly kept the longer ones. Missing, unfortunately, are some of those essays that captured the original spirit of the enterprise at its best: Jean-Paul Poisson, for example, on "the office of the notary," a fixture in every small French town and part of the life cycle of anyone with any property to inherit, bequeath, or contest—which meant a large part of the population; or Jacques Revel on "the region," a crucial constituent element in the mental and moral geography of every inhabitant of France. But these, like many of the other contributions not included in the English-language edition, are of more interest to the French reader—for whom they are, precisely, a realm of memory. Perhaps for that reason the majority of the cuts are from the middle volumes on "the Nation," whose innermost memories and concerns are least accessible to outsiders.

What the English reader gets, as a result, is something far closer to the spirit of Volume III, *Les Frances*—whose structure is used to regroup the translated essays. A few of the essays on French land and topography have been retained but hardly any of the descriptions of social or educational *rites de passage*—such as receiving one's *bachot* from a lycée or being accepted into a *grande école*—or the illuminating monographic contributions on the origins of the French fascination with their own heritage. Nora's original interest in *lieux de mémoire* like the Sacré Coeur in

Montmartre or the Fourteenth of July national holiday as commemorative objects for dissection is thus diluted, and the result is a collection of very high-quality essays on mostly conventional historical subjects: political and religious divisions and traditions; significant institutions, dates, buildings, and books.

Within these limits, this new translation makes available to English-language readers some of the best French scholarship today: Jacques Revel on the Royal Court; Mona Ozouf on "Liberty, Equality, Fraternity"; Jean-Pierre Babelon on the Louvre; Alain Corbin on "Divisions of Time and Space"; Marc Fumaroli on "The Genius of the French Language"; and others besides.

Revel and Corbin, especially, bring to their subjects great scholarly authority: Respectively, the president of the École des Hautes Études en Sciences Sociales (and longtime editor of the journal *Annales*) and the holder of the premier chair of history in France, they wear their standing and their learning lightly. Alain Corbin, who has written on everything from economic backwardness in the Limousin to the history of prostitution, illustrates divisions of time and space with a remarkable superabundance of examples. Jacques Revel recites once again the national Ur-narrative of courtly life in early modern France, but he infuses it with so much allusion, subtlety, and significance that the whole familiar story reads as though told and understood for the first time.

Even those essays that don't quite come off—like that by Antoine Compagnon on *À la recherche du temps perdu*, where the author is confronted with the precociously self-referential, realm-of-memory character of Proust's own masterpiece—are still a pleasure to read and full of wit and perception. Most impressive of all, perhaps, is the way in which all the contributions manage to cast light on a compact range of themes at the core of any attempt to grasp the French past, and France itself.

The first of these is the sheer ancientness and unbroken continuity of France and the French state (eight hundred years at the most modest estimate), and the corresponding longevity of the habit of exercising authority and control from the center. This is not merely a matter of political power, the well-known propensity of French rulers of all ideological persuasions to aggregate to themselves the maximum of sovereignty and dominion. In his essay on Reims Jacques Le Goff notes that the cathedral there—the traditional site for the coronation of French kings—is a masterpiece of "classical" Gothic, before going on to comment that "in French history 'classical' often refers to the imposition of ideological and political controls."[20]

The urge to classify, to regulate everything, from trade and language to theater or food, is what links the public sphere in France with cultural and pedagogical practices. It is not by chance that the *Guide Michelin* (green) authoritatively divides all possible sites of interest into three: interesting, worth a detour, worth a journey. Nor is it an accident that the *Guide Michelin* (red) follows the same tripartite division for restaurants—both inherited the practice from "classical" French rhetoric and philosophy, which also bequeathed it to dramatic theory and political argument. As Pascal Ory notes, "codification" in France is a *lieu de mémoire* in itself.

So is religion. Christianity—Catholic Christianity—is so long-established in France that Nora himself has no qualms about treating it, along with monarchy and peasantry, as the essence of true Frenchness. All the essays on religion in *Realms of Memory* have a robust, engaged quality: Claude Langlois even outdoes Nora, claiming that "in terms of monuments, the lesson is clear: France is either Catholic or secular. There is no middle term." André Vauchez, who has a fine essay on cathedrals, would probably agree with him—he is trenchantly committed to his subject, defending against the philistinism of the times the appropriately symbolic and otherworldly character of a great cathedral. But in the context of this collection, Vauchez has it easy—as Proust pointed out: "The cathedrals are not only the finest ornaments of our art but the only ones that are still connected with the purpose for which they were constructed"—an assertion even truer today than it was when Proust made it in 1907.[21]

But France is not just Catholic or secular—it is, and has long been, Protestant and Jewish as well, just as it is now also Islamic. Jews and Protestants are well served in the essays by Pierre Birnbaum and Philippe Joutard included here, both of which are more thoughtful and less conventional than the contributions on Catholics, perhaps because they must perforce work against the historiographical and national grain.

Joutard shows the importance of memory in French Protestant life, so marked that Protestants in rural communities typically have a stronger collective memory of ancient events than do their Catholic neighbors, even when the Catholics were more active in, and were more directly affected by, the events in question. And his essay on the longevity of victim memory is an implicit reminder to the editor that too much emphasis upon the normatively Catholic character of Frenchness can result in new forms of neglect. There is no entry in these pages for the massacre of Protestants on St. Bartholomew's Day, 1572—a French "memory date" if ever there was one.

If Catholicism is at the "center" of French memory and heretics and minorities have often sat neglected at the cultural "periphery," the same Manichaean contrast has been reproduced in a rich variety of social and geographical keys. For as long as anyone can remember, France has been divided: between north and south, along the line running from Saint-Malo to Geneva that was favored in nineteenth-century economic geography as the point of separation between modern and backward France; between speakers of French and speakers of a disfavored regional patois; between Court and country, Right and Left, young and old (it is not without significance that the average age of the members of the Legislative Assembly of the French Revolution in 1792 was just twenty-six years), but above all between Paris and the provinces.

The "provinces" are not the same thing as the countryside—*campagne* in France has had positive connotations for centuries, whereas ever since the emergence of a court, "provincial" has been a term of round abuse. In the subliminal iconography of France, the countryside is peopled by solid peasants, rooted in the soil for generation upon generation. Even today, Armand Frémont, the author of an essay, "The Land," in *Realms of Memory*, cannot resist a distinctively French response to his theme: "The land was domesticated without violence to nature's rhythms, without the large-scale transformation of the landscape sometimes seen in other countries"; the French landscape shows "unparalleled harmony," etc. The sense of loss today, as rural France vanishes from sight, is palpable.[22]

No one, however, regrets "the provinces." The typical "provincial" came from a small town and was conventionally depicted harboring the forlorn hope of "making it" in Paris—unless he stayed at home under the bovine illusion that life in his constricted little world was somehow real and sufficient. From Molière to Barrès, this is the staple tragicomic premise of French letters. It reflects, of course, a widespread prejudice shared by provincials and Parisians alike: that everything of consequence happens in Paris (which is why 92 percent of Parisian students under the "bourgeois" monarchy from 1830 to 1848 were drawn from the provinces). The capital thus was able to drain from the rest of the (provincial) nation virtually all life and energy. Much of French history, from the political economy of Louis XIV's Versailles through the atavistic ideological appeal of Marshal Pétain's anti-Parisian rural idyll to the residential preferences of French professors can more readily be understood once this fundamental polarity is grasped.

The pejorative connotation of "provincial" stands in marked contrast to the traditional French affection not just for peasants and the land, but also for the idea of France, as mapped on the territory itself. Here, of course, "traditional" should be understood as something quite recent—it was in the nineteenth century, specifically in the early years of the Third Republic, from 1880 to 1900, that the map of France was imprinted so successfully upon the collective soul of the nation. Great pedagogic works of history and geography (Ernest Lavisse's *Histoire de France* and Paul Vidal de La Blache's *Tableau de la géographie de France*, both discussed in *Realms of Memory*) provided generations of French teachers with the tools with which to hone the civic sensibility of the nation's children.[23]

The *Tour de la France par deux enfants* (first published in 1877 and required reading for every schoolchild for decades to come) and the bicycle *Tour de France* (inaugurated in 1903, the year Vidal de La Blache's *Tableau* first appeared) followed fairly closely the route traditionally taken around France by the artisan journeymen (*compagnons*) on their own *tour de France* in times past. Thanks to this contiguity of time and place—real and constructed—the French by 1914 had a unique, unmatched feel for the memory of their country, its frontiers, its variety, and its topography, as prescribed in the official cartography of the national past and present. It is the passing of this "feel," and the reality it reflected, however tendentiously, that Nora is recording and mourning in these pages.

The pedagogical efforts of the early Third Republic—proclaimed in

1870 after Napoléon III was captured by the Prussians—were under-standably more appreciated in the disfavored provinces than in the na-tion's capital. In a 1978 survey the five most popular street names in France were République, Victor Hugo, Léon Gambetta, Jean Jaurès, and Louis Pasteur: two Third Republican politicians, the pre-eminent "re-publican" scientist, the French poet whose funeral in 1885 was a high point of Republican public commemoration, and the Republic itself. But these street names show up much more frequently in provincial com-munities than in Paris, where on the contrary there is a marked bias to-ward names that are nonpolitical or from the *ancien régime*. The civic conformity of the moderate late-nineteenth-century Republic echoed and comforted the mood of small-town life.

After 1918, when the time came to commemorate the enormous French losses in World War I, the republican cult of the war dead, what Antoine Prost calls the civil religion of interwar France, was again more marked in the provinces, and not just because it was in the villages and hamlets that the human losses had been greatest. The Third Republic, and everything it stood for, mattered more in the towns and villages of France's regions and departments than it did in urbane, cosmopolitan Paris: The loss of that heritage is thus felt more deeply there.[24]

The experience and the memory of war in our century is an important clue to France's fractured heritage, and perhaps deserves more attention than it receives in *Realms of Memory*. In the words of René Rémond: "From 1914 to 1962, for nearly half a century, war was never absent from French memory, from national consciousness and identity."[25] The First World War I may have been morally untroubling, but it left scars too deep to touch for a long time: In addition to the five million men killed or wounded, there were hundreds of thousands of war widows and their children, not to speak of the shattered landscape of northeastern France. For many decades World War I lay, as it were, in purgatory—remembered but hardly celebrated. Only very recently have the battlefields of the Western Front become sites of more confident commemoration—as you enter the Department of the Somme, official roadside signs welcome you to the region, reminding you that its tragic history (and its cemeteries) are a part of the local heritage and merit a visit: something that would have been unthinkable not long ago.[26]

But World War II, not to speak of France's "dirty wars" in Indochina and Algeria, carries more mixed and ambivalent messages and memories. If Vichy is now a *lieu de mémoire* for scholars and polemicists, for most French men and women it has yet to emerge fully from the coffin of oblivion into which it was cast in 1945: "four years to be stricken from our history," in the words of Daniel Mornet, the prosecutor at the trial of Marshal Pétain. The twentieth-century past, in short, cannot easily substitute for the older, longer history whose passing is recorded and celebrated in Nora's collection.

It is not just that the recent past is too close to us. The problem is that although the land, the peasants, even the Church (though not the monarchy) survived well beyond 1918 and even 1940, something else did not. In the first half of the Third Republic, from 1871 until World War I, there was no difficulty in absorbing the trophies of an ancient royal past into the confident republican present. But there is nothing very glorious or confident about French history since 1918, despite de Gaulle's heroic efforts; just stoic suffering, decline, uncertainty, defeat, shame, and doubt, followed in very short order, as we have seen, by unprecedented changes. These changes could not undo the recent memories; but they did—and here Nora is surely right—appear to erase the older heritage, leaving only troubling recollections and present confusion.

This is not the first time France has had occasion to look back on a hectic sequence of turbulence and doubt—the men who constructed the Third Republic after 1871 had to forge a civic consensus and a national community in the aftermath of three revolutions, two monarchies, an empire, a short-lived republic, a civil war, and a major military defeat all in the span of one short lifetime. They succeeded because they had a story to tell about France that could bind the past and future into a single narrative, and they taught that story with firm conviction to three generations of future citizens.

Their successors cannot do this—witness the sorry case of François Mitterrand, president of France throughout the 1980s and for half of the 1990s. No French ruler since Louis XIV has ever taken such care and trouble to commemorate his country's glory and make it his own; his reign was marked by a steady accumulation of monuments, new museums, memorials, solemn inaugurations, burials and reburials, not to speak of gargantuan lapidary efforts to secure his own place in future national memory, from the Arch at La Défense in western Paris to the Very Large Library on the south bank of the Seine. But what, aside from his Florentine ability to survive in power for so long, was Mitterrand best known for, on the eve of his death? His inability fully and accurately to recall and acknowledge his own role as a minor player at Vichy—an uncannily precise individual reflection of the nation's own memory hole.

The French, like their late president, don't know what to make of their recent history. In this, to repeat, they are not so very different from their neighbors to the east and elsewhere. But in France these things used to seem so simple, and it is the contrast that causes the level of unease audible in Nora's great work. It also, I think, explains his juxtaposition of history and memory that I noted earlier. Memory and history used to move in unison—historical interpretations of the French past, however critical, dealt in the same currency as public memory. That, of course, was because public memory in its turn was shaped by official accounts of the national experience that derived their meaning from a remarkably consensual historiography. And by official I mean above all pedagogical—the French were taught their memory—a theme brought out in Nora's collection by the essays on French history as taught in nineteenth-century schoolbooks.

Now, in Nora's view, history and memory have lost touch, with the nation and with each other. Is he right? When we travel the French *autoroutes* and read those didactic placards, what is actually happening? There would not be much point in telling us that we are looking at Reims Cathedral, approaching the battlefield of Verdun, or driving near the village of Domrémy, for example, unless we already knew why these places were of interest; for this, after all, the panels do not say. Their transparency depends on knowledge that the passerby has already acquired—in school. We don't need to be told what these places "mean"; they take their meaning from a familiar narrative which they confirm by their presence. And therefore the narrative has to come first, or else they have no meaning.

Lieux de mémoire—"realms of memory"—cannot, in short, be separated from history. There is no *autoroute* information panel telling you when you are passing "Vichy" (as distinct from a signpost indicating the exit for the town). This is not because "Vichy" is divisive (Jeanne d'Arc, born at Domrémy, is, after all, a highly contentious symbol, currently the darling of Jean-Marie Le Pen's National Front), but because the French have no narrative to which they can attach "Vichy" that would give to it an agreed, communicable meaning. Without such a narrative, without a history, "Vichy" has no place in French memory.

In the end, then, it doesn't really matter that "old" France has gone forever, or that, in Armand Frémont's phrase, the state is "reprinting the poem of French rural society" in "eco-museums" and rural theme parks, though much is thereby lost. This isn't even new—there has always been forgetting and remembering, the inventing and abandoning of traditions, at least since the Romantic years of the early nineteenth century.[27] The problem with living in an era of commemoration is not that the forms of public memory thus proposed are fake, or kitsch, or selective and even parodic. As a deliberate attempt to both recall and outdo the Valois monarchs, Louis XIV's Versailles was all of these things and an anticipatory pastiche of every *lieu de mémoire* that has succeeded it to this day. That is just how heritage and commemoration are.

What is new, at least in the modern era, is the neglect of history. Every memorial, every museum, every shorthand commemorative allusion to something from the past that should arouse in us the appropriate sentiments of respect, or regret, or sadness, or pride, is parasitic upon the presumption of historical knowledge: not shared memory, but a shared memory of history as we learned it. France, like other modern nations, is living off the pedagogical capital invested in its citizens in earlier decades. As Jacques and Mona Ozouf gloomily conclude in their essay on Augustine Fouillée's educational classic *Le Tour de la France par deux enfants*: "*Le Tour de la France* stands as witness to that moment in French history when everything was invested in the schools. We have completely lost our faith in the realm of pedagogy, which is why Mme Fouillée's sharply etched portrait seems to us so blurred."[28]

For the moment, at least, Pierre Nora's themes are still material for a study of *lieux de mémoire*. But to judge from the virtual disappearance of narrative history from the curriculum in school systems, including the American, the time may soon come when, for many citizens, large parts of their common past will constitute something more akin to *lieux d'oubli*, realms of forgetting—or, rather, realms of ignorance, since there will have been little to forget. Teaching children, as we now do, to be critical of received versions of the past serves little purpose once there no longer *is* a received version.[29] Pierre Nora is right, after all—history does belong to everyone and to no one, hence its claim to universal authority. Like any such claim, this will always be contested. But without it, we are in trouble.

The selection of essays from Pierre Nora's Les Lieux de mémoire, *translated by Arthur Goldhammer and published in 1998 by Columbia University Press, was reviewed by me in the* New York Review of Books *in December of that year. Since then, the University of Chicago Press has published a different selection of essays from the same French work under the title* Rethinking France, *making available in English some of the essays not included in the Columbia collection. However, the Goldhammer translations are distinctly superior.*

NOTES TO CHAPTER XII

[1] James E. Young, *The Texture of Memory: Holocaust Memorials and Meaning* (New Haven, CT: Yale University Press, 1993), 5. See also Daniel Sherman, "Art, Commerce and the Production of Memory in France after World War I," in *Commemorations: The Politics of National Identity*, ed. John R. Gillis (Princeton, NJ: Princeton University Press, 1994), 186–215.

[2] Milan Kundera, *Testaments Betrayed: An Essay in Nine Parts* (New York: HarperCollins, 1995), 128.

[3] Saul Friedländer, *Nazi Germany and the Jews*, vol. I, *The Years of Persecution, 1933–1939* (New York: HarperCollins, 1997); Henry Rousso, *The Vichy Syndrome: History and Memory in France Since 1944* (Cambridge, MA: Harvard University Press, 1991).

[4] Pierre Nora, "General Introduction: Between Memory and History," in *Realms of Memory* (Paris: Gallimard, 1984–1992), 1:3.

[5] *Les Lieux de mémoire. Vol. 1, La République; Vol. 2, La Nation; Vol. 3, Les Frances*, all under the direction of Pierre Nora. In addition to the translation under review here, four volumes on the themes of the state, space, cultures and traditions, and historiography will be published by the University of Chicago Press.

[6] Philippe Burrin, "Vichy," in *Realms of Memory*, 1:182.

[7] "In France . . . the intensity of the phenomenon [of commemoration—TJ] owes less to the accidents of chronology than to the richness of the French historical repertoire, to the radical nature of the revolutionary break, and to the memorial rumination to which the country has been condemned by the feeling that it is no longer a place where history on the grand scale is made." Pierre Nora, "The Era of Commemoration," in *Realms of Memory*, 3:610.

[8] Pascal Ory, "Gastronomy," in *Realms of Memory*, 2:443.

[9] Nora, "Between Memory and History," in *Realms of Memory* 3, 6–7.

[10] "En fin de parcours, le lecteur étranger perd le fil. Qu'est-ce qui n'est pas lieu de mémoire?" Pim den Boer, "Lieux de mémoire et l'identité de l'Europe," in *Lieux de mémoire et identités na-*

tionales, ed. Pim den Boer and Willem Frijhoff (Amsterdam: Amsterdam University Press, 1993), 17. See also Pierre Nora, "Preface to the English-language edition," in *Realms of Memory,* 1:xvii.

[11] Nora, as well as being a respected teacher, is editorial director at Gallimard, France's premier publishing house, and responsible for *Le Débat,* the country's most important intellectual periodical. He has drawn on the work of some close collaborators from this enterprise.

[12] Nora, "The Era of Commemoration," in *Realms of Memory,* p. 614.

[13] Nora, "Introduction" to Volume 3 of *Realms of Memory,* xii.

[14] Pierre Nora, "La notion de 'lieu de mémoire' est-elle exportable?" in *Lieux de mémoire et identités nationales,* p. 9.

[15] Chateaubriand is quoted by Jacques Le Goff in "Reims, City of Coronation," in *Realms of Memory,* 3:245.

[16] For a fine example of what can be done with the study of towns and cities as sites of memory (or forgetting), see Sophie de Schaepdrijver, "Bruxelles, 'lieu sans identité' ou le sort d'une capital incertaine, voué à l'imitation," in *Lieux de mémoire et identités nationales,* p. 90: "Le sort de Bruxelles est, je crois, exemplaire de ce qui se passe lorsqu'une ville devient lieu d'oubli, lieu d'une course à la modernité qui n'est freinée par nul instinct de conservation (car au nom de quoi conserverait-on?)." ["Brussels' fate seems to me an exemplary instance of what happens when a town becomes a site of forgetting, of a rush to modernize restrained by no instinct for conservation—for in the name of what would one conserve?"]

[17] Though some contributors, notably Pascal Ory, make a sustained effort to apply a comparative perspective. As he writes, "It makes no sense to accumulate supposed gastronomic references taken out of context from Gallic or Gallo-Roman sources unless one can show by similar methods that other peoples were somehow different." Ory, "Gastronomy," in *Realms of Memory,* 450.

[18] Nora, "Generation," in *Realms of Memory,* 1:528.

[19] Nora, "Introduction" to Volume 3 of *Realms of Memory,* xii; see also "La notion de 'lieu de mémoire' est-elle exportable?" in *Lieux de mémoire et identités nationales,* 4: "Ni l'anglais, ni l'allemand ni l'espagnol ne peuvent lui donner d'équivalent satisfaisant. Cette difficulté à passer dans d'autres langues n'indique-t-elle pas déjà une manière de spécificité?"

[20] Jacques Le Goff, "Reims, City of Coronation," in *Realms of Memory,* 211.

[21] Claude Langlois, "Catholics and Seculars," in *Realms of Memory,* 1:116; Proust is quoted by André Vauchez in "The Cathedral," *Realms of Memory,* 2:63.

[22] Armand Frémont, "The Land," in *Realms of Memory,* 2:25, 34. In 1976 Georges Duby and Armand Wallon edited a four-volume, multiauthored, uncompromisingly scholarly history of rural France, from ancient times to the present (*La Fin de la France paysanne* was the elegiac title of the final volume). It was a national best seller.

[23] "Dans ce livre, tu apprendras l'histoire de la France. Tu dois aimer la France, parce que la nature l'a faite belle, et parce que son histoire l'a faite grande." ["In this book you will learn the history of France. You must love France because nature has endowed her with beauty and history has made her great."] From the frontispiece of the 1912 edition of Ernest Lavisse's *Histoire de France (cours moyen),* reproduced in *Realms of Memory,* 2:168.

[24] Antoine Prost, "Monuments to the Dead," in *Realms of Memory,* 2:328.

[25] See René Rémond, "Mémoire des guerres," in *Lieux de mémoire et identités nationales,* 266.

[26] In the little town of Péronne, at the heart of the Somme battlefields, there is now a "Historial" devoted to the history and memory of World War I. Unlike most such museums, its installations are not merely commemorative but deliberately and self-consciously historical; they offer historians' interpretations, sometimes controversial and from a German and British perspective as well as a French one, of aspects of the war experience that were not displayed or emphasized in traditional evocations of the grandeur and misery of the war.

27 See Armand Frémont, "The Land," in *Realms of Memory*, 28. In the 1930s there was already a gnawing sense that peasant France was receding into the past—the 1929 census had revealed that, for the first time, less than half the national population lived in communities defined as "rural." Various exhibitions and fairs displayed "working models" of farms, artisanal occupations, and village communities, and much anticipatory effort was devoted to remembering and reproducing an idealized country past. See Shanny Peer, *France on Display: Peasants, Provincials, and Folklore in the 1937 Paris World's Fair* (Albany, NY: State University of New York Press, 1998), and James D. Herbert, *Paris 1937: Worlds on Exhibition* (Ithaca, NY: Cornell University Press, 1998).

28 Jacques and Mona Ozouf, "*Le Tour de la France par deux enfants*: The Little Red Book of the Republic," *Realms of Memory*, 2:148.

29 In Patrick Hutton's words: "No culture can sustain itself with autopsies of the institutional forms and modes of discourse of its discarded past." See Patrick H. Hutton, *History as an Art of Memory* (Hanover, NH: University Press of New England, 1993), xxiv.

CHAPTER XIII

The Gnome in the Garden:
Tony Blair and Britain's "Heritage"

In the spring of 2001, during a BBC radio discussion of the forth-coming British general election, a young journalist voiced her frustration. "Don't you agree," she asked her fellow panelists, "that there's no real choice? Tony Blair believes in privatization, just like Mrs. Thatcher." "Not quite," replied Charles Moore, editor of the (Conservative) *Daily Telegraph*. "Margaret Thatcher believed in privatization. Tony Blair just likes rich people." That is indeed so, and although Moore's witticism doesn't really address the question, it points, perhaps inadvertently, to something seriously amiss in England today.

Two weeks after that exchange Blair and his New Labour Party duly won the British general election, overwhelming the hapless William Hague and his moribund Conservatives by a sweeping majority. He could hardly acknowledge it, but this famous victory, like much else in Blair's glittering political career, was only possible thanks to a threefold inheritance from Mrs. (now Lady) Thatcher. First, she "normalized" the radical dismantling of the public sector in industry and services and its replacement with the "privatized" Britain whose praises Blair enthusiastically sings. Second, and in the process, she destroyed the old Labour Party and facilitated the task of those who fought to reform it: Blair had merely to reap the reward of their work. Third, her asperity and her intolerance of dissent and disagreement have fractured her own party and rendered it unelectable. The British never much cared for the woman or her policies, but they conceded a grudging admiration for her style and they tolerated her excesses and eccentricities. Her successors, John Major and William Hague, have enjoyed no such latitude.

Even so, New Labour's performance was far from glorious. For the first time in modern British history, abstainers (41 percent of the electorate) vastly outnumbered those who voted for the winning party (25 percent). There were some good reasons to vote Labour: Blair's government has introduced a minimum wage, addressed the disgracefully high level of child poverty in Britain, taken a firm and honorable stance over Kosovo, and urged the cancellation or reduction of third-world debt. There were also credible grounds for voting against: the scandal of the Millennium Dome, political cronyism, overcozy relations with Labour Party donors, mismanagement of the foot-and-mouth disease crisis, and the embarrassing condition of public education, the National Health Service, and the railways.

But many people didn't vote at all. There are various possible explanations for this. Characteristically, Blairites sought the most "spinnable": According to Baroness Jay, Labour leader in the House of Lords, people stayed away from the polls because they were "contented" with their prosperous lot (an imprudent echo of Conservative Prime Minister Harold Macmillan's 1959 claim that the British people had "never had it so good"). Even if true this adds scant luster to Blair's achievement. He inherited a stable economy and a benevolent international economic environment; the best that can be said of his first government is that it did not squander its advantages. Meanwhile, within twenty-four hours of their victory, some Labour members of Parliament were proposing a solution to electoral apathy: Voting, they suggested, should be made obligatory.

That hint of sanctimonious compulsion—Nanny knows best—is something many people find distasteful in Blairite triumphalism. But it isn't the real problem. What seems to grate most is the ersatz quality of Tony Blair and his politics. He doesn't exactly believe in privatization (but nor is he against it . . .), he just likes rich people. He talks the talk of devolution, but as prime minister he is notoriously obsessed with control. He is a populist who shuns direct contact with the voters (witness his palpable distaste and embarrassment when confronted with unscripted questions or disapproval during carefully orchestrated walkabouts). In one preelection speech he urged Labour activists to "work not for ourselves" but "for what we can do for our country" (even his friends had the grace to find this a little much). He conveys an air of deep belief, but no one knows in quite what.[1] He is not so much sincere as Sincere.

There is nothing contrived about Tony Blair's inauthenticity. He came by it honestly, as it were. Old Labour stood for the working class, trade unions, state ownership, and the nostalgic little-England socialism of William Morris and the Webbs. Its last leader, Michael Foot, led it to electoral catastrophe in 1983 with a political program so fatuously anachronistic that one of Labour's own spokesmen famously called it "the longest suicide note in history." Blair has always seen it as his first task to put all that far behind him. *His* Labour is resolutely "New." There is frequent mention of gender but none of class.[2] Blair has experimented with various catchy identification tags—"Third Way," "Cool Britannia"— whose common message is youth and novelty. It is not quite clear what they actually mean—there is much talk of the need to be "post-tribal" and inclusive. In any case, it is their appearance that counts.

In London, this seems to work. It is an international truism today that London is once again "swinging." It is prosperous, bustling, cosmopolitan: a world-class financial and cultural mecca, etc. Among young Europeans it is *the* place to be. And something odd has happened to Londoners themselves—they actually seem to believe everything they hear about their city, which may account for Labour's success there. The skeptical, mocking Cockney has been replaced by a town full of civic cheerleaders. No one seriously denies that Britain's capital city is overpriced and overcrowded, that its transport system is inadequate, its laboring classes cannot afford housing, and its Victorian-era sewage system is dangerously dilapidated. But Londoners today happily entertain a form of cognitive dissonance: Yes, it's all true, they concede—but all the same, London is "back."

There *is* a superficial patina of prosperity about contemporary London, a glitzy, high-tech energy that makes other European capitals feel a bit dowdy and middle-aged, just as Tony Blair seems fresh and forward-looking when contrasted with some of his continental counterparts. But the gloss is two centimeters deep. The contrast between private affluence and public squalor is actually greater now than at any time I can remember. As for the often repeated assertion that what has made London (and by extension Britain) great again has been the rise of private initiative and the reduction of a debilitating dependence on the state, this is just cant. Londoners today, like everyone else in Britain, may be employed in the private sector, but they are as dependent on the state as ever.

In an economy shaped by relatively low wages for all but a few, and quite high fixed costs for everyone, they rely on the government for their education, their health, their transportation, their civic facilities and amenities. Even their "private-sector" job itself is frequently underwritten by state assistance in the form of tax indulgences or direct subsidy. And in an age of job insecurity, a very large number of people have at some time or another had occasion to draw unemployment assistance. This is a truth hidden from Londoners: partly by Blairite rhetoric and partly by the ultravisible but quite unrepresentative world of the city financial institutions. But it is a lot clearer once you go north of the capital.

Of the ten administrative regions of England, only three (London, the South East, and East Anglia) reach or exceed the national average wealth per capita. All the rest are poorer, some far, far poorer. The North East of England in 2000 had a gross domestic product per head just 60 percent that of London. After Greece, Portugal, rural Spain, southern Italy, and the former Communist countries, Great Britain is the largest current beneficiary of European Union structural funds—which is a way of saying that parts of Britain are among the most deprived regions of the EU.

Britain's healthy employment figures are skewed by the disproportionate size of the capital city: Unemployment in the North of England remains much closer to the worst levels in continental Europe. For the young it is camouflaged by state-sponsored make-work and by training schemes for which Blair can take credit. But many men over forty, particularly in the former mining, steel, and textile towns of South Yorkshire and Lancashire, will never again hold a steady job. Tony Blair's Britain offers them nothing much worth voting for. In the rock-solid Labour seat of Barnsley Central, at the heart of the defunct South Yorkshire coalfield, only two out of five people bothered to cast a ballot in 2001.

But if Tony Blair and his New Labourites ring false even to their core voters, they nonetheless mirror something all too true about the country at large. Barnsley was once an important mining town. Thirty years ago the town breathed coal—literally. Today, in Barnsley's covered market, the liveliest business is being done by a stall selling nothing but local nostalgia (to Barnsley residents—there are no tourists): old photos and prints and books with titles like *Memories of Old Doncaster, The Golden Years of Barnsley*, and the like. They are almost the only reminders of a world that has just recently been lost and yet is already half-forgotten.[3]

Outside, Barnsley's town center has been eviscerated. Like almost every other town I saw on a recent visit to the region, Barnsley has had the civic heart ripped out of it and replaced by tawdry pedestrian malls encased in concrete parking garages. Midmorning on a weekday in June the streets were filled with families window-shopping and youths loitering in clumps. No one seemed to be going anywhere. "Olde-worlde" signposts direct you to the sights of Barnsley's nineteenth-century municipal heritage. There is no longer a railway station. In its place sits a charmless "Travel Interchange." The soiled, decrepit diesel units that pass through the "Interchange" are marked with the logo ARRIVA, the name of the company that was given the local train franchise against the unfulfilled promise of private investment in the region's transport services.

On June 17, 2001, a few miles away from Barnsley, the "Battle of Orgreave" was reenacted this year for television. The June 1984 confrontation at Orgreave between striking miners and police was the most violent of the many clashes that marked Margaret Thatcher's confrontation and defeat of Arthur Scargill and the National Union of Miners that year. Since then many of the miners have been unemployed—some of them took part (for cash) in the reenactment. It seems remarkable, and a little odd, that so desperate and political a struggle should already be getting the "heritage" treatment. It took three hundred years before the English got around to reenacting the Civil War Battle of Naseby a couple of hours to the south; Orgreave was rerun for television just seventeen years later.

Barnsley figured prominently in George Orwell's *Road to Wigan Pier*, where he wrote unforgettably of the tragedy of unemployment in Britain's industrial working class. In Wigan itself there is now not only a pier (Orwell famously remarked upon its absence) but also a signpost on the highway encouraging you to visit it.[4] Next to the cleaned-up Leeds-Liverpool canal there stand The Way We Were Museum and The Orwell at Wigan Pier, a generic 1980s-era pub selling burgers and chips. Orwell's "fearful northern slums" are gone—not only from the Wigan landscape but also, apparently, from local memory: *Memories of Wigan 1930–1970*, on sale at the museum, has some very pretty sepia pictures of salesgirls and shops, but of the pits and the workers whose condition drew Orwell there and gave Wigan a dubious fame, there is no mention.

The English capacity simultaneously to invoke and to deny the past—to feel genuine nostalgia for a fake heritage—is, I think, unique. It amounts, today, to a countrywide bowdlerization of memory.[5] And the remarkable alacrity with which industry, poverty, and class conflict have been officially forgotten and paved over, such that deep social difference is denied or homogenized and even the most recent and contested past is available only in nostalgic plastic reproduction, is what makes Tony Blair credible. He is the gnome in England's Garden of Forgetting. Many British voters, when polled on the subject of their prime minister, claim to find him insincere and false; he is even, for some, dishonest—saying anything his hearers demand. But they accept him nonetheless—and anyway see nothing better on offer. Even away from London there is something about Blair that rings true—he is the inauthentic leader of an inauthentic land.

If this sounds harsh, look closely at Blair himself. Off camera, caught unawares, he has a nervous, haunted air. He is, after all, a gifted and intelligent politician and he must surely have some sense of the fragility of his own and his country's condition. Whatever the rhetoric about the great prospects awaiting his new Britain, Blair knows that his fortuitous political success has only postponed the reckoning. Riding on Mrs. Thatcher's coattails, New Labour has successfully displaced the past; and England's thriving Heritage industry has duly replaced it with "the Past." The debate on the future, however, has only just begun; and in a curious English way it is being driven by the crisis on the railways.

. . .

THERE ARE ONE HUNDRED twenty steam railways and steam railway museums in Great Britain, ninety-one of them in England alone. Most of the trains don't go anywhere, and even those that do manage to inter-weave reality and fantasy with charming insouciance (in the summer you can ride Thomas the Tank Engine up the Keighley–Haworth line to visit the Brontë Parsonage in the West Riding of Yorkshire). They are patron-ized by hundreds of thousands every year. They represent the dream face of British trains, another world: lost, but authentic.

Meanwhile, the real, existing British railway system is nothing, as *Le Monde* gleefully noted recently, but a daily nightmare. Britain—and England especially—is a small, crowded country. Trains are essential and widely used. But except for the very first investors and not always for them, railways have rarely been a source of profit; with the coming of road transport—commercial and private—most of the old railway com-panies fell into debt, and in 1948 they were nationalized into British Railways (later British Rail). Much the same happened all over Europe.

But whereas state-run railways in continental Europe have since been the object of solicitous government attention and high levels of long-term public investment, in Britain nationalization was treated (by Left and Right alike) as the end of the story rather than the beginning. Long before Mrs. Thatcher, British governments and civil servants regarded trains as an annoying budgetary item to be rationalized and reduced at every opportunity. Lines were closed, investment held to a minimum, fares pushed as high as the market would bear. As a result, in its last year of existence, 1996, British Rail boasted the lowest public subsidy for a railway in Europe. In that year the French were planning for their rail-ways an investment rate of £21 per head of population; the Italians £33; the British just £9.

Even so, the then-Conservative government chose to privatize British Rail. They were encouraged by the prospect of a quick profit from the sale of public assets into private ownership; but their chief motive was Prime Minister John Major's need to be seen to be priva-tizing *something*—Mrs. Thatcher had by then sold off just about ev-erything else, and privatization was the Conservative Party's sole and only program. The integrated network was sold off in parts: train routes to train-operating companies, rolling stock to other companies, rails and stations to a new company called Railtrack.

The outcome has been a chronicle of disasters foretold. The theory was that train companies would compete over established routes, driving efficiency up and prices down. But trains are not buses.[6] A train route, like a train schedule, is a natural monopoly. Private train companies were, in practice, being granted a free run at a captive market. Meanwhile the logic of the market was applied no less wrongheadedly to maintenance. Railtrack was divested of all repair and maintenance tasks (and thousands of experienced engineers lost their jobs[7]). These were contracted out to private companies, who in turn subcontracted to unskilled casual labor for track repairs and inspection.

Everyone had an interest in cutting corners and postponing unprofitable or labor-intensive work. Railtrack spent money on spiffing up stations—which all could see—and neglected rail replacement. The company was contractually obliged to compensate train companies if track work delayed their trains, so it discouraged inspectors from making trouble or undertaking "nonessential" repairs. Train companies, in turn, rewrote their schedules to avoid being penalized for failure to conform to a timetable. Within a few years it was obvious that the free market, far from reducing inefficiencies, had made the railways worse than ever.

And more dangerous. In October 2000 a worn rail caused an express train to derail near Hatfield, north of London. Four passengers were killed. The resulting inquiry brought to light criminal negligence and mismanagement, as well as a confession from Railtrack that most of the national network was perilously close to collapse.[8] Railtrack's shares have duly slumped from near £18 to £3.50. There is thus no private capital available to make good the damage, much less invest in improvements. As a consequence the government has once again been forced to promise heavy investment in the railways, despite having in theory divested itself of just that responsibility a mere five years ago.[9] Meanwhile, with many trains still running at reduced speeds to avoid further accidents, rail travel in Britain is passing through an interminable purgatory with no discernible light at the end of the tunnel.

In opposition, Labour attacked this botched privatization. They rightly saw Major's Railway Act of 1993 as an unworkable absurdity, a form of asset-stripping, whereby the government chopped up a public service into marketable lots, sold them off for a quick profit, and refused to contemplate the human and economic costs of its handiwork. But once in office, Blair has been curiously silent. Indeed, encouraged by the Treasury (and some of the same senior civil servants who oversaw the rail privatization), he successfully pressed for a similar model to be applied in the sell-off of London's Underground system.

Britain's privatized railways are a cruel joke. Train users pay the highest fares in Europe for some of the worst (and as it turns out, most dangerous) trains in the Western world—and now, as taxpayers, they are paying out almost as large an annual subsidy as they were when the state owned the system. This might be more tolerable were it not for the widespread British awareness of developments overseas. You can now travel by train from Paris to Marseille in great comfort and just over three hours. The same distance in Britain (from London to, say, Pitlochry in Scotland) will take at least double the time and cost twice as much. There have been only four derailments on France's peerless TGVs since they entered service in 1981; there were thirty-three deaths on the railways in Britain in 1999 alone.

Railways are a public service. That is why the French invest in them so heavily (as do the Germans, Italians, and Spanish). They treat the huge subsidy given their train system as an investment in the national and local economies, the environment, health, tourism, and social mobility. To some English observers and a few French critics too, these subsidies represent unforgivably huge losses—difficult to quantify because buried in national accounts, but a significant drag on the national budget. Most French don't see it this way, however: For them railways are not a business but a service that the state provides for its citizens at collective expense. Any given train, route, or facility may not turn a profit, but the loss is offset by countervailing indirect benefits. To treat trains like a firm, best run by entrepreneurs whose shareholders expect a cash return on their investment, is to misunderstand their very nature.

On the evidence from across the Channel, the French would appear to have by far the better of the argument. Trains, moreover, are a good index to state involvement in other public services. The French and the

Germans spend almost half as much again as the British on their health services—and this despite the size of Britain's National Health Service, one of the world's largest employers. I know from my own experience and that of my family that both the Italian and Belgian health systems are also distinctly better than their British counterpart.

The response of English[10] politicians to such embarrassing continental comparisons has been to point accusingly at the high levels of taxation, state control, and public expenditure in continental Europe. Is *that* what you want, they ask? You'll pay a high economic price. Tony Blair in particular has made a fetish of Labour's "restrained" approach to public expenditure. His government actually spends about the same on public social services, as a percentage of gross domestic product, as Mrs. Thatcher's much-maligned Tory government did in 1984—a little less on education, a little more on health. Moreover, he and his supporters have consistently talked down the public sector as somehow dowdy and unexciting—when compared to the risks and benefits of private enterprise (hence his widely noted admiration for successful businessmen). That is one reason why Labour is now finding it so hard to recruit teachers, nurses, doctors, and policemen.[11]

The mood, however, is changing. For four years Tony Blair held out the promise of a Third Way, a carefully triangulated compromise between Anglo-American private economic initiative and continental-style social compassion. Today we hear little of the Third Way: Its prophet, Professor Anthony Giddens, so ubiquitous in Blair's first term, has of late been conspicuous by his silence. Since the national trauma of the railway crisis, New Labour has instead become wholeheartedly devoted to "delivering" European levels of public service . . . but apparently at American levels of personal taxation. This is not going to happen. You can do almost anything you want with the past, but the future, like economic reality, is intractable. The British are moving inexorably toward a very hard choice.

This choice is conventionally presented as being for or against joining the euro, and so in a way it is. But the real issue is not the euro but Europe—or more precisely, the European social model. The English (unlike the Scots) still don't feel very European—which is why the Conservative leader William Hague, warning that "the pound" was in danger, thought he could capitalize on English national sentiment in his 2001 election campaign. They probably never will. And a party that could demonstrate how Britain would be better off outside Europe and its currency might yet capitalize on this sentiment in a referendum on the subject. But the electorate has something quite different on its mind.

New Labourites rightly claim that Britain is a postpolitical (actually postideological) society. From this they deduce that people aren't interested in doctrinal disputes over the state and the market. They just want whatever works—hence Blair's carefully pragmatic emphasis on mixing public sector and private profit (which is why he pulls his punches even when faced with the mess on the privatized railways, a disaster he could legitimately blame on Tory incompetence and worse). But my own feeling is that England in particular is fast becoming a post-postpolitical society.

By this I mean that Thatcher and Blair have so successfully uprooted the old Left-Right, state-market distinctions that many people can no longer remember why they need feel inhibited in favoring a return to the state. Why, they ask, should we not have a transport network/health service/school system that works as well as the Swedish or French or German one? What does it have to do with the market or efficiency or freedom? Are the French less free because their trains work? Are the Germans less efficient because they can get a hospital appointment when they need it?

Gordon Brown, the Chancellor of the Exchequer (finance minister), has built his political career on the claim that he has made Labour a party of economic responsibility. But a large minority of British voters wasn't even born the last time Britain had an economically "irresponsible" Labour government. For them that's history, and voters aren't interested in history. If economic "irresponsibility" reduces grotesquely long hospital waiting lists, makes the trains run safely at affordable prices, or gets a math teacher for your child's school, what, they ask, is wrong with it?

That is Britain's real "European" question, and British politicians will not be able to dodge it indefinitely. The German and French press have recently made great play with the British mess—one German news magazine notoriously described Britain as "third world." That isn't quite fair, but it is more accurate than the British care to admit. And *pace* widespread continental opinion to the contrary, the British are not like Americans. They expect a certain level of service from the state and are willing to pay for it. That is why the Liberal Democrat Party actually improved its vote at the 2001 election by advocating increased taxation to pay for better services.[12] Sooner or later, British politicians are going to have to provide satisfactory public services to a community that so depends upon them— or else explain just why they cannot or will not do so.

If Blair has been able to postpone such uncomfortable thoughts it is perhaps because, despite what everyone says, the English at least have changed less than they think. Their public amenities are often squalid and inadequate; their chosen prime minister is an object of widespread skepticism and mistrust; their rail network has fallen prey to an absurd scheme, cynically executed; their hospital doctors rain devastating criticism upon an understaffed, underfinanced health service; by their own admission the English think most other people are better off than themselves.[13]

In almost any other country this level of public dissatisfaction would be politically lethal. In England it has so far produced nothing worse than electoral apathy.[14] A few months ago, listening to exhausted commuters on a filthy, stalled train regale one another contentedly for nearly two hours with tales of woe and frustration at the hands of doctors, civil servants, and politicians, I concluded that the English are not just a bit different. They are truly unusual. Maybe Baroness Jay was right after all. The English are actually contented with their deteriorating lot. They are the only people who can experience schadenfreude at their own misfortunes.

This essay, written in 2001 in the immediate wake of Tony Blair's second general election victory, first appeared in the New York Review of Books *in July 2001. Since then, Blair's trajectory, culminating in his shared responsibility for the invasion of Iraq in 2003 and his embarrassingly protracted "cérémonie des adieux," has given me no cause to revise my low estimate of the man and his "legacy."*

NOTES TO CHAPTER XIII

[1] He is apparently a convinced Christian, but as beliefs go this cuts little ice in contemporary Britain.

[2] Except when it can be exploited for demagogic ends. When in the year 2000 Magdalen College, Oxford, didn't offer a place to a young woman from a state school who has since been admitted to Harvard, the government and Britain's tabloid press vigorously outbid one another in accusing Oxbridge of "elitism." Britain's two leading universities duly groveled and promised to do better in the future.

[3] Many British towns are "twinned" with continental counterparts—an excuse for town managers and local politicians to get free holidays at municipal expense. The only lasting echo of Barnsley's earnest proletarian past is a rusting sign on the main road into town: "Barnsley: twinned with Gorlavka, Ukraine."

[4] "Alas! Wigan Pier has been demolished and even the spot where it used to stand is no longer certain." George Orwell, *The Road to Wigan Pier* (London: Penguin, 1989; first published in 1937) 68. Much the same might be said of England today. . . .

[5] It is not just the North that has been given the Heritage treatment. In the West Midland Potteries district today you can learn a lot about how Josiah Wedgwood fashioned his wares; but you will look in vain for evidence of how the pottery workers lived or why it was called the Black Country (Orwell describes even the snow as turning black from the belching smoke of a hundred chimneys).

[6] Not that the "market" works for buses, either. In London and other big cities, privatized buses duplicate one another along the main roads, competing for the easy business. But no one wants the unprofitable rural routes, many of which have been canceled. This prefigures the likely future of the British postal services too, another state sector about to be opened up to the forces of competition, efficiency, and profit.

[7] One of the ways in which the privatized railway companies planned to make money was by cutting labor costs. By 1997 there were just 92,000 men and women employed on the railways, against 159,000 in 1992. Predictably, a disproportionate number of those redundancies fell on engineers and maintenance workers.

[8] For an incisive account of the Hatfield disaster and its implications, see Ian Jack, *The Crash that Stopped Britain* (London: Granta, 2001). In this excellent book Jack shows how both the Conservative and Labour governments and the private companies involved failed in their duties, while virtually all in charge emerged without being held responsible. Some went on to bigger and better-paid jobs.

[9] In June 2000 Blair's transport minister announced with great fanfare a ten-year program of new investment in transport to the value of £60 billion. This promise has a true Blairite ring to it: In the fine print it is explained that £34 billion is expected from private investment, and £10 billion represents prior commitments brought forward. That leaves just £16 billion over ten years—not much of an improvement upon the low levels of public investment that brought the crisis about in the first place.

[10] Scottish politics are different. From Edinburgh the continent feels quite close, and most Scots have no desire to see their public sector reduced.

[11] The public sector has suffered in other ways, too. The BBC, in a thankless effort to compete with the lowest common denominator of commercial and satellite television, has abandoned its commitment to enlighten and inform (another elitist legacy vigorously condemned by its political masters). Today it carries a distinctively English mix of gardening, cooking, quiz shows, home improvement, and low-end comedy, interspersed with nostalgic recollections from its better days. At its worst, it reminds one of nothing so much as Italy's RAI-Uno, minus the good looks.

[12] The Liberal Democrats increased their representation to fifty-two seats, with nearly 19 percent of the vote, their best performance since the 1920s. As always, their strongest support came from the professional and middle-class voters of the "Celtic fringe": Scotland, the Welsh borders, and the English South West. But they have also begun to win votes in "middle

England," at the expense of Tories and Labour alike. Their recent leaders (Paddy Ashdown and now the young Charles Kennedy) are more appealing than anyone in the two big parties, and their refreshing willingness actually to *promise* tax increases as the price of an improved public sector has been taken as a sign of honesty and credibility. They ought to be the biggest beneficiary of the much-heralded breakdown of old class-based voting habits. But their problem is that many people won't vote for them because they don't believe the Lib-Dems will ever win enough seats to form a government: a self-fulfilling prophecy. In the constituency-based, single-round, first-past-the-post, winner-takes-all British system the two big parties will always do better and will silently conspire to ensure that third parties are kept well out of the picture.

[13] During a year spent in the prosperous south of England, I lost count of the number of times young people in particular, on learning that I was from New York, would ask, "But why have you come back *here*?"

[14] There is no hint of a populist backlash at either extreme. True, at Oldham—a former mill town in Lancashire where race riots broke out shortly before the elections—the British National Party won 11,643 votes in two local seats, about 14 percent of the vote. Fascists have always been able to get some votes in places with a large ethnic presence. Oldham has many Asians brought there to work in the (now defunct) textile industry. In 1997 the same party won 7 percent of the vote in an East London district with a large Bengali population (which replaced the Jews who once lived there). But the neo-Fascist vote in Britain is negligible compared to that of Marseille or Antwerp. Even the Tories' desperate ploy of promising to lock away all asylum-seekers in detention centers won them no additional popular support.

CHAPTER XIV

The Stateless State:
Why Belgium Matters

Belgium gets a bad press. A small country—the size of Wales, with a population of just ten million—it rarely attracts foreign notice; when it does, the sentiment it arouses is usually scorn, sometimes distaste. Charles Baudelaire, who lived there briefly in the 1860s, devoted considerable splenetic attention to the country. His ruminations on Belgium and its people occupy 152 pages of the *Oeuvres Complètes*; Belgium, he concluded, is what France might have become had it been left in the hands of the bourgeoisie.[1] Karl Marx, writing in a different key, dismissed Belgium as a paradise for capitalists. Many other exiles and émigrés have passed through the country; few have had much good to say of it.

I am neither an exile nor an émigré, but I too had the occasion recently to spend an extended period in Belgium. Unlike most temporary visitors to the country, however, I was not in Brussels, but in a small Flemish village not far from Bruges; and in contrast to most of Belgium's transitory foreign residents today, I could claim at least a slender bond to the place since my father was born there, in Antwerp. Daily life in rural Flanders is uneventful, to say the least; it is only with time that you become aware of the uneasy, troubled soul of this little corner of the European Union. Belgium has much to commend it beyond the self-deprecatingly touted virtues of beer and waffles; but its salient quality today may be the illustration that this small country can furnish of the perils now facing states everywhere.

You do not have to be there for very long to be reminded that during the past decade Belgium has been a cornucopia of scandals. The latest of these, mass poisoning of the local food chain through the leakage of dioxin (a highly toxic substance) into chicken feed and pig swill, briefly emptied the village supermarkets last June—though English-speaking visitors were firmly assured that the health risks were negligible compared to those associated with British beef or genetically engineered American corn. But before dioxin Belgium had had other scandals: money laundering, graft and kickbacks in high places, political assassinations, kidnapping, pedophilia, child murder, police incompetence, and wholesale administrative corruption.

All of this has happened in a tiny, prosperous region of northwest Europe whose national capital is also the headquarters of "Europe" (whose bureaucracies are largely segregated from Belgium in an unsightly glass and concrete ghetto). But half the population of the country—the Dutch-speaking Flemings—have divided and federalized it to the point of near extinction, while the other half, the French-speaking Walloons, have no distinctive identity; not surprisingly, there have been suggestions that Belgium might do better just to melt away. Would it matter? Who would care?[2]

Whether Belgium needs to exist is a vexed question, but its existence is more than a historical accident. The country was born in 1831 with the support of the Great Powers of the time—France, Prussia, and Britain, among others—none of whom wished to see it fall under the others' sway. The territory it occupies had been (and would remain) the cockpit of European history. Caesar's Gallia Belgica lay athwart the line that would separate Gallo-Roman territories from the Franks. When Charlemagne's empire fell apart in the ninth century, the strategically located "Middle Kingdom"—between the lands that would later become France and Germany—emerged as a coveted territorial objective for the next millennium. The Valois kings, Bourbons, Habsburgs (Spanish and Austrian), Napoléon, Dutch, Prussian Germans, and, most recently, Hitler have all invaded Belgium and claimed parts of it for themselves, occupying and ruling it in some cases for centuries at a time. There are probably more battlefields, battle sites, and reminders of ancient and modern wars in Belgium than in any comparably sized territory in the world.

Belgians, then, could be forgiven for a degree of uncertainty about their national identity. The state that came into being at the London Conference of January 1831 was removed from the control of the Dutch, furnished with a newly minted king from Germany, a constitution modeled on the French one of 1791, and a new name. Although the term "Belgium" had older roots (the twelfth-century chronicler Jean de Guise attributed it to a legendary monarch, "Belgus," of Trojan provenance), most of the inhabitants of the region identified only with their local community. Indeed, urban or communal loyalty lay at the core of whatever was distinctive about the place. From the thirteenth century onward, Flemish towns had come together to fight off the fiscal and territorial claims of lords, kings, and emperors. Even today Belgium is the only country in Europe where identification with the immediate locality trumps regional or national affiliation in the popular imagination.

The new Belgian state rested on a highly restricted suffrage that confined power and influence to the French-speaking commercial and industrial bourgeoisie; in practice it was held together not by any common feeling of Belgianness but by hierarchically organized social groups— "pillars" (*piliers* in French, *zuilen* in Dutch)—that substituted for the nation-state. Catholics and anticlericals in particular formed distinct and antagonistic communities, represented by Catholic and liberal political parties. These parties, in turn, served not just to win elections and control the state but to mobilize and channel the energies and resources of their "pillar." In each case an electoral constituency doubled as a closed social, economic, and cultural community.

With the emergence in the 1880s of a Socialist party that sought to control the growing industrial working class, the "pillarization" of Belgium into liberal, Catholic, and Socialist "families" was complete. From the late nineteenth century until the present, Belgian public and private life has been organized around these three distinct families— with antagonism between Socialists and Catholics steadily displacing in significance the older one between Catholics and liberals. Much of daily life was arranged within hermetically separated and all-embracing nations-within-a-nation, including child care, schooling, youth groups, cafés, trade unions, holiday camps, women's groups, consumer cooperatives, insurance, savings societies, banking, and newspapers.

At election time, especially following the expansion of the suffrage (extended to all men in 1919, to women in 1948), governments could only be formed by painfully drawn-out coalition building among the parties representing these pillars. Such coalitions were typically unstable (there were eighteen governments between the world wars and there have been thirty-seven since 1945). Meanwhile, political, judicial, civil service, police, and even military appointments are made by "proportionality," which is to say that they are assigned to clients and friends within the pillars through a complex and corrupting system of agreements and deals.

Some of this story is, of course, familiar from other countries. The "culture wars" of Imperial Germany and the parliamentary instability of Fourth Republic France come to mind, as does the *proporz* system of public appointments in Austria today and the clientele-driven venality of postwar Italy (two countries likewise born in uncomfortable and contested circumstances). But Belgium has two distinguishing features. First, the pervasive system of patronage, which begins in village councils and reaches to the apex of the state, has reduced political parties largely to vehicles for the distribution of personal favors. In a small country where everyone knows someone in a position to do something for them, the notion of an autonomous, dispassionate, neutral state barely exists. As Belgium's current prime minister, Guy Verhofstadt, said in the mid-eighties, Belgium is little more than a party kleptocracy.

Second: Below, above, within, and across the social organizations and political divisions of Belgian society runs the yawning fault line of language. In the northern half of the country (Flanders, Antwerp, Limburg, and much of Brabant, the region around Brussels), Dutch is spoken; in the southern half ("Wallonia," which stretches from Hainault in the west to Luxembourg in the east), French. Living in the village of Zedelgem, close to the much-traveled tourist sites of Bruges and Ghent and just twenty minutes from the frontier with French-speaking Hainault, I encountered many Dutch speakers who cannot (or will not) speak French;

a much larger proportion of the French-speaking population of the country has no knowledge of Dutch. Brussels, officially "bilingual," is in practice a French-speaking enclave within the Dutch-speaking sector. Today these divisions are immutable, and they correspond quite closely to an ancient line dividing communities that fell respectively under French or Dutch rule.[3]

Their origins, however, are fairly recent. French, the court language of the Habsburg monarchy, became the language of the administrative and cultural elite of Flanders and Wallonia during Austrian rule in the eighteenth century. This process was reinforced by the French revolutionary occupants and their Napoleonic heirs. Meanwhile, the peasants of Flanders continued to speak (though less frequently read or write) a range of local Flemish dialects. Despite a shared language base, Flemings and Dutch were divided by religion; the Flemish Catholics' suspicion of the Protestant ambitions of the Dutch monarchy contributed to their initial welcome for an independent Belgian state. Domination by French speakers was reinforced by early-nineteenth-century industrialization; impoverished Flemish peasants flocked to Wallonia, the heartland of Belgium's wealth in coal, steel, and textiles. It is not by chance that many French-speaking Walloons today have Flemish names.

The Belgian state was Francophone, but French was not imposed—the 1831 constitution (Article 23) stated, in effect, that Belgian citizens could use the language of their choice. French was required only for government business and the law. But when a movement for Flemish-language rights and a distinctive Flemish identity began to assert itself in the mid-nineteenth century (beginning with the 1847 Declaration of Basic Principles of the Flemish movement), it had little difficulty demonstrating that in practice Dutch speakers, or the speakers of regional Flemish dialects, were at an acute disadvantage in their new state. They could not be tried in their own language; secondary and higher education was de facto a Francophone near-monopoly; and French-speaking interests looked after themselves at the expense of their Flemish co-citizens. When American grain imports began to undercut and destroy the home market for Flemish farmers, the Brussels government refused to establish protective tariffs for fear of retribution against (Walloon) industrial exports.

The conflation of linguistic rights and regional interests was thus present from the outset in Flemish resentment of "French" domination. Once a suffrage reform in 1893 gave the vote to a growing body of Dutch-speaking citizens from the north, most of whom were solidly organized within the Catholic social and political "pillar," the state was forced to compromise with their demands. By 1913 Dutch was officially approved for use in Flemish schools, courts, and local government. In 1932 a crucial step was taken, when Dutch became not just permitted but required in Flemish schools. The union of language and region—the creation of two administratively distinct unilingual territories conjoined only by the overlap in Brussels—was now inevitable.

This process, implicit in the language legislation between the two world wars, was delayed by World War II. As in World War I, radical Flemish activists tried to take advantage of the German occupation of Belgium to advance the separatist cause. On both occasions, German defeat set them back. After World War II in particular, the memory of the wartime collaboration of the ultra-separatist Vlaams Nationaal Verbond (VNV) discredited the Flemish case for a generation. At the same time, the postwar punishment of (disproportionately Flemish) collaborators rankled, as did the abdication of King Leopold III in 1950. The king's ambivalent behavior during the war had discredited him with many Belgians, but a referendum in March 1950 produced a national vote of 58 percent in favor of keeping him (among Dutch-speaking voters, 72 percent voted for the king). However, demonstrations in Wallonia and Brussels, where a majority wanted to see Leopold go, forced him to step aside in favor of his son Baudouin, leaving many Flemings resentful of the way the vote, and their preference, had been overturned.[4]

What finally doomed the unity of Belgium, however, was the reversal of economic fortunes. Where once French-speaking Wallonia had dominated, it was now in precipitous decline. During the fifties two hundred thousand jobs were lost as the mines of the Sambre-Meuse region closed. Coal mining, steel making, slate and metallurgical industries, textile production—the traditional core of Belgian industrial power—virtually disappeared; Belgian coal production today is less than two million tons per year, down from twenty-one million tons in 1961. Only the residue of what was once the continent's most profitable industrial conurbation remains, in the decrepit mills of the Meuse valleys above Liège and the gaunt, silent mining installations around Mons.

The country that built the first railway in continental Europe (from Brussels to Malines), and that still has the densest rail network in the developed world, now has little to show for it but an unemployment rate, in Wallonia, among the highest in Western Europe. In Charleroi and the neglected industrial villages to its west, middle-aged men gather listlessly in dingy, decaying cafés; they and their families owe their subsistence to Belgium's generous and vigorously defended welfare system, but they are doomed to a superannuated existence of extended, involuntary retirement and they know it.

Flanders, meanwhile, has boomed. Unencumbered by old industry or an unemployable workforce, towns like Antwerp and Ghent have flourished with the growth of service technology and commerce, aided by their location at the heart of Europe's "golden banana," running from Milan to the North Sea. In 1947 over 20 percent of the Flemish workforce was still in agriculture; today fewer than 3 percent of Dutch-speaking Belgians derive their income from the land. There are more Dutch speakers than French speakers in the country (by a proportion of three to two), and they produce and earn more per capita. This process, whereby the Belgian north has overtaken the south as the privileged, dominant region, has been gathering speed since the late fifties—accompanied by a crescendo of demands from the Flemish for political gains to match their newfound economic dominance.

These demands have been met. Through seven revisions of the constitution in just thirty years, the Belgian unitary state has been picked apart and reconstructed as a federal system. The results are complex in the extreme. There are three "Regions": Flanders, Wallonia, and "Brussels-Capital," each with its own elected parliament (in addition to the national parliament). Then there are three "Communities": the Dutch-speaking, the French-speaking, and the German-speaking (representing the approximately 65,000 German speakers who live in eastern Wallonia near the German border). These, too, have their own parliaments. The regions and the linguistic communities don't exactly correspond—there are German speakers in Wallonia and some French-speaking towns (or parts of towns) within Flanders. Special privileges, concessions, and protections have been established for all of these, a continuing source of resentment on all sides. Two of the regions, Flanders and Wallonia, are effectively unilingual, with the exceptions noted. In officially bilingual Brussels, 85 percent of the population speaks French.

There are, in addition, ten provinces (five each in Flanders and Wallonia), and these, too, have administrative and governing functions. But real authority lies either with the region (in matters of urbanism, environment, the economy, public works, transport, and external commerce) or with the linguistic community (education, language, culture, and some social services). The national state retains responsibility for defense, foreign affairs, social security, income tax, and the (huge) public debt; it also administers the criminal courts. But the Flemish are demanding that powers over taxation, social security, and justice shift to the regions. If these are granted, the unitary state will effectively have ceased to exist.

The politics of this constitutional revolution are convoluted and occasionally ugly. On the Flemish side, extreme nationalist and separatist parties have emerged. The Vlaams Blok (now Vlaams Belang), spiritual heir to the VNV, is now the leading party in Antwerp and some Dutch-speaking suburbs north of Brussels. The traditional Dutch-speaking parties have consequently been forced (or tempted) to take more sectarian positions. Similarly, in Wallonia and Brussels, politicians from the French-speaking mainstream parties have adopted a harder "community" line to accommodate Walloons who resent Flemish domination of the political agenda.

As a result, all the mainstream parties have split along linguistic and community lines: The Christian Democrats (since 1968), the Liberals (since 1972), and the Socialists (since 1978) all exist in duplicate, with a Flemish and a Francophone party of each type; the Christian Democrats dominate Flemish politics, the Socialists remain all-powerful in Wallonia, and the Liberals are prominent in Brussels. The result is further deepening of the rift between the communities, as politicians and electors now address only their own "kind."[5]

One of the crucial moments in the "language war" came in the sixties, when Dutch-speaking students at the University of Leuven (Louvain) objected to the presence of French-speaking professors and classes at a university situated within Dutch-speaking Vlaams-Brabant. Marching to the slogan of "Walen buiten!" ("Walloons get out!"), they succeeded in breaking apart the university, whose Francophone members headed south into French-speaking Brabant-Wallon and established the University of Louvain-la-Neuve. In due course the university library, too, was divided and its holdings redistributed, to mutual disadvantage.

These events, which occurred between 1966 and 1968 and brought down a government, are still remembered among French speakers—just as many Flemings continue to meet annually on August 29 in Diksmuide, in West Flanders, to commemorate Flemish soldiers killed in World War I under the command of French-speaking officers whose orders they could not understand. The memorial tower erected there in 1920 carries the inscription "Alles voor Vlaanderen—Vlaanderen voor Kristus" ("All for Flanders—Flanders for Christ"). On the Belgian national holiday—July 21, which commemorates Leopold of Saxe-Coburg's ascent to the throne in 1831 as Leopold I of Belgium—flags are still hung out in Wallonia, but I did not see many in the tidy little villages of Flanders. Conversely, the Flemish authorities in 1973 decreed that they would recognize the date of July 11 in celebration of the victory of the Flemish towns over the French king Philippe le Bel at the Battle of the Golden Spurs (Kortrijk) in 1302.

The outcome of all this is absurdly cumbersome. Linguistic correctness (and the constitution) now require, for example, that all national governments, whatever their political color, be "balanced" between Dutch- and French-speaking ministers, with the prime minister the only one who has to be bilingual (and who is therefore typically a Fleming). Linguistic equality on the Cour d'Arbitrage (Constitutional Court) is similarly mandated, with the presidency alternating annually across the language barrier. In Brussels, the four members of the executive of the capital region sit together (and speak in the language of their choice) to decide matters of common concern; but for Flemish or Francophone "community" affairs they sit separately, two by two. Whenever money in Brussels is spent on "community" affairs—schools, for example—it must always be apportioned exactly 80:20, in accordance with the officially fixed ratio of the respective language groups. Even the automatic information boards on interregional trains switch to and fro between Dutch and French (or to both, in the case of Brussels) as they cross the regional frontiers.

As a consequence, Belgium is no longer one, or even two, states but an uneven quilt of overlapping and duplicating authorities. To form a government is difficult: It requires multiparty deals within and across regions; "symmetry" between national, regional, community, provincial, and local party coalitions; a working majority in both major language groups; and linguistic parity at every political and administrative level. And when a government is formed, it has little initiative: Even foreign policy—in theory the responsibility of the national government—is effectively in the hands of the regions, since for Belgium it mostly means foreign trade agreements, and these are a regional prerogative.

JUST WHAT REMAINS of Belgium in all this is unclear. Entering the country by road, you could be forgiven for overlooking the rather apologetic signpost inscribed with a diminutive "België" or "Belgique." But you will not miss the colorful placard informing you of the province (Liège, say, or West-Vlaanderen) that you have just entered, much less the information board (in Dutch or French, but not both) indicating that you are in Flanders or Wallonia. It is as though the conventional arrangements had been inverted: The country's international borders are a mere formality, its internal frontiers imposing and very real.

The price that has been paid to mollify the linguistic and regional separatists and federalists is high. In the first place, there is an economic cost; it is not by chance that Belgium has the highest ratio of public debt to gross domestic product in Western Europe. It is expensive to duplicate every service, every loan, every grant, every sign. The habit of using public money (including EU regional grants, a rich source of provincial and local favors) on a proportional basis to reward clients of the various pillars has now been adapted to the politics of the language community: Ministers, state secretaries, their staffs, their budgets, and their friends are universal, but only in Belgium do they come attached to a linguistic doppelgänger. The latest government, top-heavy with carefully balanced representation of every possible political and regional interest, is no exception, illustrating, as one political commentator put it, the "surrealist inflation of portfolios and subdivision of responsibilities."[6]

But the cost of Belgium's peculiar politics goes beyond the charge on the Belgian franc (a lingering token of nationality, foredoomed by the coming of the euro). Belgian insouciance in the face of urban planning—the gross neglect that has allowed Brussels to become a metaphor for all that can go wrong in a modern city—is not new. Baudelaire in 1865 was already commenting upon the "tristesse d'une ville sans fleuve" as the burghers of Brussels buried the local stream under tarmac and cobblestones. But the disastrous "urban renewal" of the 1960s, and the soulless monumentalism of the "Europe" district of Brussels today, bear witness to a combination of unrestrained private development and delinquent central authority that is distinctively federal in nature—there is simply no one in charge, even in the capital.

The Dioxin Affair in the summer of 1999 ("Chickengate" to the delighted editorialists of *Le Monde*) illustrated the same problem. The troubling feature of the scandal was not just that one or more suppliers of animal feed had ignored the usual sanitary precautions and leaked a lethal substance into the food chain. It was also that the government had known about it for weeks before telling either the European Union or its own public; and when the news did come out, the government in Brussels had no idea what to do about it or how to prevent a similar occurrence in the future. The main concern of the Belgian government was how to appease and recompense infuriated farmers for the animals that had to be destroyed and the sales that were lost: Many Flemish farmers belong to the Boerenbond, a powerful organization of Flemish agribusiness, which is part of the Catholic "pillar" of Flemish politics, and was thus a power base of the Christian Democratic prime minister, Jean-Luc Dehaene.

In the absence of government oversight, the striking incidence of high-level corruption and graft is no surprise (Baudelaire again: "La Belgique est sans vie, mais non sans corruption"). Belgium has become sadly notorious as a playground for sophisticated white-collar criminals, in and out of government. At the end of the 1980s, the Belgian government contracted to purchase forty-six military helicopters from the Italian firm Agusta and to give the French company Dassault the job of refitting its F-16 aircraft; competing bidders for the contracts were frozen out. It later emerged that the Parti Socialiste (in government at the time) had done very nicely from kickbacks on both deals. One leading Socialist politician who knew too much, André Cools, was killed in a parking lot in Liège in 1991; another, Étienne Mange, was arrested in 1995; and a third, Willy Claes, a former prime minister of Belgium, sometime (1994–95) secretary general of NATO and foreign minister when the deals were made, was found guilty in September 1998 of taking bribes. A former army general closely involved in the affair, Jacques Lefebvre, died in mysterious circumstances in March 1995.

The Dassault/Agusta affair was especially significant, not just for the links between government, politics, business, and graft, but because of the apparent involvement of organized crime—something already evident in a number of murders and kidnappings through the eighties and early nineties. These were followed by a series of highly publicized crimes against children, culminating in the truly awful affair of Marc Dutroux. In prison today on charges of murder, Dutroux was at the center of an international pedophilic network running what used to be called the "white slave trade," procuring boys and girls alike for the pleasure of powerful patrons in Belgium and abroad. He and his accomplices, all based in the depressed industrial towns of southern Wallonia, were responsible between 1993 and 1996 for the kidnapping, rape, or murder of six girls, two of them starved to death in a cellar under Dutroux's house. What stirred the public to anger was not only the crimes but the astonishing incompetence of the police charged with finding the criminals—and a widespread belief that some of those responsible for finding and prosecuting them had been part of a (homosexual) ring which continued to benefit from very highly placed protection.

Belgium's police forces are characteristically many and divided. There are dozens of "communal" police forces, responsible only for their immediate vicinity. Then there is the Police Judiciaire—nationwide in theory, in practice divided by and run from local *arrondissements*. Finally there is the Gendarmerie, the only truly national police force but just eighteen thousand strong.[7] These separate police forces do not cooperate—they don't even share information. And in the

Dutroux affair they were competitive—each trying to keep a step ahead of the other in the hunt for the abductors of the girls.

As a result, they actually impeded each other's inquiries. In addition, they were inept. When Dutroux, a convicted rapist on parole, was questioned by police at his home, the house (where the children were hidden and still alive) was never searched. Later, in April 1998, when Dutroux was already under arrest, he managed to escape from the gendarmes guarding him. That he was recaptured later the same day has done little to reassure many Belgians, now convinced that Dutroux, who has yet to be tried, is being protected by friends in high places. The investigation of his crimes was hampered most recently by the unexplained suicide, in July 1999, of Hubert Massa, the Liège public prosecutor responsible for preparing the case (he also led the investigation into the Cools murder case).[8]

The horror of the Dutroux affair triggered a deep anger and frustration in the Belgian public; in October 1996 three hundred thousand people marched through Brussels to protest crime, corruption, incompetence, the heartless and ineffective response of the authorities, and the sacking of an overzealous magistrate thought to be too "sympathetic" to the victims. Since then parliamentary inquiries and administrative reforms have followed one another, to no obvious effect. But the embarrassing dioxin scandal of this past summer may have had more lasting consequences. In the elections of June 13 this year the Belgian voters finally threw Dehaene's Christian Democrats out of office for the first time in forty years. The Socialists lost votes everywhere and the Liberals (loosely comparable to Germany's Free Democrats in their business-friendly politics) came into government under Guy Verhofstadt—young (forty-six) by local standards and the first Liberal prime minister since 1884.

Moreover, the Greens (known in Wallonia as Ecolo and in Flanders as Agalev) have entered government for the first time, together with the Volksunie, a Flemish populist party founded in 1954 but somewhat moderated in tone since then. This breakthrough of such small, non-"pillar" parties, ending the throttlehold on government of the three established groupings, may be a passing reaction to the scandals, a protest vote and nothing more. The same elections also saw an increase in the vote for the Vlaams Blok in Flanders and Brussels; in the Antwerp districts, where it topped the poll, its rhetoric and even its posters eerily echo Jörg Haider in Austria, Christoph Blocher in Switzerland, and Jean-Marie Le Pen in France. Like them, the Vlaams Blok uses nationalist rhetoric as a smokescreen for anti-immigrant and racist demagogy, and its growing support does not necessarily correspond to much real interest in its separatist program. But beyond the protests and the frustration, something else is happening.

Belgium today is held together by little more than the king, the currency, the public debt—and a gnawing collective sense that things cannot continue as they have. Of course, the desire for a political house-cleaning, Italian-style, is quite compatible with demands for even more federalization—as radical Flemish politicians have not failed to point out, both the Agusta and the Dutroux scandals originated in Wallonia. But this argument no longer carries as much weight as it did—and risks the charge of cynical opportunism. The generation of the sixties, now in power, continues to play the federalist and communalist cards; but recent polls suggest that most people, even in Flanders, no longer put regional or language issues at the head of their concerns.

This is especially true of new Belgians: The children of immigrants from Italy, Yugoslavia, Turkey, Morocco, or Algeria have more pressing concerns. Even those who identify strongly with Flanders (or Wallonia) don't see a need to abolish Belgium, much less conjoin their fate to another country, or to "Europe." Language politics, then, may have blown themselves out in Belgium—though there is a risk that those who have built political careers on them may be slow to appreciate the change.

For similar reasons, the old "pillars" are in decline. Younger Belgians see the world rather differently. They are not much moved by appeals to sectoral interest—the same prosperity that has underwritten the "Flemish miracle" has defanged the politics of linguistic resentment. What is more, Belgians no longer align themselves with a single party or community in every facet of their lives. Declining religious practice, the accessibility of higher education, and the move from countryside to town have weakened Catholic and Socialist parties alike. In their place has come the rise of single-issue, "à la carte" voting. This is a desirable development—without the "pillars" Belgian politics and public life may well become more transparent, less cozy and corruption-prone. In short, they will cease to be distinctively Belgian. But what, then, will keep the country together?

One answer is prosperity. The obvious difference between Belgium and other, less fortunate parts of Europe, where politicians exploit communal sensibilities and corruption flourishes, is that Belgium is rich. Brussels may be an unappealing, seamy city, and unemployment may be high in Wallonia, but life for most people in Belgium is tranquil and materially sufficient. The country is at peace—if not with itself then at least with everyone else. If Belgium disappeared, many Belgians might not even notice. Some observers even hold the country up as a postnational model for the twenty-first century: a virtually stateless society, with a self-governing, bilingual capital city whose multinational workforce services a host of transnational agencies and companies.

Even the transportation system has a curiously decentered, self-deprecating quality. A major junction in the trans-European network, Brussels has three railway stations; but none of them is a terminus—trains to Brussels go to and through all three stations. The "Central Station" is, symptomatically, the least of them—obscure, featureless, and buried underground beneath a heap of concrete. As with its stations, so with the city itself: Brussels has successfully effaced itself. Whatever "there" was once there has been steadily dismantled. The outcome is an unaspiring anonymity, a sort of underachieving cultural incognito of which Sarajevo and Jerusalem can only dream.

But the scandals and their shadow won't go away, with their dead politicians, dead prosecutors, dead children, escaped criminals, incompetent and corrupt police forces, and widespread sense of neglect and abandonment. Last summer it seemed to many that the Belgian state could no longer perform its primary mission: the protection of the individual citizen. Swayed by political and economic forces beyond its control, caught between federalist decentralization and uncoordinated, incompetent government agencies without resources or respect, Belgium is the first advanced country truly at the mercy of globalization in all its forms. It is beginning to dawn on more than a few Belgians that in progressively dismantling and disabling the unitary state in order to buy off its internal critics, they may have made a Faustian bargain.

As we enter the twenty-first century, and an uncertain era in which employment, security, and the civic and cultural core of nations will all be exposed to unprecedented and unregulated pressures beyond local control, the advantage will surely lie with countries whose governments can offer some guarantees of protection and a sense of cohesion and common purpose compatible with the preservation of civil and political liberties. So Belgium does matter, and not just to Belgians. Far from being a model, it may be a warning: We all know, at the end of the twentieth century, that you can have too much state. But Belgium may be a useful reminder that you can also have too little.

This essay on the state of Belgium first appeared in the New York Review of Books *in December 1999. It prompted a number of exchanges on the subject of Belgian history, the Flemish language, and other matters: See in particular the* New York Review of Books *vol. 48, no. viii, May 2001.*

NOTES TO CHAPTER XIV

[1] See Charles Baudelaire, *Oeuvres Complètes* (Paris: Gallimard, Bibliothèque de la Pléiade, 1961), 1317–1469.

[2] It is not clear where Belgium would go. In our day neither the Dutch nor the French have shown any interest in acquiring it; anyway, few Flemings or Walloons feel much affinity with their fellow Dutch or French speakers across the border. For Walloons in particular the problem of just who they are is a recurrent theme in their literature; on this and much else about the dilemmas of being Belgian, see Luc Sante's fine book *The Factory of Facts* (New York: Pantheon, 1998).

[3] See Astrid von Busekist, *La Belgique: Politique des langues et construction de l'État* (Brussels: Duculot, 1998).

[4] On postwar retribution and its aftermath, see Luc Huyse and Steven Dhondt, *La Répression des collaborations 1942–1952: Un passé toujours présent* (Brussels: Crisp, 1991). Just this year, Herman Suykerbuyk, a prominent member of the (Flemish) Christian Democratic party, has been pressing for a law to indemnify the victims of "repression"—i.e., Flemish nationalists condemned after the war for collaboration with the Nazis.

[5] The main newspapers, *Le Soir* and *De Standaard,* have almost no readers outside the French- and Dutch-speaking communities respectively. As a result, neither takes much trouble to report news from the other half of the country (and when the Flemish press recently reported rumors of a royal "love child" born to King Albert of a foreign mistress, Francophone commentary treated these as politically motivated slurs upon the sole surviving symbol of Belgian unity). When someone speaks Dutch on Walloon television (and vice versa) subtitles are provided. It is only partly a jest to say that English is now the common language of Belgium.

[6] Jean-Pierre Stroobants, in *Le Soir,* July 13, 1999.

[7] It was the Gendarmerie who were responsible for the disaster at Brussels's Heysel stadium on May 29, 1985, when forty soccer spectators died in a riot that the police did not anticipate and proved unable to control.

[8] On the Dutroux affair, see Yves Cartuyvels et al., *L'Affaire Dutroux: La Belgique malade de son système* (Brussels: Editions Complexe, 1997), and Dirk Schümer, *Die Kinderfänger: Ein belgisches Drama von europäischer Dimension* (Berlin: Siedler, 1997). Dutroux is not the first notorious criminal to escape with ease from Belgian captivity: In 1979 Zelko Raznatovic, serving time for armed robbery, escaped from Verviers prison and was never recaptured. He is now better known as Arkan, leader of the paramilitary Serb terrorists in Bosnia and colleague of Slobodan Milošević.

CHAPTER XV

Romania between History and Europe

The February 2000 issue of the Bucharest men's magazine *Plai cu Boi* features one Princess Brianna Caradja. Variously clad in leather or nothing much at all, she is spread across the center pages in a cluster of soft-focus poses, abusing subservient half-naked (male) serfs. The smock-clad underlings chop wood, haul sleighs, and strain against a rusting steam tractor, chained to their tasks, while Princess Brianna (the real thing, apparently) leans lasciviously into her furs, whip in hand, glaring contemptuously at men and camera alike, in a rural setting reminiscent of Woody Allen's *Love and Death*.

An acquired taste, perhaps. But then Mircea Dinescu, editor of *Plai cu Boi* and a well-known writer and critic, is no Hugh Hefner. His centerfold spread has a knowing, sardonic undertone: It plays mockingly off Romanian nationalism's obsession with peasants, land, and foreign exploitation. Princess Brianna is a fantastical, camp evocation of aristocratic hauteur and indulgence, *Venus in Furs* for a nation that has suffered serial historical humiliation. The ironic juxtaposition of pleasure, cruelty, and a rusting tractor adds a distinctive local flourish. You wouldn't find this on a newsstand elsewhere in Europe. Not in Prague, much less Vienna. You wouldn't even find it in Warsaw. Romania is different.[1]

In December 2000, Romanians went to the polls. In a nightmare of post-Communist political meltdown, they faced a choice for president between Ion Iliescu, a former Communist apparatchik, and Corneliu Vadim Tudor, a fanatical nationalist. All the other candidates had been eliminated in a preliminary round of voting. The parties of the center, who had governed in uneasy coalition since 1996, had collapsed in a welter of incompetence, corruption, and recrimination (their leader, the former university rector Emil Constantinescu, did not even bother to stand for a second presidential term). Romanians elected Iliescu by a margin of two to one; that is, one in three of those who voted preferred Tudor. Tudor's platform combines irredentist nostalgia with attacks on the Hungarian minority—some two million people out of a population of twenty-two million—and openly espouses anti-Semitism. The magazines that support him carry cartoons with slanderous and scatological depictions of Hungarians, Jews, and Gypsies. They would be banned in some Western democracies.[2]

Both Tudor and Iliescu have deep roots in pre-1989 Romanian politics. Tudor was Nicolae Ceauşescu's best-known literary sycophant, writing odes to his leader's glory before making the easy switch from national Communism to ultranationalism and founding his Greater Romania Party in 1991 with émigré cash. Ion Iliescu is one of a number of senior Communists who turned against Ceauşescu and manipulated a suspiciously stage-managed revolution to their own advantage. President of Romania between 1990 and 1996 before winning again in 2000, he is popular throughout the countryside—especially in the region of Moldavia, where his picture is everywhere. Even urban liberals voted for him, holding their noses (and with Tudor as the alternative). There are men like these in every Eastern European country, but only in Romania have they done so well. Why?

By every measure, Romania is almost at the bottom of the European heap (above only Moldova, Belarus, and Ukraine). The Romanian economy, defined by per capita gross domestic product, ranked eighty-seventh in the world in 1998, below Namibia and just above Paraguay (Hungary ranked fifty-eighth). Life expectancy is lower in Romania than anywhere else in Central or Southeastern Europe: For men it is just sixty-six years, less than it was in 1989 and ten years short of the EU average. It is estimated that two out of five Romanians live on less than $30 per month (contrast, e.g., Peru, where the minimum monthly wage today is $40). By all conventional measures, Romania is now best compared to regions of the former Soviet Union (except the Baltics, which are well ahead) and has even been overtaken by Bulgaria. According to *The Economist*'s survey for the year 2000, the "quality of life" in Romania ranks somewhere between Libya and Lebanon. The European Union has tacitly acknowledged as much: The Foreign Affairs Committee of the European Parliament lists Romania as last among the EU-candidate countries, and slipping fast.[3]

It wasn't always thus. It is not just that Romania once had a flourishing oil industry and a rich and diverse agriculture. It was a country with cosmopolitan aspirations. Even today the visitor to Bucharest can catch glimpses of a better past. Between the 1870s and World War I the city more than doubled in size, and some of the great boulevards laid down then and between the wars, notably the Calea Victoria at its very center, once stood comparison with the French originals on which they were modeled. Bucharest's much-advertised claim to be "the Paris of the East" was not wholly spurious. Romania's capital had oil-fired streetlamps before Vienna and got its first electric street lighting in 1882, well before many Western European cities. In the capital and in certain provincial towns—Iasi, Timisoara—the dilapidated charm of older residences and the public parks has survived the depredations of Communism, albeit barely.[4]

One could speak in a comparable vein of Prague or Budapest. But the Czech Republic and Hungary, like Poland, Slovenia, and the Baltic lands, are recovering unexpectedly well from a century of war, occupation, and dictatorship. Why is Romania different? One's first thought is that it isn't different; it is the same—only much worse. Every post-Communist society saw deep divisions and resentments; only in Romania did this lead to serious violence. First in the uprising against Ceauşescu, in which hundreds died; then in interethnic street fighting in Târgu-Mures in March 1990, where eight people were killed and some three hundred wounded in orchestrated attacks on the local Hungarian minority. Later, in Bucharest in June 1990, miners from the Jiu Valley pits were bused in by President Ion Iliescu (the same) to beat up student protesters: There were twenty-one deaths and 650 people were injured.

In every post-Communist society some of the old *nomenklatura* maneuvered themselves back into positions of influence. In Romania they made the transition much more fluently than elsewhere. As a former Central Committee secretary, Iliescu oversaw the removal of the Ceauşescus (whose trial and execution on Christmas Day 1989 were not shown on television until three months later); he formed a "National Salvation Front" that took power under his own direction; he recycled himself as a "good" Communist (to contrast with the "bad" Ceauşescu); and he encouraged collective inattention to recent history. By comparison with Poland, Hungary, or Russia, there has been little public investigation of the Communist past: For many years, efforts to set up a Romanian "Gauck Commission" (modeled on the German examination of the Stasi archives) to look into the activities of the Securitate ran up against interference and opposition from the highest levels of government.

Transforming a dysfunctional state-run economy into something resembling normal human exchange has proven complicated everywhere. In Romania it was made harder. Whereas other late-era Communist rulers tried to buy off their subjects with consumer goods obtained through foreign loans, under Ceauşescu the "shock therapy" advocated after 1989 in Poland and elsewhere had already been applied for a decade, for perverse ends. Romanians were so poor they had no belts left to tighten; and they could hardly be tempted by the reward of long-term improvement. Instead, like Albania and Russia, post-Communist Romania fell prey to instant market gratification in the form of pyramid schemes, promising huge short-term gains without risk. At its peak one such operation, the "Caritas" scam which ran from April 1992 to August 1994, had perhaps four million participants—nearly one in five of the population. Like "legitimate" privatization, these pyramid schemes mostly functioned to channel private cash into mafias based in old party networks and the former security services.

Communism was an ecological disaster everywhere, but in Romania its mess has proven harder to clean up. In the industrial towns of Transylvania—in places like Hunedoara or Baia Mare, where a recent leak from the Aural gold mine into the Tisza River poisoned part of the mid-Danubian ecosystem—you can taste the poison in the air you breathe, as I found on a recent visit there. The environmental catastrophe is probably comparable in degree to parts of eastern Germany or northern Bohemia, but in Romania its *extent* is greater: Whole tracts of the country are infested with bloated, rusting steel mills, abandoned petrochemical refineries, and decaying cement works. Privatization of uneconomic state enterprises is made much harder in Romania in part because the old Communist rulers have succeeded in selling the best businesses to themselves, but also because the cost of cleaning up polluted water and contaminated soil is prohibitive and off-putting to the few foreign companies who express an initial interest.

The end of Communism has brought with it nearly everywhere a beginning of memory. In most places this started with the compensatory glorification of a pre-Communist age but gave way in time to more thoughtful discussion of politically sensitive topics from the national past, subjects on which Communists were typically as silent as nationalists. Of these the most painful has been the experience of World War II and local collaboration with the Germans—notably in their project to exterminate the Jews. Open debate on such matters has come furthest in Poland; in Romania it has hardly begun.

Romania was formally neutral in the early stages of World War II; but under the military dictator Marshal Ion Antonescu the country aligned itself with Hitler in November 1940 and joined enthusiastically in the Nazi invasion of the Soviet Union, contributing and losing more troops than any of Germany's other European allies. In May 1946, with Romania firmly under Soviet tutelage, Antonescu was tried and executed as a war criminal. He has now been resurrected in some circles in post-Communist Romania as a national hero: Statues have been erected and memorial plaques inaugurated in his honor. Many people feel uneasy about this, but few pay much attention to what would, almost anywhere else, be Antonescu's most embarrassing claim to fame: His contribution to the Final Solution of the Jewish Question.[5]

The conventional Romanian position has long been that, whatever his other sins, Antonescu saved Romania's Jews. And it is true that of the 441,000 Jews listed in the April 1942 census, the overwhelming majority survived, thanks to Antonescu's belated realization that Hitler would lose the war and his consequent rescinding of plans to deport them to extermination camps. But that does not include the hundreds of thousands of Jews living in Bessarabia and Bukovina, Romanian territories humiliatingly ceded to Stalin in June 1940 and triumphantly reoccupied by Romanian (and German) troops after June 22, 1941. Here the Romanians collaborated with the Germans and outdid them in deporting, torturing, and murdering all Jews under their control. It was Romanian soldiers who burned alive nineteen thousand Jews in Odessa in October 1941; who shot a further sixteen thousand in ditches at nearby Dalnick; and who so sadistically mistreated Jews being transported east across the Dniester River that even the Germans complained.[6]

By the end of the war the Romanian state had killed or deported over half the total Jewish population under its jurisdiction. This was deliberate policy. In March 1943 Antonescu declared: "The operation should be continued. However difficult this might be under present circumstances, we have to achieve total Romanianization. We will have to complete this by the time the war ends." It was Antonescu who permitted the pogrom in Iasi (the capital of Moldavia, in the country's northeast) on June 29 and 30, 1941, where at least seven thousand Jews were murdered. It was Antonescu who ordered in July 1941 that fifty "Jewish Communists" be exterminated for every Romanian soldier killed by partisans. And it was unoccupied Romania that alone matched the Nazis step for step in the Final Solution, from legal definitions through extortion and deportation to mass extermination.[7]

If Romania has hardly begun to think about its role in the Holocaust, this is not just because the country is a few years behind the rest of Europe in confronting the past. It is also because it really is a little bit different. The project to get rid of the Jews was intimately tied to the long-standing urge to "Romanianize" the country in a way that was not true of anti-Semitism anywhere else in the region. For many Romanians the Jews were the key to the country's all-consuming identity problem, for which history and geography were equally to blame.

Peasants speaking Romanian have lived in and around the territories of present-day Romania for many centuries. But the Romanian state is comparatively new. Romanians were for many centuries ruled variously by the three great empires of Eastern Europe: the Russian, the Austro-Hungarian, and the Ottoman. The Turks exercised suzerainty over

Wallachia (where Bucharest sits) and Moldavia to its northeast. The Hungarians and latterly the Habsburgs ruled Transylvania to the northwest and acquired the neighboring Bukovina (hitherto in Moldavia) from the Turks in 1775.

The Russians for their part pressed the declining Ottoman rulers to turn over to them effective control of this strategic region. In 1812, at the Treaty of Bucharest, Tsar Alexander I compelled Sultan Mahmud II to cede Bessarabia, then part of eastern Moldavia. "Romania" at this point was not yet even a geographical expression. But in 1859, taking advantage of continuing Turkish decline and Russia's recent defeat in the Crimean War, Moldavia and Wallachia came together to form the United Principalities (renamed Romania in 1861), although it was not until 1878, following a Turkish defeat at Russian hands, that the country declared full independence, and only in 1881 was its existence recognized by the Great Powers.

From then until the Treaty of Versailles, the Romanian Old Kingdom, or *Regat*, was thus confined to Wallachia and Moldavia. But following the defeat of all three East European empires in World War I, Romania in 1920 acquired Bessarabia, Bukovina, and Transylvania, as well as part of northern Bulgaria. As a result the country grew from 138,000 square kilometers to 295,000 square kilometers, and doubled its population. The dream of Greater Romania—"from the Dniester to the Tisza" (i.e., from Russia to Hungary) in the words of its national poet Mihai Eminescu—had been fulfilled.

Romania had become one of the larger countries of the region. But the Versailles treaties, in granting the nationalists their dream, had also bequeathed them vengeful irredentist neighbors on all sides and a large minority population (grown overnight from 8 to 27 percent) of Hungarians, Germans, Ukrainians, Russians, Serbs, Greeks, Bulgarians, Gypsies, and Jews—some of whom had been torn from their homelands by frontier changes, others who had no other home to go to. Like the newly formed Yugoslavia, Romania was at least as ethnically mixed as any of the preceding empires. But Romanian nationalist leaders insisted on defining it as an ethnically homogeneous nation-state. Resident non-Romanians—two people out of seven—were "foreigners."

The result has been a characteristically Romanian obsession with identity.[8] Because so many of the minorities lived in towns and pursued commerce or the professions, nationalists associated Romanianness with the peasantry. Because there was a close relationship between language, ethnicity, and religion among each of the minorities (Yiddish-speaking Jews, Catholic and Lutheran Hungarians, Lutheran Germans, etc.), nationalists insisted upon the (Orthodox) Christian quality of true Romanianness. And because Greater Romania's most prized acquisition, Transylvania, had long been settled by Hungarians and Romanians alike, nationalists (and not only they) made great play with the ancient "Dacian" origins.[9]

Today the Jewish "question" has been largely resolved—there were about 760,000 Jews in Greater Romania in 1930; today only a few thousand are left.[10] The German minority was sold to West Germany by Ceauşescu for between 4,000 and 10,000 deutschmarks per person, depending on age and qualification; between 1967 and 1989, 200,000 ethnic Germans left Romania this way. Only the two million Hungarians (the largest official minority in Europe) and an uncounted number of Gypsies remain.[11] But the bitter legacies of "Greater Romania" between the world wars stubbornly persist.

In a recent contribution to *Le Monde*, revealingly titled "*Europe: la plus-value roumaine*," the current prime minister, Adrian Năstase, makes much of all the famous Romanians who have contributed to European and especially French culture over the years: Eugène Ionescu, Tristan Tzara, E. M. Cioran, Mircea Eliade . . . [12] But Cioran and, especially, Eliade were prominent intellectual representatives of the Romanian Far Right in the 1930s, active supporters of Corneliu Zelea Codreanu's Iron Guard. Eliade at least, in his mendaciously selective memoirs, never even hinted at any regrets. This would hardly seem a propitious moment to invoke him as part of Romania's claim to international respect.

Năstase is not defending Eliade. He is just trying, clumsily, to remind his Western readers how very European Romania really is. But it is revealing that he feels no hesitation in enlisting Eliade in his cause. Eliade, like the Jewish diarist Mihail Sebastian, was an admirer and follower of Nae Ionescu, the most influential of the many interwar thinkers who were drawn to the revivalist mysticism of Romania's Fascists.[13] It was Ionescu, in March 1935, who neatly encapsulated contemporary Romanian cul-

tural paranoia: "A nation is defined by the friend-foe equation." Another
follower was Constantin Noica, a reclusive thinker who survived in
Romania well into the Ceauşescu era and has admirers among contemporary Romania's best-known scholars and writers. Noica, too, suppressed evidence of his membership in the Iron Guard during the
thirties.[14]

This legacy of dissimulation has left many educated Romanians more
than a little unclear about the propriety of their cultural heritage: If
Eliade is a European cultural icon, what can be so wrong with his views
on the un-Christian threat to a harmonious national community? In
March 2001, I spoke about "Europe" in Iasi to a cultivated audience of
students, professors, and writers. One elderly gentleman, who asked if he
might put his question in Italian (the discussion was taking place in
English and French), wondered whether I didn't agree that the only future for Europe was for it to be confined to "persons who believe in Jesus
Christ." It is not, I think, a question one would get in most other parts
of Europe today.

The experience of Communism did not change the Romanian problem so much as it compounded it. Just as Romanian politicians and intellectuals were insecure and paranoid and resentful about their country's
place in the scheme of things—sure that the Jews or the Hungarians or
the Russians were its sworn enemies and out to destroy it—so the
Romanian Communist Party was insecure and paranoid, even by the
standards of Communist parties throughout Eastern Europe.

In this case it was the Communists themselves who were overwhelmingly Hungarian or Russian or/and Jewish.[15] It was not until 1944 that
the party got an ethnic Romanian leader, Gheorghe Gheorghiu-Dej—
and one of the compensatory strategies of the Romanian Communists
once installed in power was to wrap themselves in the mantle of nationalism. Dej began this in the late fifties by taking his distance from the
Soviets in the name of Romanian interests, and Ceauşescu, who succeeded him in 1965, merely went further still.[16]

This led to an outcome for which the West must take some responsibility. Communism in Romania, even more under Dej than Ceauşescu,
was vicious and repressive—the prisons at Pitesti and Sighet, the penal
colonies in the Danube delta, and the forced labor on the Danube–Black

Sea Canal were worse than anything seen in Poland or even Czechoslovakia, for example.[17] But far from condemning the Romanian dictators, Western governments gave them every encouragement, seeing in Bucharest's anti-Russian autocrats the germs of a new Tito.

Richard Nixon became the first U.S. president to visit a Communist state when he came to Bucharest in August 1969. Charmed by Nicolae Ceaușescu during a visit to Romania in 1978, Senator George McGovern praised him as "among the world's leading proponents of arms control"; the British government invited the Ceaușescus on a state visit in the same year; and as late as September 1983, when the awful truth about Ceaușescu's regime was already widely known, Vice President George Bush described him as "one of Europe's good Communists."[18]

National Communism ("He may be a Commie but he's our Commie") paid off for Ceaușescu, and not just because he hobnobbed with Richard Nixon and the Queen of England. Romania was the first Warsaw Pact state to enter GATT (in 1971), the World Bank, and the IMF (1972), to get European Community trading preferences (1973) and U.S. most-favored-nation status (1975). Western approval undercut Romanian domestic opposition, such as it was. No U.S. president demanded that Ceaușescu "let Romania be Romania."

Even if a Romanian Solidarity movement had arisen, it is unlikely that it would have received any Western support. Because the Romanian leader was happy to criticize the Russians and send his gymnasts to the Los Angeles Olympics, the Americans and others said nothing about his domestic crimes (at least until the rise of Mikhail Gorbachev, after which the West had no use for an anti-Soviet maverick dictator). Indeed, when in the early eighties Ceaușescu decided to pay down Romania's huge foreign debts by squeezing domestic consumption, the IMF could not praise him enough.

The Romanians, however, paid a terrible price for Ceaușescu's freedom of maneuver. To increase the population—a traditional Romanianist obsession—in 1966 he prohibited abortion for women under forty with fewer than four children (in 1986 the age barrier was raised to forty-five). In 1984 the minimum marriage age for women was reduced to fifteen. Compulsory monthly medical examinations for all women of childbearing age were introduced to prevent abortions, which were permitted, if at all, only in the presence of a party representative.[19] Doctors in districts with a declining birth rate had their salaries cut.

The population did not increase, but the death rate from abortions far exceeded that of any other European country: As the only available form of birth control, illegal abortions were widely performed, often under the most appalling and dangerous conditions. In twenty-three years the 1966 law resulted in the deaths of at least ten thousand women. The real infant mortality rate was so high that after 1985 births were not officially recorded until a child had survived to its fourth week—the apotheosis of Communist control of knowledge. By the time Ceauşescu was overthrown, the death rate of newborn babies was twenty-five per thousand and there were upward of 100,000 institutionalized children—a figure that has remained steady to the present. At the end of the twentieth century, in the eastern department of Constanta, abandoned, malnourished, diseased children absorb 25 percent of the budget.[20]

The setting for this national tragedy was an economy that was deliberately turned backward into destitution. To pay off Western creditors, Ceauşescu obliged his subjects to export every available domestically produced commodity. Romanians were forced to use 40-watt bulbs at home so that energy could be exported to Italy and Germany. Meat, sugar, flour, butter, eggs, and much more were rationed. Fixed quotas were introduced for obligatory public labor on Sundays and holidays (the corvée, as it was known in ancien régime France). Gasoline usage was cut to the minimum and a program of horse-breeding to substitute for motorized vehicles was introduced in 1986.

Traveling in Moldavia or in rural Transylvania today, fifteen years later, one sees the consequences: Horse-drawn carts are the main means of transport, and the harvest is brought in by scythe and sickle. All Socialist systems depended upon the centralized control of systemically induced shortages. In Romania an economy based on overinvestment in unwanted industrial hardware switched overnight into one based on pre-industrial agrarian subsistence. The return journey will be long.

Nicolae Ceauşescu's economic policies had a certain vicious logic—Romania, after all, did pay off its international creditors—and were not without mild local precedent from pre-Communist times. But his urbanization projects were simply criminal. The proposed "systematization" of half of Romania's 13,000 villages (disproportionately selected from minority communities) into 558 agro-towns would have destroyed what remained of the country's social fabric. His actual destruction of a section of Bucharest the size of Venice ruined the face of the city. Forty thousand buildings were razed to make space for the "House of the People" and the 5-kilometer-long, 150-meter-wide Victory of Socialism Boulevard. The former, designed as Ceauşescu's personal palace by a twenty-five-year-old architect, Anca Petrescu, is beyond kitsch. Fronted by a formless, hemicycle space that can hold half a million people, the building is so big (its reception area is the size of a soccer field), so ugly, so heavy and cruel and tasteless, that its only possible value is metaphorical.

Here at least it is of some interest, a grotesque Romanian contribution to totalitarian urbanism—a genre in which Stalin, Hitler, Mussolini, Trujillo, Kim Il Sung, and now Ceauşescu have all excelled.[21] The style is neither native nor foreign—in any case, it is all façade. Behind the gleaming white frontages of the Victory of Socialism Boulevard there is the usual dirty gray, precast concrete, just as a few hundred yards away there are the pitiful apartment blocks and potholed streets. But the façade is aggressively, humiliatingly, unrelentingly uniform, a reminder that totalitarianism is always about sameness; which is perhaps why it had a special appeal to a monomaniacal dictator in a land where sameness and "harmony"—and the contrast with "foreign" difference—were a long-standing political preoccupation.

Where, then, does Romania fit in the European scheme of things? It is not Central European in the geographical sense (Bucharest is closer to Istanbul than it is to any Central European capital). Nor is it part of Milan Kundera's "Central Europe": former Habsburg territories (Hungary, Czechoslovakia, Galicia)—a "kidnapped West"—subsumed into the Soviet imperium. The traveler in Transylvania even today can tell himself that he is in Central Europe—domestic and religious architecture, the presence of linguistic minorities, even a certain (highly relative) prosperity all evoke the region of which it was once a part. But south and east of the Carpathian Mountains it is another story. Except in former imperial cities like Timişoara, at the country's western edge, even the idea of "Central Europe" lacks appeal for Romanians.[22]

If educated Romanians from the Old Kingdom looked west, it was to France. As Rosa Waldeck observed in 1942, "The Romanian horizon had always been filled with France; there had been no place in it for anyone else, even England."[23] The Romanian language is Latinate; the administration was modeled on that of Napoléon; even the Romanian Fascists took their cue from France, with an emphasis on unsullied peasants, ethnic harmony, and an instrumentalized Christianity that echoes Charles Maurras and the Action Française.

The identification with Paris was genuine—Mihail Sebastian's horror at the news of France's defeat in 1940 was widely shared. But it was also a palpable overcompensation for Romania's situation on Europe's outer circumference, what the Romanian scholar Sorin Antohi calls "geocultural Bovaryism"—a disposition to leapfrog into some better place. The deepest Romanian fear seems to be that the country could so easily fall right off the edge into another continent altogether, if it hasn't already done so. E. M. Cioran in 1972, looking back at Romania's grim history, captured the point: "What depressed me most was a map of the Ottoman Empire. Looking at it, I understood our past and everything else."

An open letter to Ceauşescu from a group of dissident senior Communists in March 1989 reveals comparable anxieties: "Romania is and remains a European country. . . . You have begun to change the geography of the rural areas, but you cannot move Romania into Africa." In the same year the playwright Eugène Ionescu described the country of his birth as "about to leave Europe for good, which means leaving history."[24]

The Ottoman Empire is gone—it was not perhaps such a bad thing and anyway left less direct an imprint on Romania than it did elsewhere in the Balkans. But the country's future remains cloudy. About the only traditional international initiative Romania could undertake would be to seek the return of Bessarabia (since 1991 the independent state of Moldova), and today only C. V. Tudor is demanding it.[25] Otherwise politically active people in Bucharest have staked everything on the European Union. Romania first applied to join in 1995 and was rejected two years later (a humiliation which, together with a cold shoulder from NATO, probably sealed the fate of the center-right government). In December 1999 the EU at last invited Romania (along with Bulgaria, Latvia, Lithuania, Slovakia, Malta, and Turkey) to begin negotiations to join.

Along with Bulgaria, Romania finally entered the European Union on January 1, 2007. But it will prove a hard pill for Brussels to swallow. The difficulties faced by the German Federal Republic in absorbing the former GDR would be dwarfed by the cost to the EU of accommodating and modernizing a country of twenty-two million people starting from a far worse condition. Romanian membership in the EU will bring headaches. Western investors will surely continue to look to Budapest, Warsaw, or Prague. Who will pour money into Bucharest? Today, only Italy has significant trade with Romania; the Germans have much less, and the French—oh irony!—trail far behind.

Romania today, Mr. Năstase's best efforts notwithstanding, brings little to Europe. Unlike Budapest or Prague, Bucharest is not part of some once-integrated Central Europe torn asunder by history; unlike Warsaw or Ljubljana, it is not an outpost of Catholic Europe. Romania is peripheral, and the rest of Europe stands to gain little from its presence in the union. Left outside it would be an embarrassment, but hardly a threat. But for just this reason Romania is the EU's true test case.

Hitherto, membership in the EEC/EC/EU has been extended to countries already perceived as fully European. In the case of Finland or Austria, membership in the union was merely confirmation of their natural place. The same will in time be true of Hungary and Slovenia. But if the European Union wishes to go further, to help *make* "European" countries that are not—and this is implicit in its international agenda and its criteria for membership—then it must address the hard cases.

Romania is perhaps the hardest: a place that can only overcome its past by becoming "European," which of course meant joining the European Union as soon as possible. But there was never any prospect of Romania meeting EU criteria for membership in advance of joining. Thus Brussels is constrained to set aside its insistence that applicant countries conform to "European" norms before being invited into the club. In Romania's case there is no alternative. Romanian membership will cost Western Europeans a lot of money and will expose the union to all the ills of far-Eastern Europe. In short, it will have been an act of apparent collective altruism, or at least unusually enlightened self-interest.

But without such a willingness to extend its benefits to those who actually need them, the union would be a mockery—of itself and of those who place such faith in it. The mere prospect of joining, however dim, led to improvements in the situation of the Hungarian minority in Transylvania and has strengthened the hand of reformers—without pressure from Brussels, the government in Bucharest would never, for example, have overcome Orthodox Church objections and reformed the humiliating laws against homosexuality. As in the past, international leverage has prompted Romanian good behavior.[26] And as in the past, international disappointment would almost certainly carry a price at home.

In 1934 the English historian of Southeastern Europe R. W. Seton-Watson wrote, "Two generations of peace and clean government might make of Roumania an earthly paradise."[27] Today that is perhaps a lot to ask (though it shows how far the country has fallen). But Romania needs a break. The fear of being "shipwrecked at the periphery of history in a Balkanized democracy" (as Eliade put it) is real, however perverse the directions that fear has taken in the past. "Some countries," according to E. M. Cioran, looking back across Romania's twentieth century, "are blessed with a sort of grace: everything works for them, even their misfortunes and their catastrophes. There are others for whom nothing succeeds and whose very triumphs are but failures. When they try to assert themselves and take a step forward, some external fate intervenes to break their momentum and return them to their starting point."[28]

This essay on the condition and prospects of Romania first appeared in the **New York Review of Books** *in November 2001. It has since been republished in Romania, where it provoked a certain discomfort—not least for the somewhat provocative title of the NYR version: "Romania: Bottom of the Heap." Among the considerable private correspondence generated by the essay was at least one letter of appreciation . . . from Princess Brianna Caradja (the scantily clad aristocrat described in the opening paragraph).*

NOTES TO CHAPTER XV

[1] I am deeply grateful to Professor Mircea Mihâies for bringing *Plai cu Boi* to my attention.

[2] For an excellent discussion of Tudor's politics and a selection of cartoons from *Politica* and *România Mare*, see Iris Urban, "Le Parti de la Grande Roumanie, doctrine et rapport au passé: le nationalisme dans la transition post-communiste," *Cahiers d'études*, No. 1 (2001) (Bucharest: Institut Roumain d'Histoire Récente). See also Alina Mungiu-Pippidi, "The

Return of Populism—The 2000 Romanian Elections," *Government and Opposition* 36, no. 2 (Spring 2001): 230–252.

[3] For data see *The Economist. World in Figures*. London: 2001 edition.

[4] For an evocative account of life in interwar Bukovina after its reunion with Moldavia in 1920, see Gregor von Rezzori, *The Snows of Yesteryear* (New York: Vintage, 1989).

[5] The infamous prison at Sighet, in the Maramureş region on Romania's northern border with Ukraine, has been transformed into a memorial and museum. There is full coverage of the suffering of Communist Romania's many political prisoners, rather less reference to Sighet's even more notorious role as a holding pen for Transylvanian Jews on their way to Auschwitz. This was not the work of Romanians—the region had been returned to Hungary by Hitler in August 1940—but the contrast is eloquent.

[6] "The behavior of certain representatives of the Rumanian army, which have been indicated in the report, will diminish the respect of both the Rumanian and German armies in the eyes of public [*sic*] here and all over the world." Chief of Staff, XI German Army, July 14, 1941, quoted in Matatias Carp, *Holocaust in Romania: Facts and Documents on the Annihilation of Romania's Jews, 1940–1944* (Bucharest: Atelierele Grafice, 1946; reprinted by Simon Publications, 2000), 23 n8. There is a moving account of the deportation of the Jews of Bukovina and Bessarabia, the pogrom in Iasi, and the behavior of Romanian soldiers in Curzio Malaparte, *Kaputt* (Evanston, IL: Northwestern University Press, 1999; first published 1946).

[7] See Carp, *Holocaust in Romania*, p. 42n34, and 108–109. Radu Ioanid accepts the figure of 13,266 victims of the Iasi pogrom, based on contemporary estimates. See his careful and informative *The Holocaust in Romania: The Destruction of Jews and Gypsies Under the Antonescu Regime, 1940–1944* (Chicago: Ivan R. Dee, 2000), 86.

[8] See Irina Livezeanu, *Cultural Politics in Greater Romania: Regionalism, Nation Building and Ethnic Struggle, 1918–1930* (Ithaca, NY: Cornell University Press, 1995), an important book.

[9] The reference is to the Imperial Roman province of Dacia. Romanian antiquarians claim that Dacian tribes survived the Roman occupation and maintained unbroken settlement in Transylvania; Hungarians insist that when the Magyars arrived from the east in the tenth century the place was essentially empty, with Romanians coming later. For what it is worth, both sides are probably in error. Meanwhile, the Dacia motorworks in 2000 was still manufacturing a Romanian car—the Dacia 1300—familiar to middle-aged Frenchmen as the Renault 12 (first appearance: 1969). The Hungarians have nothing remotely so ancient with which to compete.

[10] Whatever the Jewish "problem" was about, it had little to do with real or imagined Jewish economic power. The accession of Bessarabia and Bukovina in 1920 added hundreds of thousands of Jews to Romania's population. Most of them were poor. The Bessarabian-born writer Paul Goma describes his father's response to the Fascists' cry of "Down with the Jews!": "But how much further down could our little Jew get than the village shopkeeper?" See Paul Goma, *My Childhood at the Gate of Unrest* (London: Readers International, 1990), 64. Nevertheless, according to Corneliu Zelea Codreanu, founder in 1927 of the League of the Archangel Michael (later the Iron Guard), "The historic mission of our generation is the solution of the Jewish problem." Codreanu is quoted by Leon Volovici in *Nationalist Ideology and Anti-Semitism: The Case of Romanian Intellectuals in the 1930s* (New York: Pergamon, 1991), 63. Codreanu was homicidal and more than a little mad. But his views were widely shared.

[11] In 2001 the Hungarian government passed a status law giving certain national rights and privileges to Hungarians living beyond the state's borders. This has understandably aroused Romanian ire at what some see as renewed irredentist ambition in Budapest; from the point of view of the Hungarians of Transylvania, however, the new law simply offers them some

guarantees of protection and a right to maintain their distinctive identity. For a sharp dissec-
tion of identity debates and their political instrumentalization after communism, see Vladimir
Tismaneanu, *Fantasies of Salvation: Democracy, Nationalism, and Myth in Post-Communist
Europe* (Princeton, NJ: Princeton University Press, 1998), notably chapter 3, "Vindictive and
Messianic Mythologies," 65–88.

[12] Adrian Năstase, "Europe: la plus-value roumaine," *Le Monde*, July 23, 2001.

[13] On Sebastian, Eliade, and the anti-Semitic obsessions of Bucharest's interwar literati, see Peter
Gay's review of Sebastian's *Journal, 1935–1944: The Fascist Years* (Chicago: Ivan R. Dee,
2000) in the *New York Review of Books*, October 4, 2001. For a representative instance of
Eliade's views on Jews, see for example Sebastian's diary entry for September 20, 1939, where
he recounts a conversation with Eliade in which the latter is as obsessed as ever with the risk
of "a Romania again invaded by kikes" (p. 238). Sebastian's diary should be read alongside
that of another Bucharest Jew, Emil Dorian: *The Quality of Witness: A Romanian Diary,
1937–1944* (Philadelphia: Jewish Publication Society of America, 1982).

[14] On Noica see Katherine Verdery, *National Ideology Under Socialism: Identity and Cultural Politics
in Ceaușescu's Romania* (Berkeley: University of California Press, 1991), chapter 7, "The
'School' of Constantin Noica." Ionescu is quoted by Sebastian, *Journal*, 9.

[15] Among the most important leaders of the Romanian Party, first in exile in Moscow and then in
Bucharest, until she was purged in 1952, was Ana Pauker, daughter of a Moldavian *shochet*
(ritual slaughterer). See Robert Levy, *Ana Pauker: The Rise and Fall of a Jewish Communist*
(Berkeley: University of California Press, 2000).

[16] See the comprehensive analysis by Vladimir Tismaneanu, "The Tragicomedy of Romanian
Communism," *Eastern European Politics and Societies* 3, no. 2 (Spring 1989): 329–376.
Khrushchev, who had little time for Romanians, sought to confine them to an agricultural
role in the international Communist distribution of labor; Dej and Ceaușescu preferred to
secure national independence via a neo-Stalinist industrialization drive.

[17] On the peculiar sadism of prisons in Communist Romania, see Matei Cazacu, "L'Expérience de
Pitesti," *Nouvelle Alternative* 10 (June 1988); and Lena Constante, *The Silent Escape: Three
Thousand Days in Romanian Prisons* (Berkeley: University of California Press, 1995; first
published in French by Éditions La Découverte, Paris, 1990).

[18] For the American story, see Joseph F. Harrington and Bruce J. Courtney, *Tweaking the Nose of
the Russians: Fifty Years of American-Romanian Relations, 1940–1950* (New York: East
European Monographs/Columbia University Press, 1991). Even *The Economist*, in August
1966, called Ceaușescu "the de Gaulle of Eastern Europe." As for de Gaulle himself, on a
visit to Bucharest in May 1968 he observed that while Ceaușescu's Communism would not
be appropriate for the West, it was probably well suited to Romania: "Chez vous un tel régime
est utile, car il fait marcher les gens et fait avancer les choses." ("For you such a regime is
useful, it gets people moving and gets things done.") President François Mitterrand, to his
credit, canceled a visit to Romania in 1982 when his secret service informed him of Romanian
plans to murder Paul Goma and Virgil Tanase, Romanian exiles in Paris.

[19] "The foetus is the socialist property of the whole society" (Nicolae Ceaușescu). See Katherine
Verdery, *What Was Socialism and What Comes Next?* (Princeton, NJ: Princeton University
Press, 1996); Ceaușescu is quoted on p. 65.

[20] Romania's abortion rate in 2001 was 1,107 abortions per 1,000 live births. In the EU the rate
was 193 per thousand, in the U.S. 387 per thousand.

[21] And Le Corbusier.

[22] From a Transylvanian perspective, Bucharest is a "Balkan," even "Byzantine," city. I am deeply
grateful to Professor Mircea Mihaies, Adriana Babeti, and the "Third Europe" group at the
University of Timișoara for the opportunity of an extended discussion on these themes in
October 1998. Our conversation was transcribed and published last year, with a generous

introduction by Professor Vladimir Tismaneanu, as *Europa Iluziilor* (Iasi: Editura Polirom, 2000), notably 15–131.

[23] R. G. Waldeck, *Athene Palace* (New York: Robert McBride, 1942; reprinted by the Center for Romanian Studies, Iasi, 1998). The quote is from the reprint edition, p. 10.

[24] For Cioran see E. M. Cioran, *Oeuvres* (Paris: Gallimard, 1995), 1779: "Ce qui m'a le plus déprimé, c'est une carte de l'Empire ottoman. C'est en la regardant que j'ai compris notre passé et le reste." The letter to Ceauşescu is cited by Kathleen Verdery in *National Ideology Under Socialism*, 133. For Ionescu's bleak prophecy, see Radu Boruzescu, "Mémoire du Mal—Bucarest: Fragments," *Martor: Revue d'Anthropologie du Musée du Paysan Roumain* 5 (2000): 182–207.

[25] Note, though, that in 1991 Adrien Năstase (then foreign minister) committed himself to an eventual reunification "on the German model." Likewise President Ion Iliescu, in December 1990, denounced the "injuries committed against the Romanian people" (in 1940) and promised that "history will find a way to put things completely back on their normal track." See Charles King, *The Moldovans: Romania, Russia, and the Politics of Culture* (Stanford, Stanford University/Hoover Institution Press, 2000), 149–150. The Romanian-speaking population of destitute Moldova would like nothing better. But Romania just now does not need to annex a country with large Russian and Ukrainian minorities, an average monthly wage of around $25 (when paid), and whose best-known export is the criminal trade in women.

[26] Repeal of anti-Jewish laws was the price of international recognition for the newly independent Romanian state in 1881. In 1920 the Versailles powers made citizenship rights for Jews and other non-Romanians a condition of the Trianon settlement. In both cases the Romanian state avoided compliance with the spirit of the agreement, but nonetheless made concessions and improvements that would not have been forthcoming without foreign pressure.

[27] R. W. Seton-Watson, *A History of the Roumanians* (Cambridge: Cambridge University Press, 1934), 554; also cited in King, *The Moldovans*, 36.

[28] E. M. Cioran, "Petite Théorie du Destin" (from *La Tentation d'Exister*), *Oeuvres*, 850. The French original reads: "Il y a des pays qui jouissent d'une espèce de bénédiction, de grâce: tout leur réussit, même leurs malheurs, même leurs catastrophes; il y en a d'autres qui ne peuvent aboutir, et dont les triomphes équivalent à des échecs. Quand ils veulent s'affirmer, et qu'ils font un bond en avant, une fatalité extérieure intervient pour briser leur ressort et pour les ramener à leur point de départ."

CHAPTER XVI

Dark Victory: Israel's Six-Day War

T hirty-five years ago this summer, in one of the shortest wars in modern history, Israel confronted and destroyed the combined armies of Egypt, Syria, and Jordan, established itself as a regional superpower, and definitively reconfigured the politics of the Middle East and much else besides. Since we are still living with its consequences, the Six-Day War itself seems somehow familiar. Its immediacy was reinforced until very recently by the presence at the head of Israel's government of one of the generals who played an important part in the victory in 1967, and by the salience of the West Bank and the Gaza Strip (occupied in the course of the campaign) in contemporary international politics. The detailed implications of Israel's lightning victory are etched into our daily news.

In truth, however, 1967 was a very long time ago. Hitler had been dead just twenty-two years, and the state of Israel itself had not yet celebrated its twentieth anniversary. The overwhelming majority of today's Israeli citizens were not yet born or not yet Israelis. Nineteen years after its birth, the country was still shaped by its origins in turn-of-the-century Labor Zionism. The only leaders whom Israel had known were men and women of the Second Aliyah, the Russian and Polish immigrants of the first years of the twentieth century; and the country was still utterly dominated by that founding generation and its sensibilities. A time traveler returning to Israel in 1967 must traverse not just time, but also space: In many crucial respects the country still operated, as it were, on Białystok time.

This had implications for every dimension of Israeli life. The kibbutzim, curious communitarian progeny of an unlikely marriage of Marx and Kropotkin, dominated the cultural landscape no less than the physical one. Even though it was already clear to some observers that the country's future lay in technology, in industry, and in towns, the self-description of Israel drew overwhelmingly on a Socialist realist image of agrarian pioneers living in semiautarkic egalitarian communes. Most of the country's leaders, beginning with David Ben-Gurion himself, were members of a kibbutz. Kibbutzim were attached to national movements that were affiliated with political parties, and all of them reflected, to the point of caricature, their fissiparous European heritage: splitting and re-splitting through the years along subtle doctrinal fault lines.

Political conversation in Israel in those years thus echoed and recapitulated the vocabulary and the obsessions of the Second International, circa 1922. Labor Zionism was subdivided over issues of dogma and politics (in particular the question of Socialist Zionism's relationship to Communism) in ways that might have seemed obsessive and trivial to outsiders but were accorded respectful attention by the protagonists. Laborites of various hues could indulge such internecine squabbles because they had a monopoly of power in the country. There were some religious parties, and above all there were the "Revisionists," the heirs of Vladimir Jabotinsky and his nationalist followers, incarnated in Menachem Begin's Herut party (the forerunner of today's Likud). But the latter were in a permanent minority; and anyway it is significant that Begin and his like were still referred to disparagingly as "revisionist," as though it were the doctrinal schisms of the early twentieth century that still determined the colors and the contours of Israeli politics.

There were other aspects of Israeli life and Zionist education that echoed the founders' European roots. On the kibbutz where I spent much time in the mid-1960s, a fairly representative agricultural community in the Upper Galilee affiliated with one of the splinter parties to the left of the main Labor Party (Mapai), the concerns of the early

Zionists were still very much alive. The classical dilemmas of applied socialism were debated endlessly. Should an egalitarian community impose sameness? Is it sufficient to distribute resources equally to all participants, allowing them to dispose of these according to preference, or is preference itself ultimately divisive and taste best imposed uniformly by the collective? How far should the cash nexus be allowed into the community? Which resources and activities are communal in their essence, which private?

The dominant tone on the kibbutz and in the country was provincial and puritanical. I was once earnestly reprimanded by a kibbutz elder for singing "inappropriate" popular songs, that is, the latest Beatles hits; and Zionist education went to great lengths to encourage intracommunity fellow feeling and affection among the young while eviscerating it of any hint of the erotic. The prevailing ethos, with its faith in the redemptive value of Land and Labor, its scoutlike clothing and communal dances, its desert hikes and dutiful ascents of Masada (the hard way, of course), its lectures on botany and biblical geography, and its earnest weekly discussion of Socialist "issues," represented nothing so much as a transposition into the Middle East of the preoccupations and mores of the Independent Labour Party of 1890s Britain, or the *Wandervogel* walking clubs of late Wilhelminian Germany.

Not surprisingly, Arabs figured very little in this world. In discussions of the writings of Ber Borochov and the other iconic texts of Labor Zionism, much attention was of course paid to the question of "exploitation." But in accordance with the Marxist framework in which all such debates were couched, "exploitation" was restricted in its meaning to the labor theory of value: You exploit someone else by employing them, remunerating them at the minimum required to keep them working productively, and pocketing the difference as profit. Accordingly, as seen from the perspective of kibbutz-based Labor Zionists, to hire Arabs (or anyone else) for wages was to exploit them. This had been the subject of animated practical quarrels as well as doctrinal arguments among kibbutz members; historically it was part of what distinguished kibbutzim from the labor-employing village cooperatives, or moshavim. But beyond such rather abstruse considerations, which were of little relevance to the real Israeli economy, relations between Jews and Arabs were not much discussed.

It is easy, looking back, to see in this curious oversight the source of our present troubles. And critics of the whole Zionist project are quick to remark that this refusal to engage with the presence of Arabs was the original sin of the Zionist forefathers, who consciously turned away from the uncomfortable fact that the virgin landscape of unredeemed Zion was already occupied by people who would have to be removed if a Jewish state was ever to come about. It is true that a few clear-sighted observers, notably Ahad Ha'am, had drawn attention to this dilemma and its implications, but most had ignored it. Actually the matter was not quite so simple, to judge from my own recollection of the last years of the old Zionism. Many Israelis of that time rather prided themselves on their success in living peacefully alongside Arab neighbors within the national borders. Far from deliberately denying the Arab presence, they boasted of their acquaintance with Arabs, and especially with Druze and Bedouins. They encouraged the young to familiarize themselves with local Arab society no less than with the flora and the fauna of the landscape.

But that, of course, is just the point. For pre-1967 Zionists, Arabs were a part of the physical setting in which the state of Israel had been established; but they were decidedly not part of the mental template, the Israel-of-the-mind, through which most Israelis saw their politics and their environment. Taking the Jews out of Europe did not take Europe out of the Jews. Notwithstanding the presence of Yemenite and North African Jews, condescendingly tolerated by the Ashkenazi majority, Israel in 1967 was a European country in all but name. The country was born of a European project, and it was geographically and sociologically configured by the vagaries of European history. Its laws were shaped by European precedent, its leaders and ideologists were marinated in late-nineteenth-century European socialism and nationalism.

However much they had consciously turned their backs on Europe— and a significant proportion of the adult population of that time consisted of concentration camp survivors with few fond memories of the old continent—Israelis were European to the core. I do not just mean the German-speaking Jews on Mount Carmel who reproduced every little detail of life in late-Habsburg Vienna and never bothered to learn Hebrew, or the English-speaking Jews drinking tea, eating fruitcake, and playing cricket in Kibbutz Kfar Hanassi; I am speaking about the whole country.

The result was an uncomfortable tension in Israeli sensibilities. Part of the Zionist enterprise was the wholehearted commitment to Zion, after all. It entailed a root-and-branch rejection of the Old World: its assumptions, its comforts, its seductions. At first, this had been a choice; later, thanks to Hitler, Zionism became an urgent necessity. The European Jews who ended up in Palestine after 1945 were committed to adapting to life in a small state of their own making in far-western Asia. But the process of adaptation had not advanced very far by the mid-1960s, and Arabs (like the Middle East in general) were simply not at the center of most Israelis' concerns. There was nothing particularly anti-Arab about this. As I recall, many Israelis were just as prejudiced against immigrant Jews from North Africa or the Near East as they were against Arabs. Perhaps more so.

THE SIX-DAY WAR was to change all that, utterly. And yet, for all its lasting consequences, there was nothing particularly unusual about the origin of the conflict. Like its predecessor, the Suez War of 1956, the war of 1967 is best regarded in the light in which Israel's generals saw it at the time: as unfinished business left over from the War of Independence. None of the parties to that earlier conflict was happy with the outcome, and all regarded the 1948 armistice as temporary. Although Israel had succeeded in expanding its borders beyond those of the original partition, it was still left with what were regarded, in the military calculations of the time, as virtually indefensible frontiers.

In the course of the early 1950s, the Egyptians encouraged guerrilla incursions across Israel's southern border, inviting regular retaliation from Israel—whose military had by 1955 decided to provoke Cairo into open conflict. In October 1956, taking advantage of Anglo-French alarm at Gamal Abdel Nasser's nationalist ambitions, Israel conspired with Paris and London to mount an attack on Egypt. Although initially successful, the campaign was cut short under pressure from Moscow and Washington. The European powers were humiliated, and Israel was obliged to withdraw back to the 1948 line.

In these circumstances Israel was as insecure as ever. Acknowledging this, the United States undertook to guarantee that the Straits of

Tiran, leading from the Red Sea to Eilat, Israel's port on the Gulf of Aqaba, would henceforth be kept open. In the meantime United Nations forces were to be stationed along the Egypt-Israel frontier, and also at Sharm-el-Sheikh, at the entrance to the Straits on the southeastern tip of the Sinai peninsula. Thereafter the Egyptian frontier was quiet, and it was Syria—whose Ba'athist leaders nursed ambitions to displace Nasser at the head of Arab radicalism—that emerged in the early 1960s as Israel's chief antagonist.

In addition to providing hospitality to Palestinian irregulars raiding across Israel's northeast borders or through Jordan, Damascus had various well-attested plans to divert the headwaters of the Jordan River. Partly for this reason, Israeli strategists had by 1967 come to regard Syria as the main short-term threat to national security. From the Golan Heights above the Sea of Galilee, Syria could target Israeli kibbutzim and villages; and it was a destabilizing influence on neighboring states, Jordan especially. Still, Nasser's Egypt had by far the larger armed forces. Were Israel seriously to entertain going to war with Syria, it would inevitably have first to neutralize the threat from its historic enemy to the south.

There is good reason to believe now that the chain of events leading to the outbreak of war on June 5 began with at least a partial misunderstanding. In the early spring of 1967, Israeli jets struck Syrian targets. In April, Israeli generals (including Chief of Staff Yitzhak Rabin) publicly threatened Damascus with worse to come if border harassments (whose scale they exaggerated) did not stop. Rabin himself seems to have favored toppling the Syrian regime, but Prime Minister Levi Eshkol felt otherwise: Syria was a client state of the Soviet Union, and Eshkol had no desire to provoke the Russians. He was not alone. The former Chief of Staff Moshe Dayan, not yet in the government, is quoted by Michael B. Oren in his new account of the Six-Day War as regretting Rabin's outburst: "He who sends up smoke signals has to understand that the other side might think there's really a fire."*

And that, in effect, is what happened. Russian intelligence misconstrued Israeli intentions and secretly advised the Syrians that the Israelis

---

* Michael B. Oren, *Six Days of War: June 1967 and the Making of the Modern Middle East* (Oxford: Oxford University Press, 2002).

were planning to attack—an interpretation given some plausibility by
Rabin's broadcast threats, widely commented upon in the foreign press.
The Syrians duly informed Cairo. Nasser had no immediate plans to go
to war with Israel, for whose military he had a well-founded respect; but
he felt constrained to offer public backing for Syria or else lose standing
in the Arab world. In practice, such backing took the conventional and
not unfamiliar form of bombastic public expressions of full support for
Damascus and grand promises to confront Israel at some unspecified
future date.

So far, so commonplace. What ratcheted the crisis from rhetoric into
war was Nasser's grandstanding demand, on May 17, that UN forces be
withdrawn from Gaza. The Egyptian dictator almost certainly calculated
thus: Either the United Nations would do his bidding and withdraw,
giving him a cost-free and highly visible public success, or else it would
refuse the request and Egypt would score a moral victory as the aggrieved
party. Nasser surely did not anticipate the reaction of the UN's ineffective
Secretary-General U Thant, which was to order the immediate withdrawal of all UN troops the following day not just from Gaza but from
the whole Sinai peninsula.

Nasser would have preferred that UN troops not be withdrawn from
Sharm-el-Sheikh. He could hardly be seen to regret U Thant's strange
decision, which in practice returned all of Sinai to Egyptian control, but
it put him in a predicament. He was obliged to move Egyptian armies
forward to the Israeli border and down to Sharm-el-Sheikh, which he
duly did; but with Egyptian soldiers now stationed across from the island
of Tiran, Nasser could not resist the temptation, on May 22, to announce
that once again the Straits were closed to all Israel-bound shipping, as
they had been in the early 1950s.

From this point on, as Nasser probably realized, war would be hard
to avoid. From the outside Nasser's moves seemed self-evidently the
prelude to a declaration of war; and in any case the closing of the Straits
of Tiran was itself, for Israel, a casus belli. Surrounded by enemies, and
accessible from the outside only by air and sea, Israel had once again lost
its vital link to the Red Sea and beyond. But this was not the main
concern for Israel. As Foreign Minister Abba Eban explained at the time,
what mattered was not so much the Straits themselves but Israel's deter-

rent capacity, which would lose all credibility if the country accepted Nasser's blockade without a fight.

Israeli diplomats tried at first to bring international pressure to bear on Egypt to reopen the Straits; and at the same time they asked the Great Powers openly to express their backing for Israel's response. The British and the French refused point blank, de Gaulle confining himself to a warning against any preemptive Israeli strike and an embargo on all French arms deliveries to Israel. (This was a time when the Israeli air force was overwhelmingly dependent on French-made Mirage and Mystère jet fighters.)

The Americans were a bit more sympathetic. Lyndon Johnson tried unsuccessfully to round up support for an international convoy of merchant ships to "run" the Straits and to call Egypt's bluff. He assured Eshkol and Eban of American sympathy, and of American backing in the event of an unprovoked attack on Israel. But more he could not give, despite John Foster Dulles's guarantee in 1957; in the mood of the time, he pleaded, Congress would not allow an American president openly to back Israeli aggression, however justified. Privately, his military experts assured Johnson that the Israelis had little to fear: Given the freedom to "shoot first," they would win within a week. But to Eshkol, Johnson merely announced that "Israel will not be alone unless it decides to go it alone."

That, of course, is what Israel did. The Israeli military, with Dayan newly installed by popular demand as defense minister, resented being made to wait for two long weeks of "phony war," but Eshkol's diplomatic strategy surely paid dividends. The Soviet Union put considerable pressure on Egypt not to start a war, but with rather greater success—at the end of May, at the last minute, Nasser abandoned a plan to attack Israel first, and he seems to have assumed that the crisis he had half-reluctantly set in motion had been defused. Israel, meanwhile, was seen to have tried every diplomatic means to avert a fight—even though most Israeli leaders and all the generals were now committed to war unless Nasser reopened the Straits, which they rightly assumed (and in some cases hoped) he would not do.

The American military experts who anticipated an easy Israeli victory were well informed, but they were in a minority. Many civilian Israelis feared the worst. From President 'Abd al-Rahman Muhammad 'Aref of Iraq ("Our goal is clear—we shall wipe Israel off the face of the map. We shall, God willing, meet in Tel Aviv and Haifa") to Palestinian leader Ahmed al-Shuqayri ("We shall destroy Israel and its inhabitants and as for the survivors—if there are any—the boats are ready to deport them"), Arab leaders appeared united in their determination to demolish the Jewish state. Their threats seemed credible enough: Between them, the armies of Egypt, Syria, Iraq, Jordan, and their friends comprised some nine hundred combat planes, five thousand tanks, and half a million men. At best the Israelis had one-quarter that number of planes, one-fifth the tanks, and only 275,000 men.

THE STORY OF the war itself is well known. On June 5, Day One, Israeli planes struck first and demolished much of the Egyptian air force on the ground, destroying 286 combat planes and killing nearly one-third of Egypt's pilots. On Days Two and Three, the Israeli army shattered or dispersed the bulk of the Egyptian armed forces in Sinai, thanks in large measure to Israel's complete domination of the skies. Meanwhile, ignoring Eshkol's invitation to stay out of the war, Jordan's King Hussein—believing that his survival depended upon his being seen to join the struggle against Israel—aligned himself with the Arab coalition ("the hour of decision has arrived"). In the ensuing battles the Israelis, after some hard fighting, seized all of Jerusalem and Jordanian territory west of the Jordan River.

By the end of Day Four, the war was effectively over. At the United Nations, the United States and the major European powers (including the Soviet Union) had from the outset been pressing urgently for a cease-fire, as the Israelis had anticipated they would: When the war began, Abba Eban estimated that the Israeli armed forces would have at most seventy-two hours before the superpowers intervened. But the Egyptians rejected a cease-fire. Their ambassador at the United Nations, Muhammad El Kony, was assured from Cairo that things were going well for the Arabs and that time was on their side; and he in turn blithely reassured his Soviet counterpart Nikolai Federenko that the Israelis were bluffing and that the planes they had destroyed were plywood decoys.

The Israelis were lucky, and they knew it: Had the Egyptians accepted a UN cease-fire on June 6, when it was first proposed, instead of on June 8, when Nasser finally acknowledged the extent of the catastrophe, they might have saved at least part of their army, and Israel would never have occupied the Old City of Jerusalem or the West Bank. Once the cease-fire was agreed (and Israel could hardly oppose it, having fought what was officially a "pre-emptive defensive war"), Dayan took a snap decision on his own initiative to attack Syria—the real Israeli objective—before the cease-fire could take effect. This incurred the enduring wrath of Moscow and ran the risk of undoing the benefits of all Eban's painstaking prewar diplomatic maneuvers, but it paid off. After some tough hours on the slopes of the Golan, the Israelis overran the Syrian defenses and literally raced to Quneitra to occupy the Heights themselves before time ran out.

The scale of Israel's victory was unprecedented and took some time for all the parties fully to appreciate. Egyptian losses alone amounted to perhaps fifteen thousand men and eighty-five percent of the country's prewar military hardware. Between two hundred thousand and three hundred thousand Arabs fled Gaza and the West Bank into exile, many of them already refugees from 1948. Israel now controlled land covering an area four and a half times its prewar size, from the Jordan to the Suez Canal, from the Lebanese uplands to the Red Sea. The fighting had not been quite so one-sided as the brevity of the war and its outcome might suggest—had it not been for their utter superiority in the air, the Israelis might have been quite closely matched, especially by some of the Jordanian units and the best Egyptian divisions; but it was the result that counted. One outcome of the war, certainly the most important from the Israeli perspective, was this: No responsible Arab leader would ever again seriously contemplate the military destruction of the Jewish state.

Michael B. Oren, in his new history of the war, tells the story in gripping detail. He has done an immense amount of research in many sources, Hebrew, Arabic, Russian, and English, and although his narrative is keyed to the Israeli perspective, this produces only occasional distortion. The Egyptian and Jordanian viewpoints are acknowledged, and Israel's responsibility for prewar misunderstandings and wartime errors (notably the bombing of the American ship *Liberty*) is given reasonable prominence. One particular virtue of Oren's book is that it pays full attention to the international dimension of the conflict, especially the concerns and the actions of the two superpowers. This allows Oren to set what was in one sense a very local war into its wider context: The war nearly did not happen thanks to international efforts at prevention, and it certainly would not have been allowed to go on much longer, as the Israelis fully understood.

Oren is good, too, on some of the personalities of the time, especially the Israelis, for whom he has a better feel. The stories of Rabin's near-breakdown on the eve of battle, of Dayan's rakish duplicity, of Nasser's horror at the scale of his defeat, are all skillfully told. Some, such as Yigal Allon, the hawkish leader of the left-leaning Achdut Ha'Avodah Party and sometime hero of the Independence War, come off badly: hungry for battle, eager for territory, loath to relinquish any land in exchange for peace. Others, such as the much underestimated Levi Eshkol, receive a distinct boost in their reputation. It was Eshkol who admonished General Ariel Sharon (when Sharon offered to destroy the Egyptian army "for a generation") that "nothing will be settled by a military victory. The Arabs will still be here." And it was Eshkol who asked his military adviser Yigal Yadin, the day after the lightning conquest of the West Bank: "Have you thought yet about how we can live with so many Arabs?" (Yadin's reply is not recorded.)

And yet Oren's book, for all its great learning and vivid writing, is somehow unsatisfactory. This is not because of his weakness for verbal infelicities: We read of someone seeking to "palliate the Syrians," that "Hussein was once again caught between clashing rocks," and so forth. Nor is it because Oren's grasp grows insecure as he moves beyond the Middle East: France in 1956 assuredly did not conspire with Israel because its government "shared Israel's socialist ideals" (how then account for the co-conspiratorial enthusiasm of Britain's Conservative leaders?); and it was President Eisenhower's economic arm-twisting, not Marshal Bulganin's empty threat to "use missiles," that brought the Suez War to an abrupt end. These slips suggest that Oren may be out of his depth in the broader currents of international history, but they do not vitiate his project.

The problem lies in the project itself. Oren announces at the outset that he plans to put the Six-Day War back in its context, and to present its origins and its outcome in such a manner that they will never be looked at in the same way again. And with respect to the origins he does indeed offer a comprehensive, if narrowly diplomatic, account. The story of the war itself is very well told, and for its source base alone this book should now be considered the standard work of reference. Yet neither the origins nor the war come across, at least to this reader, in any strikingly novel way. More thorough than previous accounts, to be sure. Better documented, certainly. But different? Not really.

As for the long-term outcome of the most fateful week in modern Middle Eastern history, Oren does not even begin to engage it. To be fair, any serious attempt at assessing the war's consequences would require another book. But the main consequences of Israel's victory can be summarized fairly succinctly. There was a widespread belief among Arab commentators, swiftly communicated to the Arab "street," that the United States and Britain had helped Israel—how else could its air force have achieved such dazzling successes? This prepared the way for a significant increase in anti-American sentiment across the region, a change of mood that proved lasting and with the consequences of which we are living still.

The ironic outcome is that whereas American official support for Israel in June 1967 had actually been rather lukewarm—Washington feared alienating moderate Arab opinion—the two countries did draw much closer thereafter. Israel was now a force to be reckoned with, a potential ally in an unstable region; and whereas in June 1967 Johnson's advisers had warned him against committing America openly to the Zionist cause, future administrations would have no such anxieties. With Arab states increasingly hostile, the United States had less to lose. France, meanwhile, released from the embarrassment of its imbroglio in Algeria, turned its back on the Jewish state ("*un peuple sûr de lui et dominateur,*" in de Gaulle's notorious phrase) and made the strategic decision to rebuild its bridges to the Arab world.

International public opinion also began to shift. Before the war, in Europe as well as the United States, only the Far Right and the Far Left were avowedly anti-Israel. Progressives and conservatives alike were sympathetic to Israel, the underdog seemingly threatened with imminent extinction. In some circles comparisons were drawn with the Civil War in Spain just thirty years earlier, with Israel cast as the legitimate republic besieged by aggressive dictators. Throughout Western Europe and North America, in South Africa and Australia, a significant effort was mounted from May 1967 to send volunteers to help Israel, to replace in the fields the men called up to fight.

I played a very minor role in these events, returning in my own case from the United Kingdom to Israel on the last commercial flight to land there before the outbreak of hostilities. Consequently, I met a lot of these volunteers, in Europe and then in Israel. There were many non-Jews among them, and most would have classed themselves as politically "left." With the trial of Eichmann and the Frankfurt trials of concentration camp personnel a very recent memory, defending Israel became a minor international cause.

According to Abba Eban, speaking in the aftermath of victory, "Never before has Israel stood more honored and revered by the nations of the world." I am not sure that this was so. Israel was certainly respected in a new way. But the scale of its triumph actually precipitated a falling-away of support. Some might plausibly attribute this to the world's preference for the Jew as victim—and there was indeed a certain post-June discomfort among some of Israel's overseas sympathizers at the apparent ease with which their cause had triumphed, as though its legitimacy were thereby called retrospectively into question.

But there was more to it than that. The European Old Left had always thought of Israel, with its long-established Labor leaders, its disproportionately large public sector, and its communitarian experiments, as "one of us." In the rapidly shifting political and ideological currents of the late 1960s and early 1970s, however, Israel was something of an anomaly. The New Left, from Berlin to Berkeley, was concerned less with exploited workers and more with the victims of colonialism and racism. The goal was no longer the emancipation of the proletariat; it was rather the liberation of the third-world peasantry and what were not yet called "people of color." Kibbutzim retained a certain romantic aura for a few more years, but for hard-nosed Western radicals they were just collective farms and as such a mere variant of the discredited Soviet model. In defeating the Arab armies and occupying Arab land, Israel had drawn attention to itself in ways calculated to encourage New Left antipathy, at just the moment when hitherto disparate radical constituencies—Ulster Catholics, Basque nationalists, Palestinian exiles, German extra-Parliamentarians, and many others— were finding common cause.

As for the conventional Right, through the 1950s and 1960s it enthusiastically took Israel's side against Nasser—the bête noire of every Western government, Raymond Aron's "Hitler on the Nile." With Nasser thoroughly humiliated, however, and with the colonial era retreating into memory, many European conservatives lost interest in Israel and sought instead to curry favor among its oil-producing neighbors: before the energy crisis of 1973, but especially afterwards.

In a variety of ways, then, the international context after 1967 turned increasingly unfavorable for Israel, despite its dramatic victory and because of it. Yet the most important change of all, the transformation that would color all of Israel's dealings with the rest of the world, took place in the country itself. Relieved of any serious threat, ostensibly sufficient unto themselves, Israelis became complacent. The attitude of Yael Dayan, addressing her diary as the war ended, is quite typical: "The new reality in the Middle East presented Israel as the strongest element, and as such it can talk a different language and had to be talked to differently." The prickly insecurity that characterized the country in its first two decades changed to a self-satisfied arrogance.

From 1967 until the shock of the Yom Kippur War of 1973, Israel was "dizzy with success." The apparent ease of the June victory led both the public and—less forgivably—the generals to believe that they were invincible. The image of the Israeli Defense Forces was burnished to a shine. Self-congratulatory (and implicitly contradictory) myths were espoused: that the Six-Day War had been won with consummate ease thanks to the technical and cultural superiority of the Israeli forces; that the climactic battles (for Jerusalem, for the Golan) had seen heroic feats of soldiering against harsh odds.

Books such as Yael Dayan's *Israel Journal* reflected and nourished a widespread sense of spiritual superiority. Attached to Sharon's Southern

Command during the war, she sneered at the contents of captured Egyptian officers' tents: thrillers, nylons, candies. "I knew what *our* officers' bedside tables contained. An Egyptian soldier would have found a few pens, writing paper, a few books and study matter—perhaps a book of poems." Comparing the two sides, Dayan concludes that the Egyptians had the material advantage, but "we had spiritual superiority."

Perhaps. Or perhaps not. As I recall Israeli junior officers' quarters on the Golan in the late summer of 1967, there were more pinups than poems. But from encounters with soldiers at the time I can certainly confirm the astonishingly quick transition from quiet confidence to an air of overweening superiority. Sharon was not the only one to sweep his arm across the captured landscape and declare (in his case to Yael Dayan) that "all this is ours." And the new mood was reinforced by the appearance in fairly short order of a new kind of Israeli. The great victory of 1967 gave Zionism a shot in the arm, with a new generation of enthusiastic immigrants arriving from America especially; but these new Zionists brought with them not the old Socialist texts of emancipation, redemption, and community, but rather a Bible and a map. For them, Israel's accidental occupation of Judea and Samaria was not a problem, it was a solution. In their religious and jingoistic eyes, the defeat of Israel's historical enemies was not the end of the story, but rather the beginning.

In many cases their aggressive nationalism was paired with a sort of born-again, messianic Judaism, a combination hitherto largely unknown in Israel. In the heady aftermath of the capture of Jerusalem, the chief rabbi of the army, Shlomo Goren, had proposed that the mosques on the Temple Mount be blown up. The general in command on the Jordanian front, Uzi Narkiss, had ignored him; but in years to come the voice of intolerant, ultrareligious Zionism would become more insistent and not so easy to turn away.

The demography of Israel was altered in other ways, too. In the aftermath of the Six-Day War, Jews in Syria, Iraq, Egypt, Libya, and elsewhere were subjected to persecution and discrimination, and the rate of Jewish immigration to Israel from Arab lands rose sharply. Hitherto it had been mostly confined to Jews expelled or fleeing from the newly independent states of the Maghreb; these continued to come, either directly or via France, but they were no longer a small minority of the overall population. These new Israelis not only did not share the political and cultural background of the earlier European immigrants. They had strong and distinctly unfriendly opinions about Arabs. After all, relations between Jews and Arabs in the places they had come from were often based on little more than mutual contempt. When the old Labor parties predictably failed to attract their support (or did not even bother to try), they turned to the erstwhile revisionists, whose chauvinist prejudices they could appreciate. The rise to power of Menachem Begin, Yitzhak Shamir, and their successors was literally unimaginable before June 1967. Now it became possible and even inexorable.

This was the irony of the victory of 1967: It was the only war Israel ever won that gave the country a real chance to shape the Middle East to everyone's advantage, its own above all—but the very scale of the victory somehow robbed the country's leaders of imagination and initiative. The "overblown confidence" (in Oren's apt phrase) after June 1967 led to the initial disasters of the Yom Kippur War of 1973 when, unable to imagine that Arab military planning was as good as their own intelligence suggested, the Israeli general staff was caught napping. That same misplaced confidence led Israel's politicians to let policy drift in the course of the 1970s, at a time when the initiative was still very much in their hands.

As for the occupied territories, Eshkol's question to Yadin remained unanswered. The habit of encouraging frontier settlements in the name of security—a building block of the original *Yishuv* (the Jewish community in pre-1948 Palestine) and the origin of many kibbutzim—made sense in the military circumstances of the 1930s. But half a century later it was an utter anachronism. It was in this context, however, that mainstream politicians connived at the subsidized establishment in the West Bank of tens of thousands of religious and political extremists. Some politicians—Allon, Sharon—always intended to install a permanent Israeli presence on the captured lands. Others merely preferred not to oppose the mood of the hour.

Nobody thought much about how to remove the settlements when the time came to exchange land for peace, though it had been clear from the outset that come it would. On June 19, 1967, the Israeli cabinet secretly voted to accept the principle of returning occupied land in exchange for lasting peace. As Eshkol had noted when the war began: "Even if we conquer the Old City and the West Bank, in the end we will have to leave them."

It is easy to wax nostalgic for the old Israel, before the victories of 1967 and the disturbing changes they brought in their wake. The country may have had "Auschwitz frontiers" (Eban) but its identity within them was at least clear. Yet if the Jewish state was ever to be at home in the Middle East—to be the "normal" polity that its Zionist founders envisaged—then its curious European orientation, a time-space capsule in an alien continent, could not last. And there is no doubt that, for better or for worse, since June 1967 Israel has entered fully into the Middle Eastern world. It, too, has crazed clerics, religious devotees, nationalist demagogues, and ethnic cleansers. It is also, sadly, less secure than at any time in the past forty years. The idea that Jews in Israel might lead their daily lives oblivious of the Arab world, as many did before 1967, is today tragically unthinkable.

Short of forcibly expunging the Arab presence from every inch of soil currently controlled by Israel, the dilemma facing Israel today is the same as it was in June 1967, when the aging David Ben-Gurion advised his fellow countrymen against remaining in the conquered territories. A historic victory can wreak almost as much havoc as a historic defeat. In Abba Eban's words, "The exercise of permanent rule over a foreign nation can only be defended by an ideology and rhetoric of self-worship and exclusiveness that are incompatible with the ethical legacy of prophetic Judaism and classical Zionism." The risk that Israel runs today is that for many of its most vocal defenders, Zionism has become just such an "ideology and rhetoric of self-worship and exclusiveness" and not much more. Israel's brilliant victory of June 1967, already a classic in the annals of preemptive warfare, has borne bitter fruits for the losers and the winners alike.

This essay—a July 2002 review of Michael Oren's new history of the Six-Day War—was my last contribution to the New Republic. *The following year my name disappeared from the journal's masthead in the wake of my essay on the one-state solution in Israel and Palestine ("Israel: The Alternative," in the* New York Review of Books, *vol. 50, no. xvi, October 2003). Despite the largely favorable tone of my review, Michael Oren—perhaps unaccustomed to dissent or criticism—wrote a curiously vituperative, ad hominem response, which the* New Republic *published in its edition of September 30, 2002.*

CHAPTER XVII

The Country That Wouldn't Grow Up

By the age of fifty-eight a country—like a man—should have achieved a certain maturity. After nearly six decades of existence we know, for good and ill, who we are, what we have done, and how we appear to others, warts and all. We acknowledge, however reluctantly and privately, our mistakes and our shortcomings. And though we still harbor the occasional illusion about ourselves and our prospects, we are wise enough to recognize that these are indeed for the most part just that: illusions. In short, we are adults.

But the state of Israel remains curiously (and among Western-style democracies, uniquely) immature. The social transformations of the country—and its many economic achievements—have not brought the *political* wisdom that usually accompanies age. Seen from the outside, Israel still comports itself like an adolescent: consumed by a brittle confidence in its own uniqueness; certain that no one "understands" it and everyone is "against" it; full of wounded amour propre, quick to take offense and quick to give it. Like many adolescents Israel is convinced—and makes a point of aggressively and repeatedly asserting—that it can do as it wishes; that its actions carry no consequences; and that it is immortal. Appropriately enough, this country that has somehow failed to grow up was until very recently still in the hands of a generation of men who were already prominent in its public affairs forty years ago: an Israeli Rip van Winkle who fell asleep in, say, 1967 would be surprised indeed to awake in 2006 and find Shimon Peres and General Ariel Sharon still hovering over the affairs of the country—the latter albeit only in spirit.

But that, Israeli readers will tell me, is the prejudiced view of the outsider. What looks from abroad like a self-indulgent, wayward country—delinquent in its international obligations and resentfully indifferent to world opinion—is simply an independent little state doing what it has always done: look after its own interests in an inhospitable part of the globe. Why should embattled Israel even acknowledge such foreign criticism, much less act upon it? *They*—gentiles, Muslims, Lefties—have reasons of their own for disliking Israel. *They*—Europeans, Arabs, Fascists—have always singled out Israel for special criticism. *Their* motives are timeless. *They* haven't changed. Why should Israel change?

But *they* have changed. And it is this change—which has passed largely unrecognized within Israel—to which I want to draw attention here. Before 1967 the state of Israel may have been tiny and embattled, but it was not typically hated: certainly not in the West. Official Soviet-bloc Communism was anti-Zionist of course, but for just that reason Israel was rather well regarded by everyone else, including the non-Communist Left. The romantic image of the kibbutz and the kibbutznik had a broad foreign appeal in the first two decades of Israel's existence. Most admirers of Israel (Jews and non-Jews) knew little about the Palestinian catastrophe of 1948. They preferred to see in the Jewish state the last surviving incarnation of the nineteenth-century idyll of agrarian socialism—or else a paragon of modernizing energy, "making the desert bloom."

I remember well, in the spring of 1967, how the balance of student opinion at Cambridge University was overwhelmingly pro-Israel in the weeks leading up to the Six-Day War—and how little attention anyone paid either to the condition of the Palestinians or to Israel's earlier collusion with France and Britain in the disastrous Suez adventure of 1956. In politics and in policymaking circles only old-fashioned conservative Arabists expressed any criticism of the Jewish state; even neo-Fascists rather favored Zionism, on traditional anti-Semitic grounds.

For a while after the '67 war these sentiments continued unaltered.

The pro-Palestinian enthusiasms of post-sixties radical groups and nationalist movements, reflected in joint training camps and shared projects for terrorist attacks, were offset by the growing international acknowledgement of the Holocaust in education and the media: What Israel lost by its continuing occupation of Arab lands it gained through its close identification with the recovered memory of Europe's dead Jews. Even the inauguration of the illegal settlements and the disastrous invasion of Lebanon, while they strengthened the arguments of Israel's critics, did not yet shift the international balance of opinion. As recently as the early 1990s, most people in the world were only vaguely aware of the "West Bank" and what was happening there. Even those who pressed the Palestinians' case in international forums conceded that almost no one was listening. Israel could still do as it wished.

But today everything is different. We can see, in retrospect, that Israel's victory in June 1967 and its continuing occupation of the territories it conquered then have been the Jewish state's very own *nakbar*: a moral and political catastrophe. Israel's actions in the West Bank and Gaza have magnified and publicized the country's shortcomings and put them on display to a watching world. Curfews, checkpoints, bulldozers, public humiliations, home destructions, land seizures, shootings, "targeted assassinations," the Wall: All of these routines of occupation and repression were once familiar only to an informed minority of specialists and activists. Today they can be watched, in real time, by anyone with a computer terminal or a satellite dish—which means that Israel's behavior is under daily scrutiny by hundreds of millions of people worldwide. The result has been a complete transformation in the international view of Israel. Until very recently the carefully burnished image of an ultramodern society—built by survivors and pioneers and peopled by peace-loving democrats—still held sway over international opinion. But today? What is the universal shorthand symbol for Israel, reproduced worldwide in thousands of newspaper editorials and political cartoons? The Star of David emblazoned upon a tank.

Today only a tiny minority of outsiders see Israelis as victims. The true victims, it is now widely accepted, are the Palestinians. Indeed, Palestinians have now displaced Jews as *the* emblematic persecuted minority: vulnerable, humiliated, and stateless. In itself this unsought distinction does little to advance the Palestinian case (any more than it ever helped Jews); but it has redefined *Israel* forever. It has become commonplace to compare Israel at best to an occupying colonizer, at worst to the South Africa of race laws and Bantustans. In this capacity Israel elicits scant sympathy even when its own citizens suffer: dead Israelis—like the occasional assassinated South African white in the apartheid era, or British colonists hacked to death by native insurgents—are typically perceived abroad not as the victims of terrorism but as the collateral damage of their own government's mistaken policies.

Such comparisons are lethal to Israel's moral credibility. They strike at what was once its strongest suit: the claim to be a vulnerable island of democracy and decency in a sea of authoritarianism and cruelty; an oasis of rights and freedoms surrounded by a desert of repression. But democrats don't fence into Bantustans helpless people whose land they have conquered; and free men don't ignore international law and steal other men's homes. The contradictions of Israeli self-presentation—"we are very strong/we are very vulnerable"; "we are in control of our fate/we are the victims"; "we are a normal state/we demand special treatment"— are not new: They have been part of the country's peculiar identity almost from the outset. And Israel's insistent emphasis upon its isolation and uniqueness, its claim to be both victim and hero, were once part of its David vs. Goliath appeal.

But today the country's national narrative of macho victimhood appears to the rest of the world as simply bizarre: evidence of a sort of collective cognitive dysfunction that has gripped Israel's political culture. And the long-cultivated persecution mania—"everyone's out to get us"— no longer elicits sympathy. Instead it attracts some very unappetizing comparisons: At a recent international meeting I heard one speaker, by analogy with Helmut Schmidt's famous dismissal of the Soviet Union as "Upper Volta with missiles," describe Israel as "Serbia with nukes."

Israel has stayed the same, but the world—as I noted above—has changed. Whatever purchase Israel's self-description still has upon the imagination of Israelis themselves, it no longer operates beyond the country's frontiers. Even the Holocaust can no longer be instrumentalized to excuse Israel's behavior. Thanks to the passage of time, most Western European states have now come to terms with their part in the

Shoah, something that was still not true a quarter century ago. From Israel's point of view, this has had paradoxical consequences: Until the end of the cold war, Israeli governments could still play upon the guilt of Germans and other Europeans, exploiting their failure fully to acknowledge what was done to Jews on their territory. Today, now that the history of World War II is retreating from the public square into the classroom and from the classroom into the history books, a growing majority of voters in Europe and elsewhere (young voters above all) simply cannot understand how the horrors of the last European war can be invoked to license or condone unacceptable behavior in another time and place. In the eyes of a watching world, the fact that an Israeli soldier's great-grandmother died in Treblinka is no excuse for his own abusive treatment of a Palestinian woman waiting to cross a checkpoint. "Remember Auschwitz" is not an acceptable response.

In short: Israel, in the world's eyes, *is* a normal state; but one behaving in abnormal ways. It *is* in control of its fate; but the victims are someone else. It *is* strong (*very* strong); but its behavior is making everyone else vulnerable. And so, shorn of all other justifications for its behavior, Israel and its supporters today fall back with increasing shrillness upon the oldest claim of all: Israel is a *Jewish* state, and that is why people criticize it. This—the charge that criticism of Israel is implicitly anti-Semitic—is regarded in Israel and the United States as Israel's trump card. If it has been played more insistently and aggressively in recent years, that is because it is now the only card left.

The habit of tarring any foreign criticism with the brush of anti-Semitism is deeply ingrained in Israeli political instincts: Ariel Sharon used it with characteristic excess, but he was only the latest in a long line of Israeli leaders to exploit the claim. David Ben-Gurion and Golda Meir did no different. But Jews outside of Israel pay a high price for this tactic. Not only does it inhibit their own criticisms of Israel for fear of appearing to associate with bad company, but it encourages others to look upon Jews everywhere as de facto collaborators in Israel's misbehavior. When Israel breaks international law in the occupied territories, when Israel publicly humiliates the subject populations whose land it has seized—but then responds to its critics with loud cries of "anti-Semitism"—it is in effect saying that these acts are not Israeli acts, they are *Jewish* acts; the occupation is not an Israeli occupation, it is a *Jewish* occupation; and if you don't like these things it is because you don't like *Jews.*

In many parts of the world this is in danger of becoming a self-fulfilling assertion: Israel's reckless behavior and its insistent identification of all criticism with anti-Semitism is now the leading source of anti-Jewish sentiment in Western Europe and much of Asia. But the traditional corollary—if anti-Jewish feeling is linked to dislike of Israel, then right-thinking people should rush to Israel's defense—no longer applies. Instead, the ironies of the Zionist dream have come full circle: For tens of millions of people in the world today, Israel is indeed the state of all the Jews. And thus, reasonably enough, many observers believe that one way to take the sting out of rising anti-Semitism in the suburbs of Paris or the streets of Jakarta would be for Israel to give the Palestinians back their land.

If Israel's leaders have been able to ignore such developments, it is in large measure because they have hitherto counted upon the unquestioning support of the United States—the one country in the world where the claim that anti-Zionism = anti-Semitism is still echoed not only in the opinions of many Jews but also in the public pronouncements of mainstream politicians and the mass media. But this lazy, ingrained confidence in unconditional American approval—and the moral, military, and financial support that accompanies it—may prove to be Israel's undoing.

For something is changing in the United States. To be sure, it was only a few short years ago that Prime Minister Sharon's advisers could gleefully celebrate their success in dictating to President George W. Bush the terms of a public statement approving Israel's illegal settlements. No U.S. congressman has yet proposed reducing or rescinding the $3 billion paid annually to Israel (20 percent of the total U.S. foreign aid budget) which has helped sustain the Israeli defense budget and cover the cost of settlement construction in the West Bank. And Israel and the United States appear increasingly bound together in a symbiotic embrace whereby the actions of each party exacerbate their common unpopularity abroad—and thus their ever-closer association in the eyes of critics.

But whereas Israel has no choice but to look to America—it has no other friends, at best only the conditional affection of the enemies of its enemies (such as India)—the United States is a Great Power; and Great Powers have interests that sooner or later transcend the local obsessions of even the closest of their client states and satellites. It seems to me of no small significance that the recent essay on "The Israel Lobby" by John Mearsheimer and Stephen Walt has aroused so much public interest and debate. Mearsheimer and Walt are prominent senior academics of impeccable conservative credentials. It is true that—by their own account—they could still not have published their damning indictment of the influence of the Israel lobby on U.S. foreign policy in a major U.S.-based journal (it appeared in the *London Review of Books*); but the point is that ten years ago they would not—and probably could not—have published it at all. And while the debate that has ensued may generate more heat than light, it is of great significance: As Dr. Johnson said of female preachers, it is not well done, but one is amazed to see it done, at all.

The fact is that the disastrous Iraq invasion and its aftermath are beginning to engineer a sea change in foreign policy debate here in the U.S. It is becoming clear to prominent thinkers across the political spectrum—from erstwhile neoconservative interventionists like Francis Fukuyama to hard-nosed realists like Mearsheimer—that in recent years the United States has suffered a catastrophic loss of international political influence and an unprecedented degradation of its moral image. The country's foreign undertakings have been self-defeating and even irrational. There is going to be a long work of repair ahead, above all in Washington's dealings with economically and strategically vital communities and regions from the Middle East to Southeast Asia. And this reconstruction of the country's foreign image and influence cannot hope to succeed while its foreign policy is tied by an umbilical cord to the needs and interests (if that is what they are) of one small Middle Eastern country of very little relevance to America's long-term concerns—a country that is, in the words of the Mearsheimer/Walt essay, a strategic burden: "a liability in the war on terror and the broader effort to deal with rogue states."

That essay is thus a straw in the wind—an indication of the likely direction of future domestic debate here in the U.S. about the country's peculiar ties to Israel. Of course it has been met by a firestorm of criticism from the usual suspects—and, just as the authors anticipated, they have been charged with anti-Semitism (or with advancing the interests of anti-Semitism: "objective anti-Semitism," as it might be). But it is striking to me how few people with whom I have spoken now take that accusation seriously, so predictable has it become. This is bad for Jews—since it means that genuine anti-Semitism may also in time cease to be taken seriously, thanks to the Israel lobby's abuse of the term. But it is worse for Israel.

This new willingness to take one's distance from Israel is not confined to foreign policy specialists. As a teacher I have also been struck in recent years by a sea change in the attitude of students. One example among many: At New York University in 2005 I was teaching a class on twentieth-century Europe and trying to explain to young Americans the importance of the Spanish Civil War in the political memory of Europeans and why Franco's Spain had such a special place in our moral imagination: as a reminder of lost struggles, a symbol of oppression in an age of liberalism and freedom, and a land of shame that people boycotted for its crimes and repression. I cannot think, I told the students, of any country that occupies such a pejorative space in democratic public consciousness today. You are wrong, one young woman replied: What about Israel? To my great surprise most of the class (including many of the sizable Jewish contingent) nodded their approval. The times they are indeed a-changing.

That Israel can now stand comparison with the Spain of General Franco in the eyes of young Americans ought to come as a shock and an eleventh-hour wake-up call to Israelis. Nothing lasts forever, and it seems likely to me that in later years we shall look back upon the years since 1973 as an era of tragic illusion for Israel: years that the locust ate, consumed by the bizarre notion that, whatever it chose to do or demand, Israel could count indefinitely upon the unquestioning support of the United States and would never risk encountering any backlash. This blinkered arrogance is tragically summed up in an assertion by

Shimon Peres in 2003, on the very eve of the calamitous war that will in retrospect be seen, I believe, to have precipitated the onset of America's alienation from its Israeli ally: "The campaign against Saddam Hussein is a must."

From one perspective Israel's future is bleak. Not for the first time, a Jewish state finds itself on the vulnerable periphery of someone else's empire: overconfident in its own righteousness; willfully blind to the danger that its indulgent excesses might ultimately provoke its imperial mentor to the point of irritation and beyond; and heedless of its own failure to make any other friends. To be sure, the modern Israeli state has big weapons—very big weapons. But what it can do with them except make more enemies? However, modern Israel also has options. Precisely because the country is an object of such universal mistrust and resentment—because people expect so little from Israel today—a truly statesmanlike shift in its policies (dismantling of major settlements, opening unconditional negotiations with Palestinians, calling Hamas's bluff by offering its leaders something serious in return for recognition of Israel and a cease-fire) could have disproportionately beneficial effects.

But such a radical realignment of Israeli strategy would entail a difficult reappraisal of every cliché and illusion under which the country and its political elite have nestled for most of their life. It would entail acknowledging that Israel no longer has any special claim upon international sympathy or indulgence; that the United States won't always be there; that weapons and walls can no more preserve Israel forever than they preserved the German Democratic Republic or white South Africa; that colonies are always doomed unless you are willing to expel or exterminate the indigenous population. Other countries and their leaders have understood this and managed comparable realignments: Charles de Gaulle realized that France's settlement in Algeria (far older and better established than Israel's West Bank colonies) was a military and moral disaster for his country, and in an exercise of outstanding political courage he acted upon that insight and withdrew. But when de Gaulle came to that realization he was a mature statesman, nearly seventy years old. Israel cannot afford to wait that long. At the age of fifty-eight the time has come for it to grow up.

This essay was commissioned by the editors of the Israeli liberal daily Ha'aretz for a special edition on the occasion of the country's fifty-eighth birthday and was published by them in May 2006. It aroused the predictable flurry of critical responses from correspondents and bloggers reluctant to countenance any criticism of Israel or its policies and practices. Most of the hysterical responses came from the United States; as so often in these matters, Israeli reactions—both critical and supportive—were more measured.

Part Four

THE AMERICAN (HALF-) CENTURY

CHAPTER XVIII

An American Tragedy?
The Case of Whittaker Chambers

In the fall of 1993, Maria Schmidt, a young Hungarian historian in Budapest, phoned me in New York. She had a question. "Tell me about 'Alger Hiss'?" I explained as briefly as I could. "You mean that there are people in the United States who still believe that he was telling the truth?" Certainly, I replied, and not least among my fellow professors. "In that case," she said, "I am going to send you something that I have found." Schmidt is a historian of contemporary Hungary. She had gained access to the wartime and postwar archives of the Hungarian Communist Party, and there, while combing through communications and reports that passed between Hungarian secret policemen and Communist Party leaders, she had come across the name "Alger Hiss" a number of times. Assuming it to be an alias—the Hiss case does not figure prominently in European history lessons—she was surprised to discover that a man had actually existed by that name (and was at that time still alive). Schmidt's evidence has since been corroborated by material retrieved from Soviet and American government sources. For those who do not believe in fairies, the Hiss affair is now closed.

What remains is the altogether more interesting case of Whittaker Chambers. The events that brought Whittaker Chambers to public notice are well known, and in a fascinating biography Sam Tanenhaus recapitulates them in gripping detail.* A courier for the Communist underground from 1932 until 1938, Chambers "defected" from the party and told his story in 1939 to Adolf A. Berle Jr., an assistant secretary of state in the Roosevelt administration and the president's liaison for intelligence matters. Berle passed along Chambers's information, which included the names of the party's sources in the American government, among them Alger Hiss, a rising star in the State Department who had served in the early Roosevelt years in the Agricultural Adjustment Administration.

For some years nothing more was done, though Chambers was investigated and interrogated by the FBI in 1941 and again after the war. Then, in July 1948, the House Un-American Activities Committee (HUAC) called Elizabeth Bentley to testify. Bentley, who had succeeded Chambers as the underground Communist courier in Washington, D.C., offered testimony that for the first time corroborated Chambers's earlier information. Chambers was called before the committee. His own testimony implicated Alger Hiss and seven others as members of a Communist network operating in the inner circles of the New Deal administrations. At that time, Chambers did not claim to have knowledge of any espionage undertaken by the group, nor could he furnish documentary evidence in support of his testimony. Belonging to the Communist Party in the 1930s was not in itself a criminal activity.

Hiss, too, was called to testify before the committee. He made a good showing and denied ever having known Chambers. In later sessions Hiss conceded that he had indeed known him "under a different name"; and Hiss's own version of their meetings in the 1930s contained a number of contradictory details. All the same, a series of encounters between the two men, in closed and open sessions of the committee, did little to advance the case against Hiss. But when Chambers repeated his charges—that Hiss was a Communist and might still be a Communist—on a radio program, without benefit of the legal protection afforded by the House hearings, Hiss (confident that Chambers had no proof with which to back his assertions in court) sued him for slander on September 27, 1948.

---

* Sam Tanenhaus, *Whittaker Chambers: A Biography* (New York, Random House, 1997).

Obliged now to come up with something more than his recollections, even if they were confirmed by at least one other ex-Communist witness, Chambers finally recanted his earlier denial and affirmed that Alger Hiss and others had been engaged in espionage. He backed up his claim by retrieving from their hiding place documents and microfilms that he had stashed away at the time of his apostasy in 1938 as insurance against Soviet retribution. This material was temporarily reburied in a hollowed-out pumpkin on Chambers's farm (hence the notorious "pumpkin papers") before being dramatically offered up to HUAC in evidence. HUAC then passed the material, reluctantly, to a grand jury, and on December 15, 1948, Alger Hiss was indicted on two counts of perjury: for denying under oath that he had seen Chambers after January 1, 1937, and for claiming, also under oath, that he had never transmitted government documents to him. On both these points, the evidence of the new material was decisive. Hiss could not be charged with espionage, since the statute of limitations had passed, but the charge of perjury stood in for such an accusation.

Hiss's first trial, which lasted from June 1 to July 8, 1949, ended in a hung jury. A second trial began on November 17, 1949, and lasted until January 21, 1950, when Hiss was unanimously found guilty of perjury and sentenced to five years' imprisonment. He eventually served forty-four months. For the rest of his long life (he died in 1996), Hiss maintained that he was not guilty. His application for a retrial was refused, but for many people, his protestations of innocence rang true. The onus, it has sometimes seemed, was on Chambers, and on his supporters, to show why Hiss would continue to deny the charges if they were true, and to provide more than just a few documents and a partially damaged microfilm. Many suggested that there had been a miscarriage of justice, a frame-up, a conspiracy. But as Tanenhaus demonstrates convincingly, the proof is now overwhelming. The material evidence itself was damaging enough, not to mention Chambers's memory of copious crucial details about Hiss and his activities, and nobody has successfully called it into question.

The idea that the whole charge was concocted in the overheated atmosphere of the postwar years was laid to rest by those, such as Sidney Hook, who recalled Hiss being named by Chambers in private conversation as early as 1938. In *Perjury: The Hiss-Chambers Case,* published in 1978, Allen Weinstein concluded, from the evidence then available, that "Alger Hiss [was] guilty as charged." Since then, the government has released the "Venona traffic"—cables to Moscow sent by Soviet agents in the United States—and these show not only that there were indeed spy networks in the American government, and that they included high-placed New Dealers such as Harry Dexter White and Alger Hiss; but also that Hiss may have been an active agent well into the 1940s. Even Laurence Duggan, a State Department official who killed himself (or was killed) on December 20, 1948, following rumors about his Communist allegiance, and whose death prompted Reinhold Niebuhr and Arthur Schlesinger Jr. to call for an end to HUAC's investigations, now turns out to have been among the agents who can be identified from the intercepted Soviet messages.

From recently opened Soviet archives, moreover, we have further confirmation that Chambers was telling the truth about Communist sources in the United States government and about the sort of material that they were supplying. In particular, the Russian evidence corroborates Chambers's claim that his whole group was run by a Hungarian named Josef Peters. Which brings us back to Maria Schmidt. What she found was a detailed debriefing in 1954 by Hungarian intelligence operatives of one Noel Field, a former Soviet agent in the United States, who had fled to Prague from Western Europe in 1949 to avoid extradition to America and was imprisoned for five years (without trial) in Hungary, caught in the entrails of the great Stalinist purges of the era.

Field makes it unambiguously clear that Hiss, like Field himself, was a Communist operative. Field had no reason to lie, since what he said was not for public consumption. In any case, he was telling his story to men who knew more about it than he did, and who could (and did) check it out in Budapest and Moscow. After his release, Field wrote openly to Hiss from Budapest in 1957, offering to exculpate him. Hiss politely declined. Hiss's supporters made much of this letter, but it now turns out to have been a minor exercise in disinformation, with several earlier drafts kept filed away in Hungarian party archives until Schmidt came across them. Finally, Schmidt saw a handwritten autobiographical note for the Hungarian secret intelligence services by the same Josef Peters whom Chambers had identified, confirming everything the latter had said.

And so to Whittaker Chambers himself. In death as in life, he has been pursued by unfavorable comparisons with the man he brought down. In *The Great Fear*, David Caute's history of the McCarthy years, Chambers is described as "humped, shambling . . . shifty, hesitant, podgy" while Hiss is "a gentle, inquisitive, quasi-encyclopedic gentleman." The obituaries of Hiss in November 1996 obligingly echoed the emphasis on Chambers's unprepossessing physique: "portly, rumpled," according to the *New York Times*, and "overweight and unkempt" in the *Washington Post* version. As Arthur Koestler once observed, the roles in this drama were apparently miscast. Eleanor Roosevelt noted approvingly at the time of the first perjury trial that "one gets the feeling . . . that Mr. Chambers is on trial and not Mr. Hiss."

Chambers had few friends, owing to his solitary disposition and his renegade Communist past. He was also notorious for a lack of attention to his appearance, from his teeth to his shoes. Hiss, by contrast, was tall and handsome; he looked good in a suit, and he could call on references from everyone from the ghost of Oliver Wendell Holmes (for whom he clerked) to John Foster Dulles. Just as Maurice Barrès had concluded from Alfred Dreyfus's Jewishness that he must be capable of treason, so Hiss's admirers inferred from his social quality that he could *not* be capable of treason.

And yet, as Tanenhaus reminds us, the two men were almost eerily alike in certain respects. Both came from insecure, turn-of-the-century, lower-middle-class families, with the Hiss clan at best one step up the unstable social ladder. Chambers's father, Jay, was a journeyman graphic artist in New York; Hiss's father worked in a Baltimore importing firm. The two men, who were born three years apart (Chambers in 1901, Hiss in 1904), suffered parallel family tragedies. Chambers's brother Richard, four years his junior, killed himself in 1926 at the age of twenty-two, while his father died three years later, in 1929, of liver disease. Hiss's father slit his throat in 1907, when Alger was just two and a half. His brother Bosley, his senior by four years, was an alcoholic and died of kidney failure in 1926. Hiss's older sister took her own life just three years later.

Despite the patina of Harvard Law School and a glittering résumé, Hiss had a lot more in common with Chambers than contemporaries appreciated. And Chambers himself believed as much. He described Hiss in 1948 as "the closest friend I ever had in the Communist Party," and over time he came to understand their conflict as the stuff of high tragedy. In *Witness*, Chambers's extraordinary narrative of his life and his times, he claims nothing less: "At heart, the Great Case was this critical conflict of faiths; that is why it was a great case. On a scale personal enough to be felt by all, but big enough to be symbolic, the two irreconcilable faiths of our time—Communism and Freedom—came to grips in the persons of two conscious and resolute men. Indeed, it would have been hard, in a world still only dimly aware of what the conflict is about, to find two other men who knew so clearly."

This, as Philip Rahv noted at the time, is pure bathos. And it does its author a curious injustice: He was much more interesting than that. In the early 1920s, after wandering through a series of pickup jobs in the lower depths of New Orleans and Washington, Chambers had enrolled at Columbia University long enough to come to the notice of Mark Van Doren, who judged him to be the best of his students in that era—from a class that included Meyer Schapiro and Lionel Trilling. One of his contemporaries, Jacques Barzun, would note later that "we were convinced he would leap into fame," and Trilling himself wrote in 1975 that although Chambers was given to "large solemnities" and "portentous utterance," he had a mind that "was not without force" (high praise in Trillingese). Chambers's early writings—poems and short stories—are skillful and sometimes moving. *Can You Hear Their Voices?*, a play based on the Arkansas drought of 1931, was well received, and not only by the theater critic of the Moscow-based *International Literature*, who thought that it gave a "revolutionary exposition of the problem of the agricultural crisis and correctly raises the question of the leading role of the Communist Party in the revolutionary farmers' movement." Chambers abandoned his literary ambitions to devote thirteen years of his life to the Communist movement.

He joined the party in 1925, went underground in 1932, and worked assiduously for the cause for six more years. For him, as for so many others, the party offered a substitute for family, community, and faith. But Chambers came to Communism after unsuccessful efforts to find God, one of a number of ways in which he remained an outsider even in the party. In the United States, as in Europe, the early ranks of Communism were drawn disproportionately from radicalized immigrants, many of them Jewish, for whom conventional religion was not an option, before or after their entanglement with Leninism. When they abandoned the Communist movement, they tended to drift into Trotskyism, scholarly neo-Marxism, even liberal anti-Communism, as well as engagement with non-Communist labor organizations.

For Chambers, such paths of retreat were closed. It was all or nothing. This uncompromising mentality served him well when it came to understanding, ahead of most other commentators, that Stalinism was no mere perversion of the Leninist utopia, but its very essence; yet it left Chambers more isolated than ever, with few sympathizers and fewer friends. Even after the Hiss affair—during which he tried to kill himself with rat poison and thus put an end to his self-imposed calvary—he remained a loner, admired by people whose reactionary and nativist obsessions he did not share and despised by almost everyone else.

Since 1939, he had been working at *Time*, first as a book reviewer, briefly as foreign editor, and then as a senior editor of the magazine. Some of his political writings from those years have weathered well, notably a little fable from May 1945 called "The Ghosts on the Roof," in which Chambers imagined the Romanovs looking approvingly on as Stalin fulfilled their centuries-old ambitions. Yet even Henry Luce was uncomfortable with the publicity that followed Chambers's summons before HUAC, and in 1948 Chambers lost his job at *Time*. He would never again find steady work as a writer and journalist. During the 1950s, his daughter was blackballed from admission to Swarthmore (despite Chambers's own involvement with the Quakers). He died in July 1961 as lonely as he had lived.

It is understandable that Chambers should have been so hated by so many in the 1950s, and not only because of his apostasy. It was the Hiss affair that gave the decisive impetus to Joseph McCarthy and his supporters; the latter's notorious speech in Wheeling, West Virginia ("two hundred and five known Communists in the State Department"), was made on February 9, 1950, just two weeks after Hiss's conviction. And Chambers himself was not above the occasional unsubstantiated charge. In the discussion over "who lost China," he once claimed, with no first-hand knowledge, that the presence of Communist agents in Washington had "decisively changed the history of Asia." (As Irving Howe pointed out at the time, "Mao, alas, recruited his armies in the valley of Yenan, not the bars of Washington.")

But Tanenhaus, who is remarkably evenhanded in his discussion of the McCarthy era, shows very convincingly that Chambers himself was no witch-hunter. He did not initially want to appear before HUAC, and when he did appear, like Walter Krivitsky before him, he was shocked at the ignorance and the lack of political sophistication of his interrogators. He was sufficiently committed to the cause of anti-Communism to realize very quickly that McCarthy was its worst enemy, and he retained enough of his Marxism (or at least what Tanenhaus calls a "dark historicism") to see that the clever young men of the National Review were flying in the face of reality in their call to undo the New Deal and in their failure to distinguish between Josef Stalin and Nikita Khrushchev.

And Chambers stands out from his contemporaries in another respect as well. His literary and moral sensibilities were untainted by his political affiliations. Writing in 1957, he attacked Ayn Rand for her arrogance and "dictatorial dogmatism": "From almost any page of *Atlas Shrugged*, a voice can be heard, from painful necessity, commanding 'To a gas chamber, go!'" Two years later he wrote to William F. Buckley Jr. that "the spectacle of an artist like Paul Robeson, denied a passport by his own government, makes us traduced of other nations."

Still, even those who were forced to concede that Chambers was probably telling the truth about Hiss found his behavior inexcusable. For such people, Hiss was innocent even if he was guilty. The New Deal, receding into the glow of memory, was sacrosanct for liberals. If the idealistic New Dealer had given secrets to the Soviet Union, he had done so on selfless grounds. (No one ever suggested that Hiss received money for his services.) And was the Soviet Union really so unworthy a cause?

Was it proper to read back into the atmosphere of the 1930s (Chambers's knowledge of espionage and the Communist underground was confined to that decade) the sour mood and the political acrimony of the cold war? Journalists such as Walter Lippmann, Joseph Alsop, and James Reston all took up these points, neglecting to mention something already widely acknowledged in Europe: that many of the political and military secrets passed along to Moscow in the years 1934–41 found their way fairly quickly into Nazi hands.

OTHERS DID NOT NEED to read the evidence to know what they thought about Chambers. He was an ex-Communist and perforce a man of the Right, and so he had no place in the world of American letters. Mary McCarthy, whose authoritarian proclivities were restrained only by her intellectual indiscipline, urged Hannah Arendt to do a hatchet job on *Witness.* This is not just a book to be reviewed, she told her friend: "The great effort of this new Right is to get itself accepted as normal, and its publications as a normal part of publishing—some opinions among others, all equally worthy of consideration—and this, it seems to me, must be scotched, if it's not already too late." Arendt reviewed the book, but wisely declined her friend's invitation to attack the man.

Thus there were many forms of "McCarthyism" in the 1950s. Chambers was tainted as much by association with Nixon and his colleagues as by anything he himself said or did. Few gave heed to the admonition that Koestler delivered in a lecture in Carnegie Hall in 1948. "Bad" allies, he reminded his audience, are unavoidable. "You can't help people being right for the wrong reasons. . . . This fear of finding oneself in bad company is not an expression of political purity; it is an expression of a lack of self-confidence." As Chambers wrote in *Witness,* anticipating precisely the reaction of people like Mary McCarthy, "It was the 'best people' who were for Alger Hiss . . . the enlightened and the powerful, the clamorous proponents of the open mind and the common man, who snapped their minds shut in a pro-Hiss psychosis."

Decades later, the pro-Hiss psychosis can still be seen at work. Laboring under the curious illusion that the moral and historical credibility of American progressivism depends upon the exculpation of Alger

Hiss (and by extension of philo-Communism in general), two generations of liberal intellectuals have striven to clear his name at Whittaker
Chambers's expense. In 1978, the *Nation* sent a reporter to Budapest to
meet the eighty-year-old Josef Peters, Chambers's controller back in the
1930s, then living in retirement in Hungary. Under investigation by
HUAC in 1948, Peters had taken the Fifth; but when the reporter asked
him about the Hiss affair, Peters laughingly confirmed to him that the
very notion of any "secret" Communist "underground" was nonsense,
and that he had never been involved in anything of the sort. It is not
difficult to imagine Peters's thoughts as the man from the *Nation*, duly
reassured, walked away from his door: Lenin's derogatory reference to
"useful idiots" has cognates in most European languages. As Raymond
Aron ruefully noted back in 1950, "progressivism consists in presenting
Communist arguments as though they emanated spontaneously from
independent speculation."

Even today, nearly four decades after his death and with the truth of
his testimony firmly established, Whittaker Chambers remains a marked
man. Consider the review of Tanenhaus's book in the *New Yorker*. So far
as Hiss's Communist activities are concerned, Sidney Blumenthal writes,
"the room for reasonable doubt continues to shrink." Indeed. But that is
apparently not the end of the matter. Blumenthal opportunistically resur-
rects the same charge that Alger Hiss's lawyers initially intended to pursue
(and then abandoned, lest it rebound on their client): that the affair was
about unrequited homosexual attraction.

As it happens, Tanenhaus deals very well with this issue. Chambers,
like his father, was probably bisexual (he certainly admitted to numerous
homosexual activities), and some of his youthful poetry reveals markedly
homoerotic preoccupations. In the 1950s, of course, these were highly
charged matters, and hints of homosexual involvement or motivation
could destroy a man. Today things are different. Blumenthal reminds
his readers that in the 1950s "conservatism was the ultimate closet,"
shielding Roy Cohn, J. Edgar Hoover, and the rest from exposure and
scrutiny. Chambers, it is thereby suggested, is guilty by association with
such men, who overcompensated for their hidden sexual preferences by
persecuting others. Why else would he attack a man like Hiss? Thus, as
so often in the past, we are led away from the evidence and the great

political issues of the day toward an alleged private imperative of a disreputable kind.

Why did Chambers do it? According to Blumenthal, "his motives remain murky." But not the consequences of his actions: "Since the end of the Cold War, this conservative anti-Communism has become an anachronism. What endures is the fear of the enemy within: the homosexual menace." And there is more. In case the homosexual issue lacks a *bien-pensant* resonance, Blumenthal reminds us that one result of Whittaker Chambers's "outing" of State Department China experts such as O. Edmund Clubb was the latter's replacement by "the dogmatic, abstract Dean Rusk, who eventually became Secretary of State. Vietnam lay in the future, but a seed of tragedy had been planted." Thus Chambers also bears an indirect responsibility for the Vietnam War.

This is a smear, 1990s style. Blumenthal's insinuations are a reminder that there is nearly always something provincial and self-serving about the response of American intellectuals to Whittaker Chambers. Many of them simply cannot, or will not, understand Chambers and his actions in a broader international context. For the Hiss case did not happen in a vacuum. It is exactly contemporaneous, for example, with the trial in Budapest in 1949 of László Rajk, the first of the great postwar show trials that served as cover for a purge of prewar underground Communists. Hence the interrogation of Noel Field and the references to Hiss in Eastern European archives.

The Hiss affair was also a remarkable echo of the Kravchenko and Rousset affairs in France. In 1946, Viktor Kravchenko, a midlevel Soviet bureaucrat who had defected to the United States, published *I Chose Freedom*, his account of the real workings of the Stalinist autocracy. A French Communist periodical, *Les Lettres Françaises*, published an article in November 1947 claiming that the book was an American fabrication, and that the details it gave of life in Stalin's Russia were a lie. Kravchenko sued for libel and produced a string of witnesses to confirm his story. He won his case and symbolic damages, but for the vast majority of French intellectuals he remained for many years guilty of the more serious crime of slandering the Soviet Union and its French supporters.

In November 1949, in the same week that the second Hiss trial began, David Rousset, a survivor of the German camps, wrote an article

in *Le Figaro Littéraire* describing the concentration camp system in the
Soviet Union. The same Communist periodical accused him of inventing
the whole thing, and he, too, sued for libel. Among the witnesses he
produced was the remarkable Margarete Buber-Neumann, a former
German Communist who had spent three years in the Soviet forced labor
camp at Karaganda before being handed to the Germans in 1940 and
spending the war years in Ravensbrück. Buoyed by her testimony, Rousset
won his case as well, but with no discernible impact upon the philo-
Soviet sensibilities of a significant sector of the French intelligentsia.

Nobody, to my knowledge, has suggested that Margarete Buber-
Neumann, David Rousset, Viktor Kravchenko, or the many other
European ex-Communists who spoke out about Stalinism in the 1930s
and 1940s—men and women such as Victor Serge in Russia, Ruth
Fischer in Germany, and Ignazio Silone in Italy, not to mention Arthur
Koestler—were driven by some peculiar combination of ressentiment
and repressed sexuality to betray former colleagues, embarrass friends,
or avenge themselves upon an inhospitable world. Like Chambers,
however, they sacrificed something for speaking out, and they were
execrated by their erstwhile comrades on the intellectual Left. Nor have
European progressives been as keen as their American counterparts to
repress the thought that there might really have existed a secret
Communist underground. As Koestler noted, the fact that such claims
were sometimes made by people who are distasteful doesn't make them
untrue. Even in Britain, where Communism was never more than a
minority predilection, it has not occurred to many people to imagine
that the now-notorious spy network recruited among Cambridge un-
dergraduates in the 1930s was an invention of the political Right.

Whittaker Chambers himself felt some affinity for his European counterparts, who had a better understanding of his background and his dilemma. In 1959, he returned from one of his rare trips abroad exhilarated
from a meeting in Austria with Koestler and Buber-Neumann. "We," he
wrote to William F Buckley Jr., "are almost the only survivors—the old
activists who were articulate, consequent revolutionists and not merely
agents." Like Ignazio Silone, he was convinced that only Communists and
ex-Communists could truly understand each other, as one another's only
true and worthy opponents. Certainly, Chambers was giving himself airs

here—or, rather, clinging desperately in his last years to the idea that he belonged to a select group of historically important individuals and was not just the renegade informer that American intellectuals took him for. Still, he had a point. Even so subtle a critic as Irving Howe, when reviewing Chambers's autobiography in 1952, could not help faulting him for tarring Lenin with the Stalinist brush. Stalin was not Lenin's ideological heir, wrote Howe, but the maker of a "new bureaucratic ruling-class." Chambers did not have to encounter that sort of face-saving ideological maneuver among his European peers, who had seen Leninism close-up and suffered no such "revisionist" illusions.

Chambers's admiration for the Europeans was in some measure reciprocated. Koestler described *Witness* in 1953 as "a great book, in the old, simple sense of greatness"; and even before its appearance Richard Crossman had invited its author to contribute to *The God That Failed.* (Chambers declined the invitation.) What these men and others found in Chambers was an unusual degree of moral courage—Trilling described him as "a man of honor"—and occasional bursts of almost Orwell-like insight, as when he writes of progressive intellectuals that "fundamentally benevolent and humane, they loved their fellow-countrymen in distress far more than they could ever love them in prosperity."

And yet, whatever the degree of mutual respect and sympathy that bound him to his European peers, he was not "one of them." As his biographer shows with care and understanding, Whittaker Chambers was utterly American. It is not for nothing that he called his autobiography *Witness.* He had a tragic worldview, morbid even, framed by a bitter and unhappy childhood and a lifelong search for an all-embracing, all-sustaining creed. All mortal questions for Chambers depended upon finding the answer to one transcendental and ultimate question. In Communism, he found a version of that answer, the key to the human condition, and, in contrast to most ex-Marxists, he never really abandoned it. His descriptions of politics as a battle between the forces of good and the forces of evil; his eschatological evocations of the coming struggle between freedom and enslavement; his account of human history since the Renaissance as a hubristic assertion of the centrality of man for which a price must now be paid: All this is a one-dimensional version of the Manichaean creed of Leninism held up to the mirror of a renascent religious fervor.

When he wrote that the Hiss case had "religious, moral, human and historical meaning" Chambers was not grandstanding. He really meant it. And he thought that it was true for Alger Hiss too, which is why he raised his opponent, in his own imagining, to a plateau far higher than Hiss deserved. Chambers's insistence on describing Hiss's dishonesty as self-sacrifice is the best clue to his own fundamental inability to grasp the truth about the Communist ideal to which he had once devoted himself: that it meant more to him than it did for many of the others. It was this quasi-theological transubstantiation of Communism that made Whittaker Chambers so much an American figure. The educated, secular, cosmopolitan, disabused skepticism of his European friends would have kept them from coming to such pleasingly redemptive conclusions.

Sam Tanenhaus is to be congratulated on having captured so sympathetically the complexities of this troubled man. His book reads at times like a thriller, and he tells the story of the hearings and the trials with great verve and skill. He is fairer to all parties concerned than anyone else whom I have read on these matters. All this would be for naught, of course, if Tanenhaus had somehow missed the man himself. He hasn't. You cannot read this book without feeling for this solitary, unhappy character, an insecure autodidact with the sensibility of a mystic, who "hung always upon the curse of himself," as he wrote to his children in the preface of his book.

Chambers's tragedy was that his years in the entrails of the Communist movement were the high point of his life. He remained obsessed with the 1930s, he saw his own and humanity's history through the prism of the choices and the commitments of that decade, and he was crucified for that obsession by generations to come. He really did feel a duty to bear witness, but he suffered deeply for the pain and the publicity that he brought upon himself, his family, and his former friends. Tanenhaus shows just how greatly Chambers agonized over whether to tell what he knew, and it is hard to resist the thought that there is an element of Shakespearean tragedy in this otherwise unremarkable man trapped in an unforgiving era. He, too, must more than once have rued his self-assigned condition: "The time is out of joint. O cursed spite/That ever I was born to set it right."

This review of Sam Tanenhaus's admirable biography of Whittaker Chambers first appeared in the New Republic in 1997. Even at that late date it provoked anguished exchanges from readers and colleagues convinced that the case against Alger Hiss remained unproven and that the reputation of Chambers could not—and should not—be redeemed.

CHAPTER XIX

The Crisis: Kennedy, Khrushchev, and Cuba

The story of the Cuban missiles begins in April 1962, when the Soviet leader Nikita Khrushchev decided to increase very substantially the limited military support hitherto provided by the USSR to the government of Fidel Castro in Cuba. At his urging, the Soviet Presidium duly assented to a military buildup on the island, which, in its final form, was to include some fifty thousand Soviet military personnel, organized in five nuclear missile regiments, four motorized regiments, two tank battalions, one MIG-21 fighter wing, forty-two IL-28 light bombers, two cruise missile regiments, twelve SA-2 antiaircraft units with 144 launchers, and a squadron of eleven submarines, seven of them equipped with nuclear missiles.

President John F. Kennedy and U.S. intelligence analysts were aware of the growing Soviet military presence in Cuba. But it was only after August 29, 1962, when a U-2 reconnaissance plane spotted the SA-2 missile sites, that Kennedy went public, on September 4, with a warning that whereas such land-to-air defensive missiles were acceptable, the installation of *offensive* missiles in Cuba would not be. On September 13, during a press conference, he repeated the warning: "If at any time . . . Cuba were to . . . become an offensive military base of significant capacity for the Soviet Union, then this country will do whatever must be done to protect its own security and that of its allies."[1]

What Kennedy did not then know was that by September the Soviet buildup also included thirty-six SS-4 medium-range ballistic missiles (MRBMs) and twenty-four SS-5 intermediate-range ballistic missiles (IRBMs), together with their nuclear warheads. (The first nuclear warheads arrived in Mariel aboard a Soviet freighter on October 4; by October 28, when the crisis ended, all the warheads for both sorts of missiles and all the SS-4 missiles themselves were actually in Cuba—only the SS-5s remained to be delivered.) Indeed, the Kennedy administration had been assured, by Khrushchev and by Anatoly Dobrynin, the Soviet ambassador to the U.S., that no such missiles were or would be placed in Cuba. When Dobrynin in early September asked how he might reply to a private question from Robert Kennedy about the Cuban situation, he was instructed by Moscow that "in talking to the Americans you should confirm that there are only *defensive* Soviet weapons in Cuba."

Dobrynin reassured Robert Kennedy accordingly, with all the more conviction in that he, too, knew nothing about the ballistic missile emplacements. The U.S. authorities accepted these reassurances, particularly since, as George Ball notes in his memoirs, the Soviet Union had never hitherto placed offensive missile bases outside its own territory, not even in the neighboring countries of the Warsaw Pact.[2]

The significance of the MRBMs and IRBMs lay in their reach. They were designed not to hit incoming aircraft but to land on targets deep inside the U.S.; the range of an SS-4 was about 1,100 nautical miles, that of an SS-5 nearly twice that. A Soviet MRBM of that era, launched from Cuba, could hit Washington, D.C.; an IRBM could hit almost any target in the continental U.S., sparing only the far Pacific Northwest. They were useless as defensive weapons; their only possible value was offensive—or as a deterrent to the offensives of others. Thus, when a U-2 flying over San Cristobal, in western Cuba, on October 14 spotted three missile sites under construction, and when these sites were identified in Washington as identical to known MRBM launch sites in the Soviet Union, President Kennedy and his advisers drew the obvious conclusion. They had been lied to, and their warnings had been ignored.

The Soviet Union was placing offensive missiles in Cuba, missiles that could only be deployed against targets in the U.S. The Cuban missile crisis had begun.

The first, confidential phase of the crisis, from early morning on October 16, when McGeorge Bundy, Kennedy's national security adviser, woke him up with the bad news, until 7:00 p.m. on the evening of October 22, when President Kennedy announced a naval quarantine around Cuba, was confined to a handful of men in Washington, D.C.: the "Executive Committee" (ExComm) that Kennedy gathered around him to decide what to do. The deliberations of this group, secretly taped by Kennedy himself, have now been painstakingly transcribed and impeccably edited by Ernest R. May and Philip D. Zelikow.*

Curiously, and like Khrushchev, who had made no contingency plans for the eventuality of his missile buildup being discovered before completion, Kennedy and his advisers had given no thought to what they should do if just such a crisis should occur: "No one, as far as I can remember," Bundy later wrote, "thought it necessary in September to consider what we would do if our warnings were disregarded . . . . This was a failure of foresight, and one of the reasons for respecting the quality of the basic decision President Kennedy reached on October 20 is that he had to begin on the sixteenth almost from a standing start."[3] That decision, of course, was to announce a partial quarantine of Cuba, under which ships suspected of carrying military supplies would be stopped from entering Cuban waters. But among the other strategies considered—and according to Kennedy it was not until October 21 that he made his final decision—were a more comprehensive blockade than the selective one eventually imposed, an air strike on the missile sites in Cuba, a blanket air strike on the island's military bases, and a full-scale military invasion.

The Joint Chiefs of Staff favored the most extreme response, but they had little civilian backing on ExComm. The option of ignoring the buildup and continuing as before had no takers. For five days ExComm debated three unknowns: How many missiles were in place, and were

---

*Ernest May and Philip Zelikow, eds., *The Kennedy Tapes: Inside the White House during the Cuban Missile Crisis* (Cambridge, MA: Harvard University Press, 1997).

they operational? How would the NATO allies react to either an insufficient U.S. response or an excessive one, the dilemma of "credibility" that obsessed Kennedy and his close advisers? And what would Khrushchev do in response to various possible American moves?

An air strike risked missing some of the missile sites—their exact number was unknown—and thus inviting a response from those still in place, or in some part of the world where the balance of forces favored the Soviet Union, notably Berlin. Conversely, if the nuclear warheads were not yet in Cuba—and no one at this stage knew the answer to that—an air strike was excessive; a blockade on all incoming offensive weaponry would suffice. And since an invasion took some advance planning, it could be kept in reserve as an option if all else failed. Meanwhile, a naval blockade or quarantine would buy both sides time to reconsider. Following the advice of Secretary of Defense Robert McNamara, Secretary of State Dean Rusk, Under Secretary of State George Ball, and his Soviet experts (former ambassadors Charles Bohlen and Llewellyn Thompson), this was the option that Kennedy chose.

On October 22, then, having first informed senior congressmen, leading NATO allies, and the Soviet leadership of his intentions, Kennedy announced to the world the presence of offensive nuclear missiles in Cuba and the U.S. response—a limited naval quarantine (civilian necessities would be allowed through) until the offending weaponry had been removed. To justify his actions, Kennedy emphasized the threat to peace in the Western Hemisphere and the U.S. commitment to defending the West, as well as the danger now faced by Americans living under the shadow of nuclear missiles.

How would Khrushchev respond to the quarantine and the accompanying demands? Thanks to his memoirs and to the Soviet archival material presented by Fursenko and Naftali in *One Hell of a Gamble*, we know that Khrushchev was thoroughly chastened and confused by the course of events.* The men sitting in the White House did not know this, however, and even those who suspected it could not be sure. When the quarantine went into effect at 10:00 a.m. on October 24, the crisis

---

* Aleksandr Fursenko and Timothy Naftali, *"One Hell of a Gamble": Khrushchev, Castro and Kennedy, 1958–1964* (New York: Norton, 1997).

seemed to be approaching its climax. That day Khrushchev sent Kennedy a cable insisting that Soviet weaponry in Cuba was purely defensive and threatening to ignore the quarantine—"We confirm that armaments now on Cuba, regardless of classification to which they belong, are destined exclusively for defensive purposes, in order to save Cuban Republic from attack of aggressor." What, then, would happen if a U.S. destroyer hailed a Soviet vessel and it refused to stop? Kennedy himself was not optimistic. Far from expecting Khrushchev to accede to his demands, he feared a speed-up in the missile-site construction, a formal threat of Soviet nuclear retaliation if the U.S. were to attack Cuba—and possibly a move to take advantage of the crisis to squeeze the West out of Berlin.

In fact, the whole matter passed off peacefully. Kennedy and his colleagues took special care to seek out a harmless (Panamanian-owned) freighter to intercept and allow through, thus making their point without running undue risks. On the advice of his friend David Ormsby-Gore, the British ambassador to the U.S., Kennedy also reduced the quarantine zone from eight hundred miles, as initially announced, to five hundred miles, giving the Soviets more time to reflect and to call back their ships. Khrushchev, in turn, did not wish to have the U.S. discover and inspect his most advanced weaponry, and so, as Kennedy had anticipated and hoped, he ordered missile-carrying ships to stop and turn back, which they did on Thursday, October 25. The quarantine had not led to a shooting war. But the U.S. administration still had no solution to its primary concern, Soviet nuclear missiles already in Cuba. Plans for an air strike and even an invasion continued.

Then, on Friday the 26th, Khrushchev sent a long and rather rambling private communication to Kennedy in which he deplored the drift toward war: "If indeed war should break out, then it would not be in our power to stop it, for such is the logic of war. I have participated in two wars and I know that war ends when it has rolled through cities and villages, everywhere sowing death and destruction." Instead, he proposed a solution: "If assurances were given by the President and the government of the United States that the USA itself would not participate in an attack on Cuba and would restrain others from actions of this sort, if you would recall your fleet, this would immediately change everything . . . . Then the necessity for the presence of our military specialists in Cuba would disappear . . . . Mr. President, we and you ought not now to pull on the ends of the rope in which you have tied the knots of war, because the more the two of us pull, the tighter this knot will be tied. And a moment may come when that knot will be tied so tight that even he who tied will not have the strength to untie it, and then it will be necessary to cut that knot. And what that would mean is not for me to explain to you, because you yourself understand perfectly of what terrible forces our countries dispose."

Khrushchev's letter, born of a growing fear in the Kremlin that Kennedy was about to attack Cuba and force a confrontation, might have defused the crisis there and then.[4] But the next day, Saturday the 27th, it was followed by a public and more formal letter, which made any settlement contingent on a quid pro quo: withdrawal of the offensive missiles in Cuba in return for the removal of NATO's nuclear missiles in Turkey. The Soviet proposal put Kennedy in a difficult position—as he commented to George Ball that Saturday morning, "Well, *this* is unsettling *now*, George, because he's got us in a pretty good spot here. Because most people would regard this as not an unreasonable proposal."

The complications of such an exchange (to be discussed below), together with the shooting down of a U-2 reconnaissance plane over Cuba that same day, seemed to leave the crisis unresolved and the clock ticking. Kennedy's military advisers insisted that delaying an air strike beyond Monday, October 29, was imprudent; but the president himself was more concerned than ever about the acknowledged impossibility of destroying all the missiles in one strike. As he remarked on Friday, "It still comes down to a question of whether they're going to fire the missiles." In the end it was decided to reply to Khrushchev's first letter and, in essence, accept it. Meanwhile Robert Kennedy was dispatched to meet privately with Ambassador Dobrynin that Saturday evening and impress upon him the urgency of an agreement, and the possibility of coming to a confidential understanding on the "missile swap."

Dobrynin's report of this meeting—that the Americans were serious and that President Kennedy was under irresistible military pressure to commit the irreversible—may have exaggerated Robert Kennedy's message, but it had the desired result. On Sunday, October 28, Radio Moscow broadcast Khrushchev's formal acceptance of the official U.S. terms for an end to the crisis—"The Soviet Government . . . has given a new order to dismantle the arms which you described as offensive, and to crate and return them to the Soviet Union"—and work on dismantling the missiles began directly.[5] Much remained to be worked out—the exact list of matériel to be removed from Cuba, the conditions of observation and on-site supervision, which Castro (furious at the outcome) vehemently rejected, and the secret understanding to remove missiles in Turkey.

The U.S. imprudently pressed its public advantage to insist that the IL-28 light bombers be removed as well, even though Kennedy himself had privately recognized that they posed little threat. But Khrushchev conceded these terms, on November 20 the quarantine was lifted, and on December 6 the last bomber was shipped out.[6] The NATO missiles were removed from Turkey by April 1963, as unofficially promised.

Why did Khrushchev do it? It made no sense to install some of the Soviet Union's most advanced (and vulnerable) military hardware seven thousand miles away on an undefendable island, in the hope that the U.S. would not notice what was happening until it was too late. During the crisis Kennedy and his advisers came up with four possible explanations for this aberrant behavior: (i) Cuba was to be a "lever" for Soviet ambitions in Berlin: "Let go in Berlin or else"; (ii) the move was part of internal Kremlin power struggles; (iii) Khrushchev was trying to compensate for Soviet strategic inferiority; (iv) Khrushchev seriously feared a coming U.S. invasion of Cuba and was seeking ways to avert it.

Of these, only (iii) and (iv) were true, in some degree—and it is symptomatic of the near-tragedy of errors in October 1962 that most of the men in the White House were much more disposed to believe and act on the assumption of (i) or (ii). Khrushchev was certainly frustrated with his inability to shift the Western allies from Berlin, despite his threats and bluffs of the past five years; what he calls in his memoirs the "anomalous" outcome of the 1945 Potsdam accords was a source of irritation to the Soviet Union throughout the first decades of the cold war.[7] But a change in the Berlin situation would at most have been a side benefit of a Soviet nuclear presence in Cuba; it was not its main purpose.

Khrushchev's main purpose was to compensate, rather desperately, for Soviet military shortcomings. Until 1961 the USSR had seemed quite well placed. The outcome of the Suez crisis of 1956 had misled Khrushchev into thinking that his threat at the time to fire off rockets if the Anglo-French expedition didn't withdraw had played a crucial part in the denouement (it didn't). The successful launching of Sputnik in 1957 and Khrushchev's own exaggerated boasting had aroused American fears of a "missile gap"—fears that Kennedy successfully exploited in his 1960 election campaign. But high-level reconnaissance flights over the Soviet Union had convinced the Americans that Soviet intercontinental ballistic capacity had been vastly overstated, and in October 1961 Roswell Gilpatric, the U.S. assistant secretary of defense, had publicly revealed U.S. knowledge of Soviet strategic inferiority. A year later, by the time of the Cuban crisis, the Soviet Union was at a seventeen-to-one disadvantage in intercontinental missiles.[8]

Khrushchev knew this, and he knew that the Americans knew it. In John Gaddis's words, he "understood more clearly than Kennedy that the West was winning the cold war."[9] The Soviet resumption of atmospheric testing in August 1961—followed by the U.S. decision to follow suit in April 1962—did nothing to allay Khrushchev's sense of military inferiority (to which should be added his domestic agricultural failures and the chorus of Chinese attacks on Soviet "revisionism"). The temptation to place medium-range missiles (with which the Soviet Union was well supplied) just off the Florida coast seemed irresistible. After all, the U.S. had bases all around the frontiers of the USSR. As Khrushchev complained to U.S. Ambassador Thompson in April 1961, "The USA . . . believes that it has the right to put military bases along the borders of the USSR"—and a few Soviet missiles up against America's borders would serve it right. "The Americans had surrounded our country with military bases and threatened us with nuclear weapons, and now they would learn just what it feels like to have enemy missiles pointing at you."[10]

IN ADDITION TO the psychic reward of jolting the Americans—"throwing a hedgehog at Uncle Sam's pants," as Khrushchev put it to his colleagues in April 1962—Khrushchev had another motive. American experts had not fully appreciated the depth of Khrushchev's fears for Cuban security. But these were real, and by no means irrational. With some help from Castro himself, the U.S. had made of Cuba a pariah state; it had actively supported one abortive invasion and was known to be devising all manner of schemes to undermine and overthrow the local regime, including the elimination of Castro himself. The Cubans themselves had the Guatemalan coup of 1954 firmly in memory, and they never tired of warning Moscow of impending attacks and possible invasions, not all of them the product of Castro's overheated imagination.

If the Soviet Union could not protect its new (and only) friend in the Western Hemisphere against U.S. attack, how credible was it as the mainspring of progress and revolution? A year after the Bay of Pigs debacle, Khrushchev was obsessed by the fear that the U.S. might invade Cuba: "While I was on an official visit to Bulgaria [in April 1962] . . . one thought kept hammering away at my brain: what will happen if we lose Cuba?"[11] But the only protection Moscow could realistically offer Castro was a threat sufficiently terrible, immediate, and local to deter the Americans from any future aggression. Hence the decision to introduce the missiles.

Khrushchev was not just whistling in the dark when, in *The Glasnost Tapes*, he claimed to have gained something from his maneuver: "Our aim was to preserve Cuba. Today, Cuba exists." In retrospect, even some of the American participants in the missile crisis conceded the reasonable basis of Soviet fears—"After all, there was the Bay of Pigs and afterward a series of pointless 'dirty tricks' pulled on Castro by the Central Intelligence Agency and Cuban exiles."[12] But the American leadership at the time had obsessions of its own, which obscured Soviet objectives from view. To begin with, the members of ExComm were old enough to remember, and invoke, the events of the thirties and forties. The errors of appeasement, the success of the Berlin airlift of 1948–49, the lessons of the Korean War, were uppermost in their thinking. After his criticisms of Eisenhower, his failure at the Bay of Pigs, and his poor showing at the 1961 Vienna summit, Kennedy was ultrasensitive to any hint of indecision or weakness. On October 19, the third day of the crisis, General Curtis LeMay, the head of the air force, pressed him to take decisive military action: "I see no other solution. This blockade and political action, I see leading into war. . . . It will lead right into war. This is almost as bad as the appeasement at Munich."[13]

There were more recent analogies, too. American pressure on the British and French to withdraw from Suez in November 1956 had led to fears among the NATO countries that when it came to a war, the U.S. might retreat to its hemisphere, abandoning the vulnerable and exposed European allies. Hence the perceived need in Washington to "stand firm." Conversely, the fiasco of the Bay of Pigs had taught Kennedy and his advisers the wisdom of observing at least the forms of legality. Hence the decision—urged upon Kennedy by Dean Rusk in particular—that there should be no unannounced actions, and that any actions taken should be both prudent and legal, so as not to shake further the allies' confidence.

These foreign policy concerns made Kennedy simultaneously resolute and cautious. Domestic politics, however, all pointed toward a need to appear uncompromising, at least in public. Republican congressmen, notably Senator Kenneth Keating, had for some time been warning of the growing threat from Soviet missiles in Cuba; the administration's belated public acknowledgment of the extent of the danger gave its opponents a leverage over the handling of the crisis that Kennedy felt had to be offset by an appearance of granite resolve. Most of his nonmilitary advisers, with McNamara in the lead, were convinced that the missile emplacements had no impact on the United States' overall strategic superiority and thus in no way increased U.S. vulnerability. As McGeorge Bundy later observed, it was not U.S. missile superiority but the mere risk of nuclear war that kept Khrushchev from ever pushing too near the brink.[14] But President Kennedy, who was not much liked by his senior officers and who faced a midterm election the following month, could hardly say this in public. Robert Kennedy reported himself as having said to his older brother at the height of the crisis, "If you hadn't acted you would have been impeached"—a remark to which the president apparently nodded agreement. This is characteristic hyperbole from the excitable younger Kennedy, but it certainly must have been a factor in the president's decisions at the time.[15]

THESE BACKGROUND CONSIDERATIONS had a major part in determining the U.S. response to the Cuban missile crisis—indeed, they helped define for the U.S. leadership just what sort of a crisis it actually was. Thus Kennedy and his advisers were reluctant to play down the Soviet threat, or trade missiles in Turkey, or do anything else that might "let down our friends" and make them lose faith in American determination to preserve the free world. In fact the danger of allied disenchantment was vastly exaggerated—as the British ambassador to Washington reported himself saying to Kennedy at the height of the crisis, "Very few people outside the United States would consider the provocation offered by the Cubans serious enough to merit an American air attack."[16]

Nevertheless, when ExComm discussed the possibility of a missile swap as proposed in the second Soviet letter of October 27, which would mean depriving the Turks of their recently installed NATO missiles, McGeorge Bundy summed up the common view: "In our own terms it would already be clear that we were trying to sell our allies for our interests. That would be the view in all of NATO. Now, it's irrational and it's crazy, but it's a *terribly* powerful fact."

The missiles in question were the "Jupiters" of Philip Nash's new book.* They are the Rosencrantz and Guildenstern of the crisis plot, and their story is told here in full for the first time. In December 1957 NATO decided to install these intermediate-range nuclear missiles in Turkey and in Italy. Their presence fulfilled U.S. promises to provide its allies with credible defenses against the Soviet nuclear threat, plugged the apparent "missile gap" in the aftermath of Sputnik, and provided a use for an early generation of vulnerable, ground-based, liquid-fueled American missiles that were obsolete long before the last of them was deployed, after numerous delays, in March 1962. The Turks alone wanted them, and more for domestic political reasons than anything else. About the only military value of the Jupiters lay in increasing the number of targets the USSR would have to attack in the event of war.

Few had any illusions about these weapons, which were provocative to the Soviets and of no help to the West. Even Eisenhower, the president who approved their installation, thought them militarily insignificant, according to Nash. Kennedy's advisers would later try to outdo one an-

---

* Philip Nash, *The Other Missiles of October: Eisenhower, Kennedy and the Jupiters, 1957–1963* (Chapel Hill: University of North Carolina Press, 1997).

other in dismissing them: "worse than useless" (Bundy), "we joked about which way those missiles would go if they were fired" (Rusk), "a pile of junk" (McNamara—whose first defense review unsuccessfully recommended cancellation of the Jupiters' deployment).[17] When the crisis began, some officials, Rusk and McNamara especially, were initially keen to put the Jupiters on the table as a negotiating chip, and were restrained only by the collective belief that the Turks, and other NATO allies, would be disheartened by such cynical lack of attention to their feelings and needs.[18] Later, some of the ExComm members calculated that even if an air strike on Cuba brought retaliation against the Jupiters, this would be a reasonable and tolerable risk.

Khrushchev, meanwhile, was equally aware of the Jupiters' negligible military significance, and he paid them little attention. But when, on October 27, he and his colleagues thought they detected the chance of a negotiated compromise—perhaps overinterpreting as a direct hint some casual remarks in a newspaper article by Walter Lippmann—they decided to invoke the Jupiters as a way of getting something more out of the unpromising situation in which they now found themselves.

The Americans, as we have seen, were embarrassed by a suggestion that in other circumstances would not have been unwelcome, and so it was only as part of a highly secretive deal that the removal of the Jupiters was agreed to, thereby depriving the Soviets of the propaganda advantage they had sought from a public missile "swap." As Khrushchev would later conclude, "This agreement was primarily of moral significance and had no practical consequences. All those missiles were obsolete and America did not need them. The Americans would have removed them even if there were no conflict between us."[19]

Why the secrecy, then? Why did McNamara, Rusk, Bundy, and others lie to Congress and others for years to come, insisting there was no such deal (and making Kennedy look strikingly unreasonable and uncooperative as a result)? Partly, once again, to protect the sensibilities of their allies, partly to protect JFK's image and the record of uncompromised victory. And partly, if Anatoly Dobrynin is to be believed, to protect the future presidential ambitions of his brother. "Very privately, Robert Kennedy added that some day—who knows?—he might run for president, and his prospects could be damaged if this secret deal about the missiles in Turkey were to come out."[20] The secret was kept at least until the early eighties, when George Ball and others hinted at it in their memoirs. It is noteworthy that the Soviet leadership, who might have had an interest in making it more widely known, chose never to do so.

Two final considerations shaped and inhibited U.S. behavior in the crisis. One, of course, was the unhealthy obsession with Cuba. The Kennedys did much to fan this near-hysteria—it was John Kennedy who had once described Eisenhower's relatively restrained approach to Cuba as "the most glaring failure of American foreign policy." Having talked up the Cuban threat in public and (in Robert Kennedy's case) assiduously encouraged and participated in "Mongoose" and other CIA schemes in 1961–62 to destroy Castro, they were ill-placed to minimize the danger in October. For the same reason, they did not fully grasp how much their preoccupations had made Cuba one of the Kremlin's own major concerns.[21] Once Khrushchev had decided to place offensive missiles there, however, the visceral unacceptability to Americans of Soviet missiles being *that* close to home (something Europeans had lived with for many years) was itself a political element in the situation that Kennedy could hardly ignore.

Finally, there was Berlin. In retrospect it seems absurd that Kennedy and his advisers should have been so obsessed by the possibility of a Soviet move there. They were convinced that Khrushchev was engaged in a complex, Machiavellian ploy to achieve his long-standing German objectives. Hardly an hour passed during the first ten days of the crisis without ExComm reverting to the subject of West Berlin, to the need to counter Khrushchev's anticipated countermove in the divided city. As Kennedy said on October 22 to the British Prime Minister Harold Macmillan (the only foreign leader whom he consulted throughout the crisis), "I need not point out to you the possible relation of this secret and dangerous move on the part of Khrushchev to Berlin."

The lesson of 1948 had been learned too well—"To the Kennedy administration West Berlin was indeed a vital interest of the West," Bundy wrote, and of course the most vulnerable. Just as Truman and Acheson had seen the Korean incursion as a possible prelude to a Soviet probe across the divided frontier of Germany, so Kennedy and his colleagues saw in the missile emplacements in Cuba a Soviet device to blackmail a vulnerable America into giving way in Berlin.[22]

The irony is that the Berlin crisis of the early sixties was in fact already over. Ever since 1957 Khrushchev had been pressing for a "resolution" to the unfinished business of West Berlin. On more than one occasion he had threatened to sign a separate peace treaty with the East German regime and give the latter full control of access to Berlin's western half. At the Vienna summit meeting with Kennedy, he tried to use Soviet superiority in conventional forces as a threat to push the Americans out of West Berlin. In the summer of 1961, duly impressed, Kennedy even increased the national defense budget specifically to buttress the U.S. military presence there.

Khrushchev was bluffing—he did have a vast superiority of local conventional forces in Europe and could have occupied West Berlin (and most of Western Europe) any time he wished. But the U.S. had sworn to defend the freedom of West Berlin by all means—which in practice meant nuclear weapons—and Khrushchev had no intention of risking nuclear war for Germany. Instead, he resolved the local dilemma of the East German authorities—the thousands of their subjects who were voting with their feet and heading west—by putting up the Wall in August 1961. Two months later he withdrew his earlier "deadline" for a peace treaty, and nothing more was said of the matter.[23]

But the Americans, here as elsewhere, took Soviet bluster and propaganda all too seriously and—mistakenly believing that Berlin mattered as much to the Russians as it did to the West—built their understanding of U.S.-Soviet relations around the Berlin question.[24] This dramatically ratcheted up the apparent meaning of the Cuban crisis. Thus Kennedy said on October 19: "I don't think we've got any satisfactory alternatives . . . . Our problem is not merely Cuba but it is also Berlin. And when we recognize the importance of Berlin to Europe, and recognize the importance of our allies to us, that's what has made this thing be a dilemma for these days. Otherwise, our answer would be quite easy." Give him an inch on Cuba, ran the general line, and he'll take a mile on Berlin. Three days earlier, as the crisis began, Secretary of State Dean Rusk had summarized his own interpretation of the Soviet actions: "I think also that Berlin is very much involved in this. For the first time, I'm beginning really to wonder whether maybe Mr. Khrushchev is entirely rational about Berlin." Today's readers of *The Kennedy Tapes* may be more disposed to ask that question of Khrushchev's American adversaries.

The books under review, *The Kennedy Tapes* in particular, provide the opportunity for us to think afresh about men we thought we knew; the more so since they were speaking "off the record"—only the Kennedy brothers knew they were being taped. Dean Acheson, a diplomat of considerable stature during his years as secretary of state under Truman, is here revealed as a grumpy old statesman who has learned nothing and forgotten nothing. From beginning to end he presses for an immediate air strike and more. When his advice is ignored and the moderate approach is successful he attributes it ungenerously to "just plain dumb luck." Douglas Dillon, Kennedy's urbane secretary of the treasury, comes across in the tapes as an unreasoning warmonger, hungry for military action.

Senators Richard Russell and William Fulbright, who were among the senior congressmen brought in on the secret before Kennedy's October 22 press conference, express views that are quite frightening. Discussing Kennedy's choices, Russell declares, "A war, our destiny, will hinge on it. But it's coming someday, Mr. President. Will it ever be under more auspicious circumstances?" Likewise Fulbright—"I'm in favor, on the basis of this information, of an invasion, and an all-out one, and as quickly as possible." Fortunately, Kennedy was not seeking the advice of these men and their congressional colleagues, merely their support, and this, at least, they gave him.

The advice Kennedy received from his service chiefs was similarly extreme. From beginning to end they pressed for immediate and large-scale air strikes and an invasion, and even after Khrushchev's acceptance of Kennedy's terms, they voted for military intervention nonetheless, with only General Maxwell Taylor, their chairman, dissenting. Military contempt for the young president is palpable, with General LeMay's remarks bordering on insolence. Fortunately Kennedy only met with them once, as a group, on October 19, and their scorn for him was matched by his suspicion of them. His exchange with the head of the army, General Earle Wheeler, is characteristic:

General Wheeler: "From a military point of view, I feel that the low-est-risk course of action is the full gamut of military action by us. That's it."

President Kennedy: "Thank you, General."[25]

In striking contrast, Kennedy's professional diplomats gave him excellent advice. Llewellyn Thompson, the former ambassador to Moscow, is especially impressive. He was always perceptive (and virtually alone) in his estimates of Khrushchev's likely motives and coming moves, and by October 18 he had accurately described to the president the course that events should and would take:

Thompson: "I think it's very highly doubtful that the Russians would resist a blockade against military weapons, particularly offensive ones, if that's the way we pitched it before the world."

President Kennedy: "What do we do with the weapons already there?"

Thompson: "Demand they're dismantled, and say that we're going to maintain constant surveillance."

Among the inner circle of Kennedy advisers, most of whom we are predisposed to see through the dark glass of Vietnam, George Ball maintained a moderate attitude, always seeking the least provocative and most promising avenue out of the dilemma—hardly surprising to those who recall his later dissent from the Indochina policy of the Johnson years. He was one of the first, on October 18, to articulate clearly the case against a sudden surprise attack on Cuba: "It's the kind of conduct that one might expect of the Soviet Union. It is not conduct that one expects of the United States. And I have a feeling that this 24 hours to Khrushchev is really indispensable." This advice was based on the insightful conclusion, which Ball reached on the first day of the crisis, that the Soviets didn't realize what they had done. McGeorge Bundy was sharp and analytical, asking hard questions about the risks of an attack, though he curiously inclined toward the end of the first week to align himself with the hardliners, whose assumptions he nevertheless clearly questioned.

Robert McNamara's views, on the other hand, may come as a surprise to those who recall his advocacy of bombing in Indochina. Throughout the crisis he was the voice of moderate common sense. On October 16 he told his colleagues, "I would strongly urge against the air attack, to be quite frank about it, because I think the danger to this country in relation to the gain that would accrue would be excessive." After describing the naval blockade option in some anticipatory detail on the same day, he acknowledged that "this alternative doesn't seem to be a very acceptable one. But wait until you work on the others." And despite having to fulfill his role as secretary of defense and assess the pros and cons of military options, he was always among the most clearheaded of the group in understanding that the crisis, and its resolution, were and must remain above all political.

Dean Rusk, too, comes across in these pages as a force for reason and calm. He spoke most emphatically on October 24 against those (among them Robert Kennedy) who wanted to capture and inspect Soviet vessels carrying arms; the point, he reminded his colleagues more than once, was not to seize Soviet ships but simply to prevent missiles from reaching Cuba with the use of minimum force. In view of his sad performance during the Vietnam War, it is worth recalling for the record that during the Cuban crisis, at least, he always favored negotiation, a role for the United Nations, and a peaceful resolution if at all possible.

Vice President Lyndon Johnson, too, displayed an unfamiliar side during these days. He spoke little and was not one of the men to whose opinion Kennedy paid very close attention. But when he did speak he was rather impressive. On Saturday, October 27, he had a revealing exchange with McNamara, as the group debated how to respond to Khrushchev's offer of a missile "swap":

Johnson: "Bob, if you're willing to give up your missiles in Turkey, you think you ought to defuse them, why don't you say that to him and say we're cutting a trade, make the trade there, [and] save all the invasion, lives, and everything else?"

McNamara: "I said I thought it was the realistic solution to the problem."

Johnson: "Sure. Right. What we were afraid of was he would never offer this, and what he would want to do is trade *Berlin*."

Later the same day, when Dillon and others were suggesting nighttime photographic surveillance of Cuban missile sites with the use of flares, Johnson cut in heatedly:

> I've been afraid of these damned flares ever since they mentioned them. . . .
>
> Imagine some crazy Russian captain doing it. The damn thing [the flare] goes "blooey" and lights up the skies. He might just pull a trigger. Looks like we're playing Fourth of July over there or something. I'm scared of that. . . .
>
> And I don't see what you get with that photograph that's so much more important than what you . . . You know they're working at night, and you can see them working at night. Now, what do you do?
>
> Psychologically, you scare them [the Soviets]. Well, hell, it's like the fellow telling me in Congress: "Go on and put the monkey on his back." Every time I tried to put a monkey on somebody else's back, I got one. If you're going to try to psychologically scare them with a flare, you're liable to get your bottom shot at.

The flares proposal was duly abandoned.

IN CONTRAST, Robert Kennedy's political reputation can only suffer from the publication of these records. To be sure, his "back channel" conversations with Ambassador Dobrynin helped draw the crisis to a close, and toward the end he was one of those, with Thompson and Bundy, who saw the advantage of accepting Khrushchev's first communication and ignoring the more troublesome follow-up letter.[26] But in the early days of the crisis Robert Kennedy's contributions were unhelpful, to say the least. As the administration's senior figure most intimately committed to the tactic of "dirty tricks," he was angrily belligerent in response to the Soviet move. On the first day of the crisis he burst out, "If he [Khrushchev] wants to get into a war over this . . . . Hell, if it's war that's gonna come on this thing, or if he sticks those kinds of missiles after the warning, then he's gonna get into a war six months from now, or a year from now. So . . ."

This was consistent with the younger Kennedy's personal obsession with the Cuban issue. In January 1962 he had informed the CIA/Pentagon group secretly at work undermining Castro that "we are in a combat situation with Cuba." To the incoming director of the CIA, John McCone, he announced that Cuba was "the top priority in the U.S. government—all else is secondary—no time, no money, effort or manpower is to be spared." His older brother's senior advisers clearly did not think much of him. George Ball, who later claimed to be "pleasantly surprised" by RFK's caution and good sense as the crisis unfolded, conceded that "until then I had not had much respect for his judgment; he had seemed to me—particularly in comparison with his brother—immature, far too emotional, and inclined to see everything in absolute terms with too little sensitivity to nuance and qualification."

Dean Rusk, who resented the "spin" that Robert Kennedy gave to his role in the crisis in his posthumous account of it, acidly notes in his memoirs that "the emotion that Bobby Kennedy portrayed in his book *The Thirteen Days* and that was reflected in the television program 'The Missiles of October' was unique to Bobby; this was his first major crisis." Anatoly Dobrynin, who knew Robert Kennedy well and worked closely with him in these weeks, summed him up quite fairly: "He was a complex and contradictory person who often lost his temper; at such moments he behaved badly and was unpleasant to deal with. . . . He did not know the foreign policy questions in detail, but apparently thought himself to be expert in them. This at times complicated the dialogue, particularly when he spoke on behalf of the president." Dobrynin, like everyone else, recognized the necessity of getting on with the younger Kennedy. "His clear intimacy with his brother made him a very valuable channel of communication." But nothing in the recorded evidence or the recollections of the senior staff of either John Kennedy or Nikita Khrushchev suggests that Robert Kennedy's ascension to the presidency would have been an asset to the U.S. in world affairs.[27]

How near did the world come to disaster during those two weeks thirty-five years ago? The most likely cause of a shooting war would clearly have been sheer misadventure—a missile fired, a bomb dropped, a ship sunk by accident or by some unauthorized trigger-happy officer. As it was, the U.S. went to Defense Condition 2 on October 24 (one step short of general war), and the Soviets "unintentionally" brought down a U-2 over Cuba on October 27. Either of these moves, or an attempt to stop a sensitive ship in the quarantine zone, could have been fatal, if only by misleading the other side into supposing that war was imminent. But they weren't fatal. And if they weren't, it was because the top leader on each side was determined they shouldn't be.

We might also ask what would have happened if Khrushchev had not accepted within twenty-four hours Kennedy's reply/ultimatum of Saturday the 27th. At the time, it seemed as if the U.S. had no fallback position and would have had to begin air strikes and an invasion the following week, as ExComm had agreed it must, in view of the fact that construction of the missile sites was apparently continuing apace.[28] In fact, as we have only learned in recent years, Kennedy did have a secret reserve position. He would, in extremis, have authorized Dean Rusk to encourage U Thant, the UN Secretary General, to propose a *public* missile swap, which the U.S. would then have accepted. In other words, if all else failed, he would have agreed to the terms of the second, "unacceptable" Soviet letter of September 27, proposing the removal of the Jupiters and an agreement not to invade Cuba in exchange for the dismantling of the missiles there.[29]

But even if there really had been no fallback plan and Kennedy had authorized air strikes and an invasion of Cuba in the following days, a generalized nuclear war would probably not have happened, despite the strong Soviet military presence in Cuba (stronger than the Americans knew) and the nuclear weapons already there. The reason, once again, is very simple. In McGeorge Bundy's words, "The largest single factor that might have led to nuclear war—the readiness of one leader or the other to regard that outcome as remotely acceptable—simply did not exist in October 1962." Both leaders tried hard to pretend otherwise, of course, for the sake of public appearance and because their diplomatic strategies depended upon the credibility of their nuclear threats. And in *The*

Glasnost Tapes, Khrushchev does suggest that precisely because the Soviet Union could not have responded to a Cuban invasion with an effective attack on the U.S., (conventional) war might have broken out in the European theater instead.[30] But even this seems unlikely. Khrushchev's own state of mind in the crucial ninety-six hours between the start of the quarantine and his agreement to remove the missiles is now quite clear—he was horrified at the prospect of war and decided very quickly that the game was not worth the candle.

THE WHOLE CRISIS, and the degree of risk it entailed, thus hinged on a paradox. If Kennedy and his colleagues had known what Khrushchev's real purposes were, they might have been able to defuse the whole business quietly and privately (though Bundy and other commentators always insisted that Khrushchev's bluff required a public response, lest he suppose that the U.S. wasn't serious about resisting him). But had the Americans also known how many armed nuclear missiles the USSR had already installed in Cuba—and how reluctant Khrushchev was actually to fire them—the temptation to act first and talk afterward might have proven irresistible. So their partial ignorance both provoked the drama and prevented a tragic denouement.

Conversely, had the U.S. not uncovered Khrushchev's plans to install missiles in Cuba before they were complete, Kennedy would certainly have been faced, in November 1962, with a huge political dilemma: accept the indefinite presence of Soviet ballistic missiles just off the U.S. coast, or else stage a crisis under much less favorable military and diplomatic conditions. This situation might have been made worse by Khrushchev, who, with his missiles securely in situ, could have been tempted to push his advantage well beyond what was prudent; at best he would then have suffered a reversal even more humiliating and public than the one he accepted on October 28.

Given Khrushchev's decision to place nuclear missiles in Cuba (a decision taken well before Kennedy's public warnings of September 1962), an international crisis of some kind was thus unavoidable. If it took the unnecessarily terrifying form that it did, this was in large measure because of a simple American misunderstanding that can stand as a metaphor for much of the early cold war. The officials in Washington thought that their Soviet opponents were playing a complicated game of diplomatic chess, with the various pawns on the international board—Czechoslovakia, Korea, Germany, Egypt, Indochina, and now Cuba—being subtly moved around to the calculated advantage of the Moscow principals.

In fact, however, the Soviet leaders—first Stalin, now Khrushchev—were not playing chess. They were playing poker. They had a weak hand and they knew it—long before the West German Chancellor Helmut Schmidt made the observation, Khrushchev and many of his senior colleagues understood intuitively that the empire they ruled over was basically "Upper Volta with missiles." So they bluffed. The outcome of the Cuban crisis would not have been very different if the Americans had realized sooner which game they were in; but the risks encountered along the way would have been much reduced.

Poker and chess have this in common, however—that their outcome depends more on the nerve, character, and intuition of the players than on any formal disposition of resources or rules. And the more we learn of the Cuban missile crisis the more we must come to appreciate the two men who held our fate in their hands in those days. Mr. Khrushchev's role is easier to grasp. Having made a major miscalculation, he resisted the temptation to raise the stakes. When Kennedy imposed a quarantine and demanded the removal of the missiles from Cuba, the Soviet leader could have responded by threatening nuclear retaliation if Soviet ships were intercepted or Cuban territory attacked. That, after all, was the logic of the missile emplacements in the first place—the threat of a nuclear response to deter the U.S. from aggressive moves in the Caribbean.

But Khrushchev never even considered such a challenge. As he explained on October 30 to a disappointed Castro, who would have preferred an armed (and if necessary nuclear) confrontation with the Americans, "There's no doubt that the Cuban people would have fought courageously or that they would have died heroically. But we are not struggling against imperialism in order to die. . . ."[31] Other Soviet leaders might well have behaved similarly—and Stalin, at least, would never have exposed himself as thoughtlessly as Khrushchev had done. All the same, it was Khrushchev whose decisions defused and resolved the Cuban crisis, and history owes him that much recognition.

JOHN F. KENNEDY'S POSITION is more troubling. His own posturing, no less than that of Khrushchev, got the U.S. into its Cuban imbroglio in the first place, and it was in large measure Kennedy's need to seem strong, his concern for "credibility," that fueled the rhetoric swirling around Washington in the autumn of 1962. He was a young president, under great pressure to do the "right" thing, possessing imperfect information about a possible threat to his country's security, and advised by a mixed group of men (many of them older and more experienced) who had in common only their frequently reiterated awareness that this was a major crisis and that the fate of the world hung upon their decisions.

And yet *The Kennedy Tapes* reveal a remarkable coolness in John Kennedy, a willingness and a capacity to listen, question, absorb, weigh, and finally adjudicate in extraordinary circumstances. At each turn in the proceedings, Kennedy chose the most moderate available option, sometimes against the specialized advice pressing in upon him. Instead of an invasion he favored an air strike on missile bases; instead of a blanket air strike he favored selective strikes only; he insisted that no strikes, however selective, should happen until warning had been given. He opted for a naval blockade over immediate military action, and a partial naval quarantine over a blanket blockade on all shipping.[32]

It was at Kennedy's insistence that an innocuous ship of non-Soviet registry was targeted for a symbolic exercise of the quarantine, and he pressed his staff to obtain all possible legal and international support in advance of even that limited action. He ignored suggestions that the U.S. might take advantage of the quarantine to seize Soviet ships carrying missiles in order to learn more about the Soviet weapons program. He rebuffed all pressure to respond aggressively when Captain Rudolf Anderson's U-2 was shot down over Cuba on October 27, and repeatedly postponed the confidential deadline after which the countdown to U.S. military intervention would begin. He welcomed the opportunity to use the Jupiter missiles in Turkey as a secret bargaining ploy and even authorized his secretary of state to have the United Nations urge *him* publicly to accept such a trade if all else failed. And just to be sure that there were no mistakes, on October 27 he instructed that those same Jupiter missiles be defused so that if he had to authorize air strikes on Cuba, and the Soviets responded by an attack on the Turkish missile sites, there would be minimal risk of further escalation.

Each of these decisions was taken in the face of criticism from some quarter among his advisers and generals—according to George Ball the defusing of the Jupiters was ordered "much to the disgust of those eager for dramatic action."[33] With hindsight we can see that Kennedy managed to obtain the best possible outcome in the circumstances. He was not just lucky, either, *pace* Acheson—he was consistent. In rejecting the advice he was offered in hundreds of hours of secret meetings, he ran serious risks, too; as he remarked to the assembled senior congressmen on the day of his press conference revealing the crisis, "The people who are the best off are the people whose advice is not taken because whatever we do is filled with hazards."

Of course Kennedy's motives were never unmixed, and, like any politician, he sought to turn his management of the affair into a political asset. He presented himself, and his colleagues and admirers presented him, as the man who "faced down" the Soviets, who drew a line in the sand, who won the first phase of the cold war; in Dean Rusk's words, spoken on Thursday, October 25, when the Soviet ships turned back, "We [were] eyeball to eyeball and the other fellow just blinked."[34]

Just to make sure, Kennedy went to the trouble of slandering his old political opponent Adlai Stevenson, then the U.S. ambassador to the United Nations. Stevenson, it was hinted, had been "soft" during the crisis, favoring negotiations and a missile "trade," in contrast to Kennedy's own firm, virile position. The implication—that Stevenson had been unwilling to "stand up to" the Soviets and that Kennedy had been uncompromising and unyielding—was doubly misleading; but after Charles Bartlett and Joseph Alsop published it in their "inside" account of the crisis in the December 8, 1962, issue of the *Saturday Evening Post* (with John Kennedy's prior knowledge and approval), the damage was done. The irony is that Kennedy himself was no less a victim of these domestic "dirty tricks" than Stevenson: The qualities that the president did display during the crisis—patience, moderation, a capacity for independent judgment, and a steady preference for negotiation over confrontation— were kept hidden from view.

All modern U.S. presidents are perforce also politicians, prisoners of their past pronouncements, their party, their constituency, and their colleagues. Yet there are advantages to a life spent in democratic politics: What these books show is how vulnerable Khrushchev was for lack of anyone to question his more impetuous moves, and how McGeorge Bundy's logic, Dean Acheson's diplomatic experience, and even Robert McNamara's years at the head of the Ford Motor Company had furnished none of them with that "seat of the pants" instinct that John Kennedy (like Lyndon Johnson) brought to the ExComm discussions. In any case, how many recent U.S. presidents would have fared better than Kennedy, or even half as well? It is a grimly sobering exercise to insert into *The Kennedy Tapes* some of JFK's recent successors and guess at their likely conduct under such pressure. One of the side benefits of the Cuban crisis is that none of them has ever had to face similarly trying circumstances. Meanwhile, the editors of *The Kennedy Tapes* are, I think, convincing when they write, "It seems fortunate that, given the circumstances that he had helped create, Kennedy was the president charged with managing the crisis."

This extended review essay—occasioned by a flurry of publications and documents concerning the Cuba crisis of October 1962—first appeared in the New York Review of Books *in January 1998.*

NOTES TO CHAPTER XIX

[1] For the pertinent excerpts from Kennedy's statement of September 4 and his press conference on September 13, see McGeorge Bundy, *Danger and Survival: Choices about the Bomb in the First Fifty Years* (New York: Random House, 1988), 393. Under international law and the Rio de Janeiro Treaty of 1947, Cuba, like other states, had a right to obtain and install defensive weaponry so long as it did not threaten peace in the region.

[2] Anatoly Dobrynin, *In Confidence* (New York: Times Books, 1995), 69; George Ball, *The Past Has Another Pattern: Memoirs* (New York: Norton, 1982), 286.

[3] Bundy, *Danger and Survival,* 413–414.

[4] According to Fursenko and Naftali, Khrushchev alone of the Kremlin's senior leadership never really believed that Kennedy would attack Cuba—and thus forbore to make plans for such an eventuality (*"One Hell of a Gamble,"* 273). He was perhaps wrong—but his error was crucial in sparing Kennedy that decision.

[5] General Pliyev, the senior Soviet officer in Cuba, actually began dismantling his missiles at 8 a.m. EST, even before Khrushchev's letter was broadcast.

[6] Kennedy's last-minute insistence upon the removal of the planes, after the initial terms had been agreed, was resented by Khrushchev. But he nonetheless instructed the Soviet Presidium to approve their removal, which it did on November 16, despite Mr. Mikoyan's prior assurance to Castro that the Soviet Union would not concede on this point.

[7] Nikita Khrushchev, *Khrushchev Remembers* (Boston: Little, Brown, 1970), 454.

[8] Robert McNamara, in *Blundering into Disaster* (New York: Pantheon, 1986), claims that he and President Kennedy took little notice of this disparity at the time. The fact that enough Soviet missiles would survive a U.S. attack to kill millions of Americans was sufficient to deter anyone from starting a nuclear war—"No responsible political leader would expose his nation to such a catastrophe." See pp. 44–45.

[9] John Gaddis, *We Now Know: Rethinking Cold War History* (Oxford, New York: Clarendon Press/ Oxford University Press, 1997), 261. In *Khrushchev Remembers: The Last Testament* (Boston: Little, Brown, 1974), it is clear that Khrushchev was obsessed by Soviet strategic vulnerability; hence his refusal to accept any test ban agreement that required on-site inspection.

[10] See "*One Hell of a Gamble,*" 90; *Khrushchev Remembers*, 494. The logic of Khrushchev's thinking was not lost on some U.S. policymakers well before October 1962. After the Bay of Pigs, John J. McCloy remarked to Theodore Sorensen that "even if the Soviet Union had missile bases in Cuba—which it hasn't—why would we have any more right to invade Cuba than Khrushchev has to invade Turkey?" Quoted in Nash, *The Other Missiles of October*, 95.

[11] *Khrushchev Remembers*, 493.

[12] Nikita Khrushchev, *Khrushchev Remembers: The Glasnost Tapes* (Boston: Little, Brown, 1990), 180; Dean Rusk, *As I Saw It* (New York: Norton, 1990), 242.

[13] John Kennedy's father, Joseph, had been a notorious appeaser and supporter of the Munich accords. General LeMay surely knew this.

[14] The following exchange at the first meeting of ExComm on October 16th is significant: "McGeorge Bundy: 'The question I would like to ask is . . . What is the strategic impact on the United States of MRBMs in Cuba? How gravely does this change the strategic balance?' Robert McNamara: 'Mac, I asked the Chiefs that this afternoon, in effect. And they said: "Substantially." My own personal view is: Not at all.'" (*The Kennedy Tapes*, 89).

[15] See Robert Kennedy, *Thirteen Days: A Memoir of the Cuban Missile Crisis* (New York: Norton, 1969), quoted by Bundy in *Danger and Survival*, 394. What JFK himself did say, on October 16, was this: "Last month I said we weren't going to [allow it]. Last month I should have said that we don't care. But when we said we're *not* going to, and then they go ahead and do it, and then we do nothing, then I would think that our risks increase." *The Kennedy Tapes*, 92.

[16] David Ormsby-Gore, quoted in Harold Macmillan, *At The End of the Day: 1961–1963* (London: Harper and Row, 1973), 192.

[17] All quotes are from Nash, *The Other Missiles*, unless otherwise indicated. According to Bundy, "By the autumn of 1962 no senior official except General LeMay of the air force still believed that the Jupiters were good military weapons." Bundy, *Danger and Survival*, 428.

[18] President Kennedy himself did not disagree. On October 18 he commented that "the only offer we could make, it seems to me, that would have any sense, the point being to give him [Khrushchev] some out, would be giving him some of our Turkey missiles." The Turks had no objection to exchanging Jupiters for submarine-based Polaris missiles, but since the latter would not be available until the following spring they were reluctant to agree to anything until then.

[19] *Khrushchev Remembers: The Glasnost Tapes*, 179.

[20] Dobrynin, *In Confidence*, 90.

[21] Many Kremlin specialists were firmly opposed to the siting of missiles in Cuba, seeing in the decision a strategic blunder and a failure to keep Soviet eyes on the main business of relations with the U.S. This was one of the most serious charges against Khrushchev when he was deposed in 1964.

[22] See Macmillan, *At the End of the Day*, 186; Bundy, *Danger and Survival*, 369.

[23] "Kennedy overestimated the readiness of Khrushchev and his allies to take decisive actions on Berlin, the most aggressive of which really was the erection of the Berlin Wall two months after the Vienna summit," in August 1961. Dobrynin, *In Confidence*, 46. See also *Khrushchev Remembers: The Glasnost Tapes*, 35.

[24] "Those of us who feared reprisal in Berlin were taking too much counsel of our own long anxieties and too little note of demonstrated Soviet prudence." "Throughout the missile crisis the perceived connection between Cuba and Berlin was much more important in Washington than in the Kremlin. Our fear was not his hope." Bundy, *Danger and Survival*, 421–422, 449.

[25] On October 28 the Joint Chiefs of Staff (Taylor dissenting) informed Kennedy that "[we] interpret the Khrushchev statement, in conjunction with the [continuing] build-up, to be efforts to delay direct action by the United States while preparing the ground for diplomatic blackmail."

[26] The authors of *"One Hell of a Gamble"* make much play with the informal channels then used to convey hints and messages back and forth between Washington and Moscow, notably the role of one Georgi Bolshakov, whom Robert Kennedy met privately on dozens of occasions in the course of 1961 and 1962. But the editors of *The Kennedy Tapes*, like Dobrynin in his memoirs, play down this cloak-and-dagger aspect of U.S.-Soviet relations and the purported role in the resolution of the Cuban crisis of privileged American journalists, Soviet secret agents, and Washington barmen. Khrushchev's own secrecy, the fact that he had taken none of his own messengers into his confidence over the missile emplacements, undermined their credibility; the fact that Khrushchev had used confidential channels to *lie* to him was what most offended the president. In any case, the shock of coming so near to the brink radically altered the rules of the game thereafter. A hotline was set up, Ambassador Dobrynin became the main interlocutor, and confidential "feelers," and "back channels," real or imagined, lost their significance.

[27] See *"One Hell of a Gamble,"* 148, 150; Ball, *The Past Has Another Pattern*, 290; Rusk, *As I Saw It*, 231, 240; Dobrynin, *In Confidence*, 61.

[28] "The more blood-thirsty members of the ExCom were insisting that we act Sunday morning." Ball, *The Past Has Another Pattern*, 305.

[29] This, the "Cordier ploy," named after a former U.S. diplomat who was to be Rusk's secret intermediary with U Thant if circumstances required it, was described by Rusk for the first time at the end of the eighties. Kennedy's other senior advisers were unaware of it at the time and for decades afterward. See Rusk, *As I Saw It*, 240ff.

[30] See Bundy, *Danger and Survival*, 453; *Khrushchev Remembers: The Glasnost Tapes*, 182.

[31] Khrushchev is quoted in Gaddis, *We Now Know*, on page 277. In fairness to Castro, he too had been misled by Soviet nuclear posturing into believing that the strategic balance favored his Soviet protectors. But despite a certain romantic, rejuvenating enthusiasm for their energetic and idealistic young Caribbean clients, the aging Kremlin leadership had taken the measure of Castro from the start; the missiles in Cuba were always kept under exclusively Soviet command and control.

[32] When Kennedy asked his assembled advisers on October 18 whether a blockade would require a declaration of war on Cuba, they nearly all said yes, it would. But the president himself thought otherwise—once you declare war you will be compelled to invade, he warned them, and that is just the outcome the blockade was intended to help avert.

[33] Ball, *The Past Has Another Pattern*, 306.

[34] See Rusk, *As I Saw It*, 237.

CHAPTER XX

The Illusionist: Henry Kissinger and American Foreign Policy

The years 1968–75 were the hinge on which the second half of our century turned. The cultural revolt that we somewhat misleadingly call "the sixties" reached its apogee in the early seventies and entered the mainstream of public life and language. "Revisionist" or reform Communism heaved its last, optimistic breath in Czechoslovakia and Poland in 1968; its defeat signaled first the end of a chimera in Eastern Europe and then, shortly thereafter, the first stage of the dismantling of that same fond hope in the West, with the 1973 translation of Solzhenitsyn's *Gulag* and the unraveling illusions of Old and New Left alike. In the Middle East the unstable post-'67 truce between Israel and the Arab states was followed by the Yom Kippur War, the oil embargo and price rise, and a radically altered power configuration both in the region and between the Arabs and the great powers. In South Asia a new country—Bangladesh—was born, in the course of a war between India and Pakistan.

In 1968 the United States was still a major presence in Southeast Asia, with over half a million troops in South Vietnam alone. Of greater significance, it was also still the world's banker, thanks to the postwar arrangements set in place at Bretton Woods in 1944: The dollar, whose relationship to other currencies was based on fixed exchange rates, was the international reserve currency, backed by U.S. gold reserves. From August 1971 this unsustainable and increasingly symbolic role was abandoned to national and international policy initiatives and the fluctuations of trade and currency markets. In a related development, the member states of the European Community voted the following year to commit themselves to the goal, however distant, of political unity. The nervous but familiar certainties of the cold war gave way to détente: between the U.S. and the Soviet Union (SALT 1, the first international agreement to limit strategic armaments, was signed in 1972), and between Germany and its eastern neighbors following Willy Brandt's *Ostpolitik* and the treaties and agreements he secured with the Soviet Union in 1970 and the years that followed.

In Asia, the United States, after studiously ignoring Communist China for two decades, entered into a series of communications and meetings with Chinese leaders that would culminate (in 1979) in the restoration of diplomatic relations between the two countries, something that would have been unthinkable for most American politicians and statesmen of the cold war era. By April 1975 the U.S. had been evicted from Vietnam and Cambodia; two months later the Helsinki conference on security and cooperation in Europe was convened. The dramatic international developments of the 1980s were still unforeseen and unthinkable (for all but a few imprisoned dissidents in Eastern Europe); but their foundations were now in place.

Throughout this protean moment in the international and national history of our times, the foreign policy of the most important country in the world was effectively run by one man, Henry Kissinger—first as national security adviser, then as secretary of state. And for most of that time he answered to the desires of Richard Nixon, president of the United States from January 1969 until his forced resignation in August 1974, after which Kissinger stayed on in a similar capacity under Nixon's successor, Gerald Ford. Kissinger's protracted domination of state business, and the fact that Nixon's presidency coincided with such an important turning point in world affairs, make their management of U.S. foreign policy a matter of unusual general interest, and have tended to favor the claim made by both men that there was, in fact, no coincidence—that their strategic thinking and their actions played a central role in bringing about the changes I have described.

That is one reason why William Bundy's new book is important.* It is a carefully written and painstakingly researched narrative of U.S. foreign affairs as they were conducted by Nixon and Kissinger. It is not the last word on its subject—as Bundy acknowledges, many archives and papers remain inaccessible, not least those public documents reclassified by Kissinger himself as "personal" papers and closed to prying scholarly eyes until five years after his death. But nothing of importance is left out; the story is not likely to change significantly in later versions. And that story, as we shall see, is distinctly unflattering to both men.

In itself that is hardly new—Nixon has long been a soft target for journalists and historians, and Kissinger, too, has been the subject of more than one critical assessment. But William Bundy is not a journalist, and he is not, at least by profession, a historian. He was for a very long time a member of the old foreign policy "establishment" of this country; indeed his curriculum vitae is almost a caricature of the type. From 1951 to 1960 he worked for the CIA as an analyst of international political developments; from 1961 to 1964 he was in the Office of International Security Affairs, a Pentagon-based oversight committee evaluating the political and diplomatic impact of military options. From 1964 through 1969 he was the assistant secretary of state responsible for East Asian policy; according to former senator and ambassador Mike Mansfield, it was William Bundy, together with his brother McGeorge, Robert McNamara, and General Maxfield Taylor (Chairman of the Joint Chiefs of Staff), who were the "architects" of American policy in Vietnam. From 1972 until 1984 he was the editor of *Foreign Affairs*, the prestigious and influential "house journal" of that same establishment.[1]

William Bundy, then, is a consummate "insider," and this is an insider's analysis of the making of U.S. foreign policy at a time when the old foreign policy elite was losing control to a new brand of international relations "expert." It is cool, reasonable, dispassionate, sometimes quite

---

* William Bundy, *A Tangled Web: The Making of Foreign Policy in the Nixon Presidency* (New York: Hill & Wang, 1998).

technical, and at least as much concerned with how policy gets made as with its implementation. It does not blame its subjects for situations they inherited—understandably, since these, notably in Southeast Asia, were largely the work of Bundy himself and his peers and colleagues. Nor does Bundy devote overmuch space to discussing the moral and political dimensions of that inheritance. Moreover, he offers scrupulously balanced accounts of the choices Nixon and Kissinger had—and didn't have—and he gives credit where credit is due. But just for that reason his book is a devastating, and within its limits definitive, dismantling of a certain myth, and it should be read by an audience far transcending the author's fellow insiders, though they may be more startled than anyone by its conclusions.

The myth in question is that of the strategic originality, even genius, of American foreign-policymaking in the Nixon era. It is a version of history assiduously cultivated by Nixon himself, by Henry Kissinger in his memoirs, other writings, speeches, and public persona, and by their many admirers and acolytes. We found the world in a mess, it says: the cold war still frozen, the U.S. trapped in a hopeless war in Southeast Asia, incoherent and contradictory American alliances and dealings with allies and enemies alike. In six short years we executed two truly radical departures: the opening to China and détente and arms agreements with the Soviet Union. We extricated the country from its Asian imbroglio, we propounded the "Nixon doctrine," whereby the U.S. would support foreign allies without getting militarily embroiled in local conflicts, we set in place the basis for Middle Eastern dialogue, we established enduring personal and institutional relations with foreign statesmen, and we laid the groundwork for the great changes of the decades to come.

And we managed all this, the story runs, because we truly understood how a global foreign policy should be made and what its objectives ought to be. If our achievement is underestimated today it is because of domestic sniping, the failure of our successors to follow through on our initiatives and strategic design, and above all because of the tragic diversion of Watergate. In the long view, the myth concludes, the foreign policy "turn" taken in the years 1968–74 will be appreciated for the courageous and original grand strategy that it truly was.

Some of this received version can stand the test of time—most obviously the decision to make contact with the leaders of Communist China. Other claims may strike some readers as spurious; but they cannot be ignored. They are, or were, quite well received in certain circles in Europe and Asia, and in this country they have left a strong impression—witness the prestige of Kissinger himself and the curiously affectionate and even admiring eulogies that greeted Nixon's death. Their successors, in the presidency, in the National Security Council (NSC), and at the State Department, have not always been men of outstanding intelligence or integrity, and this, too, has helped. And Kissinger in particular has been a master at presenting his own thoughts and deeds to an enthusiastic and receptive audience of journalists and scholars, then and since.

A Tangled Web cuts a broad, clear swath through such claims. In the first place, Bundy shows how the way in which foreign policy was made under Nixon—the effective exclusion of professional expertise, especially that of the State Department, and Kissinger's clever reorganization of committees and hierarchies at the NSC and in the White House so as to centralize virtually all knowledge and authority in his own office—meant that foreign policy was no longer subjected to careful or contradictory debate and discussion. Hardly anyone interrogated Kissinger on the possible side effects or unintended consequences of his words and actions. Decision making was certainly rendered more "efficient," in the sense that major decisions were unlikely to be questioned or diluted before implementation, but the results, Bundy writes, were often disastrous. One clear implication of his book is that U.S. foreign policy in these years, far from growing out of brilliantly reasoned and long-mulled strategic rethinking, was a "seat-of-the-pants" operation, with much consequent effort devoted to various forms of damage control.

This, it has to be noted, is a partisan position. Kissinger and Nixon most certainly did ignore and snub qualified experts, especially those in the professional diplomatic and intelligence communities with whom William Bundy was closely identified. But the track record of such "experts" through the sixties had its own blemishes. The Communist regimes of Southeast Asia, including the one in Hanoi, were authoritarian and repressive and posed a threat to their non-Communist neighbors; and Hanoi was implacably determined to expand its power. But no one in the West had found any very convincing way to oppose those governments without propping up unsavory (and often unpopular) local non-Communist regimes, and in most cases not very successfully at that. Many American soldiers had died in Vietnam before Richard Nixon came to office, for reasons that seemed increasingly obscure to many people. The "experts" could try to explain why and how the U.S. was in Southeast Asia, but they had little to offer on what should now be done, either to save South Vietnam or to extricate American forces. And that, above all, was the problem facing the incoming Republican administration.

Bundy's second theme follows from the first. The "streamlined" decision-making process, with all power and initiative centralized under two men and their staffs, was from the outset intended to exclude not just unimaginative bureaucrats but also, and especially, those offices and agencies constitutionally empowered under U.S. law to oversee and share in the making of foreign policy, notably Congress. This would in due course be the source of Nixon's undoing, when congressional committees and even erstwhile senatorial supporters of the Vietnam War, for example, grew not just frustrated but genuinely alarmed at covert operations, unauthorized bombings, and the like and began to rein in the executive power. But it is also related to the inability of Nixon, in particular, to grasp that in a democracy the government is not only obliged but is also well advised to give a running account of what it is doing and why if it wishes to retain public confidence and support.

On the contrary, Bundy writes, foreign policy under Nixon and Kissinger was not only not adequately discussed with Congress or the electorate, it was on vital occasions deliberately hidden by what can politely be called dissimulation. The administration did not just indulge in covert acts or illegal military operations and wiretapping or otherwise persecute those whom Nixon or Kissinger suspected of leaking details of their undertakings (which in Kissinger's case included members of his own staff). When they did describe what they planned to do, and why it ought to be done—whether to a congressional committee, to a roomful of journalists, or in a televised speech—they not infrequently, Bundy writes, said one thing and then in practice did the opposite.

In the short run, Bundy observes, this gained support for their policies— as when Nixon impressed upon his domestic constituency the virtues of

"Vietnamization," or Kissinger promised great things for the Paris Peace Agreements of January 1973. But the point is that, while the Paris accords were probably the best outcome that the U.S. could get by that date, they represented an unhappy compromise and at best a holding operation, as Kissinger well understood. To claim more for them—to hold out the prospect of a free and autonomous South Vietnamese state for the foreseeable future—was disingenuous. And such deception just stored up greater frustration, disillusion, and ultimately cynicism when it turned out that the results were quite other than promised.

This chronic preference for offering self-serving, optimistic tales and then hoping no one would notice the unappetizing outcomes is one of Bundy's major themes, and he sees it as having had a corrosive effect on U.S. public life: "In the end, Richard Nixon's use of covert operations was less important than his persistent record of misrepresenting his policies and pursuing strategies and actions at odds with what he told Congress and the American people."[2] And, finally, these domestic shortcomings cannot simply be excused with the claim that at least the policies themselves were strikingly effective. Some were, but others were not. The opening to China and the arms agreements with the USSR were good in themselves, and in the Chinese case helped unfreeze U.S. domestic discussion of foreign policy. Nixon and Kissinger can rightly take credit for these accomplishments. But they never merged into some overarching grand strategy, the very idea of which turns out to have been, for the most part, an Oz-like illusion.

It is one of the strengths of Bundy's book that he manages to demonstrate how integrally related were all the separate characteristics and defects just noted. He provides many examples. We have long known about Kissinger's scorn for foreign policy professionals, his confidence in his own knowledge and understanding—in the words of one earlier commentator, he "enjoyed putting the boot in State whenever possible." When one of his staffers objected to the plan to invade Cambodia in April 1970, Kissinger responded revealingly, "Your views represent the cowardice of the Eastern Establishment."[3]

Bundy, however, is concerned not so much to offer further illustrations of such attitudes as to show their detrimental impact on policymaking itself. Better staff work and a more sensitive ear to local knowledge, he argues, might have mitigated the long-term impact on U.S.-Japanese relations of the unwelcome surprise (*shokku*) of the opening of links with China in 1971—something that Nixon and Kissinger kept very much to themselves, while leaving it to the then Secretary of State Rogers and his hapless staff to explain this turn of events to the perplexed and worried Japanese, who had been given no advance warning.

In a similar way, Bundy writes, the Senate Foreign Relations Committee only learned the full extent of Nixon's "initiatives" in Cambodia thanks to the revelations of a disgruntled army officer. Although, according to Bundy, "a very few selected members of Congress" were told about the secret bombing, none of the congressional committees constitutionally established to authorize and fund military actions had ever been informed of the military violation of a neutral state. Nor, Bundy writes, had Nixon or Kissinger thought to consult other influential congressmen about these undertakings—with the result that when they were finally and inevitably leaked, they led not just to the congressional decision in June 1973 to cut funding for future U.S. military action in Southeast Asia, but to the broader mood of frustration and resentment that contributed to Nixon's fall. Bundy is quite insistent upon this sequence of events. It was not just Watergate that brought the president down, he writes; rather, it was the accumulation of broken promises, exaggerated claims, and straightforward lying—in foreign as in domestic matters—that finally drove the other branches of government into revolt—"failures of trust brought on by years of neglect and deception," in Bundy's words.

Bundy, as befits a former official of the CIA, has nothing against "secrecy," an inevitable component of policymaking in any sensitive area, and one for which there are appropriate and legitimate institutional structures. His criticism concerns deception, and the peculiar combination of duplicity and vagueness that marked foreign policy in the Nixon era. "The essential to good diplomacy," Harold Nicolson once suggested, "is precision. The main enemy of good diplomacy is imprecision." And, paradoxical as it may seem, the main source of imprecision in this era was the obsession with personal diplomacy. Diplomacy (Harold Nicolson again) "should be a disagreeable business . . . recorded in hard print."[4]

For Kissinger, in Bundy's account, the reverse was true—he preferred to treat diplomacy as a series of confidential contacts with men with whom he could "do business," while avoiding a clear and official record wherever possible. Moreover, in Bundy's words: "Contrary to the repeated claims of Kissinger in particular, neither he nor Nixon operated solely, or even habitually, on the basis of dispassionate analysis of the U.S. national interest." Both men thought rather of people in terms of "heroes and villains," and both "were strongly influenced by personal impressions of individuals."[5]

As a result, Kissinger sidetracked professional diplomats, established back channels with all manner of persons, and took over crucial negotiations himself, often without consulting the existing negotiating team and leaving them completely in the dark. On this Bundy is quite unforgiving. The "parallel track" in Paris, where Kissinger met secretly with Le Duc Tho while the official U.S. negotiators twiddled their thumbs, or a series of interventions in arms negotiations that resulted in the frustrated resignations of senior U.S. officials—these are the occasion for some of his more forthright strictures. Of the SALT 1 talks in 1970 he writes, "It was hardly the way to conduct a major negotiation: a President not really interested, his principal assistant intervening without the knowledge or concurrence of the negotiating team, and the team left to fend for itself." Of those same SALT talks a year later: "Kissinger had left many loose ends, in another sloppy negotiating performance." And of the Vietnam peace talks and Kissinger's "personal diplomacy" in general: "Negotiations bored Nixon and fascinated Kissinger, whose enthusiasm was not always matched by his skill."

How telling are these criticisms? That Kissinger was sometimes highhanded in dealing with his staff, or that on occasion he humiliated professional negotiators in order to preserve secrecy or highlight his own role, would be neither here nor there if he had secured the desired outcomes. Bundy's emphasis on such matters may strike some readers as excessive. But on many issues his criticisms are justified by the evidence he provides of poorly executed negotiations and oversold agreements.

In order to keep direct control over everything in this way, Nixon and Kissinger did not just deceive others as to their actions; they were also, Bundy suggests, less effective than they might have been even in matters that interested them. As for places and problems in which they had no sustained interest, or about which they knew very little, the outcomes were disastrous. They were blindsided, for example, by the oil crisis of 1973–74 because, Bundy writes, neither man grasped the connection between domestic demand, U.S. domestic oil production, and the changing terms of trade in international energy (the U.S. share of world oil production fell from 64 percent in 1948 to 22 percent by 1972, even as U.S. domestic usage steadily rose). Oil—like trade, or small, peripheral countries—did not figure in their view of what counted or how the world worked, and they were consistently ineffectual or wrong, through either inaction or a badly conceived policy, when faced with such matters.

Three instances will serve to illustrate these claims. Cambodia— "Mr. Nixon's war"—is normally thought of as the major flaw in the Nixon record, and so it is. It is the occasion for Bundy's strongest condemnation—"a black page in the history of American foreign policy." In Cambodia the Nixon administration repeated all the mistakes of Vietnam on an accelerated and concentrated scale without the excuse of inexperience. It secretly authorized over 3,600 B-52 air raids against suspected (but undiscovered) Vietcong bases and against North Vietnamese forces in Cambodia in 1969–70 alone. By 1974, as Bundy shows, this policy had contributed to the rise of the Khmer Rouge—a Communist guerrilla organization whose crimes certainly cannot be laid at Nixon's door, but whose political prospects were enhanced by the devastation brought about by the war. Bundy's summary of the final stage of the Cambodian disaster is characteristic in its careful review of the record and worth quoting at length:

> General Vogt [the commander of the U.S. Seventh Air Force] and most of the senior civilians involved (including Ambassador Swank) believed that the bombing kept Lon Nol afloat in the face of the 1973 Khmer Rouge offensive. It may have been crucial in enabling the government forces, using artillery, to hold their central enclave, including Phnom Penh, into 1974 and eventually until the early spring of 1975. Massive airpower used against a lightly armed attacking force with no antiaircraft capability could be effective in preventing victory for the opposing force.

On the other hand, the intensity of the bombing—as a matter of common-sense judgement shared by many objective observers—drove the Khmer Rouge to greater military efforts. It also made them more self-reliant, more separate from North Vietnam, more alienated from Sihanouk, and altogether less subject to influence from any of their Communist supporters. The bombing surely made it more rather than less difficult for any party to persuade the Khmer Rouge to accept a cease-fire and negotiate a political compromise—which was the stated objective.

The chances of such a change of course by the Khmer Rouge were almost certainly slim already. A determined negotiating effort to enlist Sihanouk . . . combined with a much more limited program of bombing to keep the threat alive, might just have stood a chance. As it was, intense bombing with no negotiating effort, until the Khmer Rouge was even more embittered, was the worst of all worlds. As throughout the American involvement in Cambodia, the policy miscalculations alone—apart from eventual congressional reactions—were monumental. They must be laid squarely at the door of Nixon and his two principal advisers, Alexander Haig and Henry Kissinger.

Nixon, Kissinger, and Alexander Haig kept the details of the Cambodian operation to themselves and a handful of colleagues as long as they could, rarely sought advice from sources outside the military (which was uniquely concerned with blocking North Vietnamese supply routes passing through eastern Cambodia), and made, Bundy writes, imprudent and unsustainable promises to Lon Nol (Cambodia's ruler following the overthrow in March 1970 of the ostensibly neutral Prince Sihanouk in the wake of the initial bombings). They not only lost the country to the Communists anyway, following a devastating four-year war, but undermined their own support at home and their country's standing abroad. In Bundy's words, "In short, the United States was raining bombs on a small country with little prospect of a good outcome. . . . The stakes in Cambodia came down, then, almost entirely to the asserted psychological impact in South Vietnam if Cambodia fell and to Nixon's sense of personal commitment to Lon Nol."

Hardly a victory for grand strategic thinking. There were well-informed people in the State Department (and even more at the Quai d'Orsay in Paris) who might have counseled Kissinger and Nixon against doing what they proposed, but they were not asked.[6] Kissinger, even more than Nixon, held it as axiomatic that the world is run by Great Powers, to whose instructions and interests lesser states duly respond. Policy in and toward Cambodia was thus conceived and practiced with no consistent attention paid to the distinctive characteristics of any of the local interested parties. In the case of Communist states and organizations, moreover, Kissinger took it to be self-evident that the lines of communication ran straight and true, from Moscow (or Beijing) to the lowest guerrilla operative in the bush.

To be fair to Kissinger, he was not alone in this belief—and in the case of the satellite states of Eastern Europe under Stalin and his successors, or powerless and tiny Communist movements in Western Europe or the U.S., it was in large measure accurate. And the rulers of the Kremlin, at least, dearly wished it were universally true, and had an active interest in convincing outsiders that it was. But the experience of Malaysia, Indonesia, and much of Latin America might have taught otherwise, had those in power been listening. Just as the Vietnamese rulers in Hanoi were historically suspicious of China, so the Cambodian Communists were never in thrall to their Vietnamese "comrades," though the Maoist "model"—which they had experienced firsthand in China—undoubtedly shaped their thinking more directly. Zhou Enlai even tried once to convey this basic truth about Asian history and Communist politics to Kissinger in person, to no apparent avail.

The Cambodian policy, in Bundy's analysis, was thus ultimately justified by the claim that there was "linkage," that just as invasion in Cambodia might pay off in Vietnam, so pressure in Hanoi (by its Soviet or Chinese "masters") might trickle down to the Khmer Rouge and bring about some sort of truce in Cambodia itself. Hence the suggestion that one of the virtues of détente would be the leverage the U.S. could assert, through its improved relations with Moscow or Beijing, upon their ill-behaved offspring in Southeast Asia. The military and logistical links were there, but, as Bundy's account makes clear, the leverage never existed. The whole enterprise rested on an astonishing mix of overconfidence, misguided strategic theorizing, and ignorance.

Cambodia was the worst example, but it was not the only one. In March 1971 the Pakistani dictator Yahya Khan violently suppressed riots in East Pakistan; millions of refugees fled into neighboring India. Tension mounted all year until December when, following Pakistan's dispatch of large numbers of troops to quell discontent in East Pakistan, fighting broke out between India and Pakistan on India's northwest frontier. The war lasted a matter of weeks, until the Pakistani forces surrendered and withdrew, and East Pakistan declared its independence as Bangladesh, leaving a defeated, humiliated, and much-reduced Pakistani state. The indigenous sources of this conflict needn't concern us here; the point is that they were also of no concern to Washington, which nonetheless "tilted" heavily toward Pakistan, to the point of putting pressure on India and sending a U.S. naval task group to the Bay of Bengal.

Why should the U.S., which had no discernible direct interest in the conflict, resort to gunboat diplomacy and demonstrate such public support for one party—the repressive, dictatorial Yahya Khan—at the cost of alienating not just India, a major power in Asia and one of its few stable democracies, but also politicized Muslims everywhere? Why, in short, did Kissinger and Nixon engage in a piece of geopolitics that Bundy rightly describes as a "fiasco" and that has left a long and unhelpful legacy of distrust for the U.S. in the entire region? For the breathtakingly simple reason, Bundy writes, that Pakistan was perceived as a friend of China (Yahya Khan had the previous year served as the link through which Kissinger made contact with the Chinese), and India, as a notoriously "neutral" state, had cultivated good relations with the Soviet Union. In Kissinger's words, quoted by Nixon himself, "We don't really have any choice. *We can't allow a friend of ours and China to get screwed in a conflict with a friend of Russia's.*"[7]

Yahya Khan had certainly performed friendly services for Nixon and Kissinger, helping establish the early contacts between Beijing and Washington and keeping them secret at a time when leaks might have been disastrous for Nixon's China project. But even if one allows that Pakistan was a "friend of ours," it did not follow that the U.S. need line up behind a violent and (as it proved) doomed military despot. However, in Kissinger's words once again, "Why is it our business how they govern themselves?"[8] And so, in another mechanistic application of hypothetical laws of geopolitical strategy, the U.S. backed the wrong man in the wrong conflict, securing, as might have been predicted, an undesired outcome and a legacy of reduced influence.

There is no evidence that China would have reacted badly, or even cared, if the U.S. had "sat out" the Indo-Pakistan conflict; there were even less grounds for believing that the Soviet Union was poised to intervene on India's behalf—the ostensible reason for the dispatch of the naval task group. There is, on the other hand (according to Bundy), some evidence that Yahya Khan was misled, or given grounds for misleading himself, into thinking that he had American backing for his uncompromising stance, first in East Pakistan and then toward India. A fiasco indeed.

Let us allow that Southeast Asia by 1970 was a region in which the policy of any U.S. administration was probably doomed to meet an unsatisfactory and ultimately disastrous end. William Bundy, it must be said, does not suggest a strategy by which the U.S. could have brought to a better end the war he had earlier helped to set in motion. Let us further acknowledge that the Indian subcontinent was terra incognita to most Americans (though, once again, not to some scorned experts at the State Department and in other official agencies); it is not just in Washington, after all, that men have badly misjudged situations taking place in "far away countries of which they know little." But what of Europe, the centerpiece of the cold war and thus the site of Nixon's own experience of foreign policy in the fifties, as well as the region in whose history Kissinger established his scholarly reputation?

In later writings, both men took some credit for laying the groundwork of détente in Europe—in his memorial eulogy for the late president, Kissinger claimed this as one of Nixon's major achievements. William Bundy is skeptical of this view. At the time, both men were very wary of any change in Europe that they did not fully control—and whereas West German Chancellor Konrad Adenauer had always consulted fully with Washington before making the slightest move, Willy Brandt in particular, while keeping his American allies fully informed, pursued his own agenda. In the worldview of Kissinger, only one superpower—the U.S.—was fully entitled to engage its counterpart—the Soviet Union—in serious conversations that might lead to significant change. The White House was overtly displeased at Brandt's election to the Chancellery in 1969 and gave only grudging and unenthusiastic assent to his *Ostpolitik*—the treaties and agreements he negotiated between the Federal Republic and the Soviet bloc states.

One reason for this was that Kissinger, concerned with geopolitical factors in international affairs, was reluctant to accept a definitive territorial and frontier settlement in Europe. But he may, at the time, have underestimated its significance for Moscow. When the Kremlin chose to overlook Nixon's resumed bombing of North Vietnam in December 1972 and went ahead with plans for a summit meeting, the U.S. administration took credit for its successful "gamble," attributing Soviet acquiescence to Moscow's nervousness at Nixon's "China turn." This view has been disputed by such contemporary Russian officials as Anatoly Dobrynin and Georgi Arbatov. "Kissinger," Arbatov said, "thinks it was China that played the decisive role in getting us to feel the need to preserve our relationship with the USA. . . . But Berlin actually played a much bigger role, almost a decisive one. Having the East German situation settled was most important to us, and we did not want to jeopardize that."[9]

Kissinger in his memoirs concluded "with hindsight" that the Soviets did not cancel the summit for several reasons. One was that cancellation would "bring about the Soviet's worst nightmare, an American relationship with Peking not balanced by equal ties with Moscow." But he also said that renewed Soviet-American hostility "would almost certainly have upset the applecart of Brandt's policy, [and] the Soviet Union's carefully nurtured strategy for Europe would have collapsed." Bundy, for his part, concludes that Brandt's policy of *Ostpolitik* "and its coming up for final Bundestag approval at that crucial moment saved the summit. At the moment of truth, stabilizing the situation in Germany, completing a new European order, and insuring Soviet control of the Eastern European nations . . . were more important to the Soviet Union than international solidarity."

Whether or not the European version of détente was such a good thing is a debatable issue—Bundy certainly admires it unstintingly, based as it was on "slow day-to-day changes and increased contacts," in contrast to the more demonstrative U.S. version of détente, linked to high-level agreements and of questionable long-term value. I have argued elsewhere that both the West German *Ostpolitik* and the U.S. idea of détente demonstrated an inadequate grasp of the weakness and instability of Communist regimes, notably that of East Germany, and showed as well a cavalier insensitivity to the needs and hopes of the population of Europe's eastern half, for whom a "definitive" postwar settlement fixing Europe's political and ideological frontiers into place was far from desirable, and was much resented. In any case, détente's indirect contribution to the destabilizing of the Soviet Union and its satellites was not part of Kissinger's—or Brandt's—goals. The architects of Helsinki cannot take credit for that accomplishment.[10]

What is beyond question is that Kissinger in particular grew rather frustrated in his dealings with the divided and changing leadership of Europe's many states. As he put it himself, "[R]elations with Europe did not lend themselves to secret diplomacy followed by spectacular pronouncements. There were too many nations involved to permit the use of backchannels." But then that is how it is with a continent full of medium-sized pluralist democracies. Willy Brandt wrote that "Henry Kissinger did not like to think of Europeans speaking with one voice. He preferred to juggle with Paris, London and Bonn, playing them off one against another, in the old style."[11] Brandt is somewhat disingenuous here; it suited him to think of European statesmen as speaking with one voice when they didn't—and don't. But his perception of Kissinger's preferences seems no less accurate for that.

The "old style" was not very effective, however. One of its chief results was to weaken the Atlantic alliance, diminishing European trust in Washington. In April 1973, Kissinger, in a famously unfortunate speech aimed at America's continental allies, declared a "European Year" without consulting a single European leader; the speech, in Bundy's words, was "didactic, occasionally scolding and petulant, and free of any suggestion that the United States might have neglected some of its own obligations, or might have erred in some of its [own] economic policies or energy practices."

The result of Kissinger's policies and his style, Bundy concludes, was to drive a wedge between the U.S. and its only credible international supporters—opening up a gap that was widened still further when the U.S. gave its NATO allies no advance warning of the worldwide military alert of October 24, 1973 (at the time of the Middle Eastern war). Like the Japanese government following the political and economic shocks of 1971 (the opening to China, the abandoning of the dollar-gold parity, and restrictions on U.S. imports), Western European politicians in the aftermath of the oil embargo, the Kissinger speech, and the cool response to *Ostpolitik* began to rethink their relations with Washington. As a result of behaving as though America's European allies could be relied upon automatically to endorse U.S. actions, Kissinger and Nixon thus released them from the habit of doing so. The damage done to NATO and the Western alliance was still being felt well into the mid-eighties.

To be sure, Nixon and Kissinger had successes too, achievements that can be placed unambiguously to their credit. The opening to China and the first round of arms agreements with the Soviet Union are among these, and William Bundy is scrupulously fair in taking note of them, just as he is careful to defend Kissinger in particular against the more all-embracing condemnations of his critics. It was Alexander Haig, he suggests, who carried the misleading, secret pledges to Thieu and who must take most of the blame for the implementation of the Cambodian schemes. An ambitious officer raised in the MacArthur school of foreign policy, he treated legal and institutional restraints on the maximum use of military force in all circumstances as annoying and dispensable impediments. Bundy's summary is unusually severe: "That a senior military officer might be so far wrong on a central constitutional point is striking (and disturbing) even at a distance of time."

As for Kissinger, Bundy gives him full credit for disengaging the Middle East from the volatile stalemate that followed the Yom Kippur War, shuttling tirelessly between Golda Meir and Anwar Sadat, outbidding the Soviet Union for local influence, and building good relations with many important local political leaders. In his dealings with Sadat and others, Bundy writes, "it was the reasoned arguments Kissinger made, the personal rapport he established, and the sense of understanding and respect he conveyed that moved things forward. He was always well-suited to be a mediator, a position in which a diplomat is justified in shading the views of A when he reports to B, in the interest of bring-ing the two closer." A barbed compliment, perhaps, but a compliment nonetheless, followed by an unequivocally admiring conclusion: "Rarely has a statesman managed a diplomatic process so fully and to the benefit of his country." Bundy also praises Kissinger for his well-attested suspi-cion of Pentagon advocates of the concept of "strategic superiority," a skeptical position he shared with Robert McNamara, and one he sus-tained against opposition from the military lobby.

But the fact remains that no one who reads this book is going to think especially well of either Nixon or Kissinger, and certainly not nearly as well as they thought of themselves. Explaining Nixon's weaknesses may be the easier task; it certainly produces the more familiar responses.[12] By the standards of American politicians he was well versed in foreign affairs, and had been active in them ever since Christian Herter put him on a 1947 House committee investigating the impact of the Marshall Plan in Europe. He could be a quick study and in principle, at least, he was open to new ideas and approaches—especially if, like the opening to China, they offered personal political advantage into the bargain. It is true that he was unable to rid himself, when observing the present, of conventional references and examples from the recent past—Munich and the Korean War among them; but this hardly distinguished him from most public men of his generation, John F. Kennedy included.

Nixon's problem, of course, lay elsewhere. He was so absorbed in the recollection and anticipation of slights and injustices, real and imagined, that much of his time as president was taken up with "screwing" his foes, domestic and foreign alike: Even when he had a defensible plan to imple-ment, such as his "new economic policy" of 1971 (the floating of the dollar and protection against "predatory" imports), he just couldn't help seeing in it the additional benefit of "sticking it to the Japanese." He warned even his allies against offering unwanted (critical) counsel—according to Brandt, he justified his bombing of North Vietnam in 1971 as a "preventive measure"—and added "with some irritation, that advice from third parties was not wanted." Indeed, this aversion to criticism was perhaps the greatest weakness of all—it was why he surrounded himself with yes-men and hardly ever exposed his person or his policies to open debate among experts or more than one adviser at a time.[13]

In order to ward off criticism and keep his foes at bay, Nixon preferred to tell people—individually and collectively—what they wanted to hear, reserving for himself the privilege of doing just the opposite. One result was that everyone was caught off balance, unable to work out just what it was that the president was truly seeking to achieve. In a recent book Henry Kissinger recalls that the Emperor Napoléon III of France was sometimes referred to as "the 'Sphinx in the Tuileries' because he was believed to be hatching vast and brilliant designs, the nature of which no one could discern until they gradually unfolded." Something of the same thing might be said of Nixon, though the comparison flatters him; but in both cases the sphinx turns out to be an elderly, insecure man frequently overtaken by events.[14]

Henry Kissinger's is an altogether more interesting case, and there is much to be learned from it. Bundy notes the contradiction between Kissinger's reputation for brilliance and his rather checkered and much oversold record in office. Although this insistence upon the contrast itself will infuriate those for whom the former secretary of state can do no wrong, the book offers little further discussion of the matter. But the question remains: If Kissinger had such a sure grasp of international affairs, was so well versed in diplomatic history and so clear-eyed in his understanding of the tasks of the statesman, how, in the instances of failure described by Bundy, could he have been led so astray by Nixon? Or, alternatively, why did he give Nixon such poor advice?

The conventional response is to investigate the context—the mitigating circumstances of reality, as it were. That is reasonable, and no one would deny that Henry Kissinger, like every statesman before him, inherited the problems he sought to address. But what if the starting assumptions themselves were also at fault?

Henry Kissinger's first book, *A World Restored*, was a study of Metternich and Castlereagh, the Austrian and British statesmen who put together the Congress System of early-nineteenth-century Europe, named after the 1815 Congress of Vienna where the international settlement was negotiated following the defeat of Napoléon. Metternich emerges as the hero of that work, and, although Kissinger has since written many other books, in his latest publication, *Diplomacy*, Metternich and his eponymous system once again come in for some respectful discussion.

Count Metternich was without question a resourceful diplomat who served his emperor well. A skeptical student of his times, he maneuvered effectively to protect the interests of a declining Habsburg Empire in an international environment buffeted by domestic revolutions and a rapidly shifting balance of international power. He sustained Austria's international position for a third of a century, and the system of interstate relations that he helped secure at Vienna contributed to the decades of relative international tranquillity that followed the revolutionary upheavals of the years 1789–15.[15]

But Kissinger does not admire Metternich as a past statesman alone. He offers him as a model for contemporary emulation: In the aftermath of the fall of Communism, he writes, "One can hope that something akin to the Metternich system evolves." This is not an isolated, casual aside. The whole cast of American diplomacy, in Kissinger's view, has been distorted by excessive sensitivity to Wilsonian idealism. What is called for is a return to the laudable realism of an earlier age: "Victory in the Cold War has propelled America into a world which bears many similarities to the European state system of the eighteenth and nineteenth centuries." And if we are back in a nineteenth-century international situation, then there should be no doubt about the correct nineteenth-century response: "The international system which lasted the longest without a major war was the one following the Congress of Vienna. It combined legitimacy and equilibrium, shared values, and balance-of-power diplomacy."[16]

The problem with taking Count Metternich and his system as a model, as with many other references to statesmen and policies of the reasonably distant past, is that their world differed from ours in at least one crucial respect—and it is the business of the historian to understand such differences and why they matter. Austria in 1815 was a hereditary empire (though liberal by the continental standards of the time) where all power was vested in the emperor and his ministers. There were no constitutional constraints, no electoral constituencies to placate or inform, no committees to consult. The imperial foreign minister and chancellor answered only to his emperor and to their shared view of the imperial interest. Metternich, who had some inkling of the coming domestic troubles in the sprawling, multinational Central European empire, could confine his attention exclusively to foreign and diplomatic affairs. In his own formulation, "I ruled Europe sometimes, but I never governed Austria."[17]

As a consequence, Metternich could practice diplomacy in the ancient manner, based in large measure on personal relations among noblemen from different lands speaking a common language and with a shared interest in cross-border social and institutional stability. Such intra-aristocratic diplomatic dealings had for Metternich the virtue of calculated imprecision and ambiguity. Kissinger quotes him with approval: "Things which ought to be taken for granted lose their force when they emerge in the form of arbitrary pronouncements. . . . Objects mistakenly made subject to legislation result only in the limitation, if not the complete annulment, of that which is attempted to be safeguarded."[18]

Here we begin to see the outlines of the misconceived lesson that Henry Kissinger appears to have drawn from his study of international relations in the past. Secured by his own bureaucratic devices and habits of mind from having to respond to critics or other branches of government, though he could always get his opinion or policy echoed and supported by a well-placed article or interview or congressman, he indeed related to Richard Nixon much as did Metternich to the Emperor Francis II. An ambitious and intelligent courtier with the ear of an absolute ruler is in a position of unique influence, especially if he carries no responsibility for domestic affairs—this much history does indeed teach us. Moreover, although the courtier runs obvious risks if he incurs the ruler's wrath, it is the ruler himself who is truly vulnerable in a crisis. The cleverest courtiers—Talleyrand comes to mind—will survive the fall of their masters, with some quick footwork and a recasting of the historical record; and Kissinger was among the cleverest of them all.

Henry Kissinger knew perfectly well that his world was not that of Metternich or even of Woodrow Wilson—statesmen in the past had never, he writes, "been obliged to conduct diplomacy in an environment where events can be experienced instantaneously and simultaneously by leaders and their publics."[19] But far from awakening him to an appreciation of a novel set of constraints upon foreign-policymaking, this changed situation seems to have made Kissinger all the more resistant to the constraints of policymaking in a constitutional republic with multiple governing branches. Unrecorded personal undertakings, unarticulated policy shifts, covert dealings and the deception of friend and foe alike, "secret wars, secretly arrived at" (George McGovern), were undertaken not in ignorance of the claims of pluralist democracy but, in some cases, in order to circumvent them. Of course, a degree of strategic calculation and secrecy is a condition of good diplomacy in any political system; but in a liberal democracy it is the beginning of wisdom to recognize their limits.

But, Kissinger's defenders might argue, so what if he abused historical analogy? He may have miscalculated or even misunderstood the domestic context in which Nixon had to operate; but he had a sure grasp of the fundamentals of international relations. Relations between states, the argument runs, are based on interest and geopolitical facts. Transformations in the ways in which countries are governed—from monarchies to aristocratic oligarchies, from liberal democracies to Communist dictatorships—may affect the way they talk about their interests and intentions, but the underlying realities remain in place. Once you know this, you can negotiate with anyone and understand the deeper meaning of any particular crisis, secure in your grasp of your country's long-term interests and the means by which these can be advanced and protected.

In the aggregate, these are untestable propositions—you either believe them or you don't. Henry Kissinger certainly behaved in accordance with some such set of assumptions. Like Sir Halford Mackinder, the early-twentieth-century British inventor of "geopolitics," he believed that the Soviet Union/Russia, for example, constitutes a "geopolitical heartland" whose rulers will always be influenced by a certain sort of imperial territorial imperative; hence his various efforts to strike "deals," with Brezhnev in particular. His admiration for Nixon rests squarely on his view that "among postwar presidents, only Nixon consistently dealt with the Soviet Union as a geopolitical challenge." Kissinger believed that small countries (like Chile) in unimportant regions (like Latin America) require little attention or respect, so long as they stay in line. He believed, as has been seen, in "linkage"—the notion that U.S. dealings with any one country or region should always be part of a global set of policies, rather than responses to local situations on an individual basis. And he believed in the "balance of power."

A case can be made for any of these approaches, taken separately. A policy based on maintaining the "balance of power"—a concept deriving from the English strategy for dealing with European states in the nineteenth century, juggling favorites and favors so as to prevent any one continental power from becoming overmighty—could make some sense in a multipolar world. Kissinger's practice, however, was inconsistent: If unchanging national and geopolitical criteria "trump" everything else, for example, why base a foreign policy on the belief that countries sharing the same ideological form—Communism—will think or behave in concert? Sometimes Kissinger followed the "geopolitical" line, as in his dealings with China; sometimes not, as in his approach based on international Communist links and influence in Vietnam or Cambodia.

Détente, and what Kissinger calls "triangular diplomacy" among the major powers, brought more reciprocal relations with China and the USSR. But they never convinced either China or the Soviet Union to moderate or restrain their "clients" in Asia or Africa—the one thing Nixon and Kissinger sought above all else. "Linkage" secured nothing that was not gained by conventional diplomatic negotiating efforts or military might. And the overall objective—the advancement of the permanent interests of the United States—was probably further from attainment at the end of the Nixon-Kissinger era than at the outset.

Ironically, this is precisely because Kissinger was so caught up in the "big" picture that he and Nixon, as we have seen, made a cumulative series of crucial missteps in the "peripheral" zones whose significance they dismissively underestimated. William Bundy's summary of the "deplorable" American treatment of Chile in the Allende era can stand for much else: "Nixon and Kissinger never gave Chile the attention required under their own decision-making system, and acted impulsively, with inadequate reflection. Their actions were not only morally repugnant but ran grave risks of the eventual exposure that damaged the United States in Latin American eyes."

There is a revealing historical precedent for this sort of failed foreign policy, where "realism" is exposed to moral condemnation and ends up disserving its own goals. In the 1870s the British Prime Minister Benjamin

Disraeli pursued a policy of great-power "realism" in the Balkans, supporting the declining Turkish empire in its repression of the claims of national and religious minorities under its control. This policy, carried out in the name of Britain's strategic interests, was condemned by Disraeli's Liberal opponent, William Gladstone, who made a series of fiery and effective public attacks on it at the election of 1880, when Disraeli's government was brought down to defeat.

Gladstone's rhetoric is dated, but his theme is unmistakable and familiar: "Abroad they [i.e., the government] have strained, if they have not endangered, the prerogative by gross misuse, and have weakened the Empire by needless wars, unprofitable extensions and unwise engagements, and have dishonored it in the eyes of Europe." Disraeli's brazen unconcern for the behavior of his friends, or for the interests of others, especially small nations, was inimical to Britain's long-term interests, Gladstone declared: If British interests were accepted as "the sole measure of right and wrong" in Britain's dealings with the world, then the same attitude might logically be adopted by any other country, and the result would be international anarchy.

Gladstone was responding in particular to Disraeli's dismissal of national movements in the Balkans (especially the notorious "Bulgarian massacres" of 1876); at best he didn't take any interest in them, at worst he attributed the troubles to the work of foreign secret societies. As for his critics at home in Britain, Disraeli dismissed their complaints as "coffee house babble"—a striking anticipation of Spiro T. Agnew's description of similarly inspired critics of President Nixon as "nattering nabobs of negativism." But although Gladstone was able to turn Disraeli's haughty unconcern for informed opinion and public moral distaste to electoral advantage, Britain's standing as a disinterested interlocutor in European affairs was indeed significantly imperiled.[20]

That is the trouble with geopolitical realism in foreign policy, especially when it is practiced with disdain for domestic constraints. You begin with a reasonable-sounding worldliness, of the kind articulated by Metternich and quoted admiringly by Henry Kissinger: "Little given to abstract ideas, we accept things as they are and we attempt to the maximum of our ability to protect ourselves against delusions about realities."[21] You then find yourself allying with disreputable foreign rulers on the "realist" grounds that they are the people with whom you have to do business, forgetting that in so doing you have deprived yourself of any political leverage over them, because the one thing that matters most to them—how they get and keep power over their subjects—is of no interest to you. And at the last, you are thus reduced to cynicism about the outcomes not just of their actions but of your own.

Thus, William Bundy points out, some of the most vaunted achievements of "realist" foreign policy turn out to be bogus. Kissinger and Nixon could hardly have been unaware, he concludes, that the Paris settlement of 1973 that "ended" the Vietnam War was a mirage, its clauses and safeguards "toothless." It looked only to short-term political advantage, with no vision or strategy for handling the longer-term fallout. Their unstinting support for the Shah of Iran was similarly disastrous—first joining with him in misleading promises to the Kurds in order to bring pressure on Iran's western neighbor, Iraq, then abandoning those same Kurds to a bloody fate, and finally bonding the image and power of the U.S. to an increasingly indefensible regime in Tehran. Like so much else about the foreign dealings of the Nixon era, the bill fell due a little later: in 1975 in Vietnam and Cambodia, in 1979–80 in Iran. And in each case the interests of the United States were among the first victims.

This history is important, because Kissinger has always claimed that—in contrast to administrations before and since—the governments in which he served were not bemused by "idealist" mirages and kept firmly in view the chief objective of foreign policy: the pursuit and defense of the U.S. national interest. One can debate endlessly what U.S. international "interests" really are and how they are best served. But what is clear, and this was Gladstone's point as it is Bundy's, is that in a constitutionally ordered state, where laws are derived from broad principles of right and wrong and where those principles are enshrined in and protected by agreed procedures and practices, it can never be in the long-term interest of the state or its citizens to flout those procedures at home or associate too closely overseas with the enemies of your founding ideals.

Richard Nixon was in one respect a fortunate man. Felled by Watergate, he has been resurrected in some quarters as an unlikely tragic hero—the greatest foreign policy president we (nearly) had, as it were; a man whose human flaws undermined his unrealized talents in this crucial arena of presidential action. Henry Kissinger has benefited twice over from this strange beatification—the flaws are Nixon's, but the foreign policy was Kissinger's, and its failures were attributable to Nixon's domestic imbroglios. Anyone tempted to give credit to such claims should read William Bundy's book, which anticipates what one must hope will be the considered judgment of history upon a troubled and troubling era in American public affairs.

Following this review of William Bundy's study of U.S. foreign policy in the Nixon years, published in the New York Review of Books *in August 1998, Henry Kissinger penned a spirited and lengthy rebuttal to Bundy's narrative and my account of it. Kissinger's letter, along with my reply, appeared in the* New York Review of Books, *vol .45, no. xiv, September 1998.*

NOTES TO CHAPTER XX

[1] Mansfield is quoted from a conversation with Anatoly Dobrynin, the Soviet ambassador to Washington. See Anatoly Dobrynin, *In Confidence* (New York: Times Books, 1995), 137. It is perhaps also germane to add that Bundy is the son-in-law of the late Dean Acheson, that his father, Harvey Bundy, was a close adviser of Henry M. Stimson during World War II, and that his brother McGeorge was President Kennedy's national security adviser, all of which makes him a member of the innermost foreign policy elite as much by dynastic relations as by election.

[2] Bundy is for the most part ostentatiously polite in expressing his distaste for the way in which the Nixon administration went about its business, confining his strictures to the content of its actions. Only very occasionally does he let slip a note of undisguised distaste. When the last set of tapes was released, on April 30, 1974, he comments almost as an aside that "the mind-set of the White House was revealed as that of the gutter."

[3] For "putting the boot in State" see U. Alexis Johnson, *The Right Hand of Power* (Englewood Cliffs, NJ: Prentice Hall, 1984), 520, quoted by Michael Schaller in *Altered States: The United States and Japan since the Occupation* (New York: Oxford University Press, 1997), 211; for "the cowardice of the Eastern Establishment" see William Shawcross, *Sideshow: Kissinger, Nixon and the Destruction of Cambodia* (New York: Simon and Schuster, 1979), 145.

[4] See Harold Nicolson, *Peacemaking 1919* (New York: Houghton Mifflin, 1933), 207, 209.

[5] This is one possible source of Nixon's astonishing promise to Thieu that rather than let South Vietnam fall following the 1973 Peace Agreement he would resume bombing of the North—a promise he was in no position either to make or to keep, thus illustrating two of Bundy's main themes. But it is just as likely that Nixon was paying off a debt incurred in 1968, when Thieu's refusal—at Nixon's secret urging—to negotiate with the North helped doom Hubert Humphrey in the election of that year.

[6] In view of the admiration of both Kissinger and Nixon for Charles de Gaulle, it is curious how little they learned from the French experience—in Indochina and again in Algeria. The

French track record was far from admirable, but by 1969 they had learned enough to stay clear of Southeast Asia—"Get out now," as de Gaulle advised Nixon; and after a long history of failed attempts to govern Cambodia they might have been able to advise the U.S. against risking that country's fragile neutrality for the sake of a temporary interruption of a North Vietnamese supply route.

[7] See Richard Nixon, *RN: The Memoirs of Richard Nixon* (New York: Touchstone, 1978, 1990), 527, quoted by Bundy (with emphasis added) on p. 290.

[8] Kissinger's remark is quoted by Bundy on p. 272, citing Christopher Van Hollen, "The Tilt Policy Revisited: Nixon-Kissinger Geopolitics and South Asia," *Asian Survey* 20, no. 4 (April 1980): 339–361.

[9] Arbatov, the onetime ranking Soviet expert on U.S. affairs, is quoted in Walter Isaacson, *Kissinger: A Biography* (New York: Simon and Schuster, 1992), 422–423, and by Bundy on p. 321, citing Isaacson.

[10] Bundy's discussion of Willy Brandt's achievements is the occasion for the only mistake of fact that I came across in his book: The ghetto memorial in Warsaw where Brandt dropped to his knees in atonement marks the site of the desperate Jewish struggle of 1943, which Bundy confuses with the Warsaw Uprising of 1944, when Soviet troops halted on the far side of the Vistula and waited for the Germans to destroy the Polish resistance.

[11] See Henry Kissinger, *Years of Upheaval* (Boston: Little Brown, 1982), 729, quoted by Bundy on p. 415; Willy Brandt, *My Life in Politics* (New York: Viking, 1992), 178.

[12] For the latest voyages into the inner recesses of the Soul of Nixon, see, e.g., Stanley I. Kutler, *Abuse of Power: The New Nixon Tapes* (New York: Free Press, 1997), and Vamik D. Volkan, Norman Itzkowitz, and Andrew W. Dod, *Richard Nixon: A Psychobiography* (New York: Columbia University Press, 1997).

[13] See Schaller, *Altered States*, 211; Brandt, *My Life in Politics*, 365.

[14] Henry Kissinger, *Diplomacy* (New York: Simon and Schuster, 1994), 105.

[15] Kissinger's interpretation of the Congress of Vienna, and of Metternich's contribution to the transformation of the European state system, is understandably dated—*A World Restored* was published in 1957. More recent scholarship questions the very notion that what took place in 1815 was the "restoration" of anything; a revolutionary transformation in international politics is how the era is described in Paul W. Schroeder, *The Transformation of European Politics 1763–1848* (Oxford, New York: Clarendon Press/Oxford University Press, 1994); see pp. 575–582.

[16] See Henry Kissinger, *Diplomacy*, 166, 805, 811.

[17] Metternich is quoted by Harold Nicolson in *The Congress of Vienna: A Study in Allied Unity 1812–1822* (London: Constable, 1946), 277.

[18] Kissinger, *Diplomacy*, 84-85.

[19] Kissinger, *Diplomacy*, 808.

[20] See R. W. Seton-Watson, *Disraeli, Gladstone and the Eastern Question: A Study in Diplomacy and Party Politics* (New York: Norton, 1972; first published in London, 1935), 548–549, 566. Henry Kissinger interprets the affair rather differently. In his version, the moralizing Gladstone, a "Wilsonian" idealist, undercut Britain's standing and influence in international affairs. See 161–163.

[21] Kissinger, *Diplomacy*, 86.

CHAPTER XXI

Whose Story Is It?
The Cold War in Retrospect

At first glance John Lewis Gaddis is the ideal person to write a general history of the cold war: He has already written six books on the same subject. His new book* is based on a popular undergraduate course at Yale, where Gaddis is the Robert A. Lovett Professor of History. To be sure, it is not clear in what precise respect this latest version is distinctively new—*We Now Know: Rethinking Cold War History* (1997) had a decidedly stronger claim.[1] But Gaddis, the "dean of cold war historians" according to the *New York Times,* writes with consummate self-assurance. And with so much practice he has his story down pat.

The cold war, in Gaddis's account, was both inevitable and necessary. The Soviet empire and its allies could not be rolled back, but they had to be contained. The resulting standoff lasted forty years. A lot of time and money was spent on nuclear weapons and the cautious new strategic thinking to which they gave rise. Partly for this reason, there were no major wars (though there were a number of nerve-wracking confrontations). In the end—thanks to greater resources, a vastly more attractive political and economic model, and the initiative of a few good

---

* John Lewis Gaddis, *The Cold War: A New History* (New York: Penguin, 2006).

men (and one good woman)—the right side won. Since then, new complications have arisen, but we can at least be grateful to have said goodbye to all *that*.

Gaddis is most comfortable when discussing grand strategy, and the best parts of his new book are those that deal with the impact of the nuclear arms race on American policymakers. He discusses at length, and with some sympathy, Washington's decades-long preoccupation with "credibility": how to convince the Soviets that we would indeed be willing to go to war over various parts of Europe and Asia while insisting with as much conviction as possible upon our reluctance to do so. If the cold war "worked" as a system for keeping the peace it was because—albeit for slightly different reasons—Moscow had parallel preoccupations. These tense but stable arrangements, based on the apposite acronym "MAD" (mutually assured destruction), only came near to breaking down when one side temporarily lost faith in its antagonist's commitment to the system: over Cuba in 1962, when Khrushchev miscalculated and Kennedy initially misread his intentions; and in the early eighties, when Ronald Reagan's huge rearmament program and reiterated rhetorical challenges to the "Evil Empire" led Moscow to believe that the U.S. really was planning a preemptive nuclear first strike, and to prepare accordingly.[2]

Any history of the cold war that pays sustained attention to such issues of high strategy is likely to have its gaze firmly fixed upon the Great Powers. So it is with Gaddis. However, his close familiarity with the history of American foreign policy is not matched by a comparable expertise in the sources and psychology of Soviet strategic calculation. Gaddis's account of American statesmen and their doings is detailed and lively. His coverage of Soviet behavior, by contrast, is conventional and two-dimensional. What emerges is a history of the cold war narrated as a superpower confrontation, but largely from the perspective of just one of those powers.

Until the fall of the Soviet Union, such unbalanced accounts were the norm. Little reliable information was available about Soviet thinking. Political observers were thus reduced either to "Kremlinology"—scouring speeches, newspaper editorials, and podium lineups—or else to deducing Communist behavior from Marxist principles. But as Gaddis himself has demonstrated elsewhere, we now know quite a lot about the thinking behind Soviet policies—rather more, in fact, than we do about some Western undertakings, thanks to the opening of Communist archives. So if *The Cold War: A New History* is so heavily weighted toward an American perspective, this cannot be an effect of unbalanced sources.[3]

It turns out to be the product of a decidedly partial viewpoint. Gaddis is an unapologetic triumphalist. America won the cold war because Americans deserved to win it. Unlike the Russians, they were "impatient with hierarchy, at ease with flexibility, and profoundly distrustful of the notion that theory should determine practice rather than the other way around." As the cold war got under way, only America understood what "justice" meant:

> For the Americans, that term meant political democracy, market capitalism, and—in principle if not always in practice—respect for the rights of individuals. For the British and French, still running colonial empires, it meant something short of that. . . . And for Stalin's Soviet Union, "justice" meant the unquestioning acceptance of authoritarian politics, command economies, and the right of the proletariat to advance, by whatever means the dictatorship that guided it chose to employ, toward a worldwide "classless" society.

Even Gaddis is constrained to concede that in their pursuit of justice American statesmen occasionally resorted to shady dealings and tactics. But he insists that whereas politicians elsewhere (in China, in the Soviet Union, in Western Europe) might be congenital sinners and cynics, for Americans this was something new—a by-product of the cold war itself. American statesmen were forced to import the moral ambiguities of foreign conflicts into which they were being drawn:

> And so the Cold War transformed American leaders into Machiavellians. Confronted with "so many who are not good," they resolved "to learn to be able not to be good" themselves, and to use this skill or not use it, as the great Italian cynic—or patriot—had put it, "according to necessity."

No doubt intended to flatter Truman and his colleagues, this irenic account of the loss of American innocence has the reverse effect. It bathes U.S. history before the cold war in a sort of prelapsarian glow, while implausibly portraying worldly, cosmopolitan diplomats like Harriman, Acheson, Kennan, Bohlen, and others as a generation of benign provincial gentlemen reluctantly obliged to compromise their ethics and adopt the sophisticated, worldly wiles of their foes in order to overcome them.

Appropriately enough, Gaddis's way of narrating cold war history reflects the same provincialism he foists approvingly upon his American protagonists. In part this is a matter of style—the author resorts quite often to down-home cliché: Eastern Europe in 1956 was a "powder keg," Communism was "like a building constructed on quicksand." At times he edges close to bathos: Richard Nixon was defeated by "an adversary more powerful than either the Soviet Union or the international communist movement. It was the Constitution of the United States of America." But this folksy prose—while maladapted to the broad-brush historical overviews Gaddis occasionally attempts ("Karl Marx knew little about penguins, but he did acknowledge, in the sexist terminology of 1852, that 'Men make their own history'")—is also a function of his terms of reference. John Lewis Gaddis has written a history of *America's* cold war: as seen from America, as experienced in America, and told in a way most agreeable to many American readers.

As a result, this is a book whose silences are especially suggestive. The "third world" in particular comes up short. How we look at international history is always in some measure a function of where we stand. But it takes a uniquely parochial perspective—and one ill-becoming someone described by Michael Beschloss in the *New York Times Book Review* as "a scholar of extraordinary gifts" offering "his long-awaited retrospective verdict on the cold war"—to publish a history of the cold war containing not even an index entry for Argentina, Brazil, Venezuela, Panama, Grenada, or El Salvador, not to speak of Mozambique, the Congo, or Indonesia. Major events in Iran—where the CIA's 1953 coup against Mohammad Mosaddeq is still held against the U.S.—and Guatemala (where the U.S. toppled Jacobo Arbenz Guzmán on June 27, 1954, precipitating decades of armed and bloody conflict) each receive passing acknowledgment from Gaddis, summarized thus: "The consequences, in both regions, proved costly."

Indeed so. But those costs are never analyzed, much less incorporated into the author's evaluation of the cold war as a whole. For Gaddis, as for so many American politicians and statesmen, the "third world" was a sideshow, albeit one in which hundreds of thousands of the performers got killed.[4] And he seems to believe that whatever unfortunate developments took place in the course of these peripheral scuffles, they were confined to the cold war's early years. Later, things improved: "The 1970s were not the 1950s." Well, yes they were—in El Salvador, for example, not to mention Chile. But this sort of tunnel vision, tipping most of the world offstage and focusing exclusively upon Great Power confrontations in Europe or East Asia, is the price Gaddis pays for placing himself firmly in Washington, D.C., when "thinking" the cold war. For the other superpower saw the cold war very differently.

Seen from Moscow, the cold war was in very substantial measure *about* the non-European world. While President Kennedy and his advisers worried in October 1962 that Nikita Khrushchev's Cuban missiles were a diversionary prelude to an attack on Berlin, the Soviet leadership (who were irritated by their East German clients and really didn't care much about Berlin except as a diplomatic pawn) dreamed of a revolutionary front in Latin America. "For a quarter of a century," one expert writes, "the KGB, unlike the CIA, believed that the Third World was the arena in which it could win the Cold War."[5] In pursuit of local influence on the African continent, Moscow fueled a huge arms boom there from the early seventies through the onset of perestroika. Indeed, it is precisely those African countries most corrupted by the "proxy" wars of the later cold war that were to become the "failed states" of our own time—one of a number of ways in which the cold war and the post–cold war eras are intimately intertwined, though you would not learn this from Gaddis.

In Africa, as in Latin America, the cold war was a clash of empires rather than ideologies. Both sides supported and promoted unsavory puppets and surrogates. But whereas the Soviet Union treated its impoverished third-world clients with cynical disdain and did not even pretend to be in the business of promoting "democracy" or freedom, the U.S.

did—which is why it was so much more vulnerable to the charge of hypocrisy, whether supporting authoritarian regimes in Spain or Portugal, venal and corrupt rulers in Vietnam or Egypt, "terrorists" in Afghanistan, or outright dictatorships from Tierra del Fuego to the Mexican border. As a consequence, for all the very real appeal of its music, its clothes, its films, and its way of life (not to speak of its limitless resources), the U.S. would largely fail in later years to reap the benefits of its cold war engagements. It is one of the ironies of the cold war that America's victories in Europe were frequently offset by long-term damage to its reputation farther afield: in Vietnam, for example, or the Middle East. The Soviet Union was not the only "loser" in the cold war.

Again, readers will learn little of these complexities in Gaddis's account, much less of their implications for U.S. foreign policy today. To the extent that he responds implicitly to criticisms of American missteps—and worse—in Latin America and elsewhere in the course of these decades, Gaddis appears to take the view that these were unfortunate things; for the most part they had to be done; and, anyway, they are all behind us. One is reminded of Marlowe's Barabas:

Barnardine: Thou hast committed—
Barabas: Fornication? But that was in another country, and besides, the wench is dead.[6]

Gaddis pays more attention to the nations within the Soviet bloc itself. But what he has to say about them, though well intentioned, inspires little confidence. Václav Havel is described as "the most influential chronicler of his generation's disillusionment with communism." But Havel suffered no such disillusionment: He never was a Communist. The rather isolated son of a wealthy family, dispossessed and discriminated against by the Communist authorities, Václav Havel took no part in his contemporaries' flirtation with Marxism. He is said by Gaddis to have given voice to a widespread vision in Eastern Europe of "a society in which universal morality, state morality, and individual morality might all be the same thing." (Gaddis isn't very good with political abstractions, but one sees what he means.) This would be nice if it were true; but sadly, in the twelve years between its founding and the fall of

Communism, Havel's Charter 77 attracted fewer than two thousand signatures in a Czechoslovak population of fifteen million.

Havel was elected as the first post-Communist president of Czechoslovakia precisely because he had spent much of the previous two decades in prison or under house arrest and was untainted by any links to the regime's discredited past or its ideology; but his moralized rhetoric never sat comfortably with the nation at large. Though Havel had many friends in the former dissident intelligentsia of Central Europe, he aroused little popular affection outside of Bohemia itself (he was not much loved even in neighboring Slovakia). A more influential and representative chronicler of his generation's lost illusions and post-Communist trajectory would be Havel's Polish fellow dissident Adam Michnik, or even the Hungarian economist János Kornai. But neither is mentioned by Gaddis.

Gaddis's thumbnail sketches of Communist doctrine are clunky and a bit embarrassing. Of Marxism as an ideological project he has this to say: "Marxism brought hope to the poor, fear to the rich, and left governments somewhere in between. To rule solely on behalf of the bourgeoisie seemed likely to ensure revolution, thereby confirming Marx's prophecy; but to do so only for the proletariat would mean that Marx's revolution had already arrived."

He explains that Brezhnev-era Communism was justified by an appeal to "ideology: to the claim that, in Marxism-Leninism, they had discovered the mechanisms by which history worked, and thus the means by which to improve the lives people lived." Of Margaret Thatcher's electoral popularity Gaddis concludes, "[it] was a blow to Marxism, for if capitalism really did exploit 'the masses,' why did so many among them cheer the 'iron lady'?" This is history writing at one notch above the level of the tabloid editorial.[7]

And indeed, when it comes to Eastern Europe under Communism, Gaddis does little more than hastily recycle received wisdom. In a work of 333 pages, Tito's break with Stalin gets just one paragraph; the Hungarian revolution of 1956 merits a mere twenty-seven lines (whereas page after page is devoted to Watergate); meanwhile John Paul II, Margaret Thatcher, and Ronald Reagan ("one of its [the U.S.'s] sharpest strategists ever") are credited at some length with bringing down

Communism.[8] As for Mikhail Gorbachev, Gaddis's account of him gives the Reagan administration full credit for many of Gorbachev's own opinions, ideas, and achievements—as well it might, since in this section of the book Gaddis is paraphrasing and citing Secretary of State George Shultz's memoirs.[9] Here and elsewhere, as the Communist regimes fall like bowling pins and the U.S. emerges resplendent, vindicated and victorious, *The Cold War: A New History* reads like the ventriloquized autobiography of an Olympic champion.

THERE IS REMARKABLY little in this book about spies (and what there is, once again, concerns mostly American spies). This is odd, considering the importance of intelligence gathering during the cold war and since. Spying was one of the few things that the Soviet bloc could do well—the East German foreign intelligence network in particular, run for thirty-three years by the late Markus ("Mischa") Wolf, was highly regarded for its techniques by both sides. The paradoxes of intelligence, generally ignored by Gaddis, are often quite interesting. Thus the USSR, whose own scientific and technical achievements lagged behind those of the West, compensated by stealing techniques and information from the West and incorporating them into weapons systems and aeronautics in particular. This—together with disinformation, self-delusion, and professional self-interest—led Western intelligence agencies (the CIA especially) to overestimate Soviet capacities and strengths and frighten their political leaders accordingly.[10]

Had Gaddis thought more about spies and spying, he might have avoided one particularly revealing error that highlights his self-confinement within the straitjacket of American domestic experience. Although there is only one mention in his book of McCarthyism, Gaddis uses that occasion to write that "it was not at all clear that the western democracies themselves could retain the tolerance for dissent and the respect for civil liberties that distinguished them from the dictators." But Senator Joseph McCarthy was an American original. There was no McCarthyism in Britain, or France, or Norway, or Italy, or the Netherlands. Numerous victims of McCarthyism—whether actors, singers, musicians, playwrights, trade unionists, or history professors—came to live in Western Europe in these years and flourished there.[11] Tolerance and civil liberties were not under threat in all "the western democracies." They were under threat in the United States. There is a difference.

During the first decade of the cold war, espionage, subversion, and Communist takeovers in distant lands were perceived by many in the U.S. as a direct challenge to the "American Way of Life"; Senator McCarthy, Richard Nixon, and the Republican Party were able to exploit the security issue in cold war America by pointing to real spies (Alger Hiss, the Rosenbergs) as well as imagined ones. Meanwhile, across the Atlantic in Great Britain, Klaus Fuchs, George Blake, Guy Burgess, Donald McLean, Anthony Blunt, and above all Kim Philby betrayed their country, their colleagues, and hundreds of their fellow agents. Between them they did far more damage to Western interests than any American spy until Aldrich Ames. Yet the serial revelation of their treason—beginning with the arrest of Fuchs in 1950—aroused remarkably little public anxiety. It certainly never provoked in Britain collective paranoia and political conformism on the scale that seized the U.S. in these same years.

The cold war was experienced very differently in Britain from the way it was lived (and is remembered) in the U.S. And things were different again in France and Italy, where between a quarter and a third of the electorate voted for a Communist Party in those years. (The Italian case, where Enrico Berlinguer deftly led his Eurocommunist party out of the Soviet orbit and into the political mainstream, is particularly interesting—but receives no attention from Gaddis.) They were also different in the Netherlands and Denmark, where domestic Communism was nonexistent but active commitment to NATO was perfectly compatible with extensive tolerance for cultural or political difference; or in Austria and Sweden—no less "western" and "democratic" than the U.S. but ostentatiously and self-indulgently "neutral" in cold war confrontations. "Western democracy" can cover a multitude of different political cultures. America's many friends in postwar Austria were forced to watch in frustration as the libraries of the popular "America Houses" in postwar Vienna, Salzburg, and elsewhere were stripped (on instructions from McCarthy-era Washington) of works by "unsuitable" authors: John Dos Passos, Arthur Miller, Charles Beard, Leonard Bernstein, Dashiell Hammett, Upton Sinclair—and also Albert

Einstein, Thomas Mann, Reinhold Niebuhr, Alberto Moravia, Tom Paine, and Henry Thoreau.[12]

John Gaddis misses all this. In general he is rather contemptuous of Western Europe: The European Economic Community gets just one passing mention, and if Gaddis spends a little more time on Charles de Gaulle it is only in order to lump him patronizingly with Mao Zedong as the leaders of bumptious "medium powers" who performed "high-wire acrobatics without a net" in order to undermine and sabotage the strategies of their respective superpower patrons. Readers of *The Cold War: A New History* who lack prior familiarity with the subject will be at a loss to understand just why a French president should have behaved so capriciously toward his American protectors, "exasperating" Washington and "flaunting" French autonomy, or what it is about the history of the preceding decades that helps explain French irritation at the "Anglo-Saxon" powers. Nor will they learn anything about de Gaulle's unquestioning loyalty to the U.S. during the Cuba crisis or the quizzical respect (albeit much tested) with which he was regarded by Presidents Kennedy, Johnson, and Nixon. These are nuances—and John Gaddis is not much given to nuance.[13]

That is a pity, because an account of the cold war that was more sensitive to national variations might have picked up the cultural aspects of the confrontation, to which Gaddis's history is completely indifferent. The cold war was fought on many fronts, not all of them geographical and some of them within national frontiers. One of these fronts was established by the Congress for Cultural Freedom (CCF), inaugurated in Berlin in June 1950, under whose auspices Bertrand Russell, Benedetto Croce, John Dewey, Karl Jaspers, Jacques Maritain, Arthur Koestler, Raymond Aron, A. J. Ayer, Stephen Spender, Margarete Buber-Neumann, Ignazio Silone, Nicolà Chiaromonte, Melvin Lasky, and Sidney Hook set out to challenge and undercut the intellectual appeal of Communism, whose own illustrious supporters and camp followers included on various occasions Sartre, Simone de Beauvoir, Bertolt Brecht, Louis Aragon, Elio Vittorini, and many of the best minds of the coming intellectual generation—including in those years François Furet, Leszek Kołakowski, and the youthful Milan Kundera.

Not one of these names, not one—not even the CCF itself or Stalin's international Peace Movement, which it was set up to oppose—receives a single mention in Gaddis's history of the cold war. Unsurprisingly, therefore, he misses something else: not just the intense intellectual and cultural confrontations over totalitarianism, Communism, Marxism, and freedom, but also the cold war between the generations. The anti-Fascist generation of the thirties—exemplified by Klaus Mann's declaration in Paris in 1935: "Whatever Fascism is, we are not and we are against it"— was displaced and fragmented by the anti-Communist generation of the fifties . . . only for both of them to be dismissed by the new radicals of the sixties.[14]

The latter were uniquely cut off from the political past of their parents' generation. Alienated from "the West" by its (in their eyes) unbroken links back to Nazi and Fascist regimes—in West Germany, Austria, and Italy above all—and by its neocolonial wars in Africa and Indochina, they had no greater sympathy for the "*crapules staliniennes*" (Daniel Cohn-Bendit) of a discredited Communist empire. They thus hung in an uncomfortable and sometimes violent limbo, athwart the international confrontation whose terms of reference they angrily rejected.[15] This is not a uniquely European story, of course. The cold war changed the United States too, first in the formative years between 1948 and 1953 and again in the later sixties. Young Americans of the same vintage as Cohn-Bendit or Germany's Joschka Fischer experienced the "peripheral" confrontations of the cold war as a lasting schism within their own culture: One former Harvard student, looking back upon the impact of the Vietnam War on the Harvard Class of '70, wrote that her generation had "maintained a certain distance, a feeling of being in some ways outsiders to this society in which we are now adults."[16]

The cold war may have begun, in a formal sense, in the late 1940s, but its intensity and its longevity only make sense if we understand that it had far older sources. The confrontation between Leninist Communism and the Western democracies dates to 1919; and in countries where Communism struck root in the local labor movement and among the intellectual elite (notably Czechoslovakia, France, and India), it is more coherently thought of as having a domestic history that extends from World War I into the 1980s. In the Soviet Union itself the basic strategies to be deployed in relations with "bourgeois democracies" were forged not in the 1940s but in the 1920s.

Thus détente, which John Gaddis misleadingly presents as an innovation of the seventies—a response to the generational revolts and democratic movements of the previous decade—in fact had its origins in the "wars of position" in which Soviet leaders ever since Lenin saw themselves as engaging against the more powerful West: sometimes taking a conciliatory line (e.g., between 1921 and 1926, during the Popular Fronts of 1934 to 1939, and again at points in the later fifties and early seventies), sometimes presenting an uncompromising "front"—as in the so-called Third Period between 1927 and 1934 and again during the frosty "Two Cultures" standoff between 1947 and 1953. Moreover, détente, too, has its paradoxes: An externally conciliatory Soviet position was often accompanied by (and helped camouflage) the reimposition of domestic repression, as during the Popular Front years or during the antidissident crackdown of the early 1970s.[17]

To ignore the prehistory of cold war politics in this way is to miss some of the most interesting aspects of the story. But perhaps the most revealing of all Gaddis's omissions is his refusal to make the link between the cold war and what has happened since. He is quite explicit about this: "Nor does [this] book attempt to locate roots, within the Cold War, of such post–Cold War phenomena as globalization, ethnic cleansing, religious extremism, terrorism or the information revolution." But with the partial exception of the information revolution, these, *pace* Gaddis, are not "post–Cold War phenomena." Under the guise of proxy confrontations from Central America to Indonesia, both "pacification" and ethnic cleansing—not to speak of religious struggles—were a continuous accompaniment to the cold war. The mass killings of hundreds of thousands in Indonesia and Guatemala are just two egregious examples among many. And no one who knew anything about (or had merely lived in) the UK, France, Germany, Italy, Spain, Turkey, India, Colombia, Algeria, or anywhere in the Middle East could for one minute suppose that "terrorism" was a "post–Cold War phenomenon."

On the contrary: Far from "settl[ing] fundamental issues once and for all," as Gaddis would have us believe, the cold war has an intimate, unfinished relationship with the world it left behind: whether for the vanquished

Russians, whose troubled postimperial frontier zones from Afghanistan and Chechnya to Armenia, Abkhazia, and Moldova are the unhappy heirs to Stalinist ethnic cleansing and Moscow's heedless exploitation of local interest and divisions; or for the victorious Americans, whose unconstrained military monopoly ought to have made of the U.S. a universally welcome international policeman but which is instead—thanks to cold war memories as well as the Bush administration's mistakes—the source of an unprecedented level of popular anti-Americanism.

Indeed, the errors of America's own post–cold war governments have deep pre-1989 roots. The military buildup and rhetorical overkill of the cold war had their uses in the strategic game playing of those decades and in the need to repress (or reassure) client states and their constituencies. In Washington during the early cold war, influential men talked loudly of bringing democracy and freedom to Eastern Europe. But when the crunch came, in November 1956, they did nothing (and had never intended to do anything, though they neglected to explain this in advance to Hungary's doomed insurgents). Today things are very different. Big promises of support for democracy and liberty are no longer constrained by risk of nuclear war or even of a Great Power confrontation; but the habit is still with us. During the cold war, however, we were—on the whole—"against" something, reacting to a challenge. Now we are proactive, we are "for" something: an inherently more adventurous and risky position, however vague our objective.[18]

If Gaddis does not pursue these thoughts it is probably because he is not much troubled by them. To judge from what he has to say about the past, he is unlikely to lose sleep over presidential abuses of power in the present or future. Indeed, Gaddis admonishes Americans for placing restrictions on their elected rulers. Describing what he clearly sees as the regrettable overreaction to Watergate and Vietnam in the 1970s, he writes: "The United States Congress was passing laws—always blunt instruments—to constrain the use of *United States* military and intelligence capabilities. It was as if the nation had become its own worst enemy." Retrospectively frustrated by such constraints, Gaddis admires the boldness and vision of President George W. Bush. A keen supporter of the recent Iraq war, Gaddis in 2004 even published a guide for the use of American policymakers, showing how preemptive and preventive war making has an honorable place in American history and is to be encouraged—where appropriate—as part of an ongoing project of benevolent interventionism.[19]

Thus, while it may seem tempting to dismiss John Lewis Gaddis's history of the cold war as a naively self-congratulatory account that leaves out much of what makes its subject interesting and of continuing relevance, that would be a mistake. Gaddis's version is perfectly adapted for contemporary America: an anxious country curiously detached from its own past as well as from the rest of the world and hungry for "a fireside fairytale with a happy ending."[20] *The Cold War: A New History* is likely to be widely read in the U.S.: both as history and, in the admiring words of a blurb on the dust jacket, for the "lessons" it can teach us in how to "deal with new threats." That is a depressing thought.

This decidedly unsympathetic review of John Gaddis's popular new history of the cold war appeared in the New York Review of Books *in March 2006. Gaddis, understandably enough, took umbrage at my lack of enthusiasm for his latest and most commercially successful account of the cold war decades; but the fact remains that his book contributes significantly to widespread misunderstanding and ignorance in the U.S. concerning the nature of the cold war, the way it ended, and its troubling, unfinished legacies at home and abroad.*

NOTES TO CHAPTER XXI

[1] See my essay "Why the Cold War Worked," *New York Review of Books*, October 9, 1997. Gaddis's many books include *The United States and the Origins of the Cold War, 1941–1947* (New York: Columbia University Press, 1972); *Russia, the Soviet Union and the United States: An Interpretive History* (Knopf, 1978); *Strategies of Containment: A Critical Appraisal of Postwar American National Security Policy* (New York: Oxford University Press, 1982); *The Long Peace: Inquiries into the History of the Cold War* (New York: Oxford University Press, 1987); *The United States and the End of the Cold War: Implications, Reconsiderations, Provocations* (New York: Oxford University Press, 1992).

[2] Huge increases in the Pentagon budget during Reagan's first term led the KGB and GRU—Soviet military intelligence—to mount the biggest intelligence operation of the cold war in an effort to penetrate Washington's (nonexistent) plans for a nuclear attack. See Christopher Andrew and Vasili Mitrokhin, *The Sword and the Shield: The Mitrokhin Archive and the Secret History of the KGB* (New York: Basic Books, 1999), 392–393.

[3] Except insofar as these are in languages Gaddis does not read. But thanks to the publications of the invaluable Cold War International History Project at the Woodrow Wilson International Center in Washington, even this is no longer an insuperable impediment, as Gaddis himself generously acknowledges.

[4] For an alternative viewpoint, see Greg Grandin, *The Last Colonial Massacre: Latin America in the Cold War* (Chicago: University of Chicago Press, 2004).

[5] Christopher Andrew and Vasili Mitrokhin, *The World Was Going Our Way: The KGB and the Battle for the Third World* (New York: Basic Books, 2005), foreword, xxvi.

[6] Christopher Marlowe, *The Jew of Malta*, Act IV, scene i.

[7] And wrong, too. Under Margaret Thatcher the British Conservative Party's share of the vote went down at every election she contested after 1979. The reason Thatcher won anyway was because Labour's vote fell even further. The "masses" didn't switch to Thatcher; they just stopped voting.

[8] Here, as elsewhere, Gaddis's account flattens out interesting undulations in the historical record. Thus Tito's break with Stalin was more than just a revolt against "Cominform orthodoxy." Tito himself was very orthodox, ideologically speaking. Indeed, he was "more Catholic than the Pope," which was just what Stalin held against him. On this subject Gaddis's Yale colleague Ivo Banac has written a very interesting book, *With Stalin Against Tito: Cominformist Splits in Yugoslav Communism* (Ithaca, NY: Cornell University Press, 1988). Curiously, it does not figure in Gaddis's bibliography.

[9] It is true that Gorbachev's view of the Soviet system shifted sharply after 1986. But he was a convinced Communist and remained one. What changed his perspective was not George Shultz's private lectures on the virtues of capitalism (as both Shultz and, less forgivably, Gaddis appear to believe) but the catastrophe of Chernobyl and its aftermath.

[10] See Markus Wolf, *Man Without a Face: The Autobiography of Communism's Greatest Spymaster* (New York: Times Books, 1997); also Andrew and Mitrokhin, *The World Was Going Our Way*, 489.

[11] One illustration among many: Moses Finley, whom I knew at Cambridge University, came to Great Britain in 1954 from Rutgers University in New Jersey. He had been fired by Rutgers in December 1952—for invoking the Fifth Amendment when called before the House Committee on Un-American Activities the previous March—and was unable to get another post in the U.S. He settled in Cambridge, became a British citizen, succeeded to the Chair of Ancient History in 1970, and died in 1986 as Professor Sir Moses Finley CBE, the most influential ancient historian of his time. I don't believe anyone in Cambridge ever asked Finley whether he was then or had ever been a Communist.

[12] See Reinhold Wagnleitner, *Coca-Colonization and the Cold War: The Cultural Mission of the United States in Austria after the Second World War* (Chapel Hill: University of North Carolina Press, 1994), 136–139.

[13] For a corrective, see Thomas Alan Schwartz, *Lyndon Johnson and Europe* (Cambridge: Harvard University Press, 2003). This important book is missing from Gaddis's bibliography.

[14] The literature on the cultural history of the cold war is unusually rich. Among many works, see Abbott Gleason, *Totalitarianism: The Inner History of the Cold War* (New York: Oxford University Press, 1995) and Volker R. Berghahn, *America and the Intellectual Cold Wars in Europe* (Princeton, NJ: Princeton University Press, 2001). Sadly, Gaddis—whose bibliography contains ten entries under his own name—could not find room for either of these books.

[15] For a recent description of the trajectory of that generation, from street fighting to government ministries, and its heritage in contemporary interventionism undertaken in the name of liberal ideals, see Paul Berman's *Power and the Idealists: Or, the Passion of Joschka Fischer and Its Aftermath* (Brooklyn, NY: Soft Skull Press, 2005). This is an important story, but *Power and the Idealists* would be a much better book if Berman had resisted the temptation to trace back his own fervently ideological support for the recent Iraq war into the mental and political world of seventies-era German activists. (For an instance of the rather desperate lengths to which Berman goes to link Iraqi Baathists and al-Qaeda, in a chapter ostensibly devoted to Joschka Fischer and German foreign policy, see, e.g., pp. 124–125.)

[16] Martha Ritter, "Echoes from the Age of Relevance," *Harvard Magazine,* July–August 1981, 10; quoted in David L. Schalk, *War and The Ivory Tower: Algeria and Vietnam* (Lincoln: University of Nebraska Press, 2005; first published in 1991).

[17] Gaddis's historically foreshortened understanding of détente and its sources probably results from his dependence in these matters upon *Power and Protest: Global Revolution and the Rise of Détente* (Cambridge, MA: Harvard University Press, 2003), written by his former student Jeremi Suri. This is a stimulating and original study but one in which imaginative global interpretation occasionally substitutes for detailed local knowledge.

[18] For a levelheaded discussion of what happens when a proactive superpower offers to "remake everyone else's world," see Ghassan Salamé, *Quand l'Amérique refait le monde* (Paris: Fayard, 2005), notably "Conclusion," 519–547.

[19] *Surprise, Security, and the American Experience* (Cambridge, MA: Harvard University Press, 2004).

[20] The phrase is David Caute's, from his review of *The Cold War: A New History* in *The Spectator,* January 14, 2006.

CHAPTER XXII

The Silence of the Lambs: On the Strange Death of Liberal America

Why have American liberals acquiesced in President Bush's catastrophic foreign policy? Why have they so little to say about Iraq, about Lebanon, or about recent reports of a planned attack on Iran? Why has the administration's sustained attack on civil liberties and international law aroused so little opposition or anger from those who used to care most about these things? Why, in short, has the liberal intelligentsia of the United States in recent years kept its head safely below the parapet?

It wasn't always so. Back on October 26, 1988, the *New York Times* carried a full-page advertisement for Liberalism. Headed "A Reaffirmation of Principle," it openly rebuked then-President Ronald Reagan for deriding "the dreaded L-word" and treating "liberals" and "liberalism" as terms of opprobrium. Liberal principles, the text affirmed, are "timeless. Extremists of the right and of the left have long attacked liberalism as their greatest enemy. In our own time liberal democracies have been crushed by such extremists. Against any encouragement of this tendency in our own country, intentional or not, we feel obliged to speak out."

The advertisement was signed by sixty-three prominent intellectuals, writers, and businessmen: among them Daniel Bell, John Kenneth Galbraith, Felix Rohatyn, Arthur Schlesinger Jr., Irving Howe, and

Eudora Welty. These and other signatories—the economist Kenneth Arrow, the poet Robert Penn Warren—were the critical intellectual core, the steady moral center of American public life. But who, now, would sign such a protest? Liberalism in the United States today is the politics that dare not speak its name. And those who style themselves "liberal intellectuals" are otherwise engaged. As befits the new Gilded Age, in which the pay ratio of an American CEO to that of a skilled worker is 412:1 and a corrupted Congress is awash in lobbies and favors, the place of the liberal intellectual has been largely subsumed by an admirable cohort of muckraking investigative journalists—notably Seymour Hersh, Michael Massing, and Mark Danner, writing in the *New Yorker* and the *New York Review of Books*.

The collapse of liberal self-confidence in the contemporary USA can be variously explained. In part it is a backwash from the lost illusions of the sixties generation, a retreat from the radical nostrums of youth into the all-consuming business of material accumulation and personal secu-rity. The signatories of the *New York Times* advertisement were born, in most cases, many years earlier, their political opinions shaped by the thir-ties above all. *Their* commitments were the product of experience and adversity and made of sterner stuff. The disappearance of the liberal center in American politics is also a direct outcome of the deliquescence of the Democratic Party. In domestic politics liberals once believed in the provision of welfare, good government, and social justice. In foreign af-fairs they had a long-standing commitment to international law, nego-tiation, and the importance of moral example. Today a spreading me-first consensus has replaced vigorous public debate in both arenas. And like their political counterparts, the critical intelligentsia once so prominent in American cultural life has fallen silent.

This process was well under way before September 11, 2001—and in domestic affairs at least, Bill Clinton and his calculated policy "trian-gulations" must carry some responsibility for the evisceration of liberal politics. But since then the moral and intellectual arteries of the American body politic have hardened further. Magazines and newspapers of the mainstream liberal center—e.g., the *New Yorker*, the *New Republic*, the *Washington Post*, and the *New York Times* itself—fell over themselves in the hurry to align their editorial stance with a Republican president bent on exemplary war. A fearful conformism gripped the mainstream media. And America's liberal intellectuals found at last a new cause.

Or, rather, an old cause in a new guise. For what distinguished the worldview of George Bush's liberal supporters from that of his neoconservative allies is that they do not look upon the "War on Terror," or the war in Iraq, or the war in Lebanon and eventually Iran, as mere serial exercises in the reestablishment of American martial dominance. They see them rather as skirmishes in a new global confrontation: a Good Fight, reassuringly comparable to their grandparents' war against Fascism and their cold war liberal parents' stance against international Communism. Once again, they assert, things are clear. The world is ideologically divided. As before, we must take our stand on *the* issue of the age. Long nostalgic for the comforting verities of a simpler time, today's liberal intellectuals have at last discovered a sense of purpose: They are at war with "Islamo-Fascism."

Thus Paul Berman, a frequent contributor to *Dissent*, the *New Yorker*, and other liberal journals and hitherto better known as a commentator on American cultural affairs, recycled himself as an expert on Islamic Fascism (itself a newly minted term of art), publishing a book on the subject (*Terror & Liberalism*, 2003) just in time for the Iraq war. Peter Beinart, a former editor of the *New Republic*, followed in his wake with *The Good Fight: Why Liberals—and only Liberals—Can Win the War on Terror and Make America Great Again* (2006), where he sketches at some length the resemblance between the war on terror and the early cold war. Neither author had hitherto evinced any familiarity with the Middle East, much less with the Wahhabi and Sufi traditions on which they pronounce with such confidence.

But like Christopher Hitchens and other erstwhile left-liberal pundits now expert in "Islamo-Fascism," Beinart and Berman and their ilk really *are* familiar—and comfortable—with a binary division of the world along ideological lines. A world thus divided is familiar to them from their parents' time; in some cases they can even look back to their own youthful Trotskyism, when seeking a template and thesaurus for world-historical antagonisms. In order for today's "fight" (note the recycled Leninist lexicon of conflicts, clashes, struggles, and wars) to make political sense, it too must have a single universal foe whose ideas we can study, theorize, and combat; and the new confrontation must be reducible, just like its twentieth-century predecessor, to a familiar juxtaposition that eliminates exotic complexity and confusion: Democracy vs. Totalitarianism, Freedom vs. Fascism, Them vs. Us.

To be sure, Bush's liberal supporters have been disappointed by his efforts. Every newspaper I have listed and many others besides have carried editorials criticizing Bush's policy on imprisonment, his use of torture, and above all the sheer ineptitude of the President's war in Iraq. But here, too, the cold war offers a revealing analogy. Like Stalin's Western admirers who, in the wake of Khrushchev's revelations, resented the Soviet dictator not so much for his crimes as for discrediting their Marxism; so intellectual supporters of the Iraq war—among them Michael Ignatieff, Leon Wieseltier, David Remnick, and other prominent figures in the North American liberal establishment—have focused their regrets not upon the catastrophic invasion itself (which they all supported) but rather on its incompetent execution. They are irritated with Bush for giving "preventive war" a bad name.

In a similar vein, those centrist voices that bayed most insistently for blood in the prelude to the Iraq war—readers may recall the *New York Times* columnist Thomas Friedman demanding that France be voted "off the island" (i.e., out of the UN Security Council) for its presumption in opposing America's drive to war—are today the most confident when asserting their monopoly of insight into world affairs. Thus the same Friedman now (August 16, 2006) sneers at "anti-war activists who haven't thought a whit about the larger struggle we're in." To be sure, Friedman's portentous, Pulitzer-winning pieties are always carefully road tested for middle-brow political acceptability. But for just that reason they are a sure guide to the mood of the American intellectual mainstream.

Friedman is seconded by Beinart, who concedes that he "didn't realize" (!) how detrimental American actions would be to "the struggle" but insists notwithstanding that anyone who won't stand up to "Global Jihad" just isn't a consistent defender of liberal values. Jacob Weisberg, in the *Financial Times*, accuses Democratic critics of the Iraq war of failing "to take the wider global battle against Islamic fanaticism seriously at all." The only people qualified to speak in this matter, it would seem, are those who got it wrong initially. Such insouciance in spite of—indeed *because* of—your past misjudgments recalls a remark by the French ex-Stalinist Pierre Courtade to Edgar Morin, a dissenting Communist vindicated by events: "You and your kind were wrong to be right; we were right to be wrong."

It is thus particularly ironically that the "Clinton generation" of American liberal intellectuals take special pride in their "tough-mindedness," in their success in casting aside the illusions and myths of the old Left. For these same "tough" new liberals in fact reproduce some of that old Left's worst characteristics. They may see themselves as having migrated to the opposite shore; but they display precisely the same mix of dogmatic faith and cultural provincialism, not to mention an exuberant enthusiasm for violent political transformations at other people's expense, that marked their fellow-traveling predecessors across the cold war ideological divide. The use value of such persons to ambitious, radical regimes is an old story. Indeed, intellectual camp followers of this kind were first identified by Lenin himself, who coined the term that still describes them best. Today, America's liberal armchair warriors are the "useful idiots" of the War on Terror.

To be fair, America's bellicose intellectuals are not alone. In Europe Adam Michnik, the hero of the Polish intellectual resistance to Communism, became an outspoken admirer of the embarrassingly Islamophobic Oriana Fallaci; Václav Havel joined the Washington-based Committee on the Present Danger (a recycled cold war–era organization originally dedicated to rooting out Communists, now pledged to fighting "the threat posed by global radical Islamist and fascist terrorist movements"); André Glucksmann in Paris contributed agitated essays to *Le Figaro* lambasting "universal Jihad," Iranian "lust for power," and radical Islam's strategy of "green subversion." All three enthusiastically supported the invasion of Iraq.

In the European case, this trend is an unfortunate by-product of the intellectual revolution of the 1980s, especially in the former Communist East, when "human rights" displaced conventional political allegiances as the basis for collective action. The gains wrought by this transformation in the rhetoric of oppositional politics were considerable. But a price was paid all the same. A commitment to the abstract universalism of "rights"—and uncompromising ethical stands taken against malign regimes in their name—can lead all too readily to the habit of casting *every* political choice in binary moral terms. In this light George Bush's war against Terror, Evil, and Islamo-Fascism appears seductive and even familiar: Self-deluding foreigners readily mistake the U.S. President's myopic rigidity for their own moral rectitude.

But back home, America's liberal intellectuals are fast becoming a service class, their opinions determined by their allegiance and calibrated to justify a political end. In itself this is hardly a new departure, of course: We are all familiar with intellectuals who speak only on behalf of their country, class, religion, "race," "gender," or "sexual orientation," and who shape their opinions according to what they take to be the interest of their affinity of birth or predilection. But the distinctive feature of the *liberal* intellectual in past times was precisely the striving for universality; not the unworldly or disingenuous denial of sectional identification but the sustained effort to transcend that identification in search of truth or the general interest.

It is thus depressing to read some of the better-known and more avowedly "liberal" intellectuals in the contemporary USA exploiting their professional credibility to advance a partisan case. Jean Bethke Elshtain and Michael Walzer, two senior figures in the country's philosophical establishment (she at the University of Chicago Divinity School, he at the Princeton Institute), both penned portentous essays purporting to demonstrate the justness of necessary wars—she in *Just War against Terror: The Burden of American Power in a Violent World* (2003) a preemptive defense of the Iraq war; he more recently in a shameless defense of Israel's bombardments of Lebanese civilians ("War Fair," *The New Republic,* July 31, 2006). In today's America, neoconservatives generate brutish policies for which liberals provide the ethical fig leaf. There really is no other difference between them.

One of the particularly depressing ways in which liberal intellectuals have abdicated personal and ethical responsibility for the actions they now endorse can be seen in their failure to think independently about the Middle East. Not every liberal cheerleader for the Global War against Islamo-Fascism, or against Terror, or against Global Jihad, is an unreconstructed supporter of Likud: Christopher Hitchens, for one, is critical of Israel. But the marked enthusiasm with which so many American pundits and commentators and essayists have rolled over for Bush's doctrine of preventive war; offered no criticism of the disproportionate use of air power on civilian targets in both Iraq and Lebanon; and stayed coyly silent in the face of Condoleezza Rice's enthusiasm for the bloody "birth pangs of a new Middle East," makes more sense when one recalls their backing for Israel: a country that for fifty years has rested its entire national strategy upon preventive wars, disproportionate retaliation, and efforts to redraw the map of the whole Middle East.

Since its inception, the state of Israel has fought a number of wars of choice (indeed, the only exception was the Yom Kippur War of 1973). To be sure, these have been presented to the world as wars of necessity or self-defense; but Israel's statesmen and generals have never been under any such illusion. Whether this approach has done Israel much good is debatable (for a clearheaded recent account that describes his country's strategy of using wars of choice to "redraw" the map of its neighborhood as a resounding failure, see *Scars of War, Wounds of Peace: The Israeli-Arab Tragedy* [2006] by Shlomo Ben-Ami, a historian and former Israeli foreign minister). But the idea of a superpower behaving in a similar way— responding to terrorist threats or guerrilla incursions by flattening another country just to preserve its own deterrent credibility—is odd in the extreme. It is one thing for the U.S. unconditionally to underwrite Israel's behavior (albeit in neither country's interest). But for the U.S. to imitate Israel wholesale, to import that tiny country's self-destructive, intemperate response to any hostility or opposition and to make it the leitmotif of American foreign policy: That is simply bizarre.

George W. Bush's Middle Eastern policy now tracks so closely to the Israeli precedent that it is very difficult to see daylight between the two. It is this surreal turn of events that helps explain the confusion and silence of American liberal thinking on this subject. Historically, liberals have been unsympathetic to "wars of choice" when undertaken or proposed by their own government. War, in the liberal imagination (and not only the liberal one), is a last resort, not a first option. But the United States now has an Israeli-style foreign policy, and thus America's liberal intellectuals overwhelmingly support it.

The contradictions to which this can lead are striking. Thus, to take just one instance: There is a blatant discrepancy between President Bush's proclaimed desire to bring democracy to the Middle East, and his refusal to intervene when the *only* working instances of fragile democracy in action in the whole Arab world—in Palestine and Lebanon—were systematically shattered by America's Israeli ally. This discrepancy, and the bad faith and hypocrisy that it seems to suggest, have become a staple of editorial pages and Internet blogs the world over, to America's lasting discredit. But America's leading liberal intellectuals have kept silent. To speak would be to choose: between the tactical logic of America's new "war of movement" against Islamic Fascism and the strategic tradition of Israeli statecraft. This is not a choice that most American liberal commentators are even willing to acknowledge, much less make. And so they say nothing.

This blind spot obscures and risks polluting and obliterating every traditional liberal concern and inhibition. How else can one explain the appalling cover illustration of the *New Republic* of August 7, 2006: a lurid depiction of Hezbollah's Hassan Nasrallah in the anti-Semitic style of *Der Stürmer* crossed with more than a touch of the "Dirty Jap" cartoons of World War II? How else is one to account for the convoluted, sophistic defense by Leon Wieseltier in the same journal of the killing of Arab children in Q'ana ("These are not tender times")? But the blind spot is not just ethical, it is also political: If American liberals "didn't realize" just why their war in Iraq would have the predictable effect of promoting terrorism, benefiting the Iranian ayatollahs, and turning Iraq into Lebanon, then we should not expect them to understand (or care) that Israel's brutal overreaction risks turning Lebanon into Iraq.

In his new book (*Five Germanys I Have Known*, 2006) Fritz Stern—coauthor of the 1988 *New York Times* text defending liberalism—writes of his concern about the condition of the liberal spirit in America today. It is with the extinction of that spirit, he notes, that the death of a republic begins. Stern, a historian and a refugee from Nazi Germany, speaks from authority in this matter. And he is surely correct. We don't expect right-wingers to care very much about the health of a republic, particularly when they are assiduously engaged in the unilateral promotion of empire. And the ideological Left, while occasionally adept at analyzing the shortcomings of a liberal republic, is typically not much interested in defending it.

It is the liberals, then, who count. They are, as it might be, the canaries in the sulfurous mine shaft of modern democracy. And thus the alacrity with which many of America's most prominent liberals have censored themselves in the name of the "war on terror," the enthusiasm with which they have invented ideological and moral cover for war and war crimes and proffered that cover to their political enemies: All this is a bad sign. Liberal intellectuals used to be distinguished precisely by their efforts to think for themselves, rather than in the service of others. Intellectuals should not be smugly theorizing endless war, much less confidently promoting and excusing it. They should be engaged in disturbing the peace—their own above all.

This essay was initially commissioned by a daily newspaper; but when it outgrew that venue, the **London Review of Books** *was kind enough to accept it and indeed encouraged me to develop its argument at length. When it appeared in the* LRB *in September 2006, it aroused considerable animosity: not so much from its targets, even though some of them understandably resented being tarred with the brush of "useful idiocy," as from leftist intellectuals who felt underappreciated in their continued opposition to President Bush. Letters to this effect duly appeared in the* **London Review of Books** *in vol. 28, no. xxi, November 2006, together with a reply from me indicating that I had restricted my discussion to intellectuals with significant public influence or readership, i.e., those who mattered.*

CHAPTER XXIII

The Good Society:
Europe vs. America

C onsider a mug of American coffee. It is found everywhere. It can be made by anyone. It is cheap—and refills are free. Being largely without flavor, it can be diluted to taste. What it lacks in allure it makes up in size. It is the most democratic method ever devised for introducing caffeine into human beings. Now take a cup of Italian espresso. It requires expensive equipment. Price-to-volume ratio is outrageous, suggesting indifference to the consumer and ignorance of the market. The aesthetic satisfaction accessory to the beverage far outweighs its metabolic impact. It is not a drink; it is an artifact.

This contrast can stand for the differences between America and Europe—differences nowadays asserted with increased frequency and not a little acrimony on both sides of the Atlantic. The mutual criticisms are familiar. To American commentators Europe is "stagnant." Its workers, employers, and regulations lack the flexibility and adaptability of their U.S. counterparts. The costs of European social welfare payments and public services are "unsustainable." Europe's aging and "cosseted" populations are underproductive and self-satisfied. In a globalized world, the "European social model" is a doomed mirage. This conclusion is typically drawn even by "liberal" American observers, who differ from conservative (and neoconservative) critics only in deriving no pleasure from it.

To a growing number of Europeans, however, it is America that is in trouble and the "American way of life" that cannot be sustained. The American pursuit of wealth, size, and abundance—as material surrogates for happiness—is aesthetically unpleasing and ecologically catastrophic. The American economy is built on sand (or, more precisely, other people's money). For many Americans the promise of a better future is a fading hope. Contemporary mass culture in the U.S. is squalid and meretricious. No wonder so many Americans turn to the church for solace.

These perceptions constitute the real Atlantic gap, and they suggest that something has changed. In past decades it was conventionally assumed—whether with satisfaction or regret—that Europe and America were converging upon a single "Western" model of late capitalism, with the U.S., as usual, leading the way. The logic of scale and market, of efficiency and profit, would ineluctably trump local variations and inherited cultural constraints. Americanization (or globalization—the two treated as synonymous) was inevitable. The best—indeed the only—hope for local products and practices was that they would be swept up into the global vortex and repackaged as "international" commodities for universal consumption. Thus an archetypically Italian product—*caffè espresso*—would travel to the U.S., where it would metamorphose from an elite preference into a popular commodity, and then be repackaged and sold back to Europeans by an American chain store.

But something has gone wrong with this story. It is not just that Starbucks has encountered unexpected foreign resistance to double-decaf-mocha-skim-latte-with-cinnamon (except, revealingly, in the United Kingdom), or that politically motivated Europeans are abjuring high-profile American commodities. It is becoming clear that America and Europe are not way stations on a historical production line, such that Europeans must expect to inherit or replicate the American experience after an appropriate time lag. They are actually quite distinct places, very possibly moving in divergent directions. There are even those—including the authors of two of the books under review—for whom it is not Europe but rather the United States that is trapped in the past.

America's cultural peculiarities (as seen from Europe) are well documented: the nation's marked religiosity, its selective prurience,[1] its affection for guns and prisons (the EU has 87 prisoners per 100,000 people;

America has 685), and its embrace of the death penalty. As T. R. Reid puts it in *The United States of Europe*, "Yes, Americans put up huge billboards reading 'Love Thy Neighbor,' but they murder and rape their neighbors at rates that would shock any European nation."* But it is the curiosities of America's economy, and its social costs, that are now attracting attention.

Americans work much more than Europeans: According to the Organization for Economic Coorporation and Development (OECD), a typical employed American put in 1,877 hours in 2000, compared to 1,562 for his or her French counterpart. One American in three works more than fifty hours a week. Americans take fewer paid holidays than Europeans. Whereas Swedes get more than thirty paid days off work per year and even the Brits get an average of twenty-three, Americans can hope for something between four and ten, depending on where they live. Unemployment in the U.S. is lower than in many European countries (though since out-of-work Americans soon lose their rights to unemployment benefits and are taken off the registers, these statistics may be misleading). America, it seems, is better than Europe at creating jobs. So more American adults are at work, and they work much more than Europeans. What do they get for their efforts?

Not much, unless they are well off. The U.S. is an excellent place to be rich. Back in 1980 the average American chief executive earned forty times as much as the average manufacturing employee. For the top tier of American CEOs, the ratio is now 475:1 and would be vastly greater if assets, not income, were taken into account. By way of comparison, the ratio in Britain is 24:1, in France 15:1, in Sweden 13:1.[2] A privileged minority has access to the best medical treatment in the world. But forty-five million Americans have no health insurance at all (of the world's developed countries, only the U.S. and South Africa do not offer universal medical coverage). According to the World Health Organization, the United States is number one in health spending per capita—and thirty-seventh in the quality of its service.

As a consequence, Americans live shorter lives than Western Europeans.

---

* T. R. Reid, *The United States of Europe: The New Superpower and the End of American Supremacy* (New York: Penguin, 2004).

Their children are more likely to die in infancy: The U.S. ranks twenty-sixth among industrial nations in infant mortality, with a rate double that of Sweden, higher than Slovenia's, and only just ahead of Lithuania's—and this despite spending 15 percent of U.S. gross domestic product on "health care" (much of it siphoned off in the administrative costs of for-profit private networks). Sweden, by contrast, devotes just 8 percent of its GDP to health. The picture in education is very similar. In the aggregate, the United States spends much more on education than the nations of Western Europe; and it has by far the best research universities in the world. Yet a recent study suggests that for every dollar the U.S. spends on education it gets worse results than any other industrial nation. American children consistently underperform their European peers in both literacy and numeracy.[3]

Very well, you might conclude. Europeans are better—fairer—at distributing social goods. This is not news. But there can be no goods or services without wealth, and surely the one thing American capitalism is good at, and where leisure-bound, self-indulgent Europeans need to improve, is the dynamic generation of wealth. But this is by no means obvious today. Europeans work less: but when they do work they seem to put their time to better use. In 1970 GDP per hour in the EU was 35 percent below that of the U.S.; today the gap is less than 7 percent and closing fast. Productivity per hour of work in Italy, Austria, and Denmark is similar to that of the United States; but the U.S. is now distinctly outperformed in this key measure by Ireland, the Netherlands, Norway, Belgium, Luxembourg, Germany, . . . and France.[4]

America's long-standing advantage in wages and productivity—the gift of size, location, and history alike—appears to be winding down, with attendant consequences for U.S. domination of the international business scene. The modern American economy is not just in hock to international bankers with a foreign debt of $3.3 trillion (28 percent of GDP); it is also increasingly foreign-owned. In the year 2000, European direct investment in the U.S. exceeded American investment in Europe by nearly two-fifths. Among dozens of emblematically "American" companies and products now owned by Europeans are Brooks Brothers, DKNY, Random House, Kent Cigarettes, Dove Soap, Chrysler, Bird's Eye, Pennzoil, Baskin-Robbins, and the Los Angeles Dodgers.

Europeans even appear to be better at generating small and medium-sized businesses. There are more small businesses in the EU than in the United States, and they create more employment (65 percent of European jobs in 2002 were in small and medium-sized firms, compared with just 46 percent in the U.S.). And they look after their employees much better. The EU Charter of Fundamental Rights promises the "right to parental leave following the birth or adoption of a child," and every Western European country provides salary support during that leave. In Sweden women get sixty-four weeks off and two-thirds of their wages. Even Portugal guarantees maternity leave for three months on 100 percent salary. The U.S. federal government guarantees nothing. In the words of Valgard Haugland, Norway's Christian Democratic minister for children and family: "Americans like to talk about family values. We have decided to do more than talk; we use our tax revenues to pay for family values."

Yet despite such widely bemoaned bureaucratic and fiscal impediments to output, Europeans appear somehow to manage rather well.[5] And of course the welfare state is not just a value in itself. In the words of the London School of Economics economist Nicholas Barr, it "is an efficiency device against market failure:"[6] a prudential impediment to the social and political risks of excessive inequality. It was Winston Churchill who declared in March 1943 that "there is no finer investment for any community than putting milk into babies." To his self-anointed disciples in contemporary America, however, this reeks of "welfare." In the U.S. today the richest 1 percent hold 38 percent of the wealth, and they are redistributing it ever more to their advantage. Meanwhile, one American adult in five is in poverty—compared with one in fifteen in Italy.[7] The benefits don't even trickle down anymore. To many foreigners today this is a distinctly unappetizing vision: The "American way of life" is at a steep discount. As an economic model the U.S. is not replicable.[8] As a social model it offers few redeeming qualities. One is reminded of Oliver Goldsmith's mordant reflections upon an earlier age of private greed and public indifference:

> *Ill fares the land, to hast'ning ills a prey,*
> *Where wealth accumulates, and men decay.*[9]

This is the case put forward by Jeremy Rifkin and T. R. Reid. Rifkin is the more ambitious of the two, rather too much so: His book, *The European Dream*, is replete with efforts to summarize everything from church history to Enlightenment philosophy, all to the end of demonstrating that it is individualist America that is stuck in a time warp and cooperative Europe that represents the future.* I think he is fundamentally right, but the case can only be hurt by the jejune summaries of the "Making of the Bourgeoisie" or the "Rise of the Nation-State," as well as by a crassly reductionist account of American materialism, and a hodgepodge of ill-advised allusions to chaos theory, the "Great Chain of Being," Hobbes, Descartes, Hegel, and the Enclosure Acts.

The European Dream isn't as bad a book as some reviewers have suggested, and it has something important to say. Of contemporary America Rifkin writes: "With only our religious fervor to hold on to, we have become a 'chosen people' without a narrative—making America potentially a more dangerous and lonely place to be." But the book would have been a whole lot better had Rifkin stuck to what he knows about and not tried so hard to say something "important."

T. R. Reid is a journalist, and his account of European superiority, which covers much the same territory as Rifkin's, is shorter, sharper, more readable, and less pretentious. It has some amusing vignettes: notably of American innocents—Jack Welch, George W. Bush (and most recently Bill Gates)—caught up in a brave new world of European regulations they can neither understand nor ignore. And Reid, like Rifkin, demonstrates very effectively just why the European Union, with its regulatory powers, its wealth, and its institutional example, is a place Americans will need to take extremely seriously in coming decades.

But though their books are timely, neither writer is saying anything very new. Their damning bill of particulars regarding the United States is familiar to Europeans—it was in 1956 that Jimmy Porter, in John Osborne's *Look Back in Anger*, sardonically observed that "it's pretty dreary living in the American age—unless of course you're American," and one way or another, that thought has echoed down the decades to

---

* Jeremy Rifkin, *The European Dream: How Europe's Vision of the Future Is Quietly Eclipsing the American Dream* (New York: Tarcher/Penguin, 2004).

the present day. But just because there is something profoundly amiss in the U.S. today, and something no less intuitively appealing about the European social compact, this does not license us to tell fairy stories.

Anyone seeking in these books an account of the origins of the EU will be led badly astray. Reid and Rifkin trip over themselves to praise the founding fathers of Europe for their foresight and wisdom in guiding Europe to its present eminence. According to Reid, in "the years following the Schuman Declaration, the European Movement took the continent by storm." The European Coal and Steel Community was a "rip-roaring economic success." Rifkin goes further: Europe, he writes, is "a giant freewheeling experimental laboratory for rethinking the human condition. . . . "(!)

These claims are absurd.[10] The European Union is what it is: the largely unintended product of decades of negotiations by Western European politicians seeking to uphold and advance their national and sectoral interests. That's part of its problem: It is a compromise on a continental scale, designed by literally hundreds of committees. Actually, this makes the EU more interesting and in some ways more impressive than if it merely incarnated some uncontentious utopian blueprint. In the same vein, it seems silly to write, as Rifkin does, about the awfulness of American "cookie-cutter housing tracts" as yet another symptom of American mediocrity without acknowledging Europe's own eyesores. This is a man who has never stared upon the urban brutalism of Sarcelles, a postwar dormitory town north of Paris; who has not died a little in Milton Keynes; who has avoided the outer suburbs of modern Milan. Reid is right to insist that Europe has the best roads, the fastest trains, the cheapest plane fares. And yes, the EU is indeed closer, as Rifkin notes, "to the pulse of the changes that are transforming the world into a globalized society." But it isn't perfect by any means.

Indeed, Europe is facing real problems. But they are not the ones that American free-market critics recount with such grim glee. Yes, the European Commission periodically makes an ass of itself, aspiring to regulate the size of condoms and the curvature of cucumbers. The much-vaunted Stability Pact to constrain national expenditure and debt has broken down in acrimony, though with no discernible damage to the euro it was designed to protect. And pensions and other social provisions will be seriously underfunded in decades to come unless Europeans have more children, welcome more immigrants, work a few more years before retiring, take somewhat less generous unemployment compensation, and make it easier for businesses to employ young people. But these are not deep structural failings of the European way of life: They are difficult policy choices with political consequences. None of them implies the dismantling of the welfare state.[11]

Europe's true dilemmas lie elsewhere. In the Netherlands, in Paris and Antwerp and other cities, antagonism and incomprehension between the indigenous local population and a fast-growing minority of Muslims (one million in the Netherlands, over five million in France, perhaps thirteen million in the EU to date) has already moved on from graffiti and no-go zones to arson, assaults, and assassinations. Turks, Moroccans, Tunisians, Algerians, and others have been arriving in Western Europe since the 1960s. We are now seeing the emergence of a third generation: in large part unemployed, angry, alienated, and increasingly open to the communitarian appeal of radical Islam.[12]

For nearly four decades mainstream European politicians turned a blind eye to all this: to the impact of de facto segregated housing; isolated uninte-grated communities; and the rising tide of fearful, resentful white voters con-vinced that the boat was "full." It has taken Jean-Marie Le Pen, the assassinated Dutch politician Pim Fortuyn, and a flock of demagogic anti-immigrant par-ties from Norway to Italy to awaken Europeans to this crisis—and it augurs badly that the response of everyone from Tony Blair to Valéry Giscard d'Estaing has been to cry "Havoc!" and wind up the drawbridge.

For the other problem facing Europe, and the two are of course con-nected, is the pressure on its outer edges. The European Union is almost too attractive for its own good—in contrast with the United States, which is widely disliked for what it *does*, the EU appeals just by virtue of what it *is*. Refugees and illegal immigrants from half of Africa periodically drown in their desperate efforts to cross the Straits of Gibraltar or beach themselves on Italy's southernmost islands—or else they land safely, only to get shipped back. Turkey had been trying for nearly forty years to gain admission to the European club before its application was (reluctantly) taken up last month. Ukraine's best hope for a stable democratic future lies inside Europe—or at least with the prospect of one day getting there, which would greatly strengthen the hand of Viktor Yushchenko and his supporters in the aftermath of their recent victory. And the same of course is true for the remnant states of former Yugoslavia. But while Brussels is all too well aware of the risks entailed in ignoring Africa or leaving Ukraine or Bosnia to fester at its gates—much less casting seventy million Turkish Muslims into the fold of radical Islam—Europe's leaders are deeply troubled at the prospect (and the cost) of committing the EU to extending itself to the edges of Asia.

These are Europe's real challenges. The EU may be, as Reid and Rifkin suggest, a luminous model of trans-state cooperation, justice, and harmony.[13] But it will not be easy for the EU to integrate its ethnic and religious minorities, regulate immigration, or admit Turkey on workable terms.[14] Yet should it mismanage the permanent crisis on its eastern and southern borders, Europe is going to be in very serious difficulties indeed. And that, not some sort of atavistic anti-Americanism or rocket envy, is why many reasonable Europeans and their leaders are utterly enraged by President George W. Bush.

To the Bush administration "Islam" is an abstraction, the politically serviceable object of what Washington insiders now call the GWOT: the Global War on Terror. For the U.S., the Middle East is a faraway land, a convenient place to export America's troubles so that they won't have to be addressed in the "homeland." But the Middle East is Europe's "near abroad," as well as a major trading partner. From Tangier to Tabriz, Europe is surrounded by the "Middle East." A growing number of Europeans come from this Middle East. When the EU begins accession talks with Turkey, it will be anticipating its own insertion into the Middle East. America's strategy of global confrontation with Islam is not an option for Europe. It is a catastrophe.

TIMOTHY GARTON ASH would probably not dissent from much of the preceding analysis. In his engaging new book he actually goes further than Rifkin and Reid in certain respects.* As an international citizen, he

---

* Timothy Garton Ash, *Free World: America, Europe and the Surprising Future of the West* (New York: Random House, 2004).

notes, the United States is irresponsibly delinquent. The EU gave away $36.5 billion in development aid in 2003. The U.S. managed just one-third that amount—and much of that foreign aid either went to Israel or else came with strings attached: Nearly 80 percent of all American "development aid" obliges recipients to spend the money on American goods and services. On Iraq alone the U.S. spent eight times the amount it gave in overseas aid to everyone else. The U.S. is the meanest of all the rich countries on the OECD's Development Assistance Committee. The Europeans are by far the most generous.

There is more. The U.S. contains just 5 percent of the world's population (and falling), but it is responsible for 25 percent of the world's greenhouse gas output per annum. Each year our atmosphere has to absorb twenty metric tons of carbon dioxide for every American man, woman, and child; but just nine tons for every European. And the American share continues to grow, even as the Bush administration blocks any international action on pollution or global warming. The *real* weapons of mass destruction, in Garton Ash's view, are global poverty and incipient environmental catastrophe. On these genuine threats to our common civilization, the European Union has a strikingly superior record. Contemporary American pundits, the "*terribles simplificateurs*" who babble glibly of Mars and Venus or Clashing Civilizations, attract Garton Ash's amused disdain. But on the insouciant indifference of the present incumbent of the White House he is utterly unforgiving: "It was said of ancient Rome that the emperor Nero fiddled while the city burned. In the new Rome, the president fiddled while the Earth burned."

All the same, *Free World* is by no means just another indictment of America. Timothy Garton Ash knows Europe—or, rather, he knows the many different Europes, the variable geometry of squabbles and interests and alliances that limit the EU's capacity to make itself felt in world politics. He shares the widespread English suspicion of French mischief making. And he balances his remarks about the U.S. with some well-aimed shots at the Common Agricultural Fund—noting that while in the year 2000 the EU donated $8 per head to sub-Saharan Africa, it managed to set aside, in the form of subsidies, $913 for every cow in Europe.

But for all that, Garton Ash is actually quite optimistic about both Europe *and* the United States. More surprisingly, he is optimistic—even, as it seems to me, a touch irenic—about the future of the Western alliance. In part, to be sure, this is driven by what he sees as urgent necessity: The West had better stop squabbling and find a way to work together for the common good, because it only has about twenty years left before China (and then India) becomes a great power and the narcissistic minor differences between Europe and America will be lost to view: "In a longer historical perspective, this may be our last chance to set the agenda of world politics."

That agenda, in Garton Ash's account, is to set aside recent quarrels and "reinvent" the post–cold war West as an example and advocate of freedom: freedom from want, freedom from fear, freedom from human and ecological oppression (the chapter on global poverty and environmental risk is revealingly titled "The New Red Armies"). The Rooseveltian echoes are no coincidence—what Garton Ash has in mind really is a new Atlantic Alliance, and it is not by chance that Winston Churchill occupies a prominent place in his argument. For this is a very British book. The choice between Europe and America is presented as one that the British understand better than anyone else (because they have lived it for sixty years); Atlantic reconciliation is thus something that London—perched uncomfortably on the edge of continental Europe and with half an eye cast permanently on Washington—is best placed to help bring about.

But is Britain really, as Garton Ash writes, a "seismograph" or "thermometer" of European–American relations? It is true that the UK today manages both to be part of the European Union and to manifest some of the trashier aspects of American commercial culture, but I doubt that this is what Garton Ash has in mind. He appears, rather, to see London's role as mitigating the damage done by American unilateralism on the one hand and "Euro-Gaullism" on the other ("the Chiracian version of Euro-Gaullism leads nowhere"). An internationally minded "Euroatlanticism" is his ideal, and Tony Blair incarnates it: "Tony Blair has grasped and articulated this British national interest, role, and chance better than any of his predecessors." Of course, Garton Ash can hardly deny that Blair has so far ducked the challenge of selling the European Constitution to a skeptical British public. And I don't think he harbors any illusions about the "special relationship." Yet he still insists that Great Britain has this vital role to play in bridging the Atlantic gap.

I find that a very odd claim. Tony Blair is a political tactician with a lucrative little sideline in made-to-measure moralizing.[15] But his international adventures, the invasion of Iraq in particular, have alienated Britain from many of its fellow EU members without gaining any influence over Washington, where the British prime minister's visits have been exercises in futility and humiliation. Yes, in certain respects the UK today has real affinities with America: The scale of poverty in Britain, and the income gap between rich and poor, has grown steadily since the 1970s and is closer to that of the U.S. than anything found in Western Europe. British hourly productivity is well below most Western European rates. However, New Labour was supposed to combine the best of the European social model and American entrepreneurship: Garton Ash himself concedes it has not quite managed this.[16]

Free World understates the challenge facing Brits—or other Europeans—seeking to draw the U.S. back into any common international project beyond the GWOT. Timothy Garton Ash is right to insist that there is more to America than neocons and Republican know-nothings and that their present dominance will pass. But his book is about the here and now. So we can't ignore that the people making policy in Washington aren't interested in reading Timothy Garton Ash's "Declaration of Interdependence." The very last thing they want is some "common initiative" in the Middle East. And they couldn't care less about his "New Red Armies." Yes: in its own interest "America should want Europe to be a benign check and balance on its own solitary hyperpower." That is good advice. But is anyone listening?

Conservative think tanks in Washington are lobbying against any consolidated European international presence—in the words of David Frum, a fellow at the American Enterprise Institute and former Bush speechwriter, it "raises important strategic questions" (i.e., we don't like it).[17] Condoleezza Rice was widely quoted in 2003 to the effect that the United States intends to "forgive Russia, ignore Germany, and punish France." According to the authors of a recent Atlantic Council report, the Bush administration regards Europe as being "on probation," its future standing with Washington dependent on better behavior.[18] For the first time since World War II, influential voices are suggesting that a united Europe would be a threat to American interests and that the U.S. should block its emergence.

Moreover, the common European-American values upon which Timothy Garton Ash's argument rests may not be quite as common as he suggests. In its widespread religiosity and the place of God in its public affairs, its suspicion of dissent, its fear of foreign influence, its unfamiliarity with alien lands, and its reliance upon military strength when dealing with them, the U.S. does indeed have much in common with other countries; but none of them is in Europe. When the international treaty to ban land mines was passed by the UN in 1997 by a vote of 142–0, the U.S. abstained; in company with Russia and a handful of other countries we have still not ratified it. The U.S. is one of only two states (the other is Somalia) that have failed to ratify the 1989 Convention on Children's Rights. Our opposition to the international Biological Weapons Convention is shared by China, Russia, India, Pakistan, Cuba, and Iran.

Abolition of the death penalty is a condition for EU membership, whereas the U.S. currently executes prisoners on a scale matched only in China, Iran, Saudi Arabia, and the Congo. American opposition to an International Criminal Court has been supported in the UN and elsewhere by Iran, Iraq, Pakistan, Indonesia, Israel, and Egypt. The American doctrine of "preventive war" now finds its fraternal counterpart in Muscovite talk of "preventive counterrevolution."[19] And as for the United Nations itself, the jewel in the crown of international agencies set in place after World War II by an earlier generation of American leaders: As I write (2005), a scurrilous, high-decibel campaign is being mounted from Washington to bring down Kofi Annan, the UN secretary-general, and cripple his institution.

So what can Europe do? In the first place, resist the temptation to make a virtue of the present tensions. It is pointless to deny their existence. In past eras the role of Europe's "other"—the close neighbor against whom Europeans measure their own distinctive identity—was variously occupied by Turkey and Russia; today that role is being filled by the United States. But like Garton Ash, I think it would be a mistake to follow Jürgen Habermas's advice and try to build European unity around "transatlantic value differences." Europeans certainly need to find a purpose and define their common role, but there are better ways to do it.

One would be to get on with ratifying their proposed constitution or a workable substitute. This document arouses paranoia and anxiety in Washington (and London); but it is actually quite dull and anodyne. Much of it consists of practical prescriptions for decision-making procedures in a cumbersome body of twenty-five-plus separate sovereign states. The constitution also strengthens the role of European courts and extends the EU's cross-border competence in criminal law and policing (a wholly laudable objective for anyone serious about fighting terrorists). But otherwise it just gives substance and application to the EU's claim to "coordinate the economic and employment policies of the member states." It is not a very inspiring document—its leading drafter, Valéry Giscard d'Estaing, is no Thomas Jefferson—but it would do much practical good.

Above all, it would enable Europe to continue playing to its international strengths in spite of American obstruction[20] and the Bush administration's efforts to pick off or otherwise pressure individual EU member states. For the EU today isn't just an interesting blueprint for interstate governance without the drawbacks of supranational sovereignty. Europe experienced the twentieth century—invasion, occupation, civil war, anarchy, massacres, genocide, and the descent into barbarism—to a degree unmatched anywhere else. The risks inherent in a "war of choice" (Iraq), or the abandonment of international agencies in favor of unilateral initiative, or an excessive reliance on military power, are thus clearer to Europeans than to most other peoples: "Europeans want to be sure that there is no adventure in the future. They have had too much of that."[21] The United States, by contrast, had no direct experience of the worst of the twentieth century—and is thus regrettably immune to its lessons.

American-style belligerent patriotism, as Garton Ash notes, is rare in contemporary Europe. This dislike of bellicosity goes well beyond traditional pacifism: Europeans no longer even *think* about interstate relations in martial terms. But *pace* American critics, this makes Europeans and their model more rather than less effective when it comes to addressing international crises. The U.S. is still rather good at the old-fashioned art of making war. But war making is the exception in modern international affairs. The real challenge is preventing war, making peace—and keeping it. And this is something at which Europe is going to be increasingly adept.

The countries of the EU already provide the largest share of the world's peacekeepers and international policemen. Europeans have a real, if limited, military capacity—though they will need to commit more resources to the planned 60,000-man "Euro-force" if it is to be effective. The best European troops—for example, the British army—have been trained for decades to work with occupied and warring civil populations, a skill with which the U.S. Army is shockingly unfamiliar. It will be a long time before the EU develops and implements a common foreign policy—though the new constitution would facilitate that, if only by creating a European foreign minister authorized to speak for the whole union. But when it does at last speak with a single voice in international affairs, the EU will wield a lot of power.

The reason is not that the EU will be rich or big—though it already is both. The U.S. is rich and big. And one day China may be richer and bigger. Europe will matter because of the cross-border template upon which contemporary Europe is being constructed. "Globalization" isn't primarily about trade or communications, economic monopolies or even empire. If it were, it would hardly be new: Those aspects of life were already "globalizing" a hundred years ago.[22] Globalization is about the disappearance of boundaries—cultural and economic boundaries, physical boundaries, linguistic boundaries—and the challenge of organizing our world in their absence. In the words of Jean-Marie Guéhenno, the UN's director of peacekeeping operations: "Having lost the comfort of our geographical boundaries, we must in effect rediscover what creates the bond between humans that constitute a community."[23]

To their own surprise and occasional consternation, Europeans have begun to do this: to create a bond between human beings that transcends older boundaries and to make out of these new institutional forms something that really is a community. They don't always do it very well, and there is still considerable nostalgia in certain quarters for those old frontier posts. But something is better than nothing; and nothing is just what we shall be left with if the fragile international accords, treaties, agencies, laws, and institutions that we have erected since 1945 are allowed to rot and decline—or, worse, are deliberately brought low. As things now stand, boundary breaking and community making are something that Europeans are doing better than anyone else. The United States, trapped once again in what Tocqueville called its "perpetual utterance of self-applause," isn't even trying.

This essay was the culminating article in a series published in the **New York Review of Books** *between 2002 and 2006 in which I discussed the U.S. under George W. Bush, its declining international standing, and the counterexample of Europe. It may be of interest that the most heartfelt response to this piece came from American readers deeply offended at aspersions cast upon the image and products of Starbucks.*

NOTES TO CHAPTER XXIII

[1] The U.S. television network that recently broadcast a passing glimpse at Janet Jackson's anatomy was excoriated for its wanton lapse of taste; but the avalanche of accompanying commercials for products designed to enhance male potency passed quite without comment. The female breast, it seems, can rot a nation's moral core; but malfunctioning penises are wholesome family fare.

[2] See Robin Blackburn, *Banking on Death: Or, Investing in Life: The History and Future of Pensions* (London, New York: Verso, 2002) 201, table 3.2.

[3] For the 2003 PISA (Programme for International Student Assessment) report, issued by the OECD on December 6, 2004, see www.pisa.oecd.org.

[4] See Andrew Sharpe, Appendix Table 2, "Output per House Levels in the OECD Countries Relative to the United States" for 2003; Centre for the Study of Living Standards, *International Productivity Monitor*, 9 (Fall 2004), at www.csls.ca/ipm/9/sharpe-tables.pdf.

[5] Note, too, that the steadily rising cost of private medical insurance in the U.S. puts at least as much of a burden on American firms as social taxation and welfare privileges place upon their European counterparts—while providing none of the attendant social benefits.

[6] Katrin Benahold, "Love of Leisure, and Europe's Reasons," *New York Times*, July 29, 2004.

[7] Following the OECD definition of a family income, less than 50 percent of the mean personal income of the nation.

[8] Appetizing or not, the American economic model could never be replicated anywhere else. Americans are the world's consumers of last resort. But their national deficits on budget and current account are reaching unprecedented levels. The collapsing dollar is sustained only by foreigners' willingness to hold it: Americans are currently spending other people's money on other people's products. Were the U.S. any other country, it would by now be in the unforgiving hands of the International Monetary Fund.

[9] *The Deserted Village* (1770).

[10] As is Reid's description of David Beckham as "Europe's Michael Jordan." Beckham is a journeyman footballer with a first-class hairdo and a celebrity wife. He would never have made the cut in the days of Pele, Johann Cruyff, or Ferenc Puskas. His prominence on European sports

pages illustrates the power of transcontinental marketing, but in this as other respects Beckham is just a depressing monument to the spirit of our age: He is, in Camus's phrase, a *"prophète vide pour temps médiocre."* The pertinent analogy here is not Michael Jordan but Dennis Rodman.

[11] In any case, America's present indebtedness is at least as much a lien on the future as Europe's welfare commitments. And Americans who point fingers at the European pension gap should recall that were United Airlines, General Motors, or any other semisolvent company to abandon its unfundable pension commitments, it is U.S. taxpayers who would be left with the tab.

[12] For a thoughtful and rather more optimistic account of the French case, see Herman Lebovics, *Bringing the Empire Back Home: France in the Global Age* (Durham, NC: Duke University Press, 2004).

[13] Perhaps not so very harmonious: Already West European leaders are asking why they should make generous budget transfers to new members like Slovakia, only to see the latter use these subsidies to hold down their local corporate tax rates and thereby steal business and factories from their more expensive Western colleagues.

[14] The Turkish dilemma is complicated, and well-meaning European liberals can find themselves on both sides of the debate. For a sensitive and cogently reasoned summary of the case for keeping Turkey at a certain distance, see the interview with Robert Badinter, a former French minister of justice and long-standing Europhile, "L'adhésion de la Turquie serait une décision aborrante," in *Le Figaro*, December 13, 2004.

[15] At the last Labour Party conference, rather than try to defend his reasons for going to war in Iraq, Blair simply informed the audience that he "believes," that they must share his "faith," and that in any case (like Martin Luther: "Here I stand, I can do no other") he would not budge.

[16] Indeed he cites a popular joke: Britain was promised that Blair's Third Way would bring with it American universities and German prisons— what it is actually getting are American prisons and German universities.

[17] Frederick Studemann, "US Conservatives Cast Wary Eye at EU Treaty," *Financial Times*, November 5, 2004. The new tone of anxiety about a renascent Europe can even be found in august journals of mainstream foreign policy debate. See, for example, Jeffrey L. Cimbalo, "Saving NATO from Europe," in *Foreign Affairs*, November/December 2004.

[18] See Bowman Cutter, Peter Rashish, and Paula Stern, "Washington Wants Economic Reform in Europe," *Financial Times*, November 22, 2004.

[19] The phrase is used by Kremlin adviser Gleb Pavlovski to describe President Putin's emerging strategy for addressing "containment" challenges at Russia's edges. I am indebted to Ivan Krastev of the Central European University in Budapest for this reference, in his unpublished essay on "Europe's Fatal Attraction."

[20] The U.S. continues to impede European efforts to reach a nuclear settlement with Iran. Even on such a volatile issue, Washington has been more concerned about the risks of a successful European initiative than the benefits of a regional settlement.

[21] Alfons Verplaetse (governor of the National Bank of Belgium).

[22] On this, see the magisterial opening paragraphs of John Maynard Keynes's essay *The Economic Consequences of the Peace* (New York: Penguin, 1995).

[23] Jean-Marie Guéhenno, *The End of the Nation-State*, trans. by Victoria Elliott (Minneapolis: University of Minnesota Press, 1995), 139.

The Social Question Redivivus

The little town of Longwy has a ghostly air. For many years it was an important center of iron and steel manufacturing in the industrial basin of the northern Lorraine and a proud stronghold of Socialist and Communist unions. Since 1975, however, the local industry, like steelworking everywhere in Western Europe, has been in trouble. Today the steelworks are gone, and so, at first sight, are their workers. At noon on a working day the town is quiet, with empty shops, a few sad-looking bars, and a deserted railway station occupied by a gaggle of drunks. The erstwhile steelworkers, grown old, wait out their lives in bars and cafés, or else stay at home with the television. Their wives and daughters have part-time, nonunion work either in new factories and offices distributed in the fields outside the town or else at commercial centers deposited optimistically at crossroads some twenty miles away. Their sons have no work at all and mill around at these same commercial centers looking at once menacing and pitiful.

There are towns like Longwy all over Europe, from Lancashire to Silesia, from the Asturian mountains to the central Slovakian plain. What makes the shattered industrial heartland of northeastern France distinctive is the political revolution that has occurred there. In the legislative elections of 1978, when the Left was defeated nationwide, the voters of

Longwy returned a Communist deputy to Paris, as usual. Twenty years later, in the legislative elections of May 1997, the right-wing National Front—which did not exist in 1978—came within three thousand votes of overtaking the local Communist candidate. A little farther east, in the similarly depressed industrial towns and villages around Sarrebourg that abut the German frontier, the National Front did even better: moving ahead of both Communists and Socialists, its candidates secured more than 22 percent of the vote in half the local constituencies.

The neo-Fascist right, whose program constitutes one long scream of resentment—at immigrants, at unemployment, at crime and insecurity, at "Europe," and in general at "them" who have brought it all about—did better still in the decayed industrial valley of the upper Loire west of Lyons, where one in five voters favored it, and best of all in the towns of Mediterranean France. In the greater Marseilles region nearly one voter in four chose the candidates of the National Front. If France had a system of proportional representation, the front would have not one but seventy-seven deputies in the new French parliament (double its number under a short-lived system of proportional representation introduced for the 1986 elections), and the Left would not have a parliamentary majority.

All these regions, and many others where the Far Right is now the leading local party, were until very recently strongholds of the Left. The demographics of most such places have not altered significantly—former Communists, not newcomers, are now voting for Jean-Marie Le Pen. The community of these men and women has been destroyed, and they are looking for someone to blame and someone to follow. This is not Wigan Pier, the world of British industrial unemployment chronicled by George Orwell between the wars. There the economy buckled and the state withdrew from all but its most minimal commitments, but the community held fast and was even strengthened in its shared belief in itself and the justice of its claims. In postindustrial France (or Britain and elsewhere) the economy has moved on while the state, so far, has stayed behind to pick up the tab; but the community has collapsed, and with it a century-long political culture that combined pride in work, local social interdependence, and intergenerational continuity.

It is ironic but not mystifying that Le Pen, like other European demagogues, picks up some of his strongest support in frontier districts.

Longwy and Sarrebourg are right next to the vanishing borders, once so contested, between France, Belgium, Luxembourg, and Germany. In today's Europe you can live in one country, shop in another, and seek employment in a third. But the free movement of people, money, and goods that is so central to Europe's much-advertised entry into a postnational, global era has not brought prosperity to this region—indeed, the most salient economic effect on the locality has been the loss of jobs in the customs service. The Europe debate, in France and elsewhere, is thus readily cast in terms of security, stability, and protection versus vulnerability and change, with Brussels serving as a lightning rod for a broad range of criticisms directed at globalization and the hegemony of the Anglo-American model of minimal state and maximized profit—what the French nervously and revealingly label *la pensée unique.*

In fact the impact of a global economy on how Europeans, at least, will choose to conduct their lives has been exaggerated. The mantra "global market forces," the latest weapon in the conceptual armory of the forces of change, does duty on a variety of fronts, replacing the superannuated ordnance of progress, inevitability, historical necessity, modernization, and so forth. But, like them, it promises and assumes too much. To take the most popular example: When applied as part of a critique of European social policies, global market forces are presumed to require that the high-wage economies of Western Europe rethink themselves, and fast, lest jobs and investment flee the pampered, overpriced European continent in search of cheaper labor and higher rates of growth elsewhere, notably in Asia. But economic growth rates among the Asian "tigers" are slowing down, and understandably; like the high growth rates in postwar Socialist countries, they depended on the extensive mobilization and exploitation of resources, human and natural. An indefinitely increasing input of labor and local capital is not sustainable—and this even before we consider that such rates of transformation are only achieved, as in the countries of real existing socialism, by vigorous control and repression.

Moreover, the specific global market force that is advertised as most likely to scupper Western Europe—lower wages on other continents or in Eastern Europe—will not apply indefinitely. By January 1997, wages in South Korea were approaching two-thirds the level of comparable wages in Germany. Demand for skilled labor in Asian states and in certain countries of Eastern Europe is bringing wages in some sectors close to or even above those earned in the poorest parts of the European Union. Already the majority of foreign direct investment from Western Europe goes to other high-wage countries. Within a few years, wage differentials alone will not be a factor in the case for cost-cutting except for certain industries where comparative advantage will always obtain. And all this ignores the more serious likelihood that Asian and other cutting-edge economies may not long remain a model even for themselves: The social inequalities and political repression that accompany cheap labor and stable investment environments will be vulnerable to comparisons with and disapproval from abroad—global forces in their own right.

But even if global market forces worked as advertised, they could not forcibly transform Europe's public policy, because its dilemmas are not essentially economic. There are now more than eighteen million officially unemployed people in the European Union. Yet finding jobs for them is not the most serious social question in Europe today—and if jobs were found by significant reductions in wages and benefits, the better to compete with the costs of jobs in other places, the real problems would worsen. Seventeen percent of the present population of the EU lives below the official poverty line (defined as an income less than 50 percent of the average in a person's country of residence). Significantly, the highest level of official poverty, after Portugal, is in Great Britain, where 22 percent of the population—over 14 million people—lives below the poverty line; yet Britain has the best record on job creation in the EU in the past half-decade.

The social crisis, then, concerns not so much unemployment as what the French call the "excluded." This term describes people who, having left the full-time workforce, or never having joined it, are in a certain sense only partly members of the national community. It is not their material poverty, but the way in which they exist outside the conventional channels of employment or security, and with little prospect of reentering these channels or benefiting from the social liaisons that accompany them, that distinguishes them from even the poorest among the unskilled workforce in the industrial economy. Such people—whether single parents, part-time or short-term workers, immigrants, unskilled adolescents, or prematurely and forcibly retired manual workers—cannot live decently, participate in the culture of their local or national community, or offer their children prospects better than their own.

Their living and working conditions preclude attention to anything beyond survival, and they are, or ought to be, a standing remonstrance to the affluence of their "included" fellows. In France, where there are 3.5 million officially unemployed and a further 4 million in precarious work, fully 30 percent of the active population are *exclus.* The figures are significantly lower only in Scandinavia, where the welfare systems of better days are still substantially in place, albeit trimmed. Under any present version of the neoliberal project—budget cuts, deregulation, etc.—the numbers of the precarious, the excluded, and the poor (disproportionately present in communities of recent immigrant origin) are likely to increase, because work is disappearing in precisely the places, and at the occupations and skill levels, where most of the vulnerable population of Europe is now concentrated and will remain for the next generation.

In policy terms this is not purely or even primarily an economic conundrum. Rich countries can almost always find the resources to pay for social benefits if they choose, but the decision on how to do so is in the first instance a political one. There have always been two basic ways to finance these benefits. One is for the state to tax work: by charging workers and employers to help it pay for a variety of social services, including unemployment payments to those same workers if they lose their jobs. This makes labor and goods expensive (by adding to employers' costs), but it has the appeal of a certain sort of equity; it also worked rather well in the postwar era of high-wage, full-employment economies, since it padded state coffers when the unemployed and pensioners were in short supply. The alternative, universal, system bills the whole nation, through direct and indirect taxation, for social services that are then made available to those who require them.

Today, with high unemployment, it is tempting to prefer the second, universal option, since governments are trying to reduce the cost of labor to employers (and with fewer people working there are fewer paychecks to tax). But the political risks entailed in charging every voter for services from which only some (the unemployed, the aged, the infirm) will benefit are high, though perhaps not as high as providing no services at all, since the handicapped, elderly, and jobless can all vote too.

There is now a third option, a version of which has been followed in the United States and now in the United Kingdom—cut benefits and gear unemployment and other compensatory payments to a person's past work record (and income) and his or her continued willingness to find and take work if available. This is now said to be the appropriate social policy for a global economy: It penalizes unwillingness to take a job at the going rate, reduces employers' costs, and limits the state's liability.

This third alternative, however tidily it responds to global market forces, ironically presumes the very spectrum of circumstances whose disappearance has brought it about: the availability of employment, no sustained interruption of work experience by involuntary unemployment, and, above all, a normal wage high enough so that the percentage of it paid out in unemployment compensation will suffice to keep a person or family out of poverty until work is available. It presupposes the sort of worker and working profile that is now rapidly vanishing in just those places where such policies are being considered or implemented. The result can only be greater poverty, a growing gap between those with steady work and those without it, and ever more men and women excluded from the working, earning, tax-paying community that will understandably look on them with fear and suspicion.*

These are the losers—the de-skilled, the unskilled, the part-time, immigrants, the unemployed—all of whom are vulnerable because of the state of the economy but above all because they have lost the work-related forms of institutional affiliation, social support, and occupational solidarity that once characterized the exploited industrial proletariat. It is they who are least able to benefit from the hypothetical added value of a global economy, or even an integrated European one: They cannot readily go somewhere else to find work, and even if they did, they would not find the social and psychic ben-

---

* I am indebted for the above to the work of the sociologist Georg Vobruba of the University of Leipzig, who has done important studies of the impact of varieties of unemployment insurance on the postindustrial workforce. See, for example, his "Social Policy for Europe," in *The Social Quality of Europe*, ed. Wolfgang Beck, Laurent van der Maesen, and Alan Walker (Boston: Kluwer Law International, 1997) 105–120.

efits that once accompanied it but would just be *exclus* somewhere else. Capital can be separated from its owner and move around the world at the speed of sound and light. But labor cannot be separated from its owner, and its owner is not just a worker but also a member of one or more communities—a resident, a citizen, a national.

True, all labor is *potentially* mobile across job skills, space, and time. But it is wildly unrealistic to expect people to change both their working skills and their home every time global market forces dictate it. And in any case, the crucial variable here is time: The transformation of an economy may be a rapid affair, but the accompanying social changes cannot be wrought at the same rate. It is the gap between economic change and social adjustment, a gap that has already lasted half a generation and will probably endure for years to come, that is causing the present dilemma and has become, by analogy with the great Social Question of the nineteenth century, the critical issue of our time.

In late-eighteenth- and early-nineteenth-century Britain, the visible havoc wreaked on the land and the people by unrestricted economic forces was noted, regretted, and opposed by poets and radicals from Oliver Goldsmith to William Cobbett. The problem of the excluded—landless laborers, pauperized weavers, unemployed bricklayers, homeless children—was attacked in various ways, culminating in the New Poor Law of 1834, which introduced the workhouse and the principle of least eligibility, whereby relief for the unemployed and indigent was to be inferior in quality and quantity to the lowest prevailing wages and conditions of employment, a model of welfare "reform" to which President Bill Clinton's recent legislation is directly, if perhaps unknowingly, indebted. The conventional arguments against state intervention were widely rehearsed: The free workings of the economy would eventually address the distortions attendant on agricultural enclosure or mechanization; the regulation of working hours or conditions would render firms uncompetitive; labor should be free to come and go, like capital; the "undeserving" poor (those who refused available work) should be penalized, etc.

But after a brush with revolt during the economic depression of the 1840s, British governments adjusted their sights and enacted a series of reforms driven in equal measure by ethical sensibilities and political prudence. By the later years of the century the erstwhile minimalist British state had set upper limits on working hours in factories, a minimum age for child employment, and regulations concerning conditions of work in a variety of industries. The vote had been granted to a majority of adult males, and the labor and political organizations that the working population had struggled to establish had been legalized—so that in time they ceased to be disruptive to the workings of capitalism and became effective sources of social integration and political stability. The result was not planned, but it is incontrovertible: British capitalism thrived not in spite of regulatory mechanisms but because of them.

In continental Europe things worked a little differently. There, the impact of economic change, often driven from abroad, was not muted by piecemeal social legislation, both because legislatures responsive to political demands were not yet in place and because farms and factories were unable to withstand foreign competition without protection. In such places, most notably France, there was a long-standing expectation that the state would provide when all else failed, a habit of mind encouraged by the state itself. Those crucial moments when the state (or the king) failed to come through are what we associate with the great crises of the Age of Revolution: 1787–90, 1827–32, and 1846–50, when the response to economic dislocation and social protest all across the continent took the form of a repeated sequence of revolt, reform, and repression.

The nineteenth-century Social Question, as described and interminably debated in the middle decades of the last century, was this: How could the virtues of economic progress be secured in light of the political and moral threat posed by the condition of the working class? Or, more cynically, how was social upheaval to be headed off in a society wedded to the benefits that came from the profitable exploitation of a large class of low-paid and existentially discontented persons?

The response of European states to the problem of managing the social consequences of the early Industrial Revolution owed almost nothing to contemporary theories that purported to describe the inevitable, structural nature of the forces at play. Economic liberalism, whether as a description of the workings of capitalism or as a prescription for economic policies, had little impact on political decision making or even social policy. That is why we have today, or had until recently, a unique and uniquely stable combination—of market economies, precapitalist social relations and moral expectations (notably our intuitive distaste for extremes of social insecurity), and interventionist states, directly inherited from the enlightened absolutist monarchies of the not-so-distant past—that characterizes the fortunate Western inheritance.

CRITICS OF THE interventionist state today level two convincing charges against it. The first is that the experience of our century reveals a propensity and a capacity, unimaginable in earlier times, for totalitarian regulation and repression not only of people but of institutions, social practices, and the very fabric of normal life. We now know and cannot ignore what the Fabians, the founding theorists of social democracy, the utopian dreamers of collectivist systems of society, and even the well-meaning proponents of paternalist social engineering did not know, or preferred to forget: that the overmighty state, under whatever doctrinal aegis, has an alarming and probably unavoidable propensity to eat its own children as well as those of its enemies.

The other lesson we should have learned from the experience of our age is that, murderous or benevolent, the state is a strikingly inefficient economic actor. Nationalized industries, state farms, centrally planned economies, controlled trade, fixed prices, and government-directed production and distribution do not work. They do not produce the goods, and as a consequence they do not distribute them very well, even though the promise of a more equitable system of distribution is usually the basis of their initial appeal.

Neither of these lessons is entirely new. Eighteenth-century critics of mercantilism knew why state-regulated economies were inefficient and self-defeating. The opponents of autocratic monarchies, from the English Puritans through the French Enlightenment to the Russian novelists of the last century, had long since itemized the sins and deficiencies of unrestricted central power and its stifling effect on human potential. What the twentieth century teaches is simply an updated version of Lord Acton's dictum: Absolute state power destroys absolutely, and full state control of the economy distorts fully. The short-lived disaster of Fascism and the longer-lasting tragedy of Communism can be adduced in evidence of processes known to our forebears but of which Colbert's system and the ancien régime were but pale anticipations. We now know that some version of liberalism that accords the maximum of freedom and initiative in every sphere of life is the only possible option.

But that is all we know, and not everything follows from it. The lessons of 1989 obscure almost as much as they teach, and, worst of all, they tend to obscure a third lesson: that we no longer have good reason to suppose that *any* single set of political or economic rules or principles is universally applicable, however virtuous or effective they may prove in individual instances. This is not a plea for cultural or moral relativism, but it is not incoherent to believe that a system of economic management might work in one place and not another, or to recognize that, within limits, what is normal and expected behavior by a government in one free society might understandably be thought intolerable interference in another.

Thus the application of neoliberal economic policy in the United States is possible, in part, because even some of those who stand to lose thereby are culturally predisposed to listen with approval to politicians denouncing the sins of big government. The American combination of economic insecurity, social inequality, and reduced or minimal government intervention in the field of welfare legislation, for example, would prove explosive in societies where the state is expected to have a hand in such matters and gets the benefit of the doubt even when it appears to be abusing its power. Thus, for reasons that are cultural and historical rather than economic, the U.S. model is not exportable and even across the breadth of the Atlantic Ocean causes quivers of distaste and anxiety among otherwise sympathetic foreign observers.

The British case, which bears some resemblance to the U.S. one, is in certain respects a little closer to the European norm. The British *state* has never played a very important part in people's lives, at least as they perceive it; it is *society* that binds the British together, or so they had long believed. Reinforced by the myth and memory of wartime unity, British people in the postwar decades were notably sensitive to hints that selfish group claims were being favored by the state at the expense of the common good. Indeed, Margaret Thatcher effected a small revolution in her country precisely by playing on a widespread fear that some sectors of society—the labor unions in particular—had gained access to the state and were using it to sectoral advantage. That she herself expanded the role of the state in other spheres of life—notably justice and local government—and used central authority to benefit other sectoral interests is beside the point. The British were susceptible to the suggestion that their difficulties arose from the omnipresence of an inefficient and vaguely threatening central power, though they had no desire to squander the achievements of state-administered social legislation in the fields of health, welfare, and education, as the Tories' final, ignominious defeat revealed.

But the British example is equally inapplicable to the continental European case—and not just because of the amusing European propensity to speak of Anglo-American neoliberalism as though the British and U.S. experience and examples were interchangeable. There are doubtless many European Socialists and liberals who would like to emulate Tony Blair. But the price of that would be to pass through the experience of Margaret Thatcher (without whom Tony Blair would still be an obscure Labour politician with no original ideas of his own), and no European politician of any hue imagines for a moment that his own country could survive *that*. It is not just that Thatcher produced double-digit unemployment and destroyed the traditional manufacturing base of the British economy, while briefly lining the pockets of the middle class with the windfall proceeds from privatization: Some of that has already happened in France, Belgium, Spain, and elsewhere. But Thatcher demolished the theory and much of the practice of the providential state, and it is that which is unthinkable across the channel.*

In continental Europe the state will continue to play the major role in public life for three general reasons. The first is cultural. People expect the state—the government, the administration, the executive offices—to take the initiative or at least pick up the pieces. When the French demand that their government provide shorter working hours, higher wages, employment security, early pensions, and more jobs, they may be unrealistic

---

* Moreover, in John Gray's words, "Neoliberalism in Britain has proved a self-limiting project." *Endgames* (Cambridge: Polity Press, 1997), 3.

but they are not irrational. They do not generally press for lower taxes (in contrast with the U.S. political obsession with tax cuts). They recognize that high taxes are the means by which the state might meet such expectations, and they are indeed highly taxed, which is why they resent it when the state fails to deliver the social goods. Germans, too, expect the state to ensure their well-being. And although, for historical reasons, they are disposed to identify the latter with social compacts and a stable currency, they too expect the state to play an active role in maintaining job security, regulating commerce, and servicing the remarkably generous welfare net with which they have provided themselves.

Even in Italy, where the state is weak and much more politically vulnerable, it has played a crucial role in providing employment, transfer payments, regional largesse, and an intricate variety of support schemes, all of which have contributed enormously to the social stability of a country whose unity has always been in question and that has been prey to more, and deeper, political crises than the Anglo-American experience can begin to appreciate. Let us pose the counterfactual question: Where would Italy be now without its huge and inefficient civil service, its overstaffed public services, its dysfunctional and discredited systems of wage-price linkage, its underfunded pension schemes, and its corrupt and abused *Cassa per il Mezzogiorno*, established in 1950 to channel resources to the backward south but long a feeding ground for the political clients and business associates of the governing Christian Democrats?

The Italian state has stood not between Italy as we now see it and some hypothetical Italian miracle of the neoliberal imagination, but between postwar Italy and political collapse. This is not just because the country would otherwise have faced insuperable social conflicts and regional disparities, but because the long-standing cultural expectations of Italians—that the state must do what society and economy, left to their own devices, cannot—would have been unacceptably thwarted. In unsteady and fragmented societies the state is often the only means by which some measure of coherence and stability can be guaranteed. The historical alternative in such cases has usually been the military, and it has been Italy's and Europe's good fortune that *that* route has been taken infrequently in recent memory.

Thus, although the state itself has had a bad press in the recent

European past, there has been little loss of faith in the importance of the things it can do, properly led. Only a state can provide the services and conditions through which its citizens may aspire to lead a good or fulfilling life. Those conditions vary across cultures: They may emphasize civic peace, solidarity with the less fortunate, public facilities of the infrastructural or even the high cultural sort, environmental amenities, free health care, good public education, and much else. It is generally recognized that not all of these may be available in their optimal form, but in that case too it is only the state that can adjudicate with reasonable impartiality between competing demands, interests, and goods. Most important, only the state can represent a shared consensus about which goods are positional and can be obtained only in prosperity, and which are basic and must be provided to everyone in all circumstances.

These are things the market—much less the global market—cannot do. Paradoxically, the idea of an active state today represents an acknowledgment of *limits* on human endeavor, in contrast to its overweening utopian ambitions in the recent past: Because not everything can be done, we need to select the most desirable or important among what is possible. The idealization of the market, with the attendant assumption that anything is possible in principle, with market forces determining which possibilities will emerge, is the latest (if not the last) modernist illusion: that we live in a world of infinite potential where we are masters of our destiny (while somehow simultaneously dependent on the unpredictable outcome of forces over which we have no control). Proponents of the interventionist state are more modest and disabused. They would rather choose between possible outcomes than leave the result to chance, if only because there is something intuitively and distressingly callous about leaving certain sorts of goods, services, and life chances to the winds of fate.

The second case for preserving the state today is pragmatic, or perhaps prudential. Because global markets *do* exist, because capital and resources fly around the world and much of what happens in people's lives today has passed from their control or the control of those who govern them, there is a greater need than ever to hold on to the sorts of intermediate institutions that make possible normal civilized life in communities and societies. We are accustomed to understanding this point when it is directed to the need for voluntary organizations, community structures, small-scale exercises of autonomy in public life, and local civic ventures or issues of common concern, such as safety, environment, education, culture. And we understand, or think we understand, the importance of intermediate institutions when we study totalitarian regimes and notice the importance their rulers attached to the *destruction* of anything that came between the isolated, anomic subject and the monopolistic state.

What we have failed to grasp is that, on the eve of the twenty-first century, *the state itself is now an intermediary institution too*. When the economy, and the forces and patterns of behavior that accompany it, are truly international, the only institution that can effectively interpose itself between those forces and the unprotected individual is the national state. Such states are all that can stand between their citizens and the unrestricted, unrepresentative, unlegitimated capacities of markets, insensitive and unresponsive supranational administrations, and unregulated processes over which individuals and communities have no control. The state is the largest unit in which, by habit and convention, men and women can feel they have a stake and which is, or can be made to appear, responsive to their interests and desires.

Finally, the need for representative democracy—which makes it possible for a large number of people to live together in some measure of agreement while retaining a degree of control over their collective fate—is also the best argument for the traditional state. Indeed, the two are fated to live or die together. Political choices will always be made because politics, as an antithetic activity, is the proper form in which different collective preferences are expressed in open societies. And because the state is the only forum in which politics can be practiced—something that becomes obvious as soon as we envisage the alternatives—it is imprudent as well as unrealistic to seek to reduce or bypass the state. It is because the free flow of capital threatens the sovereign authority of democratic states that we need to strengthen these, not surrender them to the siren song of international markets, global society, or transnational communities. That is what many perceive as wrong with the European project, and it is what would be wrong with assigning the policymaking initiative to global market forces.

Just as political democracy is all that stands between individuals and an overmighty government, so the regulatory, providential state is all that stands between its citizens and the unpredictable forces of economic change. Far from being an impediment to progress, the recalcitrant state, embodying the expectations and demands of its citizenry, is the only safeguard of progress to date. Whatever the gains in social legislation on working conditions and hours, education, the dissemination of culture, safeguarding health and the environment, insurance against homelessness, unemployment, and old age, and the limited redistribution of wealth, they are all vulnerable and politically contingent. There is no historical law that says they may not someday be undone. For it is with social advance as with political freedoms: We must always stave off threats to what has been won, rather than presume these gains to be a secure part of some unassailable heritage.

Furthermore, it is not in the interest of proponents of global market forces to seek the dismantling of the providential state. Unregulated markets are frequently self-delegitimizing, as numerous historical examples suggest. Perceived as unfair, they can become dysfunctional and will be rejected even by those who stand to gain from their smooth operation. For social and political stability are important economic variables too, and in political cultures where the providential state is the condition of social peace, it is thus a crucial local *economic* asset, whatever its actual economic behavior. That is why "the market" has worked well, albeit in very different ways, in situations as distinct as Social Democratic Scandinavia, Christian Democratic Italy, social-market Germany, and providential-state France.

THE LOSERS IN today's economy have the most interest in and need for the state, not least because they cannot readily imagine taking themselves and their labor anywhere else. Since the political Left by convention and elective affinity is most motivated to capture the support of this constituency (and had better do so if we are to avoid a selective replay of the 1930s), the present afflictions of the European Left are of more than passing concern. And they are serious. Since the late eighteenth century the Left in Europe, variously labeled, has been the bearer of a project.

Whether this project has been the march of progress, the preparation of revolution, or the cause of a class, it has always invoked the historical process, and history itself, on its behalf. Since the decline of the industrial proletariat, and more precipitously with the end of the Soviet Union, the Left in the West has been shorn of its agent, its project, and even its story—the "master narrative" within which all radical endeavors were ultimately couched, which made sense of their programs and explained away their setbacks.

This is self-evidently the case for Communists, but it is no less serious an impediment to moderate social democracy as well. Without a working class, without a long-term revolutionary objective, however benign and nonviolent in practice, without any particular reason to suppose that it *will* succeed or a transcendent basis for believing that it *deserves* to do so, social democracy today is just what its great nineteenth-century founders feared it would become if it ever abandoned its ideological presuppositions and class affiliation: the advanced wing of reforming market liberalism. Now, just as it has been relieved by the death of Communism from the crippling mortgage of revolutionary expectations, is the European Left to be reduced to defending hard-won sectoral gains and glancing nervously and resentfully at a future it cannot understand and for which it has no prescription?

The reconciliation between the European Left and capitalism is still fresh and long overdue. We should recall that as recently as 1981 François Mitterrand's Socialist Party came to power on the promise and expectation of a *grand soir*: a radical and irreversible anticapitalist transformation. And anyone who supposes that this was a peculiarly and typically French aberration should reread the British Labour Party's 1983 election manifesto—the "longest suicide note in history," in Labour Member of Parliament Gerald Kaufman's felicitous phrase. But today the Left is no longer shackled to irrelevant, ineffective, or unpopular policies. On the contrary, the sort of society that the French, Swedish, Italian, and even the German socialists claim to seek is a fairly accurate reflection of the generalized preferences of the majority of their fellow citizens.

The real problem facing Europe's Socialists (I use the term purely for its descriptive convenience, since it is now shorn of any ideological charge) is not their policy preferences, taken singly. Job creation, a more "social" Europe, public infrastructural investment, educational reforms, and the like are laudable and uncontroversial. But nothing binds these policies or proposals together into a common political or moral narrative. The Left has no sense of what its own political success, if achieved, would mean; it has no articulated vision of a good, or even of a better, society. In the absence of such a vision, to be on the left is simply to be in a state of permanent protest. And since the thing most protested against is the damage wrought by rapid change, to be on the left is to be a *conservative*.

The brief success story of European social democracy and British Labour over the past half-century can be seen in retrospect to have depended on the same fortuitous circumstances as the welfare states they helped create. Now the Left wants to preserve its positions and its hard-won sectoral gains. In defending these acquired rights and supporting those who would add to them—like railway engineers and truck drivers in France who demand retirement on full pensions at fifty-five or even fifty—the Left (and sometimes the Right) in France, Germany, Spain, and elsewhere confuses and discredits itself and its case by a failure to choose between ultimately incompatible claims. It is not so much fighting the ideological battle against neoliberal heartlessness as it is seeking to conserve privileges on behalf of the broadest possible constituency of well-organized voters who are anxious at the prospect of reduced income and services.

This paradox, if it is one, is not original. The left was often *socially* conservative—notably during the French Revolution, when some of the most radical moments occurred on behalf of artisans' struggles to preserve established claims and privileges, and again during the early Industrial Revolution. Trade unions, especially those in the skilled trades, were always instinctively conservative—even when supporting radical political solutions. But theirs is an unconvincing posture, and given the impossibility of avoiding *some* unsettling changes in coming years, it is an improvident one.

In these circumstances the dangerous illusion of a radical center or "third way" has taken hold. Like the French Socialists' 1997 slogan "Changeons d'avenir" ("Let's Have a Different Future"), Tony Blair's "radical centrism" is an empty vessel, clanging noisily and boastfully around the vacant space of European political argument. But whereas the French Left's clichés are familiar, those of New Labour are seductively novel at first hearing. Of course, there are political advantages to being in the center. In normal times that is where the winning votes are to be found in any binary representative system. But if times become somewhat less normal, as seems likely, the center will be quickly evacuated in favor of more extreme options. For the moment, Blairism consists of the successful displacement of the old, discredited Left by what might be termed the *bien-sentant* center: the politics of good feeling, in which lightly retouched Thatcherite economics are blended with appropriately well-intentioned social adjustments borrowed from the neighboring liberal tradition. In this way the charge of heartless realism is avoided without any need to imagine alternatives.

It is a tempting solution; but it is a mistake. Like the "as if" and "civil society" language of the Czech, Polish, and Hungarian opposition in the 1980s, it is a good and effective weapon in the struggle against insensitive or authoritarian governments. But once those governments have been overthrown or defeated, the morally unimpeachable advocates of antipolitics find themselves confronted with political choices for which their previous experience has not prepared them. They must either compromise—and lose their credibility—or else quit public life. For most of the past century, the European Left has somehow managed to do both. If it is to do better in the future, to avoid repeating its historical pattern of morally redeeming failure, it must return to the drawing board and ask itself these questions: What sort of social improvement is both desirable and envisageable under the present international configuration? What sort of economically literate policies are required to bring such an objective about? And what sort of arguments will be sufficiently convincing to make people vote to see these policies implemented?

The fact that the Left is in office in most of Europe today is irrelevant to these requirements. Many of the Socialists who now govern (in France, Britain, and Italy, for example) got there because of the collapse or splits of the local Right. In Britain and France a system of proportional representation would have deprived the present Labour and Socialist parties of their parliamentary majority in the elections of 1997. In that sense, they are minority governments without mandates or long-term policies, whose strongest suit is the promise that they can undo some of the damage wrought by their predecessors in office, simply by doing something different. They will not be reelected indefinitely if they fail to come up with something better than their present offerings.

To begin with, the Left might want to make a virtue of the necessity entailed in abandoning the project by which it has lived and died this century. History is the history of more than just class struggle, and the economic identity of social beings that was so central for nineteenth-century social theorists—whose encumbered heirs we remain—is now distinctly peripheral for ever more people. The disappearance of work—something the nineteenth-century utopians could only dream about!—is a crisis, but it is also an opportunity to rethink social policy. Some members of the European Left have latched quite effectively onto the idea of protecting the *exclus*: but they still think of them as just that—excluded from the norm, which remains that of fully employed, wage-earning, socially integrated workers. What needs to be grasped is that men and women in precarious employment, immigrants with partial civil rights, young people with no long-term job prospects, the growing ranks of the homeless and the inadequately housed, are not some fringe problem to be addressed and resolved, but represent something grimly fundamental.

There must, therefore, be a role for the state in incorporating the social consequences of economic change, and not merely providing minimum compensatory alleviation. This has two implications. Given the limited range of policymaking initiative in monetary and fiscal matters now open to any one government, the control or regulation of production in all its modern forms is not only undesirable but impossible. But it does not follow that we should divest the state of *all* its economic controls. The state cannot run a car company or invent microchips, but it alone has the incentive and the capacity to organize health, educational, transportation, and recreational services. It is in the social interest to have a flourishing *private* productive sector, yes. But the latter should provide the means for a thriving *public* service sector in those areas where the state is best equipped to provide the service, or where economic efficiency is not the most appropriate criterion of performance.

The proper level of state involvement in the life of the community can no longer be determined by ex hypothesi theorizing. We don't know what degree of regulation, public ownership, or distributive monopoly is appropriate across the board, only what works or is required in each case. Intervention mechanisms inherited from decisions that were appropriate when first made but that have since become anachronisms, like farm price supports or early retirement on full pay for state employees, are indefensible, above all because they inhibit the growth required to provide truly necessary benefits. Conversely, reductions in state involvement in the provision of public housing, medical facilities, or family services—cuts that seemed to make demographic, economic, and ideological sense when first introduced in the 1970s and 1980s—now look perilously socially divisive, when those who need them have no access to any other resources.

The modern state still has a considerable say over how the economic growth generated in private hands might best be collectively distributed, at least at the local level. If the Left could convincingly argue that it had a set of general principles guiding its choices in the distribution of resources and services and could show that those principles were not merely stubborn defenses of the status quo, making the best of someone else's bad job, it would have made a considerable advance. It would need to show that it understood that some must lose for all to gain; that a desire to sustain the intervention capacities of the state is not incompatible with acknowledgment of the need for painful reconsideration of the objects of that intervention; that both "regulation" and "deregulation" are morally neutral when taken in isolation. As things now stand, the continental Left merely records its (and its electors') discomfort at the prospect of rearranging the social furniture; while Britain's New Labour clings to power on the bankrupt promise that in these tricky matters it has no (unpopular) preferences of any kind.

Reconsideration of principles is notoriously hard, and it is unfortunate, if not altogether accidental, that the Left finds itself confronted with the need to reimagine its whole way of thought under less than propitious economic circumstances. But there is never a good moment for untimely thoughts. For some years to come, the chief burden on the government of any well-run national community will be ensuring that those of its members who are the victims of economic transformations over which the government itself can exercise only limited control nevertheless live decent lives, even (especially) if such a life no longer contains the expectation of steady, remunerative, and productive employment; that the rest of the community is led to an appreciation of its duty to share that burden; and that the economic growth required to sustain this responsibility is not inhibited by the ends to which it is applied. This is a job for the state; and *that* is hard to accept because the desirability of placing the maximum possible restrictions upon the interventionary capacities of the state has become the cant of our time.

Accordingly, the task of the Left in Europe in the years to come will be to reconstruct a case for the activist state, to show why the lesson for the twenty-first century is *not* that we should return, so far as possible, to the nineteenth. To do this, the Left must come to terms with its own share of responsibility for the sins of the century that has just ended. It was not so long ago, after all, that West German Social Democrats refused to speak ill of the late, unlamented German Democratic Republic, and there are still French and British Socialists who find it painful to acknowledge their erstwhile sympathy for the Soviet project in precisely its most state-idolatrous forms. But until the European Left has recognized its past propensity to favor power over freedom, to see virtue in anything and everything undertaken by a "progressive" central authority, it will always be backing halfheartedly and shamefacedly into the future: presenting the case for the state and apologizing for it at the same time.

Until and unless this changes, the electors of Longwy and Sarrebourg, like their fellows in Austria, Italy, and Belgium (not to speak of countries farther east), will be tempted to listen to other voices, less timid about invoking the nation-state and "national-capitalism" as the forum for redemptive action. Why are we so sure that the far political Right is behind us for good—or indeed the far Left? The postwar social reforms in Europe were instituted in large measure as a barrier to the return of the sort of desperation and disaffection from which such extreme choices were thought to have arisen. The partial unraveling of those social reforms, for whatever reason, is not risk-free. As the great reformers of the nineteenth century well knew, the Social Question, if left unaddressed, does not just wither away. It goes instead in search of more radical answers.

This essay was first published in 1997 in the journal Foreign Affairs, at the invitation of its then managing editor Fareed Zakaria. He asked me to write about any problem or development in foreign affairs likely to be of significance in years to come. I opted to discuss the new "social question" of poverty, underemployment, and social exclusion and the failure of the political Left to reassess its response to these and other dilemmas of globalization. Nothing that has happened in the intervening decade has led me to moderate my gloomy prognostications—quite the contrary.

PUBLICATION CREDITS

The essays in this book were first published in the following journals:

Chapter I: "Arthur Koestler, the Exemplary Intellectual" in *The New Republic*, January 2000

Chapter II: "The Elementary Truths of Primo Levi" in *The New York Review of Books*, May 20, 1999

Chapter III: "The Jewish Europe of Manès Sperber" in *The New Republic*, April 1, 1996

Chapter IV: "Hannah Arendt and Evil" in *The New York Review of Books*, April 6, 1995

Chapter V: "Albert Camus: 'The best man in France'" in *The New York Review of Books*, October 6, 1994

Chapter VI: "Elucubrations: The 'Marxism' of Louis Althusser" in *The New Republic*, March 7, 1994

Chapter VII: "Eric Hobsbawm and the Romance of Communism" in *The New York Review of Books*, November 20, 2003

Chapter VIII: "Goodbye to All That? Leszek Kołakowski and the Marxist Legacy" in *The New York Review of Books*, September 21, 2006

Chapter IX: "A 'Pope of Ideas'? John Paul II and the Modern World" in *The New York Review of Books*, October 31, 1996

Chapter X: "Edward Said: The Rootless Cosmopolitan" in *The Nation*, July 19, 2004

Chapter XI: "The Catastrophe: The Fall of France, 1940" in *The New York Review of Books*, February 22, 2001

Chapter XII: "*À la recherche du temps perdu*: France and Its Pasts" in *The New York Review of Books*, December 3, 1998

Chapter XIII: "The Gnome in the Garden: Tony Blair and Britain's 'Heritage'" in *The New York Review of Books*, July 19, 2001

Chapter XIV: "The Stateless State: Why Belgium Matters" in *The New York Review of Books*, December 2, 1999

Chapter XV: "Romania between History and Europe" in *The New York Review of Books*, November 1, 2001

Chapter XVI: "Dark Victory: Israel's Six-Day War" in *The New Republic*, July 29, 2002

Chapter XVII: "The Country That Wouldn't Grow Up" in *Ha'aretz*, May 5, 2006

Chapter XVIII: "An American Tragedy? The Case of Whittaker Chambers" in *The New Republic*, April 14, 1997

Chapter XIX: "The Crisis: Kennedy, Khrushchev, and Cuba" in *The New York Review of Books*, January 15, 1998

Chapter XX: "The Illusionist: Henry Kissinger and American Foreign Policy" in *The New York Review of Books*, August 13, 1998

Chapter XXI: "Whose Story Is It? The Cold War in Retrospect" in *The New York Review of Books*, March 23, 2006

Chapter XXII: "The Silence of the Lambs: On the Strange Death of Liberal America" in *The London Review of Books*, September 21, 2006

Chapter XXIII: "The Good Society: Europe vs. America" in *The New York Review of Books*, February 10, 2005

Envoi: "The Social Question Redivivus" in *Foreign Affairs*, September/October 1997

INDEX

KFN
5658
G76
1988

Cover design by Kat Dalton

Library of Congress Cataloging-in-Publication Data
Gross, James A., 1933–
    Teachers on trial.

    (ILR paperback ; no. 20)
    Includes index.
    1. Teachers—Legal status, laws, etc.—New York
(State) 2. Teachers—Malpractice—New York (State)
3. Actions and defenses—New York (State) I. Title.
II. Series.
KFN5658.G76   1988   344.747'078   88-13673
ISBN 0–87546–142–5 (alk. paper) 347.470478

The paper used in this publication meets the minimum requirements
of American National Standard for Information Sciences—Perma-
nence of Paper for Printed Library Materials, ANSI Z 39.48-1984.

                                                              ∞

Copies may be ordered from
ILR Press
New York State School of
Industrial and Labor Relations
Cornell University
Ithaca, NY 14851-0952

Printed in the United States of America
5 4 3 2 1

ILR Paperback Series Number 20

TEACHERS ON TRIAL

VALUES, STANDARDS, & EQUITY IN JUDGING CONDUCT AND COMPETENCE

James A. Gross

ILR PRESS
New York State School of
Industrial and Labor Relations
Cornell University